Criminology and Public Policy

Edited by

SCOTT H. DECKER and KEVIN A. WRIGHT

CRIMINOLOGY AND PUBLIC POLICY

Putting Theory to Work

SECOND EDITION

TEMPLE UNIVERSITY PRESS
Philadelphia • Rome • Tokyo

TEMPLE UNIVERSITY PRESS
Philadelphia, Pennsylvania 19122
www.temple.edu/tempress

Published 2018

Library of Congress Cataloging-in-Publication Data

Names: Decker, Scott H., editor. | Wright, Kevin Andrew, 1982- editor.
Title: Criminology and public policy : putting theory to work / edited by Scott H. Decker, Kevin A. Wright.
Description: Second Edition. | Philadelphia : Temple University Press, 2018.

| Revised edition of Criminology and public policy, 2010. | Includes bibliographical references and index. |
Identifiers: LCCN 2017055082 (print) | LCCN 2017057186 (ebook) | ISBN 9781439916599 (E-Book) | ISBN 9781439916575 (hardback : alk. paper) | ISBN 9781439916582 (paper : alk. paper)
Subjects: LCSH: Criminology. | Crime—Government policy. | Crime prevention.

| Criminal justice, Administration of. | BISAC: SOCIAL SCIENCE / Criminology. | POLITICAL SCIENCE / Public Policy / Social Policy. | SOCIAL SCIENCE / Penology.
Classification: LCC HV6025 (ebook) | LCC HV6025 .C7458 2018 (print) | DDC 364--dc23
LC record available at https://lccn.loc.gov/2017055082

♾The paper used in this publication meets the requirements of the American National Standard for Information Sciences—Permanence of Paper for Printed Library Materials, ANSI Z39.48-1992

Printed in the United States of America

9 8 7 6 5 4 3 2 1

Contents

Part II Theories of the Criminal Justice System

Acknowledgments

Every book is the product of diverse inputs. This book is no different. There are many people to thank for their contributions to this volume. First, we want to acknowledge Hugh Barlow, who pioneered the first edition and played a supportive role in putting the second edition together. He graciously agreed to step aside and provide Dr. Kevin Wright with the role of coeditor. Hugh recruited a great group of authors for the first edition and set a high standard for subsequent editions. Second, we wish to acknowledge the chapter contributors. We appreciate their hard work, patience, revisions, and general goodwill toward the process of pulling this book together. Indeed, they are the "dream team" of criminologists. Third, we wish to acknowledge the helpful contributions of Ryan Mulligan of Temple University Press. He struck just the right tone of encouragement, support, and nagging to get this book over the finish line. Fourth, we were assisted by really great graduate assistants, Caitlin Matekel, Cassandra Philippon, and Genevieve McKenzie. They provided support in a number of areas that was instrumental to the completion of the book at its high level of quality.

We are particularly grateful to Temple University Press. The Press has shown a long-standing commitment to quality scholarship. We are proud to be a part of the historic tradition at the Press.

There are a number of individuals we wish to thank. Scott wishes to thank his wife JoAnn for her patience in dealing with the excessive amount of time he spent away from her while working on this book. A special thanks to William. Kevin would like to thank Scott Decker for constantly encouraging him to think about how his work may translate into practice.

Introduction

Why Theory Matters for Policy and Why Policy Matters for Theory

Kevin A. Wright

WHY THEORY MATTERS FOR POLICY

I remember learning about "Coleman's Boat" as a sociology master's student at Washington State University as if the seminar had taken place yesterday. The boat, essentially an upside-down trapezoid, is a diagram meant to show the relationship between social structure and individual agency (see Figure I.1). Macro-level factors (the top left of the boat) influence the belief systems and values of individual actors (the bottom left of the boat), those individual beliefs translate into individual actions (the bottom right of the boat), and those individual actions then accumulate and unintentionally create the macro-level again (the top right of the boat) (Coleman 1990). Bourdieu, Giddens, and Habermas are a bit fuzzier, but I remember that boat—perhaps there is indeed something to be written about theoretical parsimony (or whether a theory lends itself to simple, nautical representations). Still further back in my memory are psychologists Bandura, Skinner, and Kohlberg. More recent and accessible after my permanent transition into criminology are Merton, Sutherland, Shaw and McKay, Agnew, Akers, and Hirschi.

The truth is that these theories never really leave one's memory—boat or no boat—because the human behavior that they attempt to explain is observable on a daily basis. Good theories are empirically supported by the social facts that surround us in everyday life. We see that people repeat behaviors for which they have been rewarded in the past; they put on presentations that may not be representative of their true selves but are ones that they wish

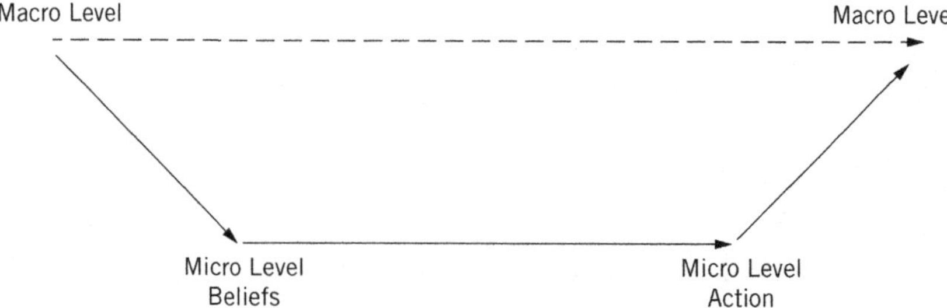

Figure I.1 Basic macro and micro level propositions adapted from Coleman (1990).

others to interpret as being reality; and they respond to pain, victimization, and trauma in a variety of ways that otherwise might appear abnormal. Many of us enter the field of criminology because we are fascinated by human behavior. We want to understand, prevent, respond to, or correct *deviant behavior* in particular. What this means is that programs and policies are needed that acknowledge, for example, that crime can be rewarding and may continue until prosocial behaviors replace that reward structure, that incarcerated men may portray themselves as ultra-masculine and refuse any assistance in the form of treatment, and that "career victims" may exist, alongside career criminals, due in part to their response to previous victimizations.

I remember something else from graduate school that I imagine has happened before and probably has happened since: I grossly misjudged the amount of time I would need to spend reading for each of my comprehensive exams. I read just about everything on the provided list for the criminological theory exam. I still have it; it's 16 pages single-spaced and lists 57 books, 168 articles, and 14 book chapters (thank you, Travis Pratt and Leana Bouffard). Of course, students were also "expected to be familiar with the most current information regarding these theoretical traditions," which meant that you could never really be "done reading." Finally satisfied that I was in fact done reading, I looked at the calendar and knew that my criminological theory comprehensive exam was in three weeks . . . and so was my corrections comprehensive exam. I had read virtually nothing in corrections beyond a seminar I had taken during the previous semester. I scurried my way through the corrections list for two weeks and I faked my way through that exam. Sure, I read Beccaria (1764), I probably wrote something about risk assessment or intensive supervision, and I cited Frank Cullen a bunch, but I faked that thing (please forgive me, Jeff Bouffard).

I did, however, pass my corrections exam, and I did so in a particular way that would influence my approach to my work going forward: I relied heavily on all the reading that I had done for my criminological theory exam. This led me to the realization that the correction of crime was very rarely tied to the actual causes of crime. Life-course theories of crime, macro-level theories of crime, feminist theories of crime—all had something to say about why people engage in crime but were surprisingly absent when it came time to doing something about it. Stated differently, policy was not informed by theory. This is not to say that theorists in those traditions were not suggesting policies based on their chosen explanation of human behavior; however, for whatever reasons, their suggestions didn't seem to take hold in corrections.

"Coleman's Boat" must have been somewhere in my head while I was writing my dissertation. How could we expect to rehabilitate individuals while returning them to the same neighborhood, family, or peer setting that likely contributed to their criminal behavior in the first place? Community disadvantage influences individual beliefs and behaviors (e.g., Wilson 2010), and the accumulation of that behavior and its response contributes to further and perhaps worsened community disadvantage and instability (e.g., Clear 2007), which then again impact individual-level criminal behavior in the form of recidivism (e.g., Kubrin and Stewart 2006). If we are to meaningfully reduce recidivism, programs and policies would need to account for individual rehabilitation while also acknowledging the influence of criminogenic settings (Wright et al. 2012). Theory and policy are linked, criminology and criminal justice are linked, and answers to the social and economic problems brought on by crime and its response will require multiple methods of reasoning to account for these linkages. This is accomplished in the second edition of *Criminology and Public Policy*, and the names of the authors in this text should be added to our recent criminological memories.

WHY POLICY MATTERS FOR THEORY

The paragraph that begins "The policy implications of the current work..." often appears right before the concluding paragraphs of a research article. Should a book-length manuscript provide policy implications, these too often appear in a chapter toward the end or even in an appendix. The translation of findings to practice is an afterthought. Worse still, the "so what?" question is often left unanswered entirely. Sometimes this is because the research question or problem addressed was never worthy of additional study in the first place. Sometimes this is due to logistical issues such as "space constraints" of a journal or a desire to present objective evidence and not make claims to how it might inform policy. Sometimes, however, this is because the theory and its implications are so out of touch with the messy reality of human behavior—and the political, social, and fiscal challenges of responding to that behavior (Sampson, Winship, and Knight 2013)—that it is difficult to put findings into practice in any meaningful way. This is the bane of the ivory tower, and it can contribute to the implementation of wasteful policies and programs that are created based on ideology rather than on science when the "policy implications of the current work" are underdeveloped or nonexistent.

You know DARE, right? Well, I won't write about the specific shaky theoretical foundations of the program (see Akers 2010) or the lack of systematic evidence supporting its effectiveness (see Rosenbaum 2007). Instead, I'd rather share an amusing but troubling anecdote of my own experience with DARE as a ten-year-old. Admittedly, I don't remember much from DARE, but one specific component has always stuck with me since "learning" it in the early 1990s. At its core, DARE relies on resisting the temptations of drugs and alcohol (e.g., Drug Abuse Resistance Education; "Just Say No"). As part of this education, my fellow students and I received a handout with strategies of resistance should we be offered the opportunity to partake in the use of drugs and alcohol. Listed were the *cold shoulder* approach, the *walk away* approach, and the simple *no thanks* approach. But it was a suggested phrase within the *give an excuse* approach regarding saying no to beer in particular that I always remember:

> "No thanks, the bubbles hurt my throat."

Each time I picture a kid saying that phrase today they're laughed at or worse. I've shared this anecdote with my students—at both the college and high school levels—and they confirm the ridiculousness of the strategy. Part of the shaky theoretical foundations of DARE include ignoring the social contexts in which kids are pressured into using drugs and alcohol (Pratt, Gau, and Franklin 2011). Whatever the theoretical foundations, the program in practice suggests that they may need revision. DARE, Scared Straight, juvenile boot camps—each of these has been written about before with these concerns in mind (e.g., Finckenauer and Gavin 1999; Lutze 2006). They are not, however, the only examples where policies or programs rest on theoretical foundations that are unable to keep up with the complexity of human interaction. Much of restorative justice policy requires a sense of community that may not exist in the communities where it's most needed. Policies that encourage deportation or restricted immigration often rely on questionable theoretical assumptions regarding the criminality of those born outside the country. And in an adult DARE parallel, strategies to avoid confrontation that are rewarded in cognitive behavioral therapy sessions—like walking away—may be met by violence in the street. Policy matters for theory because it is an added check on our theoretical work; it can validate theoretical principles or suggest that a revision is needed.

Instead of piling on DARE, I want to write about the other thing that I remember from my experience as a ten-year-old in the program: Officer Frank Pezzimenti. I was fortunate that the uniformed officer who led DARE represented one of my first police interactions in the relatively crime-free village of Fairport, New York; others aren't so fortunate. We had many individuals share their time with us in elementary through high school—folk singers, motivational speakers, and monster truck drivers. I don't remember any of their names, but I remember Officer Pezzimenti. I remember him as witty and funny, kind and caring—a supportive figure of trust and authority in the community. DARE may not do a great job of diverting youth away from drugs and alcohol, but its programmatic elements might be conducive toward building police legitimacy at an early age (see, e.g., Birkeland, Murphy-Graham, and Weiss 2005). Rather than simply just saying no to DARE, the program might be examined to determine what works and what doesn't and, therefore, what might be kept and what might be discarded when creating a theory to then guide future programming (be it for preventing substance abuse or establishing police legitimacy).

Fortunately, the state of criminologists and their work is not as dismal as portrayed at the beginning of this section. A fair number of criminologists do indeed worry about the policy implications of their findings. Tittle (2016) suggests that "problem-solving criminology" is likely the second-most popular style of criminology (behind the more traditional "theoretical science criminology"—although he offers that problem-solving criminologists may even represent a majority). The journal *Criminology & Public Policy* is devoted to publishing works that engage in policy discussions of research findings. I especially enjoy the November 2007 issue that asked criminologists to make policy propositions based on their work and gave them the freedom to do so with brevity and candor (can we do this again, please?). Websites like the Office of Justice Programs (https://www.crimesolutions.gov/) organize what works based on the scientific evidence. Problem-solving criminology is being aimed at the highest levels of government—in March 2017, twenty-five former presidents of the American Society of Criminology urged the president of the United States to "promote criminal justice policies, programs, and practices that are evidence based." Whether it be called problem-solving criminology, problem-oriented criminology, public criminology, policy-relevant criminology, or translational criminology, it's clear that the policy implications of criminological findings won't always be left to languish on the last page.

A good theory is abstract. It's logically consistent. It's simple, has a broad scope, and it doesn't take you in circles. It's testable and empirically valid.

Good theories generate good hypotheses, and with good data we may be in a position to better understand a particular phenomenon. Conceivably, then, we should be in good position to identify policies and programs based on theory that may affect that phenomenon. In criminology, this means informing public policy designed to address the problems brought on by criminal behavior and the response to that behavior. In some instances, however, it may be easier to start with the problem and work backward to develop or modify theory. Lest one be accused of selecting on the dependent variable or engaging in tautological reasoning, the theory can then be tested in other settings to see how well it holds up to the empirical data: from the specific to the general and back again.

REFERENCES

Akers, R. 2010. Nothing is as practical as a good theory: Social learning theory and the treatment and prevention of delinquency. In *Criminology and Public Policy: Putting Theory to Work*, edited by H. Barlow and S. Decker, 84–105. Philadelphia: Temple University Press.

Beccaria, C. (1764) 1963. *On crimes and Punishments*, trans. H. Paolucci. New York: Pearson Education Limited.

Birkeland, S., E. Murphy-Graham, and C. Weiss. 2005. Good reasons for ignoring good evaluation: The case of the drug abuse resistance education (D.A.R.E.) program. *Evaluation and Program Planning* 28: 247–256.

Clear, T. 2007. *Imprisoning Communities: How Mass Incarceration Makes Disadvantaged Communities Worse*. New York: Oxford University Press.

Coleman, J. 1990. *Foundations of Social Theory*. Cambridge, MA: Harvard University Press.

Finckenauer, J., and P. Gavin. 1999. *Scared Straight: The Panacea Phenomenon Revisited*. Prospect Heights, IL: Waveland Press.

Kubrin, C., and E. Stewart. 2006. Predicting who reoffends: The neglected role of neighborhood context. *Criminology* 44: 165–197.

Lutze, F. 2006. Boot camp prisons and correctional policy: Moving from militarism to an ethic of care. *Criminology and Public Policy* 5: 389–400.

Pratt, T., J. Gau, and T. Franklin. 2011. *Key Ideas in Criminology and Criminal Justice*. Thousand Oaks, CA: Sage.

Rosenbaum, D. 2007. Just say no to D.A.R.E. *Criminology and Public Policy* 6: 815–824.

Sampson, R., C. Winship, and C. Knight. 2013. Translating causal claims: Principles and strategies for policy-relevant criminology. *Criminology & Public Policy* 12: 587–616.

Tittle, C. 2016. Introduction: Theory and contemporary criminology. In *Handbook of Criminological Theory*, edited by A. Piquero, 1–17. New York: Wiley.

Wilson, W. 2010. *More Than Just Race: Being Black and Poor in the Inner City*. New York: W. W. Norton.

Wright, K., T. Pratt, C. Lowenkamp, and E. Latessa. 2012. The importance of ecological context for correctional treatment programs: Understanding the micro- and macro-level dimensions of successful offender treatment. *Justice Quarterly* 29: 775–798.

Criminology and Public Policy

PART I

Theories of Offender Behavior

Introduction to Part I

The chapters in Part I of this book remind us that programs and policies are only as good as the theoretical foundations on which they rest. They take a deductive method of reasoning by beginning with an abstract theory of criminology or criminal justice and applying that theory to a specific problem and then suggest an answer to the problem. Thus, many of the authors organize their chapters by answering "What's the theory?" "What's the problem?" and "What's the answer?" in that order. A deductive method usually starts with some abstract theory and then works forward to a conclusion that offers an explanation for crime. For example, Travis Hirschi began with the idea that all humans are self-interested and thus capable of committing criminal acts, so he sought to explain why most people *do not* engage in crime. Hirschi's social bond theory organized some existing ideas about stakes in conformity to provide a more comprehensive understanding of the social controls that keep people from acting on their criminal instincts. The theory was tested and validated through self-report surveys of high school students who demonstrated a relationship between attachment to others and delinquent behaviors. The answer, then, was to increase prosocial attachments: after-school programs, mentoring programs, summer jobs, and the like. Most of the general theorists in criminology follow this approach—Merton, Akers, Agnew, and all the way back to Beccaria—and the chapters in Part I cover an impressive amount of ground to show the utility of broad explanations of human behavior.

In Chapter 1, Anthony Braga and Kevin Drakulich zoom out to the community level in order to explain the problems of racial and ethnic disparities in offending and criminal justice processing at the individual level. They draw from macro-level theories of structure and culture to argue that it is place, and not race, that best explains these disparities. However, they go beyond the typical explanation that white people and black people live in qualitatively different neighborhoods to add theory that suggests that race itself fundamentally structures these differences. The impacts of slavery, segregation, and an overall prejudice toward people of color mean that racial disparities in offending cannot be reduced to disparities in socioeconomic class. Their answer is to "change places rather than people," but to do so in a way that challenges the racial hierarchy through community policing and a narrative on urban crime that is rooted in good data rather than bad press.

Amy Farrell, Patricia Warren, and Shea Cronin continue this focus on race in Chapter 2 as they apply critical race theory to address the problems of racial profiling and police brutality. Also at the macro-level, the authors more firmly argue that race organizes society, the institutions within society, and the practices within those institutions—definitively concluding that "race permeates the criminal justice system." Borne out of frustrations with the stalled civil rights movement, critical race theory emerged in the 1980s and argues that racism is hidden in society and thus is resistant to equal opportunity approaches that will only affect the most blatant instances of racism. When applied to racial profiling and police brutality, this means that explicit racism on the part of police is difficult to prove and thus remedy through traditional legal means, and instead a better understanding of implicit bias and the hidden and more pervasive forms of racism is required. Farrell and colleagues conclude by suggesting an answer in the form of increased voice by people of color to inform equality efforts, alongside community policing and restorative justice approaches, to ensure that the more subtle forms of societal racism are made visible and addressed.

Chapters 3 and 4 describe a very different type of environment with Ron Clarke, Justin Kurland, and Lauren Wilson writing about wildlife crimes and Rob White writing about global warming. Clarke and colleagues show just how general deductive approaches can be when they apply situational crime prevention to understand the illegal taking, killing, trading, or sale of flora or fauna. Situational crime prevention is a problem-solving methodology that focuses on modifying opportunity structures of crime instead of altering the motivation to engage in crime. Increasing the risk of engaging in crime should decrease the likelihood of it happening, for example, and mobile apps like WildScan can extend guardianship by allowing anyone to report poached animals in markets. Clarke and colleagues identify a number of challenges to establishing a fully supported, situational, crime prevention approach, and they conclude with a call for more usable data to answer the questions posed by a routine activity theory understanding of wildlife crime.

White identifies climate change—a potentially more devastating danger to flora and fauna (and humans)—as "the most important international issue facing humanity today." He draws from theoretical perspectives at the individual, situational, and structural levels to show the far reaches of temperature changes across the criminological spectrum. To these he adds some critical criminology ("the key perpetrators and responders to global warming tend to be one and the same") and demonstrates that answers are difficult to come by when those in power refuse to acknowledge their contributions to "ecocide." White's answer comes in the form of ecological crime prevention and a problem-solving approach that explicitly recognizes the political contexts that contribute to global warming.

Jillian Turanovic shifts the focus to human victims more explicitly in Chapter 5 by applying a life-course perspective to understand how victimization unfolds across time. Turanovic sagely cautions against merely replacing the dependent variable of crime with victimization in the life-course literature and instead presents a series of principles that might guide a theory of victimization across the life course. These principles draw upon lifestyle and routine activity theories, structural conditions such as disadvantage and the cultural adaptations to those conditions such as criminal subcultures, the structured nature of choice and personal agency, social ties and social support, and desistance. Turanovic suggests that the data to best understand victimization over time with any amount of scientific rigor are currently unavailable, and part of the answer—for the time being—is to think creatively about how to use the data that are available. In particular, she identifies the Pathways to Desistance Study and Add Health data sets as being especially useful, considering Pathways contains victimization among a particularly risky population and Add Health contains victimization across life stages that move beyond childhood and adolescence. Finally, Turanovic advocates for a better understanding of the dynamic causal processes between victimization and its consequences to put us one step closer toward developing a life-course theory of victimization.

Desistance from crime is the focus for Megan Kurlychek and Megan Denver in Chapter 6 as they apply a number of theoretical perspectives to better understand the process of disengagement from crime. Similar to Turanovic, they weave a variety of seemingly dissimilar interdisciplinary approaches together—labeling, social bonds, cognitive transformation, and rational choice—to show some commonalities in the theoretical desistance literature. First, adherence to a criminal label is a barrier to desistance. Second, individuals need to have both the willingness to change and the opportunities to do so.

Third, structural constraints influence the degree to which these opportunities are available to certain individuals. Despite these commonalities, there exist some serious divides between these perspectives—especially to the degree to which they consider desistance as a natural process of aging—and the answers for Kurlychek and Denver are numerous and focus on promoting desistance through policies that limit the negative stigma of system involvement, providing social support for key transition periods within and after system involvement, and rewarding and legitimizing change among those individuals who have left crime in their past.

Cody Telep and David Weisburd link criminology with criminal justice in Chapter 7 by asking "Why does crime occur at particular places?" and providing an answer that lends support for hot spots policing. They present a theory of place that organizes the existing literature from structural and opportunity theories of crime, but they do so with an explicit focus on "micro places" within the typically examined structures of communities, neighborhoods, and census tracts. Telep and Weisburd argue that crime is highly concentrated in specific street segments—even indicating wide variability of the distribution of crime within so-called high-crime neighborhoods—leading to a call for police to devote extra attention and resources to these micro places. They also indicate that the most useful hot spots interventions take a problem-oriented approach that moves beyond mere increased presence to also supplement existing situational crime prevention efforts. Importantly, Telep and Weisburd conclude by suggesting that hot spots policing can be designed to increase the perceived legitimacy of criminal justice actors within the places that they are so often needed.

Glenn Trager and Charis Kubrin demonstrate the significant implications for policy when theory does not meet reality in Chapter 8 on the immigration-crime relationship. Drawing from social disorganization theory, local labor market theory, and cultural explanations of crime, they show how negative images in the media and anti-immigrant rhetoric are to some degree supported by existing social theory. Specifically, each of these approaches suggests that increased immigration means increased crime—a reality that is not supported by the empirical data at either the individual or macro-level. Trager and Kubrin provide a specific policy example to demonstrate that this divergence is due in part to "the very strategies immigrant groups have used to successfully navigate life in the United States and keep crime rates low." The visibility of immigrants within the normal, political life of Costa Mesa, California, made it difficult to demonize foreign-born residents and instead served to increase community cohesion against true threats. Trager and Kubrin conclude that such findings can be used to modify theory—perhaps in the form of the immigrant revitalization thesis—that recognizes how the social ecology of a community can shape the rhetoric of immigration and crime.

Finally, Grant Duwe concludes Part I by writing about the "new" American crime problem of mass shootings in Chapter 9. As with immigration, mass shootings have been a topic of significant national social concern, and Duwe expertly sifts through the data to show that, while there has not been an increase in the number of mass shootings, there has been an increase in the number of mass shootings with larger victim counts—leading to more news coverage and the perception that mass shootings are now more commonplace. He thus takes a social constructionist perspective to show how mass shootings are a new name for mass murder, which went through a similar news cycle in the late 1980s and 1990s. The problem is that, like immigration, this popular discourse and its legislative and policy response are not borne out by the data. Using the FBI Supplementary Homicide Reports in conjunction with news coverage, Duwe sets the record straight regarding prevalence and severity of mass shootings and mass public shootings and in the process demonstrates how our social construction of crime can be just as important for policy as theories of criminality.

1

Race Differences in Crime

Anthony A. Braga and
Kevin M. Drakulich

WHAT'S THE THEORY?

Five basic facts inform theory about racial differences in criminal offending. First, racial differences in offending do exist for some crimes, including several types of violent crime that are among the most frequently discussed both in academic and popular discourse, particularly homicide and robbery. This "fact," however, comes with the important caveat that academic and popular discourses have historically focused disproportionately on violent "street" crimes—those most likely to be committed by disadvantaged and marginalized groups—while ignoring forms of state and corporate violence that may inflict far more damage on the health and well-being of the populace (e.g., Hagan and Palloni 1986). In this light, the claim that street crimes may be more common among disadvantaged and marginalized groups appears somewhat tautological.

The second fact is that race itself is not useful as a causal explanation for race differences in offending, at least as conceived in a fundamental biological or phenotypical sense. Its real importance lies in its social construction and meaning rather than its use as a marker of a biological category (Haney-López 1994; Smedley and Smedley 2005; Yudell et al. 2016). Third, the overarching conclusion of research on racial differences in offending is that the source of the differences in offending is to be found in the environment rather than the individual (Sampson and Wilson 1995; Krivo and Peterson 1996; Sampson and Lauritson 1997; Sampson, Morenoff, and Raudenbush 2005; McNulty, Bellair, and Watts 2013). The fourth relevant and related fact is that people of different races tend to live in dramatically different environments in the United States (e.g., Peterson and Krivo 2010). The fifth and final fact is that most violent crimes are intra-racial rather than inter-racial; thus, there are also significant race differences in victimization that fall along the same lines as offending—a side of the story we return to later in the chapter.

Given that race differences in crime exist primarily as a result of the various environments in which members of different races tend to live, one of the most important theoretical debates concerns what, specifically, matters about the very different environments inhabited by citizens of different races. This debate is not a recent one but instead is among the very first questions tackled by sociological researchers in the United States. Until recently, many popular histories of sociology in the United States began with the Chicago School and the work of Robert Park, Ernest Burgess, Louis Wirth, and others (e.g., Park and Burgess 1925). Popular histories of criminology in the United States also often begin around this same point with the work of Clifford Shaw and Henry McKay.

Shaw and McKay (1942) were centrally interested in the disproportionate levels of juvenile delinquency in some communities in Chicago (and later in other cities), particularly communities inhabited by black migrants from the South and European immigrants (especially those who had arrived recently and were burdened with an ethnic stigma). They argued against classical and biologically deterministic explanations for crime that located the cause of crime in the individual and led to popular explanations for crime rooted in race and ethnicity. Instead, they suggested that "the significantly higher rates of delinquents found among the children of Negroes, the foreign born, and more recent immigrants are closely related to existing differences in their respective patterns of geographic distribution within the city" (Shaw and McKay 1942, 162). In sum, they rooted the causes of the delinquency firmly in the different social environments inhabited by recent immigrants and marginalized groups that largely occupied the most disadvantaged neighborhoods of the new industrial cities. Their story was an optimistic one: as one immigrant group was displaced by the arrival of another, the older group moved off to better neighborhoods and experienced lower levels of delinquency.

Recent work has complicated and criticized this story about the origins of American sociology and criminology, pointing out that W.E.B. Du Bois had already established an "Atlanta School," the contributions of which were actively minimized and erased by members of the Chicago School (Morris 2015). In particular, Du Bois (1899) had already tackled the question of disproportionate crime in neighborhoods inhabited by racial minorities in his groundbreaking study *The Philadelphia Negro*. Like Shaw and McKay (1942),

Du Bois (1899) points to the relevance of the very different social conditions found in black neighborhoods. However, while Shaw and McKay seem to imply an economic essentialism—that the larger economic forces that were driving poor rural residents to cities were a sufficient explanation for the racial and economic composition of the most disadvantaged neighborhoods—Du Bois (1899) ascribed greater importance to race and racism. In a chapter titled "The Causes of Crime and Poverty," Du Bois begins with a discussion of the economic forces—including macroeconomic shifts—that affect both white people and black people. But he continues on to problems arising "from the peculiar history and condition of the American Negro," including slavery, emancipation, segregation, and racial economic exclusion, but also to something more general related to color prejudice: "the wide-spread feeling all over the land . . . that the Negro is something less than an American and ought not to be much more than what he is" (282–284).

This question about the relevance of the racial environment is echoed in later discussions, particularly in the classic debate between William Julius Wilson (1987) and Doug Massey and Nancy Denton (1993) about the high levels of concentrated disadvantage in black inner-city communities in the 1970s, 1980s, and 1990s. The debate fell along similar lines to the one in the earlier part of the century. Wilson (1987) gives primary explanatory power to economic forces, in particular deindustrialization's destruction of working-class jobs in these inner-city neighborhoods and the subsequent class-linked out-migration as those with resources fled the destruction wrought by the macroeconomic shift. This explanation is contested by Massey and Denton (1993), who suggest that it ignores the powerful role of segregation, a force resulting from choices of white policy makers, economic actors and institutions, and residents.

Sampson and Wilson (1995) reiterate Wilson's theory with regard to crime, arguing for the importance of environmental context in explanations of crime, and claiming that the causes of black and white crime are not unique. However, in a shift from Wilson's earlier (1987) work, they add segregation to their list of community-level factors relevant to crime. Among their major theoretical contributions is the identification of social disorganization and cultural social isolation as the key mechanisms linking these environmental factors to crime.

Sampson and Wilson's (1995) central claim, then, is that if white people and black people live in the same kind of environment, they would experience identical rates of crime. When researchers set out to test this hypothesis, however, they ran into a basic problem, one to which Sampson and Wilson (1995) and even Shaw and McKay (1942, 1949) had alluded: there are very few white communities in which there exists the level of extreme disadvantage suffered by many black communities. A variety of work by Ruth Peterson and Laurie Krivo attempted to resolve this methodological problem by testing the basic hypothesis of racial invariance in the environmental sources of crime (e.g., Krivo and Peterson 1996). Peterson and Krivo (2010) eventually came to the conclusion that this basic fact—that black and white Americans live in fundamentally divergent social contexts—is, rather than a methodological problem, the story itself. Their contention, drawing on a long history of theoretical work on racial structures (e.g., Bonilla-Silva 2010) and a wealth of data on community-level racial inequalities, is that "U.S. society is fundamentally structured in ways that serve to maintain white privilege, African-American oppression, and a racial hierarchy in which other nonwhite groups generally fall in between," a hierarchy that is "imprinted in the spatial and social fabric of urban neighborhoods," expressed in high levels of segregation and inequality, and that "undergirds the dramatic differentials in crime among these distinct types of areas" (Peterson and Krivo 2010, 111). In short, what does it mean to say that environmental differences "explain" racial differences in crime if those environmental differences are fundamentally structured by race?

Further challenging a purely economic model, a variety of work has also suggested a more direct role of racism in the causation of crime—that racism may be a unique factor in that it may impact offending among stigmatized and subordinate racial groups but not members of privileged or dominant racial groups. Unnever and Gabbidon (2011, 187), for instance, argue that "African-American offending emerges from their unique worldview—that is, their peerless racialized daily experience," a worldview that "arose because of their inimitable racial oppression . . . the lived experience of blacks residing in a conflicted racially stratified society." Starting from this premise, they draw on components of classic criminological theories, including social bonds, learning, and strain, to develop a model for how this worldview produces criminal offending.

Other work has suggested that racial disparities and racism in the policies and practices of law enforcement and the greater criminal justice system may play a causal role in the generation of crime. Anderson (1999), for instance, identifies a fundamental lack of faith in law enforcement to provide for the safety of residents in poor black communities as a reason for residents of those communities, particularly adolescent males, to take responsibility for their own personal safety by developing a tough reputation through picking fights with others and carrying a gun. More recent work has suggested the prevalence of a sense of *legal cynicism* in poor black communities—"a cultural orientation in which the law and the agents of its enforcement, such as the police and courts, are viewed as illegitimate, unresponsive, and ill equipped to ensure public safety" (Kirk and Papachristos 2011, 1191). One significant implication of this phenomena is that it may result in people feeling more free to violate the law—especially to achieve specific ends such as resolving grievances—and it may make others less likely to cooperate with law enforcement in ways that the justice system depends on to control crime (Bobo and Thompson 2006; Kirk and Matsuda 2011; Kirk and Papachristos 2011; Desmond, Papachristos, and Kirk 2016). Additionally, this lack of faith in the police may even be hurting one of the traditional mechanisms thought to link community characteristics to crime: the ability of a neighborhood to act informally to confront crime problems. Drakulich and Crutchfield (2013) find that a lack of confidence in the effectiveness of the police is associated with a reduced assessment of the effectiveness of informal actions to confront crime—and that these perceptions of the police explain lower rates of informal social control in neighborhoods with a higher African American population.

In sum, we know that there are racial differences in criminal offending, and we know that these differences appear rooted in the very different contexts in which members of those different racial groups tend to live (e.g., Sampson, Morenoff, and Raudenbush 2005). Theoretical work has made several core claims about why this context matters. One argument is that the environmental causes of crime are identical for black people and white people (e.g., Sampson and Wilson 1995). This argument has the benefit of suggesting that there's nothing fundamentally different about people on the basis of race and implies that members of more advantaged racial groups living in the same conditions of less advantaged groups would experience the same levels of criminal offending. It also has the advantage of empirical support: it does appear that environmental differences can largely explain racial differences in violent crime. However, a major critique is that this argument glosses over the basic fact that black and white Americans do not, on average, live in the same kinds of neighborhoods, and this reality is not a mere accident or happenstance. Instead, the racial order structures the socioeconomic conditions of black versus white neighborhoods in fundamental ways (Peterson and Krivo 2010). Some even suggest a direct role of racism in the causation of crime, whether from racial disparities in police practices or through the influence of racial oppression and injustice on a unique African American worldview.

WHAT'S THE PROBLEM?

The first and most obvious problem is the basic disproportions in offending and victimization by race. In 2015, for example, just over 13 percent of the U.S. population was black, but of those murders for which the race of the offender was reported to Uniform Crime Reports, 53 percent were black (U.S.

Department of Justice 2016). Similarly, 53 percent of race-identified murder victims were black (U.S. Department of Justice 2016). The vast majority of these murders were intra-racial: in cases where the race of the offender and victim were both known, 91 percent of black victims were killed by black offenders (U.S. Department of Justice 2016). Serious but nonfatal violence also disproportionately affected black citizens. In 2015, black citizens were 40 percent more likely than non-Hispanic white citizens to be the victim of a rape, robbery, or aggravated assault (Truman and Morgan 2016).

A second problem is the massive disproportions in contact with the criminal justice system. African Americans are overrepresented in every stage of contact with the criminal justice system: among those arrested, sentenced, on probation, in prison, and those put to death (e.g., Rosich 2007; Crutchfield, Fernandes, and Martinez 2010). These disparities begin early: in 2013, the arrest rate for black juveniles was 2.4 times higher than the arrest rate for white juveniles (Puzzanchera and Hockenberry 2016). Many scholars have noted the strong disparities in incarceration. In 2010, black imprisonment rates were 4.1 times higher than white imprisonment rates (National Research Council 2014). Exposure to incarceration is particularly high at the intersection of race, class, gender, and age. In 2010, more than 35 percent of black men between the ages of twenty and thirty-nine who did not finish high school were incarcerated—the equivalent number for white men was around 12 percent, and the number for white men with a college education was close to zero (National Research Council 2014). The lifetime risks are even more striking: among black men born in the latter half of the 1970s who did not finish high school, 68 percent would serve time in prison at some point in their lives, while the same was true for about 28 percent of white dropouts. The absolute numbers are lower among college graduates, but the disparities are actually greater: 6.6 percent of this age cohort of black men versus 1.2 percent of white men (National Research Council 2014). Importantly, in addition to these raw disparities—that are themselves a problem—research tends to suggest that racial disproportions in the criminal justice system exceed racial differences in offending (e.g., Rosich 2007; Crutchfield, Fernandes, and Martinez 2010).

A third problem involves public understandings of the first two problems and in particular the view that the first problem justifies the second. The simplest challenge to this view is the fact that, as described previously, differences by race in contact with the criminal justice system *exceed* differences in offending. More fundamentally, however, this view ignores the *reasons* for the racial differences in crime. As the review of theory suggested, racial differences in crime are the product of fundamental differences in the environments in which members of different racial groups tend to live, and those environmental differences are the product of a racial order that serves to maintain white privilege and African

American oppression. To the degree that contact with the criminal justice system is damaging (and there is a wealth of literature on the damages caused by contact with the criminal justice system), this fact represents another kind of injustice: systematically marginalizing a group and then punishing those in that group for the consequences of this marginalization. In other words, instead of the problem of differential offending justifying the problem of differential contact, these problems are additive: differential criminal justice contact worsens the inequities already reflected in higher rates of offending and victimization. Like the broader inequalities in environments, this basic problem of understanding is also no accident. Those with racial animus or biases against black people are more likely to view crime as a predominantly black phenomenon, are more likely to prefer individualistic or dispositional explanations for crime rather than explanations that account for the racial or economic environment, and are more likely to support harsh punitive approaches to crime as a problem (e.g., Chiricos, Welch, and Gertz 2004; Unnever, Cullen, and Jonson 2008; Drakulich 2015a, 2015b).

A fourth and related problem is the misperception that crime and violence are pervasive in black communities. Careful within-city research facilitates a deeper understanding of the situations, dynamics, and relationships associated with elevated rates of violent crimes committed by black offenders against black victims. For instance, in Boston, gun violence is driven by gang conflicts and is highly concentrated among a small number of high-risk places and high-risk people (Braga 2003). Roughly 5 percent of Boston's street segments and intersections generated about 74 percent of fatal and nonfatal shooting incidents between 1980 and 2008 (Braga, Papachristos, and Hureau 2010). These gun violence hot spots were in and around gang turf and drug market areas and occupied very small geographies within disadvantaged neighborhoods. In 2006, only 1 percent of Boston's population between the ages of fifteen and twenty-four were members of street gangs involved in gun violence; however, gang-related disputes generated half of all homicides and gang members were involved as offenders, victims, or both in nearly 70 percent of nonfatal shootings (Braga, Hureau, and Winship 2008). In a recent study of gang members and their associates in one disadvantaged Boston community, roughly 85 percent of all gunshot victims were in a single social network where every handshake away from a gunshot victim reduced one's odds of gun victimization by 25 percent (Papachristos, Braga, and Hureau 2012).

The patterns observed in Boston parallel distributions seen in many other cities. Criminological research has long documented that crime is highly concentrated among a small number of people (Wolfgang, Figlio, and Sellin 1972; Laub and Sampson 2003) and at a small number of places in cities (Sherman, Gartin, and Buerger 1989; Weisburd, Groff, and Yang 2012).

Even within high-crime neighborhoods, a series of studies suggests that crime clusters at a few discrete locations, leaving many blocks in those areas relatively crime free (Weisburd 2015). Further, very small proportions of youth report participating in street gangs (Klein and Maxson 2006). However, relative to non-gang delinquent youth, gang members have much higher rates of violent offending and violent victimization (Thornberry et al. 2003), and gang conflicts generate disproportionate shares of homicides in many cities (Howell and Griffiths 2016). Street gangs tend to be concentrated in disadvantaged urban neighborhoods (Bursik and Grasmick 1993). These areas, as described earlier, are disproportionately populated by minority residents due to an unfortunate history of racism, exclusion, and isolation.

A fifth problem centers on the diminished capacity of law enforcement agencies to provide justice to victims of serious violent crime and their families. Black homicide victimizations are less likely to be cleared by arrest than white homicide victimizations (Roberts and Lyons 2011). In general, the circumstances of homicide incidents powerfully influence clearance rates. For example, offenders in gang-related and drug-related homicides are much less likely to be arrested by homicide detectives (Wellford and Cronin 2000; Braga and Dusseault 2018), in part due to lack of witness cooperation. Further, black males are more likely than white males to be involved in these kinds of homicide incidents (Cook and Laub 2002). Without citizens coming forward to provide detectives with much needed information, investigations of gang and drug homicides can hit dead ends quickly with no substantive leads. As noted earlier, disadvantaged urban neighborhoods can be characterized by high levels of legal cynicism (Kirk and Papachristos 2011). Cynical views of police, prosecutors, and courts in a neighborhood may influence whether witnesses are willing to share information on homicide incidents and testify in court against charged suspects.

Some analysts suggest that the killings of black male victims receive less investigative time and effort from homicide detectives (Roberts and Lyons 2011), whereas others suggest that white female homicide victims receive more investigative time and effort (Holcomb, Williams, and Demuth 2004). Most available research on clearance rates finds little evidence of homicide detectives valuing or devaluing victims based on race (Puckett and Lundman 2003; Litwin 2004; Lundman and Myers 2012), but there are some noteworthy exceptions. For instance, a multivariate analysis of homicides in Los Angeles County between 1990 and 1994 suggested that white homicide victims received additional investigation attention and, as a result, their cases were more likely to be solved than those involving nonwhite homicide victims (Lee 2005).

It is worth noting here that the criminal dynamics that characterize high levels of homicides and lower clearance rates in black neighborhoods are not based on race. Indeed, disadvantaged white neighborhoods of Boston have been known to exhibit similar patterns of violence and lack of cooperation with the police. For instance, the Charlestown, South Boston, and North End neighborhoods of Boston were noted strongholds of Irish and Italian organized crime organizations during the 1960s through the 1980s that were characterized by repeated, unsolved killings by warring factions of the organizations (O'Neill and Lehr 1989; MacDonald 1999; Lehr and O'Neill 2000). Criminal subcultures that embrace violent norms in settling disputes and promote anti-police attitudes exist in impoverished neighborhoods with varied racial compositions. However, black neighborhoods suffer more intense rates of this kind of criminal network violence due to the more intense concentration of disadvantage in these neighborhoods (Sampson and Wilson 1995).

WHAT'S THE ANSWER?

There are no simple answers to the problems outlined above. It is clear that racial differences in criminal victimization and offending, especially for violence, must be studied from a more complex, multilevel perspective. The available scientific evidence suggests that the relationship between race and violent offending varies substantially across ecological contexts. Within disadvantaged neighborhoods, serious violence is highly concentrated among a very small group of highly active offenders who largely commit their crimes at very specific locations. Unfortunately, popular discourse on race and crime differences tends to be overly simplistic and highly reactionary. Indeed, some compelling evidence suggests that racial disparities in the administration of justice involve political responses to community and national constructions of "moral panics." As Tonry (1995) suggests, the politically charged "war on drugs" in the late 1980s and early 1990s can be viewed as racially discriminatory in its intent and consequences given its legislative and budgetary emphasis on a specific type of drug (crack cocaine) most likely to be used and detected in disadvantaged black neighborhoods. As conflict theorists argue, close attention to how crime is defined and how crime "problems" are socially constructed is essential in the study of racial differences in crime and understanding the nature of racial disparities in criminal justice (Goode and Ben-Yehuda 1994; Chambliss 1995).

Poor analyses and inappropriate descriptions of urban violent crime problems can lead to the adoption of problematic criminal justice policies and programs that exacerbate racial disparities in the criminal justice system and diminish confidence and trust in its institutions. Moreover, careless discussions of the nature of urban violence can further alienate law-abiding black residents who need and desperately want to partner with the police and other governmental institutions to create safer communities. For instance, as Braga and Brunson (2015) suggest, the term "black-on-black" violence, while statistically correct, is a simplistic and emotionally charged definition of urban violence that can be problematic when used by political commentators, politicians, and police executives. To the vast majority of urban black residents who are not involved in violence or criminal behavior, the term invokes visions of indiscriminate and aggressive police enforcement responses applied to a broad range of black people. The term also seems to marginalize serious urban violence as a "black problem" that, in the minds of some black residents, may only receive a cursory response or, worse yet, be ignored by police departments entirely.

An important step in enhancing our ability to diagnose, understand, and respond to race differences in crime and racial disparities in the criminal justice system would involve the improved collection of race and ethnicity data. Throughout this essay, we focus largely on black and white comparisons. This crude categorization stems from a lack of crime data that consistently classify information for Hispanics and non-Hispanics as well as for Asians and Native Americans (Lauritsen and Sampson 1998). Investments need to be made in criminal justice data collection systems that facilitate our understanding of differences across a more refined set of race and ethnicity categories. More nuanced theoretical and policy-relevant insights on race and crime differences have been developed by the limited data that do exist. Immigrants have long been accused of disproportionate involvement in criminal and disorderly behavior. For instance, a growing body of research suggests that neighborhoods characterized by larger concentrations of immigrants, such as Latinos and Asians, tend to have lower levels of violence, controlling for other factors (e.g., see Kubrin and Ishizawa 2012).

A number of criminal justice policy debates could be better informed by more careful consideration of the connections between race and underlying ecological variations in neighborhood contexts. For instance, careful analysis has revealed the deleterious impact of mass incarceration on the capacity of vulnerable neighborhoods to self-regulate through large-scale churning of men and women in and out of prison and jail systems (Clear 2010). Space limitations preclude a full examination of the varied ways in which criminal justice policies can have differential racial impacts and how clearer descriptions of underlying conditions and dynamics might be used to address these disparities. Nevertheless, we illustrate our point by briefly considering how theory and analysis can begin to address seemingly intractable problems in the way urban neighborhoods are policed. This discussion is then followed by a concise summary of broader approaches to improving the capacities of disadvantaged communities to address underlying problems that cause differential involvement in violence.

Careful analysis can lead to clarity in describing urban violence patterns and can thus improve police-minority community relations in at least two important ways (see Braga and Brunson 2015). First, police executives can better frame and communicate to constituents the true nature of serious violent crime problems. Second, careful analysis can lead to the development and implementation of effective and appropriately focused crime reduction strategies. The type of crime analysis work described above is well within the reach of most urban police departments. Inappropriate framing of urban criminal violence problems, and the policies and practices that result, constitute substantial obstacles for police departments and for minority communities struggling to solve these critical issues.

The extant research reviewed here suggests effective policing may require a focus on particular people and places. Thus, police departments should pursue strategies artfully tailored to specific risks such as hot spots, repeat victims, high-rate offenders, or gang hostilities (Braga 2008). However, *how* police departments choose to address these recurring problems may either improve or further damage their relationships with minority residents. Police departments can adopt crime prevention strategies that seek to engage the community in changing the underlying conditions, situations, and dynamics that cause violence to recur. Alternatively, police departments can simply "put cops on dots" through directed patrols or carry out enforcement blitzes aimed at potential offenders in high-violence areas. Unfortunately, these kinds of enforcement initiatives sometimes become unfocused in practice as entire neighborhoods can be defined as hot spot locations and young minority males simply using public spaces can be regarded as potential high-risk offenders (Brunson and Gau 2014).

Community policing should be the foundation of any focused violence-prevention approach. While community policing programs have not been found to be effective in reducing crime, they have been found to generate positive effects on citizen satisfaction, perceptions of disorder, and police legitimacy (Gill et al. 2014). Moreover, community engagement strategies implemented as part of community policing initiatives can provide important input to help focus problem-oriented policing, hot spots policing, and focused deterrence approaches, which do seem to reduce violence (Braga 2015). Developing close relationships with community members would help the police to gather information about crime and disorder problems, understand the nature of these problems, and solve specific crimes. Community members can also help with key components of strategies tailored to specific problems by making improvements to the physical environment and through informal social control of high-risk people. In this way, police strategies focusing on particular people and places would cease to be a form of profiling and become a generator of community engagement projects. Indeed, a central idea in community policing is to engage residents so they can exert more control over situations and dynamics that contribute to their own potential for victimization and, by doing so, influence neighborhood levels of violence.

Preventing violence by addressing underlying violent crime–producing situations and dynamics reduces harm to potential victims as well as harm to would-be offenders by not relying solely on arrest and prosecution actions. Community engagement in developing appropriately focused strategies would help to safeguard against indiscriminate and overly aggressive enforcement tactics and other inappropriate policing activities, which erode the community's trust and confidence in the police and inhibit cooperation. Collaborative partnerships between police and community members improve the transparency of law enforcement actions and provide residents with a much needed voice in crime prevention work. Ongoing conversations with the community can ensure that day-to-day police-citizen interactions are conducted in a procedurally just manner that enhances community trust and compliance with the law (Tyler 2006).

Given the powerful role of neighborhood conditions on race differences in violent behavior and victimization, one clear set of policy implications involves building community social organization to prevent violence. The key idea here is to change places rather than people. Underlying social and structural characteristics of neighborhoods can be addressed through a variety of social and health interventions such as diminishing economic deprivation through local investment incentives, rehabilitating deteriorating housing, promoting stable housing, ameliorating social and physical disorder, enhancing municipal services, dispersing concentrated public housing, and building human capital through neighborhood-based child development strategies (Sampson 2011). These kinds of community investments can help to reverse concentrated disadvantage and stabilize neighborhoods.

Neighborhood violence can also be addressed by improving the social organization and capacity of residents to exert informal social control over public spaces. The presence of community-based organizations, which draw membership from individuals from within and outside specific neighborhoods, predicts collective efficacy and collective civic action (Sampson 2012). These organizations, which include community newspapers, family planning clinics, alcohol/drug treatment centers, counseling or mentoring services (e.g., Big Brother), neighborhood watch groups, and other local agencies, typically act to ensure the well-being of larger community areas. For instance, Sampson suggests the key to fostering informal social controls and collective efficacy "is to increase positive connections among youth and adults in the community"

(2011, 226) and recommends initiatives such as parent involvement in after-school and nighttime youth programs, adult youth mentoring systems, and organized supervision of leisure time youth activities.

However, as suggested in the section on theory, the problem appears to be much larger than basic differences in resources and capacity between communities occupied by members of different racial groups. If those differences are the product of an underlying racial hierarchy, then solutions that are more than superficial will not be possible without directly challenging that hierarchy and dismantling the structure that preserves it. The good news is that overt and open support for a system of racial discrimination and subjugation has declined. In the "Jim Crow" era, open support for segregation and policies that distributed benefits on the basis of race was high, as was open opposition of racial mixing and interracial marriage, but open expressions of these views have declined dramatically in the intervening decades (Schuman et al. 1997). Although a new system of laissez-faire or color-blind racism arose in its place to maintain the racial hierarchy (Bobo, Kluegel, and Smith 1997; Bonilla-Silva 2010), overt disavowals of racism present at least the opportunity for change. As a recent example, in the summer of 2015, in the wake of a string of high-profile police shootings of black citizens, Pew Reports found that perceptions that the country needs to make more changes to give black people equal rights increased sharply and in fact became a majority view even among white Americans (Pew Research Center 2015). Moving forward will be challenging, but the current political climate seems to be becoming more open to such discussions and investments.

REFERENCES

Anderson, E. 1999. *Code of the Street: Decency, Violence, and the Moral Life of the Inner City*. New York: W. W. Norton.

Bobo, L. D., J. R. Kluegel, and R. A. Smith. 1997. Laissez-faire racism: The crystallization of a kinder, gentler, antiblack ideology. In *Racial Attitudes in the 1990s: Continuity and Change*, edited by Steven A. Tuch and Jack K. Martin, 15–41. Westport, CT: Praeger.

Bobo, L. D., and V. Thompson. 2006. Unfair by design: The war on drugs, race, and the legitimacy of the criminal justice system. *Social Research: An International Quarterly* 73: 445–472.

Bonilla-Silva, E. 2010. *Racism without Racists: Color-Blind Racism and the Persistence of Racial Inequality in the United States*. 3rd ed. New York: Rowman & Littlefield.

Braga, A. A. 2003. Serious youth gun offenders and the epidemic of youth violence in Boston. *Journal of Quantitative Criminology* 19 (1): 33–54.

———. 2008. *Problem-Oriented Policing and Crime Prevention*. 2nd ed. Boulder, CO: Lynne Rienner Publishers.

———. 2015. Crime and policing revisited. *New Perspectives on Policing*. Washington, DC: U.S. Department of Justice, National Institute of Justice.

Braga, A. A., and R. K. Brunson. 2015. The police and public discourse on "black on black" violence. *New Perspectives on Policing.* Washington, DC: U.S. Department of Justice, National Institute of Justice.

Braga, A. A., and D. Dusseault. 2018. Can homicide detectives improve homicide clearance rates? *Crime & Delinquency* 64 (3): 283–315. https://doi.org/10.1177%2F0011128716679164.

Braga, A. A., D. Hureau, and C. Winship. 2008. Losing faith? Police, black churches, and the resurgence of youth violence in Boston. *Ohio State Journal of Criminal Law* 6 (1): 141–172.

Braga, A. A., A. V. Papachristos, and D. M. Hureau. 2010. The concentration and stability of gun violence at micro places in Boston, 1980–2008. *Journal of Quantitative Criminology* 26 (1): 33–53.

Brunson, R. K., and J. M. Gau. 2014. Race, place, and policing the inner-city. In *Oxford Handbook on Police and Policing,* edited by Michael D. Reisig and Robert J. Kane. New York: Oxford University Press.

Bursik, R. J., Jr., and H. G. Grasmick. 1993. *Neighborhoods and Crime: The Dimensions of Effective Community Control.* New York: Lexington Books.

Chambliss, W. 1995. Crime control and ethnic minorities: Legitimizing racial oppression by creating moral panics. In *Ethnicity, Race, and Crime: Perspectives across Time and Place,* edited by Darnell Hawkins. Albany: State University of New York Press.

Chiricos, T., K. Welch, and M. Gertz. 2004. Racial typification of crime and support for punitive measures. *Criminology* 42: 358–390.

Clear, T. R. 2010. *Imprisoning Communities: How Mass Incarceration Makes Disadvantaged Neighborhoods Worse.* New York: Oxford University Press.

Cook, P. J., and J. Laub. 2002. After the epidemic: Recent trends in youth violence in the United States. In *Crime and Justice: A Review of Research,* vol. 29, edited by M. Tonry. Chicago: University of Chicago Press.

Crutchfield, R. D., A. Fernandes, and J. Martinez. 2010. Racial and ethnic disparity and criminal justice: How much is too much? *Journal of Criminal Law & Criminology* 100: 903–932.

Desmond, M., A. V. Papachristos, and D. S. Kirk. 2016. Police violence and citizen crime reporting in the black community. *American Sociological Review* 81 (5): 857–876.

Drakulich, K. M. 2015a. Explicit and hidden racial bias in the framing of social problems. *Social Problems* 62 (3): 391–418.

———. 2015b. The hidden role of racial bias in support for policies related to inequality and crime. *Punishment & Society* 17 (5): 541–574.

Drakulich, K. M., and R. D. Crutchfield. 2013. The role of perceptions of the police in informal social control: Implications for the racial stratification of crime and control. *Social Problems* 60: 383–407.

Du Bois, W.E.B. 1899. *The Philadelphia Negro.* Philadelphia: The University of Pennsylvania Press.

Gill, C., D. L. Weisburd, C. Telep, Z. Vitter, and T. Bennett. 2014. Community-oriented policing to reduce crime, disorder and fear and increase satisfaction and legitimacy among citizens: A systematic review. *Journal of Experimental Criminology* 10 (4): 399–428.

Goode, E., and N. Ben-Yehuda. 1994. Moral panics: Culture, politics, and social construction. *Annual Review of Sociology* 20: 149–171.

Hagan, J., and A. Palloni. 1986. Toward a structural criminology: Method and theory in criminological research. *Annual Review of Sociology* 12: 431–449.

Haney-López, I. F. 1994. The social construction of race: Some observations on illusion, fabrication, and choice. *Harvard Civil Rights-Civil Liberties Law Review* 29: 1–62.

Holcomb, J., M. Williams, and S. Demuth. 2004. White female victims and death penalty disparity research. *Justice Quarterly* 21: 877–902.

Howell, J. C., and E. Griffiths. 2016. *Gangs in America's Communities.* 2nd ed. Newbury Park, CA: Sage Publications.

Kirk, D., and A. V. Papachristos. 2011. Cultural mechanisms and the persistence of neighborhood violence. *American Journal of Sociology* 116 (4): 1190–1233.

Kirk, D. S., and M. Matsuda. 2011. Legal cynicism, collective efficacy, and the ecology of arrest. *Criminology* 49: 443–472.

Klein, M., and C. Maxson. 2006. *Street Gang Patterns and Policies.* New York: Oxford University Press.

Krivo, L. J., and R. D. Peterson. 1996. Extremely disadvantaged neighborhoods and urban crime. *Social Forces* 75: 619–48.

Kubrin, C. E., and H. Ishizawa. 2012. Why some immigrant neighborhoods are safer than others: Divergent findings from Los Angeles and Chicago. *Annals of the American Academy of Political and Social Science* 641: 148–173.

Laub, J. H., and R. J. Sampson. 2003. *Shared Beginnings, Divergent Lives.* Cambridge, MA: Harvard University Press.

Lauritsen, J., and R. Sampson. 1998. Minorities, crime, and criminal justice. In *Handbook of Crime and Punishment,* edited by Michael Tonry. New York: Oxford University Press.

Lee, C. 2005. The value of life in death: Multiple regression and event history analyses of homicide clearance in Los Angeles County. *Journal of Criminal Justice* 33: 527–534.

Lehr, D., and G. O'Neill. 2000. *Black Mass: The Irish Mob, the FBI, and a Devil's Deal.* New York: Public Affairs Press.

Litwin, K. 2004. A multilevel multivariate analysis of factors affecting homicide clearances. *Journal of Research in Crime and Delinquency* 41: 327–351.

Lundman, R., and M. Myers. 2012. Explanations of homicide clearances: Do results vary dependent upon operationalization and initial (time 1) and updated (time 2) data? *Homicide Studies* 16: 23–40.

MacDonald, M. P. 1999. *All Souls: A Family Story from Southie.* Boston: Beacon Press.

Massey, D. S., and N. A. Denton. 1993. *American Apartheid: Segregation and the Making of the Underclass.* Cambridge, MA: Harvard University Press.

McNulty, T. L., P. E. Bellair, and S. J. Watts. 2013. Neighborhood disadvantage and verbal ability as explanations of the black–white difference in adolescent violence: Toward an integrated model. *Crime and Delinquency* 59: 140–160.

Morris, A. D. 2015. *The Scholar Denied: W.E.B. Du Bois and the Birth of Modern Sociology.* Oakland, CA: University of California Press.

National Research Council. 2014. *The Growth of Incarceration in the United States: Exploring Causes and Consequences. Committee on Causes and Consequences of High Rates of Incarceration*, edited by J. Travis, B. Western, and S. Redburn. Committee on Law and Justice, Division of Behavioral and Social Sciences and Education. Washington, DC: National Academies Press.

O'Neill, G., and D. Lehr. 1989. *The Underboss: The Rise and Fall of a Mafia Family*. New York: Public Affairs Press.

Papachristos, A. V., A. A. Braga, and D. M. Hureau. 2012. Social networks and the risk of gunshot injury. *Journal of Urban Health* 89 (6): 992–1003.

Park, R. E., and E. W. Burgess. 1925. *The City: Suggestions for Investigation of Human Behavior in the Urban Environment*. Chicago: University of Chicago Press.

Peterson, R. D., and L. J. Krivo. 2010. *Divergent Social Worlds: Neighborhood Crime and the Racial-Spatial Divide*. New York: Russell Sage Foundation.

Pew Research Center. 2015. Across racial lines, more say nation needs to make changes to achieve racial equality. August. Available at http://www.people-press.org/files/2015/08/08-05-2015-Race-release.pdf.

Puckett, J., and R. J. Lundman. 2003. Factors affecting homicide clearances: Multivariate analysis of a more complete conceptual framework. *Journal of Research in Crime and Delinquency* 40: 171–193.

Puzzanchera, C., and S. Hockenberry. 2016. National Disproportionate Minority Contact Databook. Developed by the National Center for Juvenile Justice for the Office of Juvenile Justice and Delinquency Prevention. Available at http://www.ojjdp.gov/ojstatbb/dmcdb/.

Roberts, A., and C. J. Lyons. 2011. Hispanic victims and homicide clearance by arrest. *Homicide Studies* 15: 48–73.

Rosich, K. J. 2007. *Race, Ethnicity, and the Criminal Justice System*. Washington, DC: American Sociological Association.

Sampson, R. J. 2011. The community. In *Crime and Public Policy*, edited by J. Q. Wilson and J. Petersilia, 210–236. New York: Oxford University Press.

———. 2012. *Great American City: Chicago and the Enduring Neighborhood Effect*. Chicago: University of Chicago Press.

Sampson, R. J., and J. Lauritson. 1997. Racial and ethnic disparities in crime and criminal justice in the United States. *Crime and Justice* 21: 311–374.

Sampson, R. J., J. D. Morenoff, and S. Raudenbush. 2005. Social anatomy of racial and ethnic disparities in violence. *American Journal of Public Health* 95: 224–232.

Sampson, R. J., and W. J. Wilson. 1995. Toward a theory of race, crime, and urban inequality. In *Crime and Inequality*, edited by John Hagan and Ruth Peterson. Stanford, CA: Stanford University Press.

Schuman, H., C. Steeh, L. D. Bobo, and M. Krysan. 1997. *Racial Attitudes in America: Trends and Interpretations*. Cambridge, MA: Harvard University Press.

Shaw, C. R., and H. D. McKay. 1942. *Juvenile Delinquency in Urban Areas*. Chicago: University of Chicago Press.

———. 1949. Rejoinder. *American Sociological Review* 49: 261–72.

Sherman, L. W., P. Gartin, and M. Buerger. 1989. Hot spots of predatory crime: Routine activities and the criminology of place. *Criminology* 27 (1): 27–55.

Smedley, A., and B. D. Smedley. 2005. Race as biology is fiction, racism as a social problem is real: Anthropological and historical perspectives on the social construction of race. *American Psychologist* 60: 16–26.

Thornberry, T. P., M. Krohn, A. Lizotte, C. Smith, and K. Tobin. 2003. *Gangs and Delinquency in Developmental Perspective.* New York: Cambridge University Press.

Tonry, M. 1995. *Malign Neglect: Race, Crime, and Punishment in America.* New York: Oxford University Press.

Truman, J. L., and R. E. Morgan. 2016. Criminal victimization, 2015. U.S. Department of Justice, Bureau of Justice Statistics. Available at http://www.bjs.gov/content/pub/pdf/cv15.pdf.

Tyler, T. 2006. *Why People Obey the Law.* 2nd ed. Princeton, NJ: Princeton University Press.

Unnever, J. D., and S. L. Gabbidon. 2011. *A Theory of African-American Offending.* New York: Routledge.

Unnever, J. D., F. T. Cullen, and C. L. Jonson. 2008. Race, racism, and support for capital punishment. *Crime and Justice* 37: 45–96.

U.S. Department of Justice, Federal Bureau of Investigation. 2016. *Crime in the United States, 2015.* Available at https://ucr.fbi.gov/crime-in-the-u.s/2015/crime-in-the-u.s.-2015/home.

Weisburd, D. L. 2015. The law of crime concentration and the criminology of place. *Criminology* 53 (2): 133–157.

Weisburd, D. L., E. Groff, and S. Yang. 2012. *The Criminology of Place: Street Segments and Our Understanding of the Crime Problem.* New York: Oxford University Press.

Wellford, C., and J. Cronin. 2000. Clearing up homicide clearance rates. *National Institute of Justice Journal* 243 (April): 2–7.

Wilson, W. J. 1987. *The Truly Disadvantaged: The Inner City, the Underclass, and Public Policy.* Chicago: University of Chicago Press.

Wolfgang, M. E., R. Figlio, and T. Sellin. 1972. *Delinquency in a Birth Cohort.* Philadelphia: University of Pennsylvania Press.

Yudell, M., D. Roberts, R. DeSalle, and S. Tishkoff. 2016. Taking race out of human genetics. *Science* 351: 564–565.

2

Critical Race Theory and the Limits of Liberal Legal Remedies to Address Racial Disparities in Police Violence

AMY FARRELL, PATRICIA WARREN, AND SHEA CRONIN

In January 2017 the U.S. Department of Justice, Civil Rights Division, released a scathing report on the Chicago Police Department's (CPD) inappropriate and racially disparate use of force, including deadly force (U.S. Department of Justice 2017). The investigation followed the release of a dashboard camera video that showed a white CPD officer fatally shooting Laquan McDonald, a black teenager who was walking away from the police at the time he was killed. The release of the video shocked community leaders and the public, many of whom had expressed concern about racial profiling and inappropriate use of force within the context of growing rates of violent crime and significant public safety challenges in Chicago. In the wake of the video release, community members and national leaders joined together to protest the CPD, the superintendent of the CPD resigned, and criminal charges were filed against the officer who shot Laquan McDonald and seven additional officers who were charged with covering up the incident (Austen 2016). The event was a horrific and dramatic illustration of the dangers of police use of force and the deepening distrust between the police and the communities they serve. This distrust has been magnified as communities of color face growing threats from violent crime coupled with unequal and often racially disparate criminal justice system responses (Bobo and Thompson 2006; Nellis 2016). Race permeates the criminal justice system through practices of racial profiling and the aggressive stop and search practices ruled unconstitutional in *Floyd v. City of New York* (2013), through sentencing disparities and mass incarceration (Alexander 2012), or more aptly hyper-incarceration where social control efforts of the state target particularly vulnerable groups such as the poor and people of color (Wacquant 2008).

Police violence includes acts of brutality by the police related to the inappropriate escalation of force. Police officers are routinely called to situations that involve threats to their safety or the safety of others. In these situations, police have a right and sometimes an obligation to use appropriate force to protect themselves and the public from harm. Of particular concern is the targeting of people of color or communities of color for enforcement, which increases the risks of police violence. The inappropriate use of force by the police, resulting in disproportionate injury or death to people of color or other disenfranchised community groups, is a growing concern as these incidents are increasingly captured on video and shared widely through social media. The shooting of unarmed black men and women, notably the killing of Michael Brown by police in Ferguson, Missouri, in 2014 sparked community outrage, protests, and calls for police reform. Since Michael Brown's death, police departments across the country have been called to account for numerous deaths of unarmed black people including James Boyd, a homeless man in Albuquerque, New Mexico; John Crawford, a customer purchasing a rifle at Walmart in Beavercreek, Ohio; Tamir Rice, a twelve-year-old playing with a toy gun in a public park in Cincinnati, Ohio; Terence Crutcher, who was returning to his broken-down car in Tulsa, Oklahoma; and Walter Scott, who was fleeing from the police following a traffic stop in North Charleston, South Carolina.

Because the police do not generally release use of force data to the public and submission of such data to the federal government is voluntary, it is difficult to determine if police use of force or deadly use of force is rising or becoming increasingly racially disparate. Despite the lack of systematic national data about police use of force, community concerns have been supported by empirical research. For example, a study of thousands of police encounters in twelve U.S. cities found that, while force was used in less than 3 percent of all police interactions, African Americans were 3.6 times more likely to have force used against them compared to whites even controlling for racial differences in police contact (Goff et al. 2016). Reexamining data collected by the *Washington Post*, Wesley Lowery (2016) found that since 2015, police across the United States have shot and killed 175 young black men (24 of whom were unarmed). During that same time, the police shot and killed 172 white men (18 of whom were unarmed) (Lowery 2016). Despite the fact that the number of young black and white men who were killed by police is roughly equivalent, according to the *Washington Post* data, black men were overrepresented because they comprised 40 percent of the victims but only 6 percent of the U.S. population.

At various points in our history concerns about police violence have culminated in demonstrations and confrontations between police and minority community members, sometimes resulting in violence and property damage and often resulting in the loss of community trust. Numerous commissions have been appointed to examine issues related to racial discrimination and violence by the police including the Katzenbach Commission (President's Commission on Law Enforcement and Administration of Justice 1967), the Kerner Commission (Report to the National Advisory Commission on Civil Disorders 1968), and the Christopher Commission (Los Angeles, California, 1991). In 2015 President Barack Obama convened the President's Task Force on 21st Century Policing (2015) in the wake of a series of officer-involved shootings. The commission made numerous recommendations aimed at reducing tension between police and communities of color and creating systems of accountability around police use of force.

Criminologists have utilized various theoretical approaches to explain racial disparities in police violence. Critical race theory offers a macro-level perspective distinct from explanations focused on individual causes of police violence and instead focuses on institutional or structural explanations of and remedies to police use of deadly force. Critical race theory posits that the maintenance of racial hierarchies is central to the work of institutions of the state, including the criminal justice system. Moreover, they emphasize several principles: (1) race is a central factor in the way our society is organized; (2) racism is an institutional part of the social systems in American culture; (3) everyone contributes to the racialized system through everyday practices, and (4) race and ethnicity are social constructions that are created and revised based on a group's own self-interests (Brown 2003; Bonilla-Silva 2009). This chapter describes the historical roots of critical race theory, examines its application to the problems of racial disparities in police violence, and explores models for reform informed by this theoretical perspective.

CRITICAL RACE THEORY

Critical race theory (CRT) scholars seek to understand how racism and racial discrimination continue to exist despite policies of the state and norms of society that condemn racist beliefs and practices (Harris 2012). They argue that racism is not isolated or aberrant. Rather, it is built into the daily life and structures of American society (Delgado and Stefanic 2001). In turn, white supremacy and the legal and institutional mechanisms that support it have been rendered invisible and the impacts of white hegemony are no longer seen as oppressive. Critical race theory directs attention to structural and institutional arrangements that contribute to and maintain racial inequalities.

white dominance

Through their scholarship, CRT scholars expose the limits of formal law for addressing racial inequality and propose alternative remedies, based largely on restorative justice principles.

Historical Roots and Key Principles

Critical race theory emerged in the 1980s as an offshoot of the vanguard critical legal studies tradition. Critical legal theorists were predominately left-wing, white, male legal scholars who challenged the traditions of American legal liberalism as mechanisms to overcome social oppression (Crenshaw 1988, 2002). Frustrated with the stalled progress of the civil rights movement, critical legal theorists argued that the bedrocks of the American liberal legal traditions, including key consensus values such as representative democracy, consent of the governed, equal citizenship, and guaranteed liberties (Hartz 1955), failed to bring about meaningful social reform. Critical legal theorists posited that the law is a political tool, used by those in power to obscure oppression through the façade of neutrality in order to maintain dominance (Kelman 1987).

As scholars of color entered the academy in greater numbers during the 1970s and 1980s, they were drawn to critical studies because it resonated with their dissatisfaction with the stalled progress of the civil rights movement that frequently motivated their study (Harris 2012). Frustrated with the inability of critical legal theorists to engage meaningfully around issues of race and essentialism and angered by the marginalization of scholars of color within the legal academy, critical race scholars broke off from their critical legal theory peers to expose how American liberal legal traditions that advance notions of color-blind law and personal merit have perpetuated racial inequalities.

Since its origin in the 1980s, CRT has grown beyond legal scholarship to encompass fields of sociology, education, criminology, and women's studies. There is significant variation among critical race theorists, but three main principles can be found across the tradition. First, formal, color-blind law is dangerous in a society where white supremacy is invisible and people of color have historically been treated differently due to their membership in a group or class. Color-blind law obscures the structures that create and perpetuate social and political inequality and is insufficient to address forms of discrimination beyond the most flagrant racism. Second, legal reforms that benefit people of color generally only occur when they benefit whites—a phenomenon of "interest convergence" (Bell 1980). For example, Bell argues that the Supreme Court was willing to end a long-standing policy of "separate but equal" in *Brown v. Board of Education* in 1954 in part because it bolstered the U.S. image as a defender of civil and human rights in the face of growing

Communists' threats across the globe (Bell 1980, 524)—an interest of white Americans that converged with the desire for equality demanded from black Americans. Third, CRT scholars suggest that race is a socially constructed concept utilized to create differences among people for the purposes of group domination. CRT advances anti-essentialism, meaning that people do not occupy single identities but rather have intersecting identities and allegiances.

Application of CRT to Civil Rights Concerns

CRT scholars have consistently attacked the jurisprudence of the U.S. Supreme Court on race as perpetuating and facilitating racism under the guise of civil rights jurisprudence. They criticize the integrationists who led the nonviolent civil rights movement of the 1960s for accepting highly proscribed legal gains shrouded in a false promise of legal neutrality (see Matsuda and Lawrence 1993) and instead share closer alliances with the black liberation or "black power" movement leaders who demanded racial equality through any means necessary. Central to the CRT critiques of civil rights law as a mechanism to remedy racial injustice is the notion that equal opportunity principles—laws that require individuals of different racial groups to be treated alike, for example—can only remedy the most blatant forms of racial discrimination. Civil rights approaches, pursued through constitutional case law or legal traditions following the enactment of the 1964 Civil Rights Act, require plaintiffs to prove the animus or bad intention of state actors or others that led to racially disparate outcomes or harm to a group based on race. CRT scholars argue that because racism is hidden in modern society, such a color-blind approach to racial injustice will fail to remedy the more pervasive and usual forms of racism that people of color experience that emerge through unconscious bias and/or structures of institutionalized racism (Lawrence 2015). Additionally, modern antidiscrimination doctrine struggles to recognize and remedy the harms experienced because of one's membership in multiple disadvantaged identities. Discrimination claims rely on proof that "but for" a person's membership in a group a person would not experience harm. Such claims are difficult if not impossible to advance for those who experience discrimination or disparate treatment because of their membership in multiple groups. For example, black women's claims of discrimination are measured against standards for differential treatment of women as a class or black people as a class, ignoring the unique nature of discrimination based on a person's status as a black woman (Crenshaw 1989).

Within the realm of criminal justice, critical race theorists are suspicious of the law as a mechanism through which people of color receive justice. The adversarial system of criminal trials disadvantages people of color, particularly when judges, prosecutors, and jurors are overwhelming white (see Ward, Farrell and Rousseau 2009 for discussion of the impact of court workgroup race on case processing and outcomes). In response, some CRT theorists have suggested that jurors should acquit black defendants accused of victimless crimes to remedy racially unjust enforcement practices and the disproportionate harm of incarceration to communities of color (Butler 1995). Others have argued for limits on hate speech and crime motivated by bias, despite concerns about the protection of freedom of speech central to the liberal legal tradition (Delgado and Stefanic 1997). Despite these efforts, hate speech regulations and hate crime laws are poorly enforced and arguably have done little to stem harassment and violence directed at people of color (Bell 2002) and the criminal justice system continues to be utilized to control communities of color (Alexander 2012).

POLICY IMPLICATIONS OF CRITICAL RACE THEORY

Racial Profiling

Are racial and ethnic minorities disproportionately targeted by police? This has been a long-standing question since the 1960s during the height of the civil rights era when the role of police was to keep black citizens out of predominately white spaces. In 1968, the Kerner Commission found that police were racially biased and often used excessive force against minority citizens. Although the Kerner Commission report was released more than fifty years ago, the more contemporary story of racially biased policing emerged during the war on drugs when police organizations used racial profiles to decide whom to place under police suspicion. This practice, known as racial profiling, became more widespread in the 1990s when officers were trained by the Drug Enforcement Administration on how to use race as a signal of criminality (Smith et al. 2003). The federal government through the Drug Enforcement Agency and Operation Pipeline eventually trained more than twenty-five thousand police officers from forty-eight states to use racial profiles.

Opponents of racial profiling, like the American Civil Liberties Union (ACLU), have challenged the use of racial profiles, arguing that they are inherently discriminatory and that their use leads to a disparate number of minority citizens being stopped, searched, and arrested. As a result, many states passed legislation banning the use of racial profiles. In addition, the U.S. Department of Justice entered into consent decrees with a number of jurisdictions, explicitly prohibiting discriminatory police-citizen encounters (see the section Addressing Institutional and Structural Bias to learn more about the origin and use of consent decrees). Consent decrees required data collection in order to monitor institutional compliance (Ramirez, McDevitt, and Farrell 2000). Since 2000, more than four thousand law enforcement agencies across the United States have been involved in data collection efforts.

Allegations of racial profiling have prompted law enforcement agencies across the United States to collect police-stop data in order to study the extent of bias in police outcomes (Amnesty International 2004; Smith 2005; Withrow 2004). In addition, criminology scholars have explored the impact of race and ethnicity on a variety of police outcomes (Smith and Alpert 2002; Rojek, Rosenfeld, and Decker 2004; Tillyer and Engel 2012). This research has generally found that black people and Hispanics are disproportionately stopped, searched, and arrested. In a study of the stop practices of the New York Police Department (NYPD), the New York Attorney General found that although black people represented 25.6 percent of New York's population, they comprised 51 percent of all persons stopped by the NYPD. In 2014, the Department of Justice found that Missouri police officers were 73 percent more likely to stop and search black drivers compared to white drivers (U.S. Department of Justice 2015).

While evidence of racial disparities has been consistently found in explorations of police-citizen encounters (Lamberth 1997), it remains unclear whether racial bias or discrimination is undergirding these disparities (Engel and Cohen 2014). Despite this lack of clarity, police organizations must place race and race sensitivity in the forefront of officer training. This can be achieved both through education and accountability. Citizen and police review boards can play a proactive role in monitoring individual police behavior as well as problematic organizational practices. In addition, aggressive enforcement of civil rights laws will also play an important role in encouraging law enforcement agencies to monitor and address bias inside their organizations. Filing lawsuits against cities and states with persistent patterns of racially biased policing will send a message to all police organizations that the routine harassment of minority citizens is unacceptable.

Police Use of Force

Police use of force is an important tool used by law enforcement because it is a necessary source of power required to enforce law and order. Police officers are entitled to use force in certain circumstances; however, several questions remain: (1) when should it be utilized, (2) to what degree should it be used, and (3) are there disparate outcomes when it is used? Prior research has demonstrated that the most significant predictor of police use of force is citizen resistance (National Institute of Justice 1999). In the Project on Policing Neighborhoods, citizen resistance was the most compelling factor that influenced police use of force (Terrill 2000). In addition to resistance, officers are more likely to use force when they feel a situation or an individual is threatening to them. Currently, the idea of threat influencing police use of force has garnered a great deal attention because of the notable deaths of Michael Brown, Freddie Grey, and Tamir Rice. In each of these lethal force deaths, police organizations argued that force was necessary because the officers felt threatened either by the presumption that a gun was present or that they were in a position that could cause them harm. In each of these cases, the controversy not only surrounded whether the police had used excessive force but also whether race had influenced their decision to do so.

In the context of trying to better understand the circumstances under which police use force, scholars have identified three broad approaches: (1) individual, (2) situational, and (3) organizational. The individual approach focuses on officer characteristics including race, gender, and prior years of experience (Garner, Maxwell, and Heraux 2002; Paoline and Terrill 2007). Situational factors explain the use of force by highlighting the relevance of offender characteristics such as race, age, and gender, as well as the circumstances surrounding the police encounter (i.e., nature of the offense, whether the offender was compliant or resistant, and number of officers on the scene) (Klinger 2009). Finally, the organizational approach argues that police use of force is in part a by-product of the environment in which the force occurred (Terrill and Reisig 2003). Environments with higher rates of crimes and incivilities are more likely to have community members subjected to police force. Additionally, in William Westley's (1970) study of police violence, he notes that a police culture that condones police use of force will have officers who rely on it more heavily.

Critical race theorists are most interested in the complex ways that race and ethnicity influence force used by police. Currently, the empirical evidence is mixed. For nearly every study that finds no race or ethnic effects (Engel, Sobol, and Worden 2000; McCluskey, Terrill, and Paoline 2005), other studies find that racial and ethnic minorities are more likely to be subjected to force compared to white people (Terrill and Reisig 2003). Garner, Maxwell, and Heraux (2002) found that black suspects were more likely to have force used against them even in circumstances in which they were compliant with the officer. Similarly, Terrill and Reisig (2003) found that minority suspects are more frequently subjected to force by the police, but this effect is mediated by neighborhood context. In terms of lethal force, Tagaki (1974) suggests that police have a lower threshold of suspicion for black people because of the presumptions of criminality, which leads to higher odds of using lethal force against them. This is especially true among black males who have become the symbols of crime in the United States (Kennedy 1997).

Efforts to Stop Police Violence and Discrimination

Recognizing the Limits of Modern AntiDiscrimination Law

Traditionally, claims of police violence and discrimination by the police have been addressed through civil lawsuits against individual police officers or police agencies with liability to oversee offending officers. The primary civil rights law utilized to hold police accountable is known as Section 1983, designated as such because of the section where the law has been published within Title 42 of the *United States Code*. Originating from the 1871 Civil Rights Act, Section 1983 makes it unlawful for police, or anyone acting under the authority of the state, to deprive someone of his or her constitutional rights. Following the liberal legal tradition of promoting equality through safeguarding rights, individuals can file civil lawsuits against the police in federal court as a mechanism to hold police agencies accountable, but the success of such claims has been varied.

There are several limits of Section 1983 as a mechanism for remedying racialized police violence. First, individual officers are usually indemnified by their contract or union against legal liability for actions that occurred through the course of their regular duties. In turn, federal civil rights lawsuits are generally levied against police agencies or cities that are liable for the misconduct of the officers they employ and supervise. Second, although some larger agencies have paid tens of millions of dollars to settle legal claims of unconstitutional use of force and racial bias when the evidence of misconduct was unequivocal, beyond providing some compensation to aggrieved families, legal settlements do little to change institutional practices that cause harm (U.S. Commission on Civil Rights 1995). When police agencies settle civil rights claims, they generally refuse to acknowledge that officers or the agency were in the wrong and plaintiffs commonly must agree to keep secret the terms of the settlement and any information discovered through the legal process (Human Rights Watch 1998). In some cases, offending officers even retain their positions or move to positions in other police agencies. Third, Section 1983 claims are often unsuccessful because the mechanism for holding police agencies accountable is burdensome. Plaintiffs must prove that the actions or inactions of police agencies or municipalities caused the civil rights violation. Recent case law extends the burden on plaintiffs, requiring proof of "deliberate indifference" toward a civil rights violation that was known to the department or city (*City of Canton v. Harris* 1989; *Board of Commissioners of Bryan County v. Brown* 1997). Finally, because civil litigation requires individuals harmed by the police to hire attorneys and expend resources to pursue civil rights claims, this legal recourse is often not feasible to people in structurally disadvantaged communities who may be at most risk for police violence.

Recognizing the Role of Implicit Bias

CRT scholars work to expose the limitations of liberal legalism in addressing racial bias beyond the most overt forms of racism. Proof of animus or intent to harm is central to U.S. antidiscrimination law, but racism is taboo in modern society and few public officials assert claims that are overtly or explicitly racist. Instead, claims of discrimination tend to focus on racially disparate outcomes interpreted as evidence of discriminatory intent. Concerns about racial profiling and racialized police violence suggest that bias in some form continues to influence decision making in the criminal justice system. In response, CRT scholars increasingly draw upon the work of social psychologists to understand and expose how racial disparities in police enforcement and use of force may be the result of implicit or unconscious biases that are commonly asserted by broad cross sections of the American public (Robinson 2008).

Human beings depend on cognitive shortcuts such as stereotypes to help navigate a complex world. Every day people must make hundreds of quick decisions, often with incomplete information. Stereotypes or attitudes that we hold about situations or groups based on previous experience or messages we receive living in a society structured by racial inequality affect our actions and decisions, often without our awareness of their influence. Research in social psychology and behavioral economics suggests the unconscious influence of racial stereotypes on our behavior. The Implicit Association Test (IAT), which requires subjects to quickly pair positive and negative words with pictures of black and white faces, has now been taken by millions of people through studies or via internet portals. The IAT confirms that unconscious racial bias is extremely widespread (Greenwald, McGhee, and Schwartz 1998).

Implicit bias has become an increasingly important explanation for understanding racial disparities in police shootings, though evidence of its direct impact is still unclear. Social scientists have identified racially disparate decision making in numerous laboratory settings that cannot be explained by traditional measures of explicit bias or racism. For example, Eberhardt and colleagues (2004) found that respondents more quickly were attuned to black faces compared to white faces when primed to think about violent crime. In a series of studies utilizing video simulations, participants were shown images of black or white people holding different objects and were asked to make quick determinations of whether the video subject was holding a gun or a non-gun object such as a cell phone or wallet. If the object was a gun, they were instructed to shoot, but if the object was not a weapon, they were instructed not to shoot. The shooting studies confirmed that people were more willing to shoot unarmed black subjects compared to unarmed white subjects (Greenwald, Oakes, and Hoffman 2003; Plant, Peruche, and Butz 2005) and measures of overt racism do not explain these differences. Yet recent studies utilizing IAT measures have not found a relationship between implicit bias and racial disparities in shooting decisions (James, Klinger, and Vila 2014). More research is needed to understand the causal mechanisms behind observed racial disparities in police use of force and the role that unconscious biases may play in explaining that relationship. CRT scholarship affirms the need to pursue this line of inquiry and develop reform measures sensitive to biases that do not emerge through animus or explicit racism prohibited by traditional antidiscrimination law.

CRIMINAL JUSTICE REFORM INFORMED BY CRITICAL RACE THEORY

Addressing Institutional and Structural Problems

One of the most significant changes in the federal government's effort to address racial disparities in police use of force was congressional authorization for the U.S. Department of Justice to bring civil actions against law enforcement agencies thought to have engaged in a "pattern or practice" of behavior that deprives individuals of their civil rights as part of the 1994 Violent Crime Control and Law Enforcement Act (42 U.S.C. § 14141).[1] Dual public concern about high crime rates and police accountability led to the passage of the Crime Control Act along with the provisions that came under Section 14141. High rates of violence, particularly highly visible gun violence associated with the illegal drug trade and concentrated in disadvantaged urban communities, placed crime on the national agenda in the late 1980s and early 1990s. National politicians, both liberal and conservative, sought legislation that would send a message to constituents that they were responding to this problem. Several incidents during the same period, the most salient of which was the beating of Rodney King by Los Angeles police officers, severely diminished public trust in the police. Video of the infamous beating in March 1991 was widely seen, and the subsequent acquittal of the four officers indicted for their participation sparked one of the most destructive riots to have ever occurred in the United States. As a result, the legislation that ushered in many "tough" crime-control measures also included compromise accountability provisions.

Following the enactment of the 1994 Violent Crime Control law, attorneys in the Special Litigation Section of the Civil Rights Division (CRD) of the Justice Department began to conduct investigations of law enforcement agencies alleged to have engaged in discriminatory patterns or practices of conduct. If an investigation turned up wrongdoing, the CRD could seek to compel the agency to enter into a consent decree (which does not require the agency to accept the investigation's findings) or to bring ligation against an agency that refuses to cooperate. In the case of a consent decree, often a court-appointed monitor was put in place to oversee the agency's efforts to meet mandated improvements. The Justice Department also settled some matters privately with a Memorandum of Agreement (MOA) that does not carry with it the judicial enforceability of a consent decree and does not require the law enforcement agency to admit culpability. While often reactive responses to widespread misconduct in an organization, Section 14141 actions are aimed at initiating comprehensive, organization-wide change within the agency.

Since 1994 the Justice Department has investigated or is currently monitoring forty-six law enforcement agencies because of complaints stemming from a pattern or practice of civil rights violations (U.S. Department of Justice 2017). The Justice Department entered into the first of such consent decrees with the Pittsburgh Bureau of Police in April 1997 following high-profile incidents involving the shooting of minority community members and other incidents of misconduct committed. The set of remedies required by the resulting consent decree, including establishment of a comprehensive early warning system, implementation of a use of force policy, and improved investigative practices concerning officer misconduct, represented an attempt not just to improve disciplinary rules but also to rework the organizational environment in which officers exist. Since the first sets of Section 14141 actions, the Justice Department has sought to implement a common set of reforms within agencies, many of which have also become part of the President's Task Force on 21st Century Policing (President's Task Force 2015).

Section 14141 actions are based on several premises that are unique in comparison to other legal accountability mechanisms. First, Section 14141 actions are necessary because it is difficult for isolated individuals to bring successful suits against police agencies and in many instances agencies simply absorb the penalties as the "cost of doing business." Following the model of other civil rights era reforms (e.g., Voting Rights Act), Section 14141 gives the federal government the tools to address practices that violate rights as a mechanism to bring about change. Second, these suits are uniquely aimed at instilling reforms that seek organization-wide change such that agencies implementing reforms would become self-reinforcing over time (Walker and Archbold 2013). As part of what Walker terms the "new paradigm" in police accountability, once implemented, even internal processes such as early intervention systems (EIS) are thought to promote a culture of fair and legal practices. Finally, less frequently discussed is the potential diffusion effect that Section 14141 actions can have on other local law enforcement agencies.

While other lawsuits brought by individuals can be settled for monetary damages that can be absorbed by the agency or local government, Section 14141 actions can bring agencies under court monitoring—the closest thing to losing autonomy in public administration. CRD sees this threat as a promising tool to motivate agencies to adopt the reforms frequently implemented within agencies under consent decree or MOAs (U.S. Department of Justice 2017). Since proportionately few agencies have come or will come under CRD scrutiny, the broad effect of Section 14141 as a force for change in American law enforcement rests on this diffusion process.

The success of Section 14141 actions is uncertain. The reform package represents some of what are thought to be best practices for police accountability. Case studies from Los Angeles (Stone, Foglesong, and Cole 2009), Pittsburgh (Davis et al. 2005), and Washington, DC (Bromwich Group 2016), for example, suggest the processes produced positive changes in the accountability systems of investigated agencies. However, significant questions remain about the degree with which the reforms are institutionalized within police agencies through Section 14141 action (Walker and Archbold 2013; Walker and McDonald 2008). Even more uncertain is the effect these actions have had on agencies not directly targeted for Section 14141. We know very little about the ways in which the threat of Section 14141 actions have led police agencies to adopt changes that would improve their accountability systems on their own. Police leaders may or may not be motivated to seek reforms beyond what they see as necessary and perhaps may not have the capital to overcome barriers and achieve change within their organizations.

Part of the challenge of successful police reform has to do with having the correct "technology" of reform. The common toolkit of most Section 14141 actions—use-of-force policy development, early intervention systems, and complaint systems—may not be effective even though it is clear that police reformers see them as the best practices. But part of the challenge also lies outside the organization and is grounded in the pessimistic view of successful reform contemplated by critical race theory scholars. CRT, in part, points to the pressures placed on police agencies in a society with high levels of racial and class inequality as a cause of disparate practice and forms of misconduct. Liberal legalism assumes the courts can be a force to overcome the power differentials inherent in representative governance; giving the authority to powerful institutional actors to bring suits helps to overcome the problem of relying on individuals to bring cases. Yet the reform efforts within agencies coming under investigation take place in the local contexts that gave rise to the accountability challenges in the first place and do little to overcome the central problem of needing to increase the voice of disadvantage groups in police governance over the long term. Walker and Archbold's (2013) recommendation based years of experience evaluating consent decree reform efforts is to strengthen the use of police auditors. Establishing strong external mechanisms to document and monitor the agency's internal reforms approach no doubt goes a long way toward institutionalizing reforms because such procedures may be able to offset the institutional pressures that facilitate weak accountability approaches, but reformers also must consider the political contexts that CRT views as inhibiting fair and legal policing. It is not clear that lasting reforms can occur without local agencies reevaluating their choices of strategy and without a strong local political context to compel them to make changes.

Attention to Enforcement Strategies

Critical race theory informs mechanisms to address racialized police violence that move beyond the limits of legal reform. Because context is critical to CRT, scholars in this tradition place experiences of people of color at the center of their inquiry, seeking to understand how police policies and practices are experienced by those in communities targeted for aggressive police enforcement. Privileging the voices of people traditionally marginalized by dominant legal narratives exposes the limitations of pattern and practice investigations and consent decrees to advance change. Beyond the internal mechanisms of control that can be established through consent decrees and federal monitoring of police agencies, such as training, hiring practices that promote diversity, and establishing accountability mechanisms, a CRT perspective suggests that persistent patterns of racially disparate treatment continue despite reform because they are a direct result of specific crime control strategies. For example, aggressive stop and search practices, zero-tolerance policing, and order maintenance policing—all part of a package of police strategies employed in the last decade to stop crime by targeting minor infractions that are predicted by "broken windows theory" (Wilson and Kelling 1982) to create environments where crime flourishes—have led to aggressive police enforcement in neighborhoods of color (Fagan and Davies 2002; Gelman, Fagan, and Kiss 2007). Despite court rulings finding aggressive stop and frisk practices such as those carried out by the New York City Police Department to be unconstitutionally biased, city officials maintain aggressive enforcement efforts are necessary to control crime, particularly in neighborhoods of color (Kelly 2013). Similarly, smart policing or information-driven policing strategies such as COMPSTAT that utilize statistics to inform rapid deployment of officers to address crime problems (McDonald, Greenberg, and Bratton 2002) remove decision making about how to fight crime and where to concentrate police enforcement efforts away from community-police partnerships that are central to community policing strategies (Skogan 2006). In place of communication with local residents, crime mapping, predictive policing, and other and data-driven intelligence tools inform enforcement decisions. These tools are designed to bring science, objectivity, and neutrality to policing but they have also created greater social distance between police and the communities they serve. In turn, efforts to employ color-blind techniques privilege dominant group experiences and marginalize the harms experienced by communities of color that are disproportionately the subjects of aggressive enforcement. By failing to understand and take into account the local context, smart policing tools may in fact perpetuate racially biased enforcement and create conditions where police may utilize force. Critical race theorists instead suggest that police reform attentive to concerns about racial bias and police violence against communities of color must utilize community policing models that empower residents and build relationships between the police and communities they serve.

Advancement of Alternative Justice Models

Although CRT informs efforts to monitor and improve policing, this perspective is ultimately skeptical of the state as the primary mechanism to address racial disparities because of the interest of dominant groups in maintaining racial hierarchies. Instead, CRT suggests that the experiences of people of color should inform efforts to promote equality. This subjective perspective is critical for understanding the lived experiences of people of color and deconstructing white perspectives that are often portrayed as truth. Alternative models of justice that prioritize giving voice to the experiences of people of color include public accountability through social movement and protest such as the #BlackLivesMatter movement. Since its inception in 2012 following the murder of Trayvon Martin, a seventeen-year-old, unarmed, African American youth pursued by a community vigilante who was later acquitted based on a claim of self-defense, the #BlackLivesMatter movement mobilized thousands of African Americans and their supporters to fight against police brutality and violence. This movement and others have utilized social media platforms such as Facebook and Twitter to expose police violence.

Restorative justice approaches are another strategy proposed by CRT scholars that is less reliant on the mechanisms of the state to prevent harm. Although there are many restorative justice models in practice throughout the world, the underlying principle proposes that communities take a larger role in addressing harms to the victim, restoring the offending into the community, and preventing crime (Braithwaite 2002). Those who advocate restorative justice approaches are less concerned about the harms of crime to the state and are more attentive to healing communities and addressing the

Shift in focus ~

underlying social problems that create conditions where crime flourishes. Investment in alternative justice approaches such as restorative justice can promote voice and provide access to mechanisms of power traditionally unavailable to marginalized groups.

Critical race theory provides a new lens through which communities can pursue racial justice. It does not provide easy answers but rather exposes the limitations of modern antidiscrimination law, illuminates structural and institutional racism, and gives voice to the subjective experiences of people of color who experience discrimination, subordination, and violence.

NOTE

1. Prior to 1994, the U.S. Department of Justice had the authority to investigate racial disparities in police use of force under the Civil Rights Act of 1964, 42 U.S.C. § 2000d (Title VI), and the Omnibus Crime Control and Safe Streets Act of 1968, 42 U.S.C. 3789d (Safe Streets Act). Title VI and the Safe Streets Act prohibit police practices that are found to have a disparate impact on people based on their race or ethnicity or other protected statuses unless these practices are necessary to achieve legitimate, nondiscriminatory objectives.

REFERENCES

Alexander, M. 2012. *The New Jim Crow: Mass Incarceration in the Age of Colorblindness.* New York: New Press.

Amnesty International USA. 2004. *Threat and Humiliation: Racial Profiling, Domestic Security and Human Rights in the United States.* New York: Amnesty International USA.

Austen, B. 2016. Chicago after Laquan McDonald. *New York Times Magazine,* April 20. Available at https://www.nytimes.com/2016/04/24/magazine/chicago-after-laquan-mcdonald.html?_r=0.

Bell, D. 1980. *Brown v. Board of Education* and the interest convergence dilemma. *Harvard Law Review* 93: 518–533.

Bell, J. 2002. *Policing Hatred: Law Enforcement, Civil Rights and Hate Crime.* New York: New York University Press.

Board of the County Commissioners of Bryan County v. Brown, 520 U.S. 397 (1997).

Bobo, L. D., and V. Thompson. 2006. Unfair by design: The war on drugs, race, and the legitimacy of the criminal justice system. *Social Research* 77: 445–472.

Bonilla-Silva, E. 2009. *Racism without Racists: Color-Blind Racism and the Persistence of Racial Inequality in the United States.* Lanham, MD: Rowan and Littlefield.

Braithwaite, J. 2002. *Restorative Justice and Responsive Regulation.* New York: Oxford University Press.

Bromwich Group. 2016. *The Durability of Police Reform: The Metropolitan Police Department and Use of Force, 2008–2015.* Washington, DC: Bromwich Group LLC. Available at http://www.dcauditor.org/sites/default/files/Full%20Report_2.pdf.

Brown, T. 2003. Critical race theory speaks to the sociology of mental health: Mental health problems produced by racial stratification. *Journal of Health and Social Behavior* 44 (3): 292–301.

Butler, P. 1995. Racially-based jury nullification: Black power in the criminal justice system. *Yale Law Review* 105: 677–725.

City of Canton v. Harris, 489 U.S. 378, 385–86 (1989).

Crenshaw, K. 1988. Race, reform and retrenchment: Transformation and legitimation in antidiscrimination law. *Harvard Law Review* 1010: 1331–1387.

———. 1989. Demarginalizing the intersection of race and sex: A Black feminist's critique of antidiscrimination doctrine, feminist theory and anti-racist policy. *The University of Chicago Legal Forum* 140: 139–167.

———. 2002. The first decade: Critical reflections, or "a foot in the closing door." In *Crossroads, Directions, and a New Critical Race Theory,* edited by F. Valdes, J. M. Culp, and A. P. Harris, 9–31. Philadelphia: Temple University Press.

Davis, R. C., C. W. Ortiz, N. J. Henderson, J. Miller, and M. K. Massie. 2002. *Turning Necessity into Virtue: Pittsburgh's Experience with a Federal Consent Decree.* Washington, DC: Vera Institute of Justice.

Delgado, R., and J. Stefanic. 1997. *Critical White Studies: Looking Behind the Mirror.* Philadelphia: Temple University Press.

———. 2001. *Critical Race Theory: An Introduction.* New York: New York University Press.

Eberhardt, J. L., P. A. Goff, V. Purdie, and P. G. Davies. 2004. Seeing black: Race, crime, and visual processing. *Journal of Personality and Social Psychology* 87: 876–893.

Engel, R. S., and D. Cohen. 2014. Racial profiling. In *The Oxford Handbook of Police and Policing,* edited by M. D. Reisig and R. J. Kane, 383–416. Oxford: Oxford University Press.

Engel, R. S., J. J. Sobol, and R. E. Worden. 2000. Further exploration of the demeanor hypothesis: The interaction effects of suspects' characteristics and demeanor on police behavior. *Justice Quarterly* 17 (2): 236–258.

Fagan, J., and G. Davies. 2002. Street stops and broken windows: Terry, race, and disorder in New York City. *Fordham Law Journal* 28: 457–503.

Floyd v. City of New York, 959 F. Supp. 2d 668 (S.D.N.Y. 2013).

Garner, J. H., C. D. Maxwell, and C. G. Heraux. 2002. Characteristics associated with the prevalence and severity of force used by the police. *Justice Quarterly* 44 (4): 703–746.

Gelman, A., J. Fagan, and A. Kiss. 2007. An analysis of the New York City Police Department's "stop and frisk" policy in the context of claims of racial bias. *Journal of American Statistical Association* 102: 813–823.

Goff, P. A., T. Llyod, A. Geller, S. Raphael, and J. Glaser. 2016. *The Science of Justice: Race, Arrests, and Police Use of Force.* Los Angeles, CA: Center for Policing Equality.

Greenwald, A., M. Oakes, and H. Hoffman. 2003. Targets of discrimination: Effects of race on response to weapons holders. *Experimental Social Psychology* 39: 399–405.

Greenwald, A. G., D. E. McGhee, and J.L.K. Schwartz. 1998. Measuring individual differences in implicit cognition: The Implicit Association Test. *Journal of Personality and Social Psychology* 74: 1464–1480.

Harris, A. P. 2012. *Critical Race Theory.* Davis, CA: University of California, Davis.

Hartz, L. 1955. *The Liberal Traditional in America. An Interpretation of American Political Thought since the Revolution.* New York: Harcourt, Brace.

Human Rights Watch. 1998. *Shielded from Justice: Police Brutality and Accountability in the United States.* New York: Human Rights Watch.

The Independent Commission on the Los Angeles Police Department (Christopher Commission Report). 1991. The Report of the Independent Commission on the Los Angeles Police Department.

James, L., D. A. Klinger, and B. Vila. 2014. Racial and ethnic bias in decisions to shoot seen through a stronger lens: Experimental results from high-fidelity laboratory simulations. *Journal of Experimental Criminology* 10: 323–340.

Kelly, R. 2013. Opinion, the NYPD: Guilty of saving 7,383 lives. *Wall Street Journal*, July 23, 2013, at A17.

Kelman, M. 1987. *A Guide to Critical Legal Studies.* Cambridge: Harvard University Press.

Kennedy, R. 1997. *Race, Crime, and the Law.* New York: Random House.

Klinger, D. A. 2009. Can police training affect the use of force on the streets? The Metro-Dade violence reduction field experiment. In *Holding Police Accountable*, edited by C. McCoy, 95–107. Washington, DC: Urban Institute Press.

Lamberth, J. 1997. *A Report of the American Civil Liberties Union.* New York: ACLU.

Lawrence, C. R. 2015. Local kine implicit bias: Unconscious racism revisited (yet again). *University of Hawaii Law Review* 37: 457.

Lowery, W. 2016. Aren't more white people than black people killed by police? Yes, but no. *Washington Post*, July 11, 2016.

Matsuda, M., and C. R. Lawrence. 1993. *Words That Wound: Critical Race Theory, Assaultive Speech and the First Amendment.* Boulder CO: Westview Press.

McCluskey, J., W. Terrill, and E. A. Paoline. 2005. Peer group aggressiveness and the use of coercion in police-suspect encounters. *Police Practice and Research: An International Journal* 6 (1): 19–37.

McDonald, P., S. Greenberg, and W. J. Bratton. 2002. *Managing Police Operations: Implementing the New York Crime Control Model—Compstat.* Belmont, CA: Wadsworth.

National Institute of Justice. 1999. *Use of Force by Police: Overview of National and Local Data.* Research Report NCJ 176330. Washington, DC.

Nellis, A. 2016. *The Color of Justice: Racial and Ethnic Disparities in America's State Prisons.* Washington DC: The Sentencing Project. Available at http://www.sentencingproject.org/publications/color-of-justice-racial-and-ethnic-disparity-in-state-prisons/.

Paoline, E. A., and W. Terrill. 2007. Police, education, experience and the use of force. *Criminal Justice and Behavior* 34 (2): 179–196.

Plant, A., M. Peruche, and D. Butz. 2005. Eliminating automatic racial bias: Making race non-diagnostic for responses to criminal suspects. *Journal of Experimental Psychology* 41: 141–156.

President's Commission on Law Enforcement and Administration of Justice. 1967. The Challenge of Crime in a Free Society [Katzenbach Commission].

President's Task Force on 21st Century Policing. 2015. Final Report of the President's Task Force on 21st Century Policing. Washington, DC: Office of Community Oriented Policing Services. Available at https://cops.usdoj.gov/pdf/taskforce/TaskForce_FinalReport.pdf.

Ramirez, D., J. McDevitt, and A. Farrell. 2000. *A Resource Guide on Racial Profiling Data Collection Systems: Promising Practices and Lessons Learned.* NCJ 184768. Washington, DC: U.S. Department of Justice.

Report to the National Advisory Commission on Civil Disorders [Kerner Commission]. 1968.

Robinson, R. 2008. Perceptual segregation. *Columbia Law Review* 108: 1093–1180.

Rojek, J., R. Rosenfeld, and S. Decker. 2004. The effect of driver race on traffic stops in Missouri. *Police Quarterly* 7: 126–147.

———. 2012. Policing race: The racial stratification of searches in police traffic stops. *Criminology* 50: 993–1024.

Skogan, W. 2006. The promise of community policing. In *Police Innovation: Contrasting Perspectives,* edited by David Weisburd and Anthony Braga, 27–43. Cambridge: Cambridge University Press.

Smith, M. R. 2005. Depoliticizing racial profiling: Suggestions for the limited use and management of race in police decision-making. *George Mason UCRLJ* 15: 219–260.

Smith, M. R., and G. Alpert. 2002. Searching for discretion: Courts, social science, and the adjudication of racial profiling claims. *Justice Quarterly* 19: 673–703.

Smith, W. R., D. Tomaskovic-Devey, M. Zingraff, H. M. Mason, P. Y. Warren, C. P. Wright, H. McMurray, and C. R. Felon. 2003. *The North Carolina Highway Traffic Study. Final Report to the National Institute of Justice.* Washington, DC: U.S. Department of Justice.

Stone, C., T. Foglesong, and C. M. Cole. 2009. *Policing Los Angeles Under a Consent Decree: The Dynamics of Change at the LAPD.* Available at http://assets.lapdonline.org/assets/pdf/Harvard-LAPD%20Study.pdf.

Takagi, P. 1974. A garrison state in "democratic society." *Crime and Social Justice: A Journal of Radical Criminology* 1 (Spring–Summer): 27–33.

Terrill, W. 2000. *Police Coercion: Application of the Force Continuum.* New York: LFB Scholarly Publishing.

Terrill, W., and M. D. Reisig. 2003. Neighborhood context and police use of force. *Journal of Research in Crime and Delinquency* 40: 291–321.

Tillyer, R., and R. S. Engel. 2012. Racial differences in speeding patterns: Exploring the differential offending hypothesis. *Journal of Criminal Justice* 40: 285–295.

U.S. Commission on Civil Rights. 1995. *Racial and Ethnic Tensions in American Communities: Poverty, Inequality, and Discrimination, Volume III: The Chicago Report,* September, 139.

U.S. Department of Justice. 2017. Investigation of the Chicago Police Department. United States Department of Justice Civil Rights Division and United States Attorney's Office Northern Illinois, January 13, 2017. Available at https://www.justice.gov/opa/file/925846/download.

U.S. Department of Justice Civil Rights Division. 2015. The Ferguson Report: Department of Justice Investigation of the Ferguson Police Department. Washington, DC: U.S. Department of Justice.

———. 2017. The Civil Rights Division's Pattern and Practice Police Reform Work: 1994–Present. Available at https://www.justice.gov/crt/file/922421/download.

Wacquant, L. 2008. Racial stigma in the making of America's punitive state. In *Race, Incarceration and American Values,* by Glen Loury. Cambridge, MA: MIT Press.

Walker, S. 2012. Institutionalizing police accountability reforms: The problem of making police reforms endure. *Saint Louis University Public Law Review* 32: 57–92.

Walker, S., and C. Archbold. 2013. *The New World of Police Accountability*, 2nd ed. Los Angeles, CA: Sage Publications.

Walker, S., and M. Macdonald. 2008. An alternative remedy for police misconduct: A model state "pattern or practice" statute. *George Mason University Civil Rights Law Journal* 19: 479–552.

Ward, G., A. Farrell, and D. Rousseau. 2009. Does racial balance in workforce representation yield equal justice? Race relations of sentencing in federal court organizations. *Law and Society Review* 43: 757–804.

Westley, W. 1970. *Violence and the Police.* Cambridge, MA: MIT Press, 111–152.

Wilson, J. Q., and G. L. Kelling. 1982. Broken windows: The police and neighborhood safety. *The Atlantic* (March): 29–38.

Withrow, B. 2004. A comparative analysis of commonly used benchmarks in racial profiling: A research note. *Justice Research and Policy* 6: 71–92.

3

Situational Prevention of Wildlife Crimes

The Policy Challenges

Ronald V. Clarke, Justin Kurland, and Lauren Wilson

This chapter addresses a relatively unfamiliar criminological topic—crimes related to wildlife—which, for present purposes, can be defined as all living species of flora and fauna that occur in the wild outside human cultivation. Many categories of wildlife are protected by law for reasons of maintaining biodiversity, for tourism, because they are iconic species, or due to their value as commodities, such as rare timber or commercial fish. Crimes against protected wildlife fall into two main categories: (1) illegal killing and poaching and (2) more distant trading of live species or parts of species such as skins, ivory, or the flesh of tuna and pangolins.

We describe a small program of research undertaken at the Rutgers School of Criminal Justice based on situational crime prevention (SCP), the science and art of reducing opportunities for crime (Clarke 1980). Because the program seeks ways to reduce wildlife crime and ultimately to implement solutions, it differs from "green criminology" (South and Brisman 2013), which, broadly speaking, seeks to expose corporations and governments that follow policies or practices that harm the environment. In this respect, green criminology follows an "enlightenment" approach to influencing policy, whereas SCP seeks a more direct, interventionist role. As discussed below, this key difference complicates the task for SCP.

While it may be difficult to distinguish our program from green criminology, it is equally difficult to define the relationship between our program and the much larger field of conservation biology. While much of the work in this latter field consists of monitoring the extent and condition of threatened species, it is undertaken with an implicit policy agenda: first and foremost, to halt habitat loss and degradation and, second, to seek protection for endangered species under law. These policies are necessary but not sufficient on their own to deter determined illegal hunters and poachers—as shown by the current poaching crises of protected elephant ivory and rhino horn (Lemieux and Clarke 2009). We believe that tailored interventions emerging from detailed situational analyses of specific wildlife crimes are also needed.

This is the rationale for our program, but in its pursuit we have faced many challenges beginning with the legitimacy of the topic. Thus, we are often asked why we seek to benefit wildlife when there are so many human victims of crime who need help. Our first answer would be that our wildlife work involves only a tiny proportion of all criminological effort, which is overwhelmingly focused on human victims. Second, poaching and illegal killing of protected animals not only infringe animal rights but also can involve much cruelty and unnecessary suffering. For example, it is estimated that around 75 percent of parrots taken from the wild die before being brought to market as a result of shock or careless treatment (Cantu et al. 2007). Third, the ecological balance of ecosystems and thus the conservation of biodiversity frequently depend upon the survival of particular endangered species in the wild. Fourth, species that are endangered include many charismatic animals that play an important part in the cultural heritage of the world. We would guess that more children's books, comics, and TV programs feature tigers than the numbers that presently exist in the wild. If iconic species such as tigers were to disappear, not only would cultures be impoverished but also nongovernmental conservation agencies may find it more difficult to obtain the funds required to protect less charismatic species. Fifth, many wildlife crimes directly impact human welfare. Poaching of elephants and rhinos harms the ecotourism industry on which some African countries depend. Illegal fishing by international corporations in the coastal waters of some other African countries has destroyed the artisanal fishing that supplies these countries with much needed protein, and illegal logging has deprived Indonesia of vast sums in taxable revenue (Magrath et al. 2007). Sixth, it has been widely claimed that the illegal trade in wildlife is second only in value and volume to the illegal trade in drugs and that it finances organized crime and terrorism. While the evidence is weak (Reuter and O'Regan 2016), the claim has galvanized international support for curbing the wildlife trade and for this reason alone demands the attention of criminologists.

Challenges to legitimacy have been compounded by practical and professional concerns likely to be shared by those pushing at the margins of their discipline. We have worried about obtaining relevant data, whether it will be possible to publish papers in the leading journals, whether conservation biologists will understand the need for a criminological input, whether doctoral students will be attracted to this topic, and whether they will succeed in obtaining academic posts. While we have encountered some hostility to our work, from both criminologists and conservation biologists, this may be no greater than the usual academic resistance to work beyond the mainstream. We have been able to publish papers and our PhDs have obtained academic posts in universities with graduate programs. The much larger problem that we discuss below is the difficulty of finding ways to have a direct impact on policy and practice.

In the sections that follow we provide an introduction to SCP, discuss the challenge of responding to the great variety of wildlife crimes, analyze the conditions in which SCP has had its greatest effect on policy, and argue that there may be limited scope for meeting these conditions in the field of wildlife crime. We illustrate these points with a case study of rhino poaching in South Africa and conclude with a brief account of our current strategy in the face of these challenges. Along the way we attempt to make some more general points about the difficulties for criminology of directly impacting policy.

SITUATIONAL CRIME PREVENTION

Kurt Lewin's (1936) observation that behavior is a function of the interaction between an organism and its environment is at the heart of SCP. In criminological terms, Lewin's observation holds that crime results from a combination of offenders' propensities and their immediate situations or living circumstances. While propensity and situation might be equally important in producing crime, this does not mean that they are equally important in preventing it. While most attempts have sought to change the offender, either through punishment or remedial treatment, preventing crime has proven to be very difficult. In contrast, SCP seeks only to change the situation,[1] which has proved to be considerably easier with many successful case studies published since its inception more than thirty-five years ago (Guerette and Bowers 2009; Johnson, Bowers, and Guerette 2012).

Early studies focused on everyday property offenses, such as residential burglary and vehicle theft, leading to questions about the utility of the approach beyond that of reducing instrumental crimes. Over time, however, it has expanded to cover such disparate crime types as computer fraud (Willison 2000), organized crime (Van de Bunt and Van der Schoot 2003), terrorism (Clarke and Newman 2006), and child sex abuse (Wortley and Smallbone 2006) and, in the process, has repudiated early claims about the limited application of the approach.

SCP adopts a problem-solving methodology in which the "opportunity structure" for a highly specific crime problem is analyzed to provide an indication of which interventions might be most effective for preventing the crime. With greater experience in implementing SCP, allied with developments in theory, researchers have progressively revised a classification system that assists in the process of selecting interventions for the prevention of crime (Smith and Clarke 2012). The latest version consists of twenty-five different opportunity-reducing techniques nested within five SCP mechanisms. The original classification (Clarke 1992) identified three crime-reducing mechanisms: increasing the risk, increasing the effort, and reducing the rewards of crime that are implicit in the rational choice assumptions of SCP. These mechanisms work on the premise that crime is always a choice and occurs when various necessary conditions converge in space and time. It follows that offender-situated decision making can be altered and crime reduced by changing the offender's perceptions of the balance of risk, effort, or reward.

Subsequently, the classification was extended to include a fourth category, or mechanism—removing excuses—that speaks to Sykes and Matza's (1957) and Bandura's (1973) suggestions that rationalization can facilitate criminal behavior. This mechanism can be applied by inducing guilt or shame at the point when criminal decisions are made. For example, notices posted at the boundaries of a protected animal reserve announcing that intruders will be arrested and fined are likely to affect the situational calculus of potential offenders. A fifth mechanism—reducing provocations—was added in response to Wortley's (2001) evidence about the ways in which the immediate environment can actively encourage or induce individuals to commit crimes. One of these ways—generating emotional arousal—is particularly relevant to wildlife crime. Considerable evidence exists about the role of emotional arousal in retaliatory killings of predatory wildlife (Inskip and Zimmerman 2009) and the mechanism of reducing provocations can be applied in a number of wildlife crime contexts. For example, establishing electric fences around crop fields in Namibia can reduce the anger of villagers whose crops are regularly raided by elephants (O'Connell-Rodwell et al. 2000). The fences limit crop-raiding and, in turn, reduce villager anger and the likelihood of retaliation against elephants.

Table 3.1 classifies SCP's various mechanisms and crime inhibitors and provides examples of how these might be utilized to prevent the innumerable forms of wildlife crime. Unfortunately, very few of these preventative interventions or recommendations have been evaluated, so the table serves merely to illustrate how SCP could be applied. While SCP is easier to implement than long-term initiatives that seek to alter criminal dispositions, its implementation is still difficult (Knutsson and Clarke 2006). This is especially

Application of SCP to wildlife crime

TABLE 3.1. THE 5 SITUATIONAL CRIME PREVENTION MECHANISMS AND 25 CRIME INHIBITORS FOR WILDLIFE CRIME

Increase the Effort	Increase the Risk	Reduce the Rewards	Reduce the Provocations	Remove the Excuses
1. Harden Target • Collars that allow escape from metal snares	***6. Extend Guardianship*** • WildScan, a mobile app, to report likely illegally sourced or poached animals in markets • "Bush Watch" schemes modeled after Neighborhood Watch programs	***11. Conceal Targets*** • Avoid providing location data for potential poachers	***16. Reduce Frustration and Stress*** • Ecotourism provides monetary incentives • Business alternatives • Boost availability of affordable legal fuel wood and introduce sustainable alternatives	***21. Set Rules*** • Making locals aware of laws and conservation objectives • Require third-party evidence of legal procurement for public timber purchases
2. Control Access to Facilities • Screening entrance points into Protected Areas (PAs) • Securing rhino horn and elephant ivory stockpiles • Docking protocol at ports to check for illegal fishing gear	***7. Assist Natural Surveillance*** • Monetary rewards for whistle-blowers who disclose wildlife law violations • Publicize contact information (e.g., "hotline") for civic reports of wildlife offenses	***12. Remove Targets*** • Translocation of species • Dehorning • Tusk trimming	***17. Avoid Disputes*** • Relief schemes to compensate farmers for livestock killed • Road mitigation such as guardrail gaps and under/overpasses to reduce wildlife-motorist conflict	***22. Post Instructions*** • "Protected Area" • Road signage warning motorists of wildlife crossing zones • "Buyer Beware" campaigns using billboards and social media to engage the public
3. Screen Exits • Departure protocols at ports to check for illegal fishing gear • License plates recorded upon exit from PAs • Manned checkpoints and random investigations on forest area exit roads	***8. Reduce Anonymity*** • Ranger IDs • GPS devices for rangers and PA visitors so movement can be tracked • Log personnel who access data or evidence relating to wildlife investigations	***13. Identify Property*** • Branding legally sourced timber • Marking antique ivory • Identifying "captive-bred" animals as wild-caught based on health, behavior, and blood/stool tests	***18. Reduce Emotional Arousal*** • Corrals/fences to prevent livestock predation • Educate herding communities about best practices	***23. Alert Conscience*** • Public awareness campaigns • Social marketing campaigns targeted to wildlife consumers and their networks

4. Deflect Offenders • Road blockades for car/truck checks along roadways identified as wildlife trafficking routes • Automate customs checking systems documentation to reduce corruption	***9. Utilize Place Managers*** • Trade show officials must report animals (and vendors selling them) identified as protected • Provide equipment, training, and mentoring for park guards	***14. Disrupt Markets*** • Monitoring markets • Increasing the availability/affordability of substitute protein (chicken, fish) • Surveillance of internet markets and advertisement websites	***19. Neutralize Peer Pressure*** • Anticorruption units and multi-agency task forces to undermine corruption in police culture • Anonymous whistle-blowing mechanisms to neutralize peer intimidation and coercion	***24. Assist Compliance*** • Accessible fact sheets for tourists identifying region-specific illegal wildlife products • Plan tour routes and amenities to direct visitors away from at-risk areas
5. Control Tools/Weapons • Prohibiting the sale of fishing gear prone to by-catch • License system for timber processing facilities	***10. Strengthen Formal Surveillance*** • Alarms in facilities that house ivory/rhino horn stockpiles • CITES Identification Guides for state customs officials • Spatial Monitoring and Reporting Tool (SMART)	***15. Deny Benefits*** • Disfiguring the carapaces of ploughshares tortoises • Dying rhino horn • Increase profitability of sustainable harvest through subsidiaries and tax reductions	***20. Discourage Imitation*** • Censure details of modus operandi	***25. Control Drugs and Alcohol*** • N/A

true given the various ecological conditions that should be considered when trying to prevent even just a single type of wildlife crime such as poaching. For instance, the mechanisms and crime inhibitors that might be deployed to prevent tiger poaching at Corbett National Park in India will be different from those needed to prevent poaching of rhinos at Kruger National Park in South Africa. More specifically, not only are the physical landscapes markedly different and the mobility, foraging, and overall behavioral pattern of tigers and rhinos dissimilar, but also the poachers themselves frequently use different hunting techniques (e.g., snares versus rifles). The following section discusses the diversity of wildlife crimes and the challenge of specificity.

THE DIVERSITY OF WILDLIFE CRIME AND SCP'S NEED FOR SPECIFICITY

Wildlife crime is the illegal taking, trading, exploiting, possessing, or killing of flora or fauna in contravention of national or international laws. Thus, nests of threatened Amazonian parrot species are raided to provide nestlings for the pet trade. Poached freshwater turtles from Cambodia are mixed with legally farmed turtles in Hong Kong fish markets. Despite a recent ban on the international trade, large-scale seizures persist of frozen pangolin taken from Asia and Africa, whose scales are used for wallets, belts, and handbags and whose meat is sold clandestinely in upscale restaurants in numerous Asian countries. The bones of tigers poached from Indian nature reserves are sold in China as ingredients for Traditional Chinese Medicine. And valuable tuna is harvested from the oceans of poor countries by international fishing conglomerates and sold in Europe and Asia. These are just a few of the varied environments, species, and purposes behind some wildlife crimes, all of which need to be prevented in specific but different ways. As with urban crimes, the mechanisms and crime inhibitors that may help prevent one particular wildlife crime may not be suitable for another.

For purposes of study, it is useful to divide crimes against protected wildlife into two broad categories: (1) the initial acts of poaching and illegal killing and (2) the more distant trading of live species or their parts such as skins and ivory. The first category, poaching and illegal killing, represents the most direct ecologically impactful stage of the wildlife crime process, but these crimes are quite different from one another. Poaching is the permanent removal of flora or fauna from the wild for consumption or for sale—and even fairly specific forms of poaching can prove to be quite varied on closer inspection. For example, primate poaching in African tropical forests may at first seem straightforward, but poaching monkeys for consumption is quite different from the capture of live chimpanzees to supply the international pet trade. As for illegal killing, this typically occurs when farmers are provoked by the loss of livestock and retaliate by killing protected predators. For example, villagers living in close proximity to tiger reserves in India sometimes kill tigers that have predated their cattle, either by shooting them when they return to feed on the carcass or by poisoning the carcass. The main difference between retaliatory killing and poaching is that the former is not primarily motivated by financial gain or sustenance. This is important because, once again, the mechanisms most likely to be effective for preventing each type of crime will be different. For instance, improved livestock management, such as the use of corrals for cattle, has been shown to reduce predation by protected carnivores and in turn reduce retaliatory killing of these species. While they might effectively reduce illegal killings, corrals would have a limited value in reducing most forms of poaching.

Poaching and retaliatory killing are also quite different from the trade or trafficking of protected species. Trafficking occurs subsequent to the poaching event and can take many forms (Moreto and Lemieux 2015). Thus, "bushmeat" may be sold in local markets near to the poaching location. On the other hand, a large portion of rhinoceros horn and elephant ivory taken from sub-Saharan Africa is transported to Asia before being sold. Interventions meant to target this type of trafficking may require extensive cooperation between the origin and destination countries involved that may be separated by thousands of miles. The interventions are often undermined by the unwillingness of foreign governments to intervene in the trade, by corruption, and sometimes by the inherent difficulty of accurately identifying illegally traded wildlife parts.

The implications for our program's need for specificity in seeking to understand and prevent wildlife crimes are considerable. We stumbled unwittingly into a vast field of criminal behavior, far larger than we could conceivably impact given SCP's requirement for crime specificity. For example, breaking down the apparently unitary problem of rhino poaching into its constituent parts involves determining the species of rhino, their geographic ranges, the poachers and the means they employ, and the various subsequent processes and stages of trafficking. A sample of these difficulties is given in the annex at the end of the chapter, which describes our frustrations when attempting to analyze rhino poaching in South Africa.

SCP'S INFLUENCE ON POLICY AND THE REALITIES OF WILDLIFE CRIME

Any researcher seeking to influence policy has to recognize that research findings are only one of the many factors weighed by policy makers when making their decisions. These factors include the media and public opinion, politics and pressure groups, available budgets, and the difficulties of new policies, including the investment in existing arrangements on the ground. Faced with these realities, policy-oriented researchers in the field of criminology have generally followed the "enlightenment" model that seeks to provide a deeper background of information on policy questions. SCP is different. As a form of piecemeal social engineering (Tilley 2004), it seeks to bring about discrete policy changes by following an action-research model through which a specific problem is carefully analyzed, potential solutions are explored, the most practical and socially acceptable solutions are implemented, and the results are evaluated.

This process requires a much closer relationship between researchers and policy makers than in the enlightenment model. Laycock and Clarke (2001) have described how a systematic program of SCP research undertaken in the Home Office succeeded in changing crime prevention policy in the United Kingdom. The principal lesson of this experience was that the findings of research are most likely to have an impact on policy when policy makers (i.e., the "customers") have played a direct role in formulating the research, including the questions to be explored and the means of answering them. Many researchers would resist this arrangement because they might fear losing too much autonomy, but the clout wielded by policy makers can greatly speed up and smooth the way for research. In addition, when policy makers have had a significant part in formulating the research, they are also more likely to implement the results. This is more likely to happen when the following occur:

1. The policy makers can clearly understand the results and have confidence in them.
2. They can recognize good news in the findings.
3. The researchers are willing to speculate more widely about the implications.
4. Cost data are included in evaluations.
5. Resources are available for the policy changes.
6. Broad agreement from the various stakeholders is anticipated.
7. No insuperable political difficulties are envisaged.

How different are these conditions from the reality of seeking to bring about situational changes in wildlife crime policy! The successful SCP program described above took place in a stable Western democracy with all that implies in terms of the institutions of government, whereas much of the needed wildlife crime work is in poor countries and sometimes failed states, where governance is rudimentary and corruption is ever present.

Conservation might be seen as a Western ideal, but even when its needs are recognized, resources for it will be limited, and it must compete with the everyday needs of local people. Accepting foreign aid for conservation is not without cost, since this often comes with strings, whether political or practical. Such aid can also be the source of high-level corruption in the receiving country. From our perspective, however, more important than any of these conditions is that in the successful SCP implementation in the United Kingdom, the researchers were in regular contact with the policy makers concerned. This direct contact enabled an understanding to develop between the researchers and the policy makers about their respective goals and how these goals might be reconciled in the service of effective policy. To date, in our own work, we have never experienced this intensity of contact with those responsible for conservation in the countries where wildlife crime is most troubling.

CONCLUSIONS

In the light of these realities, our ambitions will need to be scaled back, not just for our own program but more generally for SCP wildlife crime research as well. The resources may never be available, either in terms of trained researchers or research funds, to undertake more than a few of the studies needed. It is true that governments and private foundations for conservation disburse considerable amounts of money, but most of the funds are allocated to nongovernmental organizations (NGOs) for undertaking action projects, few of which include a research or evaluation component.

In terms of our own program, we will continue to make use of available data to undertake and publish SCP analyses of the opportunity structures for specific wildlife crimes and, on the basis of these studies, will seek to identify feasible situational interventions. This might represent an "enlightenment" model of policy influence, but at least the enlightenment would be filtered through an SCP lens. Then in making the case to biologists and conservation scientists for the greater involvement of criminology in their domain, we will continue to undertake studies that demonstrate the magnitude of poaching's contribution to the endangerment of species. These studies might help us to develop links with conservation scientists, which could only enrich our research. Finally, we will continue to look for possible "customers" for our work by seeking opportunities to undertake field research in countries where problems exist, rather than simply analyzing data collected by others. Graduates of our program have already undertaken work of this kind (Moreto, Lemieux, and Nobles 2016), involving interviews with park rangers in Africa and elsewhere, and are presently engaged in a small study of human-elephant conflict in Tamil Nadu, India, which involves interviewing affected villagers about possible solutions. Even if these three strands of projected work represent only a tiny proportion of the SCP work that needs to be done, we believe they will still make a real a contribution to the prevention of wildlife crimes.

ANNEX: THE MURKY CASE OF RHINO POACHING IN SOUTH AFRICA

The two African rhinoceroses—the black rhino (*Diceros bicornis*) and the white rhino (*Cerototherium simum*)—have attracted much international attention, partly due to the increased number of poaching incidents that have taken place in South Africa since 2008. This upsurge is a function of growing demand for rhino horn in Asian markets and the associated increase in its black market value (Emslie et al. 2016). The International Union for Conservation of Nature (IUCN) now lists the black rhino as Critically Endangered due to poaching in the remainder of Africa, but contrary to public perception, its population has been increasing steadily in South Africa, from a low of 2,140 in 1995 to its present size of 5,250 (Emslie and Brooks 1999; Emslie et al. 2016). The white rhino is categorized as Near Threatened by IUCN and includes two subspecies: the northern white rhino (now functionally extinct due to poaching) and the southern white rhino (*C. s. simum*). The population of the latter in South Africa is around 20,000, up from its historic low in 1895 when there were fewer than 100 individuals found in the Kwazulu-Natal province of South Africa.

Within South Africa rhinos are therefore not under the immediate threat of extinction. South Africa contains the largest population of white rhinos in Africa (90 percent) and more than a third of the black rhinos (Emslie et al. 2016). As many as half of these rhinos might be in private reserves, while the rest are in public reserves such as Kruger National Park. Encouragingly, and again in contrast with public perceptions, range-wide population declines in South Africa have not been found for either species (Emslie et al. 2016), though declines have occurred in some areas, including Kruger National Park (Ferreira et al. 2015; Emslie et al. 2016). It can therefore be concluded that, while poaching of rhinos across the continent of Africa has been rampant, there is no immediate extinction crisis in South Africa—though this, of course, does not disregard the very real need to address the significant increase in poaching that began there in 2008. Figure 3.1 provides the annual count of rhinos poached in South Africa between 1990 and 2015. In 2015, 1,175 rhinos were poached, which was more than thirty times the number in 2006 (Emslie et al. 2016), though the rate of increase now appears to be slowing.

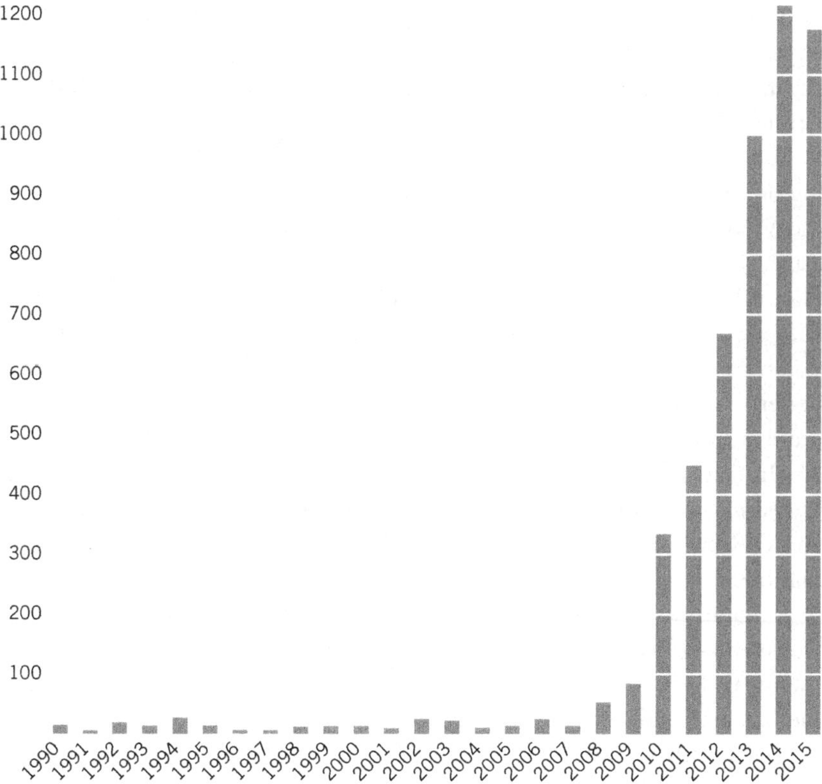

Figure 3.1 The count of rhino poaching incidents in South Africa from 1990 to 2015 (Milliken and Shaw 2012).

Little concrete information has been made public about who might be responsible for this increase in poaching and, worse, in many instances, the narratives surrounding the problem are suspect. This includes "evidence" put forward by NGOs (e.g., "Mozambique's Role in the Poaching Crisis" by Save the Rhino), journalists (e.g., Macleod 2014), researchers (Hübschle 2016), and the South African Department of Environmental Affairs (2013, a press release highlighting Mozambican poachers and downplaying South African poachers). This so-called evidence is in fact a collection of anecdotes suggesting Mozambicans are the driving force behind the poaching problem. They allegedly make long, arduous journeys (upward of 150 kilometers) across the border into South Africa to poach rhino in Kruger National Park, the only reserve that shares a border with Mozambique. The anecdotes run contrary to the overwhelming empirical evidence from the journey-to-crime literature that is best summarized by two findings: *most crime trips are short* and *offenders do not travel far to commit crime* (see Rossmo 2000). Worse, no empirical evidence available supports this narrative. In fact, the only recent criminological study on rhino poaching in Kruger National Park demonstrates that the majority of those arrested for poaching were South African (see Eloff and Lemieux 2014).

Vietnamese "hunters" have also been blamed for the epidemic of poaching but on very little evidence. For example, 185 *legal* permits were given to the Vietnamese to hunt a single rhino each between July 2009 and April 2012.[2] However, over this same period a thousand rhinos were poached (see Figure 3.1). Another scapegoat has been "international organized criminals" who are said to use helicopters and military-trained poachers with night-vision goggles. These stories might garner greater public interest and serve better to attract "anti-poaching" funds from overseas than the likely and more mundane reality of poaching by locals or perhaps even corrupt rangers. In fact, recent studies have found little evidence that wildlife crime is linked to international organized crime syndicates (Schneider 2012; Reuter and O'Regan 2016). Furthermore, the only empirical study on rhino poaching in South Africa found that over 90 percent of incidents occurred within two kilometers of a road (Eloff and Lemieux 2014), suggesting that cars and trucks, not helicopters, were the poachers' mode of transport. It seems that the organized crime stories are examples of what Felson (2002) would call the "dramatic fallacy."

Each of these narratives has contributed to what can only be misguided responses to prevention. For example, in 2012 South Africa passed legislation banning Vietnamese hunters; however, as seen in Figure 3.1, the poaching not only continued following the ban but also worsened. The story about helicopters and night-vision goggles has convinced some that the solution to rhino poaching lies in technology. For example, the South African Council for Scientific and Industrial Research (CSIR) has developed "Cmore," sophisticated detection software to track incidents and coordinate missions (CSIR 2016), which requires extensive ranger training, along with formal evaluations on ranger use and effectiveness that have either not been conducted or published.

As discussed above, specificity is critical to the application of SCP, yet empirical studies of poaching have been hampered by the lack of usable data. Even before the South African DEA stopped reporting basic information in 2015, including counts of rhinos poached and poachers arrested, little could be gleaned about the problem other than it continued to worsen.[3] Research would be assisted by the data summarized in Table 3.2, which under the influence of routine activity theory (Cohen and Felson 1979) would tease apart the dynamics of rhino poaching—where it happens, when it happens, who is involved, what they did, why they did it, and how they went about it.

TABLE 3.2. THE DYNAMICS OF RHINO POACHING IN SOUTH AFRICA: INFORMATION NEEDED

	WHO	WHAT	WHEN	WHERE	HOW	WHY
Motivated Offender	• Poacher name, age, nationality, current residential address • Previous poaching arrests		• Arrest date and time • Estimated poaching event date • Moon phase	• X, Y coordinates of poaching location • Arrest distances from park border, national border, and roadway	• Weapon used • Horn removal method • Method of transportation	• Type of payoff by smugglers (money, food, etc.)
Capable Guardian	• Number of rangers within park, geo-location of rangers while working • Ranger profiles (local community members, former soldiers, etc.)		• Ranger shifts	• Deployment patterns of patrols (ranger routines) • Placement of camera traps	• Use of technologies (drones, security programs, etc.) • Ranger equipment (weapons, night-vision goggles, etc.)	• Training and experience of rangers • Weak bureaucracy (judicial loopholes, "slap on the wrist" sentencing) • Convictions and sentencing for complicit park rangers and government employees
Suitable Target		• Species identification (black or white) • Rhino sex		• Distances of carcass from park border, national border, roadway, human settlement, and body of water • Habitat type (shrubland, grassland, etc.)		

Such data would be critical in the development of SCP strategies for park management and enforcement that depart from the "traditional" approaches typical of the last decade.

NOTES

1. The focus on the situation is characteristic of environmental criminology, the broader field of theories and interventions to which SCP belongs (Wortley and Townsley 2017).

2. Americans were provided with the highest number of legal permits to hunt rhino in South Africa, yet no concern has been expressed about this continuing trend. At the same time the media and NGOs continued to point the finger at Thai "organized crime syndicates" for using Thai sex workers to pose as big game hunters to obtain licenses for the *legal* rhino horn permit system (Milliken and Shaw 2012).

3. The safeguarding of information on the spatial distribution of poached rhinos would be understandable if their roaming patterns were relatively limited and might tip off poachers to target rich locations. However, home-range size for both rhino species is highly variable and can extend upward of 500 km^2 (Owen-Smith 2004).

REFERENCES

Bandura, A. 1973. *Aggression: A Social Learning Analysis.* Englewood Cliffs, NJ: Prentice-Hall.

Cantu, J. C., M. A. Sanchez, M. Grosselet, and J. Silva. 2007. *Trafico Ilegal de Pericos en Mexico: Una Evaluacion Detallada.* Mexico City: Defenders of Wildlife and Teyeliz.

Clarke, R. V. 1980. "Situational" crime prevention: Theory and practice. *British Journal of Criminology* 20 (2): 136–147.

———. 1992. *Situational Crime Prevention: Successful Case Studies.* Albany, NY: Harrow and Heston.

Clarke, R. V., and G. R. Newman. 2006. *Outsmarting the Terrorists.* Portsmouth, NH: Greenwood Publishing Group.

Cohen, L. E., and M. Felson. 1979. Social change and crime rate trends: A routine activity approach. *American Sociological Review* 44: 588–608.

CSIR. 2016. Cmore team recognized at Rhino Conservation Awards. July 15. Available at https://www.csir.co.za/csir-cmore-team-recognised-rhino-conservation-awards.

Eloff, C., and A. Lemieux. 2014. Rhino poaching in Kruger National Park, South Africa. In *Situational Prevention of Poaching,* edited by A. M. Lemieux, 18–43. New York: Routledge.

Emslie, R., and M. Brooks. 1999. African rhino: Status survey and action plan. IUCN/SSC African rhino specialist group. IUCN, Gland, Switzerland.

Emslie, R. H., T. Milliken, B. Talukdar, S. Ellis, K. Adcock, and M. H. Knight. 2016. African and Asian rhinoceroses—status, conservation and trade. A report from the IUCN Species Survival Commission (IUCN/SSC) African and Asian Rhino Specialist Groups and TRAFFIC to the CITES Secretariat pursuant to Resolution Conf. 9.14 (Rev. CoP15). Report to CITES 16th meeting (Johannesburg, September-October 2016), CoP 17 Doc. 68 annex 5: 1–21.

Felson, M. 2002. *Crime and Everyday Life*. Thousand Oaks, CA: Sage Publications.

Ferreira, S. M., C. Greaver, G. A. Knight, M. H. Knight, I. P. Smit, and D. Pienaar. 2015. Disruption of rhino demography by poachers may lead to population declines in Kruger National Park, South Africa. *PloS one* 10 (6): e0127783.

Guerette, R. T., and K. J. Bowers. 2009. Assessing the extent of crime displacement and diffusion of benefits: A review of situational crime prevention evaluations. *Criminology* 47 (4): 1331–1368.

Hübschle, A. 2016. *A game of horns: Transnational flows of rhino horn*. Doctoral Dissertation University of Cologne.

Inskip C., and A. Zimmerman. 2009. Human-felid conflict: A review of patterns and priorities worldwide. *Oryx* 43: 18–34.

Johnson, S. D., K. J. Bowers, and R. Guerette. 2012. Crime displacement and diffusion of benefits: a review of situational crime prevention measures. In *Oxford Handbook of Crime Prevention*, edited by B. C. Welsh and D. P. Farrington. Oxford: Oxford University Press.

Knutsson, J., and R. V. Clarke, eds. 2006. *Putting Theory to Work: Implementing Situational Prevention and Problem-Oriented Policing*. Boulder, CO: Lynne Rienner Publishers.

Laycock, G., and R. V. Clarke. 2001. Crime prevention policy and government research: A comparison of the United States and United Kingdom. *International Journal of Comparative Sociology* 42 (1): 235–255.

Lemieux, A. M., and R. V. Clarke. 2009. The international ban on ivory sales and its effects on elephant poaching in Africa. *British Journal of Criminology* 49 (4): 451–471.

Lewin, K. 1936. *Principles of Topological Psychology*. New York: McGraw-Hill.

Macleod, F. 2014. Kruger's rhino poaching "highway." November 7. Available at http://oxpeckers.org/2014/11/krugers-rhino-poaching-highway.

Magrath, W., R. Grandalski, G. Stuckey, G. Vikanes, and G. Wilkinson. 2007. *Timber Theft Prevention: Introduction to Security for Forest Managers*. Washington, DC: World Bank.

Milliken, T., and J. Shaw. 2012. The South Africa-Viet Nam rhino horn trade nexus: A deadly combination of institutional lapses, corrupt wildlife industry professionals, and Asian crime syndicates, 134–136. Johannesburg: Traffic.

Moreto, W. D., and A. M. Lemieux. 2015. From CRAVED to CAPTURED: Introducing a product-based framework to examine illegal wildlife markets. *European Journal on Criminal Policy and Research* 21 (3): 303–320.

Moreto, W. D., A. M. Lemieux, and M. R. Nobles. 2016. "It's in my blood now": The satisfaction of rangers working in Queen Elizabeth National Park, Uganda. *Oryx* 1–9.

Mozambique's role in the poaching crisis. 2016. Available at https://www.savetherhino.org/rhino_info/thorny_issues/mozambiques_role_in_the_poaching_crisis.

O'Connell-Rodwell, C. E., T. Rodwell, M. Rice, and L. A. Hart. 2000. Living with the modern conservation paradigm: Can agricultural communities co-exist with elephants? A five-year case study in East Caprivi, Namibia. *Biological Conservation* 93 (3): 381–391.

Owen-Smith, N. 2004. Functional heterogeneity in resources within landscapes and herbivore population dynamics. *Landscape Ecology* 19 (7): 761–771.

Reuter, P., and D. O'Regan. 2016. Smuggling wildlife in the Americas: Scale, methods, and links to other organized crimes. *Global Crime* 18 (2): 1–23.

Rossmo, K. D. 2000. *Geographic Profiling.* Boca Raton, FL: CRC Press.

Schneider, J. L. 2012. *Sold into Extinction: The Global Trade in Endangered Species.* Santa Barbara, CA: ABC-CLIO.

Smith, M. J., and R. V. Clarke. 2012. Situational crime prevention: Classifying techniques using "good enough" theory. In *Oxford Handbook of Crime Prevention,* edited by B. G. Welsh and D. P. Farrington, 291–315. Oxford: Oxford University Press.

South African Department of Environmental Affairs. 2013. South Africa and Mozambique agree to improved cooperation on combating rhino poaching within the Great Limpopo Transfrontier Conservation Area. June 15. Available at https://www.environment.gov.za/safricamozambique_cooperation_oncombatingr hinopoaching.

South, N., and A. Brisman, eds. 2013. *Routledge International Handbook of Green Criminology.* New York: Routledge.

Sykes, G. M., and D. Matza. 1957. Techniques of neutralization: A theory of delinquency. *American Sociological Review* 22 (6): 664–670.

Tilley, N. 2004. Karl Popper: A philosopher for Ronald Clarke's situational crime prevention? *Israel Studies in Criminology* 8: 39–56.

Van de Bunt, H. G., and C.R.A. van der Schoot. 2003. *Prevention of Organised Crime.* Den Haag, Netherlands: Boom.

Willison, R. 2000. Reducing computer fraud through situational crime prevention. In *Information Security for Global Information Infrastructures,* edited by S. Qing and J. Eloff, 99–109. New York: Springer.

Wortley, R. 2001. A classification of techniques for controlling situational precipitators of crime. *Security Journal* 14 (4): 63–82.

Wortley, R., and S. Smallbone. 2006. *Situational Prevention of Child Sexual Abuse.* Monsey, NY: Criminal Justice Press.

Wortley, R., and M. Townsley, eds. 2017. *Environmental Criminology and Crime Analysis.* 2nd ed. New York: Routledge.

4

Global Warming and Criminological Theory and Practice

Rob White

Addressing potential climate-related crimes has implications for law reform, policy development within criminal justice agencies, and contemporary environmental management practices. The aim of this chapter is to elaborate on what criminology offers conceptually (e.g., concepts such as ecocide, general strain theory, state-corporate crime) and practically (e.g., situational crime prevention, environmental law enforcement) in relation to global warming and its consequences (that include old crimes such as trafficking and assaults and new crimes such as water theft and carbon emission scheme fraud). These issues, in turn, can be framed and responded to by suitable policy and intervention strategies—but only if the political will is there.

Global warming describes the rising of the earth's temperature over a relatively short time span. *Climate change* describes the interrelated effects of this rise in temperature from changing sea levels and changing ocean currents to the impacts of temperature change on local environments that affect the endemic flora and fauna in varying ways (e.g., the death of coral due to temperature rises in seawater or the changed migration patterns of birds). *Weather* is the name given to the direct local experience of phenomena such as sunshine, wind, rain, snow, and the general disposition of the elements. It is about the short term and personal, not the long-term patterns associated with climate in general. As the planet warms up, the climate will change in ways that disrupt previous weather patterns and will in some places even bring colder weather although overall temperatures are on the rise (Lever-Tracy 2011).

Climate change is the most important international issue facing humanity today and in the long term. However, until recently criminology has devoted very little attention to this particular issue. This is changing (Stretesky and Lynch 2009; Lynch, Burns, and Stretesky 2010; Ferrell and French, 2012; Agnew 2011, 2012, 2013; White 2011, 2012a, 2012b, 2015), indeed so much so that a leading criminologist recently observed that climate change will become one of the major, if not *the* major, forces driving crime as the twenty-first century progresses (Agnew 2011).

WHAT'S THE THEORY?

The impacts of climate change imply a reconceptualization of environment-related criminality. Criminology can offer insight into the definitions and dynamics of this behavior and outline potential areas of redress. However, if it is to do so, then two key issues must first be acknowledged. The first relates to the sheer scale of the problem—global warming is a planetary issue. The second pertains to the vested interests embedded in the existing status quo—the contributors to and perpetrators of global warming are powerful and unlikely to be easily persuaded about the right course of action to prevent and respond to it. Each of these considerations should be borne in mind throughout the course of this chapter.

The Anthropocene

Temperatures are changing quickly and human activity is the main cause. The science of global warming tells us, for example, that July 2016 was the hottest month in recorded history around the world (Colangelo 2016). This is part of a longer-term and rapidly accelerating trend toward even greater warming. The key drivers of global warming are carbon dioxide emissions and deforestation (McGarrell and Gibbs 2014), although it is the former that is generally seen to be of crucial importance and is the focus of public debate and government policy (see Intergovernmental Panel on Climate Change 2013, 2014). Even if human emissions were stopped right now at this moment, the atmosphere would continue warming for another twenty-five years (Boyer 2012).

The global changes caused by human activity, especially over the last couple of centuries, have recently been described as delimiting a period referred to as the "Anthropocene" (Shearing 2015). The basis for this distinction rests upon the rapidity of the global warming and the human contributions to escalating temperatures. The most common reference point for the beginning of the Anthropocene Epoch is the Industrial Revolution from the mid-1700s in Europe (Shiva 2008). Over two hundred years of industrial revolution have been driven and underpinned by powerful forces (nation-states, companies, armies) pursuing sectional interests. This has been achieved through global imperialism, colonialism, and militarism that have served to entrench a dominant worldview and the material basis for producing and consuming natural resources in particular ways—what today is referred to as global capitalism (Greig and van der Velden 2015).

The impacts of these trends historically have been dramatic. For example, people who for thousands of years had lived in harmony with nature (i.e., through intrinsically adopting ecologically sustainable practices), including in some of the most humanly inhospitable places in the world (such as Arctic tundra and sand deserts), were subjected to dispossession, displacement, and destruction of their communities. These processes are mirrored in the contemporary exploitation of natural resources worldwide (Gedicks 2005; Klare 2012; Le Billon 2012). The impact of human activity on global warming is now clear and unequivocal (Shearing 2015), as are the specific contributions of so called "dirty industries" such as coal and gas (Heede 2014). Biophysical changes have been and will continue to be accompanied by various threats to human security, including crime.

The concept of environmental insecurity refers to actions and conditions that undermine the ability to exploit or use nature sufficiently to meet human needs. Scarcity, for example, is tied to the overexploitation of natural resources. It is also increasingly linked to the consequences of global warming (Klare 2012). Shortages of food, water, and nonrenewable energy sources can trigger nefarious activities involving organized criminal networks, transnational corporations, and governments at varying political levels (South and Brisman 2013; White and Heckenberg 2014). Yet the consequence of such activities contributes to even more ruthless exploitation of rapidly vanishing natural resources, as well as to the further diminishment of air, soil, and water quality, thereby exacerbating the competition by individuals, groups, and nations for what is left (Klare 2012; White 2014). Diminished human security stems from the biophysical and socioeconomic consequences of various sources of threat and damage to the environment including and especially climate change (South 2012). Associated with the emergent insecurities, a range of new and old crimes is apparent and criminological thought has recently turned to explaining them.

Criminological Perspectives

There are three broad levels of criminological explanation: the individualist (e.g., psychological and biological factors), the situational (e.g., labeling processes, interactions between specific individuals and groups), and the structural (e.g., social inequalities, institutional arrangements pertaining to health, education, welfare, and employment) (White, Haines, and Asquith 2017). Different theories within criminology tend to locate their main explanation for criminal behavior or criminality at one of these levels. Occasionally, a theory may attempt to combine all three levels in order to provide a more sophisticated and comprehensive picture of crime and criminality. The individualist, the situational, and the structural approaches will lead to quite different policies because of their particular perspectives. The vantage point from which one examines crime—a focus on personal characteristics through to societal institutions—thus shapes the ways in which one thinks about and acts upon criminal justice matters. This extends to criminality associated with global warming as it does to other types of criminal behavior.

There are several criminological perspectives that have recently been applied to the study of crime, criminality, and climate change. These include, for example, weather-related individualist and situational theories, general strain theory, and critical criminology. Other approaches are more oriented toward identification and description of climate-related crime and are discussed in the next section. Studies of the nexus between climate change and crime tend to focus on either the consequences of climate change for crime (i.e., climate change leads to certain sorts of crime) or the causes of global warming (i.e., certain sorts of behavior lead to climate change).

Crime as a Consequence of Climate Change

Temperature changes and human behavior. Criminological research exploring the nature and dynamics of criminality associated with climate change has included examination of the relationship between temperature changes and human behavior. This has involved three types and foci of analysis.

1. *Individuals.* The issue here is whether extreme weather conditions, especially heat waves, are related to increases in aggression and thereby criminal violence (Boyanowsky 1999; Rotton and Cohn 2003). The implications for this are far reaching. For example, a study examining the effect of weather on monthly crime patterns in the United States predicted that climate change will lead to substantial additional numbers of murders, rape, aggravated assaults, and robberies, among other serious crimes (Ranson 2014).
2. *Place-based activities.* The focus in this instance is on local weather, indoor/outdoor routines, the specific places where people spend their time and with whom, and how this affects their propensity

to engage in certain types of crime (Peng et al. 2011). This will vary depending upon ambient temperature and place. For example, a study in Dallas, Texas, found that higher temperatures may encourage people to seek shelter in cooler indoor spaces and street crimes and other crimes of opportunity are thereby subsequently decreased (Gamble and Hess 2012).

3. *Communities and change.* Consideration is given here to matters such as systemic crop failure and resultant survival and migration strategies. Changes in local weather conditions are seen to affect how people behave psychologically and socially, including participation in activities that may involve poaching and illegal harvesting for the purposes of subsistence (Mares 2013). Migration induced by climate change may lead people to fight over diminished resources in one area (Barnett and Adger 2007) and/or to leave affected areas with possible conflict arising in the receiving areas (Barnett and Adger 2007; Reuveny 2007).

Impacts of strains associated with climate change on human behavior. Analysis of criminality and climate change has likewise been provided by general strain theory (Agnew 2011). This approach invokes multifactor explanations for the relationship between crime and climate change. Three categories of strain are identified in general strain theory: (1) loss of legal avenues to attain goals (such as loss of secure employment, or autonomy), (2) loss of positively valued stimuli (such as friends, romantic partners, money), and (3) experiences of negatively valued stimuli (such as verbal and physical abuse). According to Agnew and Brezina (2010), strains are most likely to result in criminal behavior if they are thought by the individual to be (1) insurmountable, (2) unjust, (3), subject to limited social control, and (4) subject to pressure or incentive to act negatively. Within this framework, importantly, strains do not inevitably lead to crime or criminality. Some individual- and social-level factors "immunize" individuals from responding to strain through crime.

Focusing specifically on climate change, general strain theory provides a sophisticated attempt to combine observations about different levels of analysis and substantive areas of criminality (Agnew 2011). This work explicates the impact of climate change on crime in terms of the following:

- *Factors associated with climate change:* rising temperature, rising sea level, extreme weather events, changing patterns of precipitation, habitat change, negative health effects, food/water shortages, loss of livelihood, migration, social conflict

- *Factors linked to criminogenic mechanisms:* increased strain, reduced control, reduced social support, beliefs/values favorable to crime traits or conducive to crime, opportunities for crime, social conflict
- *Results:* higher levels of individual, group, corporate, and state crime

This perspective thus attempts to analyze and explain the consequences of climate change through explication of its effects at different levels—from the individual to the situational and structural—and to make a direct connection between certain biophysical changes and the likely consequences for human behavior.

Global Warming as a Consequence of Carbon Criminality

Critical criminological perspectives emphasize the connection between crimes of the powerful and global warming. A key defining feature of crimes of the powerful is that such crimes involve actions (or omissions and failures to act) that are socially harmful and carried out by elites and/or those who wield significant political and social authority in the domain of their influence (Rothe and Kauzlarich 2016). Recent criminological work highlights the fact that the key perpetrators and responders to global warming tend to be one and the same: namely, nation-states and transnational corporations, both of which are primarily concerned with maintaining the economic status quo (Kramer and Michalowski 2012). Globally, for example, there is widespread state support for businesses that contribute to global warming such as the oil and coal industries. Moreover, even though climate change is rapidly and radically altering the basis of world ecology, very little substantive action is being taken by states or corporations to reign in the worst contributors to the problem. This is deemed to be substantially a crime against humanity.

Contrarianism as denial of crime and criminality. Concern about global warming had been expressed for many years by many scientists in different disciplines. Yet it had been systematically denied and downplayed by contrarians, many of whom have friends in high places. For example, analysis of how big business has responded to global warming reveals a multipronged strategy to deter or defer action on climate change (Bulkeley and Newell 2010). Indeed, work done on the politics of climate change in the United States has demonstrated close connections between business and the government culminating in a form of state-corporate contrarianism (Brisman 2012, 2013; Kramer 2013a, 2013b). Specifically, corporate and state actors in interaction with each other create harms in four ways (Kramer and Michalowski 2012):

1. By denying that global warming is caused by human activity
2. By blocking efforts to mitigate greenhouse gas emissions
3. By excluding progressive, ecologically just adaptations to climate change from the political arena
4. By responding to the social conflicts that arise from climate change by transforming themselves into fortress societies that exclude the rest of the world

State-corporate crime relates to both *acts* (e.g., reliance upon dirty energy sources) and *omissions* (e.g., failure to regulate carbon emissions). Failure to act, now, to prevent global warming—and climate change denial or contrarianism itself—has been described as criminal (Brown 2010; Tucker 2012). This is because there is a close intersection of global warming, government action or inaction, and corporate behavior (Lynch, Burns, and Stretesky 2010; Kramer 2013b) and these contribute to the overall problem of climate change. In this instance the state is itself implicated as a perpetrator of harm. In the light of the existing scientific evidence on global warming, continued encouragement of fossil fuel industries, for example, represents intentional harm that is immoral and destructive of collective public interest in the same moment that particular industries and companies benefit.

Crimes of the powerful as drivers of global warming. Exploitation of natural resources is big business, and big business ensures that its interests (i.e., private interests) are protected across many different spheres of activity. This is evident, for example, in the continued resistance by powerful businesses to global agreements on carbon emission reductions and use of carbon taxes. Rather than tackling global warming, quite the opposite has been happening at a systems level. While some capitalist enterprises have embraced "green capitalism" and new technologies that are meant to be more environmentally benign, the overarching trend has been continued reliance upon the "old" extraction industries such as coal, gas, and oil. These are being supplemented by newer forms of energy extraction, the so-called "extreme energy" industries. This refers to novel forms of ecologically unsound energy extraction: mountaintop removal, deep-water drilling, and hydraulic fracking (Crook and Short 2014).

In response, there is the argument that those countries that have most benefited from past industrialization should also bear the burden of compensation. Taken together, it is argued that there is a broad convergence of reasons why certain countries should pay more: "Developed countries were *causally responsible* for climate change; they are the main *beneficiaries* of activities that cause climate change; and they have the *ability* to tackle the causes and effects of climate change" (Page 2008, 564). Importantly, however, such accounts largely ignore political economy and the dominance of transnational corporations in the global sphere. For instance, quantitative analysis of historic fossil fuel and cement production records of the fifty leading investment-owned, thirty-one state-owned, and nine nation-state producers of oil, natural gas, and cement from 1854 to 2010 showed that they produced 63 percent of cumulative worldwide emissions of industrial carbon dioxide and methane (Heede 2014). The largest investor-owned and state-owned companies produced the most carbon emissions.

Yet class politics still tends to be refracted through the lens of nation-state responsibilities. Moreover, the discussion tends to be pitched around compensation rather than regulation and control. Little is said about democratization of those decisions—about air, water, land, and energy—that are the most fundamental and decisive in determining the fate of the planet. Yet, as critical criminologists insist, it is precisely these decisions that are decisively important in mitigating the effects of global warming (White 2017). Greenhouse gas (GHG) emissions come from a variety of sources and include direct emissions, indirect emissions that arise as a consequence of a corporation's activities, and other indirect emissions from sources not owned or controlled by a corporation but that occur as a result of its activities (Mascher 2016). The largest five hundred companies account for over 10 percent of total GHG emissions produced each year, and 31 percent of GHG emitted globally each year is attributed to the thirty-two energy companies among the top five hundred companies (Mascher 2016). We know, therefore, who the main culprits are. But much remains yet to be done to address these issues.

WHAT'S THE PROBLEM?

Criminology needs to critically examine the consequences of global warming for the sake of national security, societal peace, and social and ecological well-being. The task for research, as Agnew points out, is to "examine the impact of climate change on particular types of crime and harmful activity in more detail" (2011, 27). Developing an integrated and detailed picture of environment-related crime and criminality is already a major project of green criminology (South and Brisman 2013; White and Heckenberg 2014), and climate change is viewed as one area deserving highest priority.

Typologies of climate-related crimes need to reference diverse situations, settings, offenders, and offenses. For example, consideration needs to be given to crimes such as water theft for family farm use related to basic survival (caused by lack of rain and changes in temperatures) to new opportunities for organized crime networks to be involved in activities such as carbon emission fraud and illegal trade in water. Suitable crime prevention techniques and approaches to match the nature of the problems foreseen to accompany climate change also need to be developed. A vital component of any criminological project concerned with global warming is an orientation toward building social resilience within and among communities and as part of this enhancing the capabilities of institutions and agencies in dealing with the foreseeable and unanticipated consequences of climate change.

Some work at developing concepts and typologies pertinent to analyses of global warming and climate-related crime has already been initiated (Sollund 2012; White 2012a; Crank and Jacoby 2015). For example, specific criminal and environmental offenses associated with the phenomenon of climate change have been categorized as the following (White 2012a):

- Offenses that contribute to climate change (e.g., unlicensed pollution, illegal felling of trees)
- Offenses arising from its consequences (e.g., water theft, wildlife poaching)
- Offenses pertaining to civil unrest and organized criminal activities (e.g., food riots, migration and people smuggling)
- Offenses of regulation and law enforcement associated with mitigation and adaptation strategies (e.g., carbon trade fraud, regulatory corruption)

It is further anticipated that there will be changes in the type, rate, and frequency of offenses as climate alters (Bergin and Allen 2008). Environmental conflicts will largely center on the allocation and struggle over resources, accompanied by attendant crimes.

Climate change has been associated with the advent of varying types of "natural disaster," which are projected to increase in intensity and frequency in the foreseeable future. These include such phenomenon as floods, cyclones, long droughts, and extreme heat spells. Study of disasters (both human created and natural) has revealed substantial instances of criminality (see, for example, Green 2005; Rodriquez, Quarantelli, and Dynes 2007; Thornton and Voigt 2007; Harper and Frailing 2012; Heckenberg and Johnson 2012). These include crimes that occur before the disaster (e.g., poor construction standards such as omission of steel reinforcing in concrete); during the disaster (e.g., looting, rape); and after the disaster (e.g., insurance fraud, misappropriation of aid funds, sex trading for aid). The scale of recent disasters (e.g., the extensive floods in Pakistan in 2011 in which one-third of the country was inundated) indicates additional forms of criminality associated with these events, including the collapse of public order, enforced climate-induced migration, and the prevalence of local gang cultures.

The terrible situation in contemporary Syria is indicative of what may portend elsewhere (Gleick 2014). Since 1975, Turkey's dam and hydropower construction has cut water flow to Syria by 40 percent and drought and poor water management have been drying up water sources everywhere. Between 2003 and 2009 the Tigris-Euphrates Basin—comprising Turkey, Syria, Iraq, and western Iran—lost water faster than any other place in the world except northern India. Frictions started to emerge as different groups and rural clans lay claim to water resources, and the dictatorship, imposed rule, and corruption were met by growing dissent. Meanwhile, Syria's population grew from 3 million in 1950 to 22 million in 2012, further decreasing the country's total per capita renewable water availability. In the 2006–2011 period, Syria experienced multiseason, multiyear periods of extreme drought, contributing to agricultural failures and further economic and population displacements. The trend toward privatization of agricultural lands corroded customary law over boundary rights, and more than 1.5 million people, mostly agricultural workers and family farmers, moved from rural lands to cities and camps on the outskirts of major cities (Gleick 2014). Civil war eventually erupted with diverse rebel factions and major political differences, including the opportunism of the so-called Islamic State and its attempts to establish a regional caliphate. War has seen the reduction of many cities to rubble, there are few services outside of emergency provision, and survival is a priority for those trapped in the conflict zones. Is this our future?

Another approach within criminology is to describe crime related to climate change from the point of view of the perpetrators (White and Heckenberg 2014). Such analysis includes reference to the following:

- *Crimes by the less powerful*—basic survival (e.g., loss of land, lack of rain, change in temperatures) through illegal migration, foraging for food in reserves, water theft, and street riots
- *Crimes by the powerful*—protection of privilege and defense of the profit motive through enclosures of land, hording of food and other basics, and the establishment of private armies/security
- *Crimes by organized criminals*—new criminal opportunities, such as carbon emission fraud, illegal trafficking of people and substances, dumping of waste, and illegal trade in food and water
- *Crimes by the state*—collusion with powerful interests, denial of human/ecological rights, failure to intervene or regulate, buying of land for food production/consumption somewhere else

In addition to this classification of climate-related crimes is the notion that a *bifurcation of crime* will occur. The rich and powerful will use their resources to secure productive lands, restrict access to food and water, exploit the financial hardships of others, and impose their own coercive rule (private security and private armies are a contemporary growth industry worldwide). Crimes of the less powerful will be crimes of desperation, and child soldiers and armed gangs will flourish in conditions of welfare collapse or nonexistent government support. Vulnerable people will flee and be criminalized for seeking asylum; others will stay to fight for dwindling resources in their part of the world (as has happened in Syria, described above). Communities will be pitted against each other as well as industries against communities. Law and order will be increasingly more difficult to maintain, much less to enforce, in other than repressive ways.

In the face of such nightmarish visions, the contemporary destruction of the environment through global warming can be conceptualized as a specific type of crime—namely, *ecocide.* This refers to the systematic destruction of environments (Higgins 2010, 2012). A key feature of this crime is that it occurs in the context of foreknowledge and intent. That is, ecocide arising from global warming, while marked by uncertainty in regard to specific rates and types of ecological change, is nonetheless founded upon generalized scientific knowledge that profound change is unavoidable unless carbon emissions—the key source of global warming—are not radically reduced now.

The biggest contributors to carbon emissions remain those of the transnational corporation and the nation-state. The "choices" ingrained in environmental exploitation (of human beings and of the nonhuman world) stem from systemic imperatives to exploit the environment for production of commodities for human use (Tombs and Whyte 2015). Placed within the larger global context of climate change, the scale and impact of the Alberta tar sands project, for example, fit neatly with the concept of ecocide as well as the concept of state-corporate crime. The project is based upon efforts to extract and refine naturally created tar-bearing sand into exportable and consumable oil. It involves the destruction of vast swathes of boreal forest, it contributes greatly to air pollution, and it is having negative health impacts on aquatic life and animals and on humans who live nearby (Smandych and Kueneman 2010). Most importantly, it is the single largest contributor to the increase of global warming pollution in Canada (Klare 2012). The role of the federal and provincial governments has been crucial to the project, and in propelling it forward, regardless of manifest negative environmental consequences.

The issue of state/corporate collusion can also be examined through the criminological lens that focuses on *techniques of neutralization* (Sykes and Matza 1957; Cohen 2001). This refers to the ways in which business and state leaders join up in attempts to prevent action being taken on climate change. The politics of denial (at both the level of ideology and policy) is propped up by various techniques of neutralization:

- *Denial of responsibility* (against anthropocentric or human causes as source of the problem)
- *Denial of injury* ("natural" disasters are "normal")
- *Denial of the victim* (failure to acknowledge differential victimization especially among the poor and the Third World)
- *Condemnation of the condemners* (attacks on climate scientists)
- *Appeal to higher loyalties* (national economic interests ought to predominate)

The net result is inaction on addressing the key factors contributing to climate change, such as carbon emissions.

Other criminological considerations of "the problem" question for whom it is a problem. Here analysis points to forms of "universal victimization" (i.e., everyone is affected by global warming) and "differential victimization" (i.e., some are affected much more than others) (White 2011). For example, peasants, indigenous peoples, and artisans who live outside the industrialized globalized economy, who have caused no harm to the earth or other people, are among the worst victims of climate change consequences (Shiva 2008). Vulnerabilities to victimization are due to other factors as well. For example, many countries have coastal areas that are vulnerable to sea-level rise. But the Netherlands has the technological and financial capacity to protect itself to greater extent than does Bangladesh. Thus, not only are poorer countries less responsible for the problem, but also they are simultaneously less able to adapt to the climate impacts they will suffer because they lack the resources and capacity to do so. This raises three key questions surrounding matters of justice: the question of responsibility (e.g., the North owes the South an "ecological debt"); the question of who pays for action on mitigation and adaptation; and the question of who bears the costs of actions and inactions (Bulkeley and Newell 2010).

WHAT'S THE ANSWER?

Criminology is obliged not only to take global warming seriously but also to propose preventative interventions that can be adopted and/or adapted to mitigate and prevent future harms. This will require a concerted effort to build capabilities (i.e., techniques, methods, platforms, and technologies) in the specific area of environmental crime prevention.

Environmental Horizon Scanning

As part of this, it is important to further develop skills and capacities in environmental horizon scanning—to anticipate issues that are yet to appear over the horizon but that can nonetheless be foreseen (White and Heckenberg 2011). Responding to criminality related to climate change will necessarily involve an eclectic synthesis of ideas and strategies, consisting not only of situational prevention techniques but also of theoretically informed responses to state and corporate crime. Importantly, best-practice crime prevention planning involves close consideration of offenders, victims, communities, and service provision and criminal justice agencies—these are an ingrained part of any investigation into specific crimes.

How to interpret, respond to, and prevent the range of environmental harms and crimes associated with climate change is part of the mandate of those criminologists with an interest in analyzing and understanding imminent threats to social and ecological well-being. From the perspective of horizon scanning, the focus of analysis is on current developments pertaining to the environment and extrapolating from these the potential harms and transgressions that may be problematic in the future. Underpinning this process is the use of a mixed-methods approach that draws upon a variety of sources and data collecting strategies (see Sutherland and Woodroof 2009). Within a criminological context such methods have long been evident (see, for example, Australian Crime Commission 2009; United Kingdom Government Office for Science 2009). The use and need for horizon scanning as an intellectual exercise and planning tool are related to the idea that many threats and opportunities are presently poorly recognized (Sutherland and Woodroof 2009). Accordingly, a more systematic approach to the identification and solution of the issues is required rather than reliance upon ad hoc or reactive approaches. For instance, initial work in this area has been undertaken by the Australian Strategic Policy Institute (Bergin and Allen 2008) and individual police practitioners (Chambers 2011) but very little from a criminological perspective as such.

The process of horizon scanning in relation to climate change involves drawing upon a wide variety of sources (e.g., cross-disciplinary, multijurisdictional, and cross-cultural methods) to investigate matters such as conflicts over resources, climate-induced migration, and the social effects of radical shifts in weather patterns. Information and data that are collated can be analyzed and interpreted in the light of broad eco-global criminological considerations (e.g., transgressions against humans, ecosystems, and animals) (White 2011), as well as specific patterns of environmental victimization involving particularly vulnerable groups (e.g., women, children, disadvantaged groups, and ethnic minorities). Steps can be taken to theorize the findings in relation to anthropogenic causes (e.g., human responsibility for harm, specific perpetrators, and degrees of culpability). Investigation of water crimes provides an illustration of this process.

Water Crimes

Crimes against water are an emerging global issue (Interpol 2016; Panjabi 2014; European Water Crimes Project 2016) and will be exacerbated by global warming. Already, pressures on water supply and quantity and quality are creating major consternation in countries such as Australia (which is, after all, the driest continent on earth). This will only intensify in the coming years given the effects of climate change.

Policy responses must be based on research that provides informed commentary on potential crime prevention and intervention measures. Research should therefore aim to collect water crime case studies, alongside an inventory of water crimes. This research would contribute to policy recommendations on mitigation strategies and promote the sustainable use of water. Key questions for such a project include the following:

- What is the relationship between water and crime?
- What types of crimes are being committed? What are the drivers for these crimes and what is their impact?
- How are water crimes being dealt with by state (provincial and regional) and federal agencies?
- Which federal and state agencies are responsible for legislation and compliance in relation to water crimes?
- How are different federal and state agencies responding to water crimes?
- Which criminological theory or theories best explain the water crimes revealed by the data and case studies?
- What can be done to proactively prevent water crimes and their impact?

This kind of project would involve systematic identification of law enforcement agencies involved in environmental and water crime–related policing (e.g., water theft), the changing legislative parameters within which they work (e.g., water and energy conservation), and the experiences and exposure of special emergency services to crimes arising from or related to climate-related disasters (e.g., profiteering from water distribution). It would require consultation with agencies such as federal and state police, departments of environment, Interpol and the UN Interregional Crime and Justice Research

Institute, as well as international nongovernmental organizations (NGOs) such as the Institute for Environmental Security. Relevant agencies and personnel in each jurisdiction (police, environmental protection agencies, state emergency services, and fire services) would also need to be contacted in relation to the nature and scope of enforcement practices in regard to issues related to water crimes. For the sake of forward planning and training and resource needs, they would also have to be consulted in regard to the nature of strategic plans vis-à-vis crime prevention, harm minimization, and social restoration.

A water crimes project would need to incorporate concurrent activities directed at constructing a water crimes criminal typology and identification of suitable crime prevention measures in relation to this typology, based upon criminological literature and investigation into present and proposed agency practices. Its anticipated outcomes and benefits would include the refinement of definitions, concepts, explanations, and examples of water crime; the development of heightened awareness of the importance of such crimes among key stakeholders and official agencies; further development of research tools and instruments, such as interview schedules and information gathering templates; and an outline of possible policy and crime prevention initiatives flowing from the information provided in project documents. It would enhance public policy in strategic areas pertaining to national security, economic well-being, and human health.

Environmental Crime Prevention

One of the key lessons from conventional crime prevention is that it ought to be based largely on a *problem-solving*, rather than policy-prescribed, model of intervention (Sutton, Cherney, and White 2014). For this reason a criminological intervention must also include discrete case studies of offenses stemming from or associated with climate change (such as water theft), in the process developing new and innovative ways to investigate these (such as environmental horizon scanning). Place-based and other situational techniques are vital to the conceptual modeling envisaged for dealing with global warming, along with social crime prevention measures (White 2008). This is because different places and people are vulnerable to different sorts of environmental harms and crimes. A problem-solving approach to crime prevention and deterrence therefore demands a certain level of specificity in regards to sites and harms.

Criminalizing Ecocide

Carbon emissions that lead to global warming occur in the pursuit of "normal" business outcomes and involve "normal" business practices (Tombs and Whyte

2015; Rothe and Kauzlarich 2016). Ecocide describes an attempt to criminalize human activities that destroy and diminish the well-being and health of ecosystems and the species within these ecosystems, including humans (Higgins 2010, 2012). Climate change and the gross exploitation of natural resources are leading to the general demise of the ecological status quo—hence increasing the need for just such a crime (Tekayak 2016). If carbon emissions are at the forefront of the causes of global warming, then the obvious question is why continue to emit such dangerous planet-altering substances into the atmosphere. Introducing ecocide as a crime against humanity would mean that "individuals in a position of superior or command responsibility will be criminally liable if they carry out an activity covered by such a provision, disregarding knowledge or intent" (Hellman 2014, 278). Ecological destruction accompanying natural resource extraction such as the oil and gas industries, coal mining, logging, and so on could be proceeded against under an international law of ecocide.

Prosecuting cases against those most responsible for global warming is not only politically fraught but also marked by complex questions. For example, the question is not only who is to blame for global warming but also how we apportion blame. A series of overlapping issues here needs to be unpacked. These issues revolve around acknowledgment of both nation-states and corporations as the major contributors to the problem, assessment of the criteria used to apportion responsibility and costs, prior and ongoing knowledge of the harm, ability to pay, and the beneficiaries of past damaging activities (Page 2008; Baatz 2013). Legal action in support of enforcement of climate policies is also another area where litigation is possible and in fact is happening (Lambrecht and Ituarte-Lima 2016). Importantly, in any such accounting, legal challenge, or regulatory intervention, it is vital not to ignore the dominance of transnational corporations on a global scale (Mascher 2016).

CONCLUSION

The election of Donald Trump to the Office of President of the United States is not in and of itself criminal. But his early days in office did involve several actions that will only reinforce the ecocidal tendencies of late capitalism. These included, for example, deletion of any mention of climate change from the White House website on the day of his inauguration. It included the appointment of former pro-industry figureheads to lead government bodies such as the Environmental Protection Agency and the Department of Energy. It included the appointment of the former chief executive officer of Mobil Oil to secretary of state. The voices of climate change contrarians have systematically and consciously been elevated within the Trump administration, while those who speak for and on behalf of the environment have been cowed or silenced. Things do not bode well for Planet Earth, at least not in the immediate future, given the contribution of the United States to global warming and its unrealized potential to take a leading role in climate change mitigation and adaptation.

From a criminological policy perspective, to effectively combat global warming requires a series of interrelated developments. These need to occur over the short term, medium term, and long term, and involve interventions across various areas of criminal justice (White and Kramer 2015). For example, with respect to law and legal reform the kinds of measures that are needed include innovative use of public litigation and public trust laws as well as the establishment of a new international convention on climate justice that incorporates the crime of ecocide. In regard to law enforcement, policy should be directed at strengthening collaborative networks involving key environmental law enforcement agencies (government as well as NGOs) and establishing permanent operational bodies at the national level to tackle environmental security issues, such as the Interpol National Environmental Security Taskforce (NEST) model (Higgins and White 2016). For courts and adjudication, measures could include the expansion of specialist environment courts and tribunals at the national domestic level, accompanied by the establishment of an international environment court (or its equivalent, such as an environmental division of the International Criminal Court).

Across the institutions of criminal justice, it is also possible to put into place and/or enhance concrete measures that serve to reduce the carbon footprint of policing, courts, corrections, and community corrections. Thus, in addition to exposing the links between climate change and crime types, and the crimes of the powerful in regard to global warming, criminological research also provides insight into other potential areas of redress. For example, work on "greening justice" has explored how the institutions of criminal justice can themselves be transformed in ways that diminish carbon emissions (such as through use of alternative energy sources and energy-efficient buildings and vehicles) and how offender rehabilitation can be directed toward ecologically beneficial projects (such as tree planting and community gardens) (White and Graham 2015).

Fundamentally, however, policy change and reform in relation to global warming are bounded by one essential consideration—politics. This, too, is reflective of the conditions that created the problem in the first place and that require radical transformative change if global warming is to be substantially addressed.

Electing and appointing people who continue to deny the basic realities of global warming and whose first acts are to tear down the institutions of environmental regulation and law enforcement are fundamentally backward steps that put one and all into jeopardy. In the light of this, it is undoubtedly a time when citizens must be even more active politically in support of sensible climate change policies. There is much to defend and protect. There is much to struggle for and against. But how people intervene and interact in the political life of their society is also complicated by the undermining of the ordinary conventions of truth and knowledge. The most powerful person on the planet tweets daily and the world listens attentively. In this post-fact era, the veracity of what is said seems to matter less than the attention that his comments garner. Evidence and contradiction matter naught. The medium is indeed the message insofar as what counts is presence, not content. A criminology for the future thus also requires media literacy and a search for truth that is not sidetracked by trivialization, slander, and bullying. This, too, is part of the challenge and struggle for climate justice.

REFERENCES

Agnew, R. 2011. Dire forecast: A theoretical model of the impact of climate change on crime. *Theoretical Criminology* 16 (1): 21–46.

———. 2012. It's the end of the world as we know it: The advance of climate change from a criminological perspective. In *Climate Change from a Criminological Perspective*, edited by R. White, 13–25. New York: Springer.

———. 2013. The ordinary acts that contribute to ecocide: A criminological analysis. In *Routledge International Handbook of Green Criminology*, edited by N. South and A. Brisman. London: Routledge.

Agnew, R., and T. Brezina. 2010. Strain theories. In *SAGE Handbook of Criminological Theory*, edited by E. McLaughlin and T. Newburn, 96–113. London: Sage.

Australian Crime Commission. 2009. *Horizons: Scanning Categories and Indicators 2009*. Canberra: ACC.

Baatz, C. 2013. Responsibility for the past? Some thoughts on compensating those vulnerable to climate change in developing countries. *Ethics, Policy & Environment* 16 (1): 94–110.

Barnett, J., and W. Adger. 2007. Climate change, human security and violent conflict. *Political Geography* 26: 639–655.

Bergin, A., and R. Allen. 2008. *The Thin Green Line: Climate Change and Australian Policing*. Canberra: Australian Strategic Policy Institute.

Boyanowsky, E. 1999. Violence and aggression in the heat of passion and in cold blood. *International Journal of Law and Psychiatry* 22 (3–4): 257–271.

Boyer, P. 2012. Wake up call from real world. *The Mercury*, October 23, 14–15.

Brisman, A. 2012. The cultural silence of climate change contrarianism. In *Climate Change from a Criminological Perspective*, edited by R. White, 41–70. New York: Springer.

———. 2013. The violence of silence: Some reflections on access to information, public participation in decision-making, and access to justice in matters concerning the environment. *Crime, Law and Social Change* 59 (3): 291–303.

Brown, D. 2010. Is climate science disinformation a crime against humanity? *The Guardian/UK*, November 3. Available at http://www.commondreams.org/view/2010/11/03-9.

Bulkeley, H., and P. Newell. 2010. *Governing Climate Change*. London: Routledge.

Chambers, D. 2011. Policing and climate change. *Australian Journal of Emergency Management* 26 (3): 52–59.

Cohen, S. 2001. *States of Denial: Knowing about Atrocities and Suffering.* Cambridge: Polity.

Colangelo, A. 2016. Warm August arrives in Australia as 2016 tipped to hit new highs. *The New Daily*, August 16.

Crank, J., and L. Jacoby. 2015. *Crime, Violence, and Global Warming.* London: Routledge.

Crook, M., and D. Short. 2014. Marx, Lemkin and the genocide-ecocide nexus. *International Journal of Human Rights* 18 (3): 298–319.

European Water Crimes Project. 2016. Available at http://www.watercrimes.eu/.

Farrell, S. T., and D. French, eds. 2012. *Criminological and Legal Consequences of Climate Change.* Oxford: Hart Publishing.

Gamble, J., and J. Hess. 2012. Temperature and violent crime in Dallas, Texas: Relationships and implications of climate change. *Western Journal of Emergency Medicine* 8 (3): 239–246.

Gedicks, A. 2005. Resource wars against native peoples. In *The Quest for Environmental Justice: Human Rights and the Politics of Pollution*, edited by R. Bullard. San Francisco: Sierra Club Books.

Gleick, P. 2014. Water, drought, climate change, and conflict in Syria. *Weather, Climate, and Society* 6: 331–340.

Green, P. 2005. Disaster by design: Corruption, construction and catastrophe. *British Journal of Criminology* 45 (4): 528–546.

Greig, A., and J. van der Velden. 2015. Earth hour approaches. *Overland*, March 25. Available at https://overland.org.au/2015/03/earth-hour-approaches/.

Harper, D., and Frailing, K. 2012. *Crime and Criminal Justice in Disaster.* Durham, NC: Carolina Academic Press.

Heckenberg, D., and I. Johnston. 2012. Climate change, gender and natural disasters: Social differences and environment-related victimization. In *Climate Change from a Criminological Perspective*, edited by R. White. New York: Springer.

Heede, R. 2014. Tracing anthropogenic carbon dioxide and methane emissions to fossil fuel and cement producers, 1854–2010. *Climate Change* 122: 229–241.

Hellman, J. 2014. The fifth crime under international criminal law: Ecocide? In *Regulating Corporate Criminal Liability*, edited by D. Brodowski, M. Espinoza de los Monteros de la Parra, K. Tiedman, and J. Vogel. New York: Springer.

Higgins, D., and R. White. 2016. Collaboration at the front line: Interpol and NGOs in the same NEST. In *Environmental Crime and Collaborative State Intervention*, edited by G. Pink and R. White. Basingstoke: Palgrave Macmillan.

Higgins, P. 2010. *Eradicating Ecocide: Laws and Governance to Prevent the Destruction of Our Planet.* London: Shepheard-Walwyn Publishers Ltd.

———. 2012. *Earth Is Our Business: Changing the Rules of the Game.* London: Shepheard-Walwyn Publishers Ltd.

Intergovernmental Panel on Climate Change. 2013. Working Group I Contribution to the IPCC Fifth Assessment Report Climate Change 2013: The Physical Science Basis: Summary for Policymakers. September 27.

———. 2014. Climate Change 2014 Synthesis Report Approved Summary for Policymakers. November 1.

Interpol. 2016. Environmental crime. Available at http://www.interpol.int/Crime-areas/Environmental-crime/Environmental-crime.

Klare, M. 2012. *The Race for What's Left: The Global Scramble for the World's Last Resources*. New York: Metropolitan Books, Henry Holt and Company.

Kramer, R. 2013a. Public criminology and the responsibility to speak in the prophetic voice concerning global warming. In *State Crime and Resistance*, edited by E. Stanley and J. McCulloch, 41–53. London: Routledge.

———. 2013b. Carbon in the atmosphere and power in America: Climate change as state-corporate crime. *Journal of Crime & Justice* 36 (2): 153–170.

Kramer, R., and R. Michalowski. 2012. Is global warming a state-corporate crime? In *Climate Change from a Criminological Perspective*, edited by R. White, 71–88. New York: Springer.

Lambrecht, J., and C. Ituate-Lima. 2016. Legal innovation in national courts for planetary challenges: Urgenda v. State of the Netherlands. *Environmental Law Review* 18 (1): 57–64.

Le Billon, P. 2012. *Wars of Plunder: Conflicts, Profits and the Politics of Resources*. New York: Columbia University Press.

Lever-Tracy, C. 2011. *Confronting Climate Change*. London: Routledge.

Lynch, M., R. Burns, and P. Stretesky. 2010. Global warming and state-corporate crime: The politicalization of global warming under the Bush administration. *Crime, Law and Social Change* 54: 213–239.

Mares, D. 2013. Climate change and crime: Monthly temperature and precipitation anomalies and crime rates in St. Louis, MO 1990–2009. *Crime, Law and Social Change* 59 (2): 185–208.

Mascher, S. 2016. Climate change justice and corporate responsibility: Commentary on the International Bar Association recommendations. *Journal of Energy & Natural Resources Law* 34 (1): 57–69.

McGarrell, E., and C. Gibbs. 2014. Conservation criminology, environmental crime, and risk: An application to climate change. *Oxford Handbooks Online: Criminology and Criminal Justice, Criminological Theories*. https:/doi.org/10.1093/oxfordhb/9780199935383.54.

Page, E. 2008. Distributing the burdens of climate change. *Environmental Politics* 17(4): 556–575.

Panjabi, R.K.L. 2014. Not a drop to spare: The global water crisis of the twenty-first century. *Georgia Journal of International and Comparative Law* 42 (2): 277–424.

Peng, C., S. Xueming, Y. Hongyong, and L. Dengsheng. 2011. Assessing temporary and weather influences on property crime in Beijing, China. *Crime, Law and Social Change* 55: 1–13.

Ranson, M. 2014. Crime, weather and climate change. *Journal of Environmental Economics and Management* 67: 274–302.

Reuveny, R. 2007. Climate change-induced migration and violent conflict. *Political Geography* 26: 656–673.

Rodriquez, H., E. Quarantelli, and R. Dynes, eds. 2007. *Handbook of Disaster Research*. New York: Springer.

Rothe, D., and D. Kauzlarich. 2016. *Crimes of the Powerful: An Introduction*. London: Routledge.

Rotton, J., and E. Cohn. 2003. Global warming and U.S. crime rates: An application of routine activity theory. *Environment and Behavior* 35 (6): 802–825.

Shearing, C. 2015. Criminology and the Anthropocene. *Criminology and Criminal Justice* 15 (3): 255–269.

Shiva, V. 2008. *Soil Not Oil: Environmental Justice in an Age of Climate Crisis*. Brooklyn: South End Press.

Smandych, R., and R. Kueneman. 2010. The Canadian-Alberta tar sands: A case study of state-corporate environmental crime. In *Global Environmental Harm: Criminological Perspectives*, edited by R. White, 87–109. Collumpton: Willan.

Sollund, R. 2012. Oil production, climate change and species decline: The case of Norway. In *Climate Change from a Criminological Perspective*, edited by R. White. New York: Springer.

South, N. 2012. Climate change, environmental (in)security, conflict and crime. In *Climate Change: Legal and Criminological Implications*, edited by S. Farrall, D. French, and T. Ahmed. Oxford: Hart.

South, N., and A. Brisman, eds. 2013. *Routledge International Handbook of Green Criminology*. New York: Routledge.

Stretesky, P., and M. Lynch. 2009. A cross-national study of the association between per capita carbon dioxide emissions and exports to the United States. *Social Science Research* 38: 239–250.

Sutherland, W. J., and H. J. Woodroof. 2009. The need for environmental horizon scanning. *Trends in Ecology and Evolution* 24 (10): 523–527.

Sutton, A., A. Cherney, and R. White. 2008. *Crime Prevention: Principles, Perspectives and Practices*. Melbourne: Cambridge University Press.

Sykes, G., and D. Matza. 1957. Techniques of neutralization: A theory of delinquency. *American Sociological Review* 22 (6): 664–670.

Tekayak, D. 2016. From "polluter pays" to "polluter does not pollute." *Geoforum* 71: 62–65.

Thornton, W. E., and L. Voigt. 2007. Disaster rape: Vulnerability of women to sexual assaults during Hurricane Katrina. *Journal of Public Management & Social Policy* 13 (2): 23–49.

Tombs, S., and D. Whyte. 2015. *The Corporate Criminal: Why Corporations Must Be Abolished*. London: Routledge.

Tucker, W. 2012. Deceitful tongues: Is climate change denial a crime? *Ecology Law Quarterly* 39: 831–894.

United Kingdom Government Office for Science. 2009. To arms: The growing use of lethal force in violent crime across Europe, The Sigma Scan. London: Government Office for Science. Available at http://www.sigmascan.org/Live/Issue/ViewIssue.aspx?IssueId=142&SearchMode=1.

White, R. 2008. *Crimes Against Nature: Environmental Criminology and Ecological Justice*. Devon: Willan.

———. 2011. *Transnational Environmental Crime: Toward an Eco-Global Criminology*. London: Routledge.

———. 2012a. The criminology of climate change. In *Climate Change from a Criminological Perspective*, edited by R. White. New York: Springer.

———. 2012b. Climate change and paradoxical harm. In *Criminological and Legal Consequences of Climate Change*, edited by S. Farrall, T. Ahmed, and D. French. Oxford: Hart Publishing.

———. 2014. Environmental insecurity and fortress mentality. *International Affairs* 90 (4): 835–851.

———. 2015. Climate change, ecocide and crimes of the powerful. In *Routledge International Handbook of the Crimes of the Powerful*, edited by G. Barak. London: Routledge.

———. 2017. Carbon criminals, climate change and ecocide. In *Criminology and the Anthropocene*, edited by C. Holley and C. Shearing. London: Routledge.

White, R., and H. Graham. 2015. Greening justice: Examining the interfaces of criminal, social and ecological justice. *British Journal of Criminology* 55 (5): 845–865.

White, R., F. Haines, and N. Asquith. 2017. *Crime and Criminology*. South Melbourne: Oxford University Press.

White, R., and D. Heckenberg. 2011. Environmental horizon scanning and criminological research and practice. *European Journal of Criminal Policy and Research* 17 (2): 87–100.

———. 2014. *Green Criminology: An Introduction to the Study of Environmental Harm*. London: Routledge.

White, R., and R. Kramer. 2015. Critical criminology and the struggle against climate change ecocide. *Critical Criminology* 23: 383–399.

5

Toward a Life-Course Theory of Victimization

Jillian J. Turanovic

Victimization has not always been a topic of great discussion among criminologists. Although discourse on crime and criminality can be traced back several centuries (Jeffrey 1959), despite a few scattered exceptions (e.g., von Hentig 1947; Wolfgang 1958), scholarly research on victimization did not really take off until the 1970s (Hindelang, Gottfredson, and Garofalo 1978; Cohen and Felson 1979). The study of victimization is therefore still pretty "young" by criminological standards. Even so, we have learned quite a bit over the past four decades. For example, we now have a decent understanding of how much victimization occurs in the United States each year, how much of that victimization is reported to the police, and where victimization is most concentrated within U.S. cities (Doerner and Lab 2015). We also know that victimization rates vary across particular groups in society and that they are highest among males and people of color (Truman and Morgan 2016). And we know that, much like the age-crime curve, victimization rates peak during the adolescent years and decline into adulthood (Macmillan 2001). Theoretical perspectives on victimization have also been put forth to explain these patterns, including routine activity and lifestyle theories (Hindelang, Gottfredson, and Garofalo 1978; Cohen and Felson 1979), which continue to dominate the study of victimization today.

Yet despite all that we have learned, there is still a lot we do not know. Theoretical advancements have largely stalled in recent years, and fundamental questions remain about how individuals' experiences with victimization vary over time, why this variation takes place, and how we can best intervene to prevent people from being victimized. The answers to these questions are important given that victimization remains a significant social problem—one that takes a significant toll on victims financially, emotionally, physically, and psychologically. But what if we could better understand stability and change in victimization and its consequences over time? If we could, perhaps we would be in a better place to develop and guide effective policies and support interventions for victims. Yet such an understanding would first require organizing the knowledge about what we know about the nature of victimization as we live our lives through time. In essence, what it seems we might need is a *life-course theory* of victimization.

WHAT'S THE THEORY?

The life-course perspective is a broad intellectual paradigm that encompasses ideas and observations from a variety of disciplines. The life course refers to a sequence of age-graded stages and roles that are socially constructed and have been found to differ substantially from one another in important ways. Tied to dynamic concerns and the unfolding of biological, psychological, and social processes through time, issues of age and aging occupy a prominent position in this perspective (Elder 1975). As individuals age and grow older, they cultivate ties to different social institutions (e.g., marriage and employment) and experience changes in cognitive capabilities (e.g., future-oriented thinking) that affect how they process and respond to life events.

Ideally a theory should be put forth in terms of a series of empirically testable propositions that are rooted firmly in the existing literature. The problem, however, is that given the state of existing research, it would be premature to put forth a formal life-course theory of victimization at this time. We simply don't know enough yet to do it. Beyond the childhood and adolescent years, we still know relatively little about how victimization unfolds across time, how victimization impacts people's lives in the short term and long term, and how social contexts shape victimization and its consequences over the life span. Accordingly, it might make more sense at this point to take a different strategy—one that presents a set of principles designed to guide us toward a better understanding of victimization over the life course. The discussion that unfolds ahead offers *eight principles* that are intended to serve as the beginning of a set of ideas as to what a theory of victimization over the life course might entail.

Principle 1: Lifestyle Patterns Can Help Explain Victimization over the Life Course

It's no big secret that individuals' risks of victimization can vary according to their lifestyles and routine activities. People who spend more of their time differentially exposed to "high risk times, places, and people" have a greater chance of coming into contact with potential offenders and experiencing victimization (Hindelang, Gottfredson, and Garofalo 1978, 245). The kinds of lifestyles that are most likely to put people in these situations are those that are risky, in that they entail a certain degree of deviance (Pratt and Turanovic 2016). These might include behaviors such as staying out late at night drinking, hanging around people who break the law, frequently being drunk or high in public, and routinely engaging in various violent and aggressive behaviors. While it is true that victimization does not *require* engaging in these risky behaviors, doing so certainly increase the odds of it happening. Prior research has shown that risky behaviors are linked to victimization across various stages of the life course (e.g., adolescence, adulthood, and old age) (Kennedy and Silverman 1990; Turanovic, Reisig, and Pratt 2015).

And across the life span, lifestyle and routine activity patterns can change considerably. They can vary with age, with risky behaviors often peaking during adolescence and then tapering off into adulthood, and they can vary along with individuals' changing motivations (e.g., Baumeister and Tierney 2011), situational factors, and life transitions (e.g., moving to a new neighborhood, being unemployed, getting married, having a child, or enrolling in school). Lifestyles and routine activities are therefore dynamic processes that should be conceptualized as such in any theory that is put forth to explain victimization over the life course.

Principle 2: Certain Lifestyles Can Carry Different Risks for Victimization over the Life Course

As the social contexts of people's lives change across the life span, the behaviors and lifestyles that are linked to victimization can change as well. Indeed, what constitutes a "risky lifestyle" at one point in the life course might not be so risky at another point in time. Take drinking alcohol, for instance. During the teenage years, drinking can be pretty risky when it comes to victimization. And there are a couple of reasons why: for one thing, teen drinking is a party behavior that is known to come with social rewards among youth, including peer group status and popularity (Kreager, Rulison, and Moody 2011). This means that teen drinking is highly likely to occur in the presence of other teens who are also drinking. At the same time, since youth in the United States cannot legally purchase alcohol or consume it publicly (usually until the age of twenty-one), they risk being punished—either formally, by the criminal justice system, or informally, by parents, teachers, and other authority figures—if they are caught getting drunk. This means that, in addition to being with peers, teens tend to drink in covert, unmonitored settings where there are no adults around to supervise them (Mayer et al. 1998). These sorts of situations can be highly conducive to victimization (Pratt and Turanovic 2016).

Drinking alcohol later in the life course, however, such as in middle or late adulthood, might not be as risky when it comes to victimization. Unlike teenagers, adults have more opportunities to consume alcohol legally in less precarious settings—like at brunch, a holiday office party, or even while watching TV at home. The social rewards that stem from drinking in adulthood might also be different in that adults are not always praised by their peers for consuming alcohol—particularly if they drink a lot of it (Demers and Bourgault 1996). What this means is that, since the situational contexts surrounding drinking can be quite different in middle or late adulthood, drinking during these stages in the life course might not be as strongly linked to victimization as in adolescence.

There is not a lot of empirical research that examines whether the strength of the relationship between certain lifestyles and victimization can change over the life course. More work is certainly needed in this regard. And, of course, we would not expect that all lifestyles have age-specific effects on victimization. Perhaps regularly walking alone downtown at night while drunk or high might be something that can be considered high risk at any age. But the point here is that some lifestyles might be much riskier during specific stages of development, and a theory of victimization over the life course should recognize this.

Principle 3: The Risk of Victimization Is Shaped by Social Contexts over the Life Course

Countless facets of people's lives are shaped and constrained by social contexts (Sampson 2012), and victimization is no exception. Hindelang and colleagues (1978) recognized this long ago when they put forth the idea of "structural constraints" in relation to personal victimization. They theorized that the lifestyle patterns that influence victimization manifest as individual- and group-level adaptations to role expectations and various aspects of the social structure. People learn attitudes and behaviors in response to their social environment, and once learned, they are incorporated into their routine activities. Hindelang and colleagues explained this idea as follows:

> Structural constraints originating from [the social structure] can be defined as limitations on behavioral options that result from the particular arrangements existing within various institutional orders, such as the economic, familial, educational, and legal orders. For example,

> economic factors impose stringent limitations on the range of choices that individuals have with respect to such fundamentals as area of residence, nature of leisure activities, mode of transportation, and access to educational opportunities. (Hindelang, Gottfredson, and Garofalo 1978, 242)

Across the life course and within economically deprived communities in particular, there are structural constraints that shape daily life in important ways. These constraints can encourage criminal attitudes and beliefs and limit the extent to which individuals are able to avoid coming into contact with risky people and risky settings (Turanovic, Pratt, and Piquero 2018). Structural constraints can also affect economic opportunities and can limit both the legitimate and illegal avenues of employment that are available in an area. With few viable options to make a living, community residents are more likely to adopt certain risky lifestyles—such as dealing drugs, stealing things, or selling stolen property—which can increase their risk of victimization.

Moreover, lifestyles can also be shaped by cultural responses to these structural conditions. In highly disadvantaged neighborhoods a "street code" value system can emerge, which places intense social pressures on residents (particularly on young males) to develop a tough, aggressive persona and to retaliate against those who show disrespect (Anderson 1999). Residents will adopt these sorts of behaviors because they perceive that they do not have much choice in the matter. And yet behaving in such a way, which is a response to structurally induced and culturally prescribed social processes (Wilson 2009), elevates the odds of being victimized (Berg et al. 2012).

So whether considering structural conditions (e.g., concentrated disadvantage) or the cultural adaptations to those conditions (e.g., street code), the point here is that victimization does not occur in a vacuum (Turanovic et al. 2018), and understanding individuals' lifestyles separate from where they live is "an almost impossible task" (Farrall and Calverly 2006, 162). Therefore, any complete theory of victimization over the life course must recognize and account for the importance of social context.

Principle 4: Individuals' Autonomy to Alter Their Risks of Victimization Can Vary over the Life Course

Constraints on lifestyles and victimization can also be imposed by age (Hindelang, Gottfredson, and Garofalo 1978). That is, during certain stages of the life course—particularly in early and late life—individuals' autonomy to alter their risk of victimization can be severely restricted. For example, children do not have much autonomy over their day-to-day lives. They generally cannot make their own decisions about where to live, whom to live with, where to go to school, or those they may encounter on a daily basis. Adults make these decisions for them. So when children experience victimization at home or at school—the most common places for child maltreatment to occur (U.S. Department of Health and Human Services 2016)—there is often little that children can do *on their own* to restructure their lives in ways that prevent them from being victimized again. Caring adults have to intervene and make these changes on their behalf.

As youth age out of childhood, however, they gain more autonomy over their daily routines, living situations, and their social interactions. Adolescence and emerging adulthood are marked by increasing self-sufficiency and independence from parents and the family home, and in adulthood, people tend to have more of a say over whom they spend time with on a regular basis. But as people age into late life, they can once again experience a loss of autonomy. In the face of declining health and cognition elderly individuals can be placed in the care of others who assume complete control over their daily lives. These situations often increase vulnerability to elder maltreatment and abuse (Choi and Mayer 2000). To be sure, perpetrators of elder abuse are most likely to be their caretakers—professional care providers and family members—whom older persons can do little to avoid (Cooper, Selwood, and Livingston 2007). Once again, as in childhood, the onus is on someone else to intervene and make changes on the victim's behalf. Thus, individuals' autonomy to alter their own risk of victimization can vary tremendously by age.

Principle 5: The Consequences of Victimization Vary across the Life Course

There is a large body of literature linking victimization to adverse consequences, including behavioral problems (e.g., aggression, crime, and substance abuse), social problems (e.g., school failure, job loss, financial hardship), psychological problems (e.g., depression, low self-esteem, and suicidality), and health problems (e.g., somatic complaints, obesity, and cardiovascular issues)—serious issues that tend to persist over time (Macmillan 2001; Turanovic and Pratt 2015). Several explanations have been put forth for why victimization is linked to such a lengthy roster of negative life outcomes. Perhaps the most well-supported ideas are those that come from the developmental and stress-coping literatures, where victimization is considered a traumatic and stressful life event. According to these perspectives, victimization elicits strong negative emotions (e.g., anxiety, depression, anger, and frustration) that victims will feel pressured to alleviate through some form of coping. Broadly speaking, coping can be defined as the process by which people regulate their behaviors and emotions under conditions of psychological distress (Agnew 2006). Coping techniques can be action oriented or internal, and they seek to reduce or minimize the various demands of a stressful situation.

Coping strategies can vary widely in response to victimization, where healthy coping techniques—such as participating in therapy or seeking comfort from family or friends—tend to be more successful at reducing long-term distress (Ong et al. 2006). Alternatively, unhealthy coping strategies might include behaviors like binge drinking, exacting revenge against the person who wronged you, and using drugs—all of which can result in more problems in the long run. Due to the intensity of negative emotions that many victims feel and because healthy coping can take more effort and resources, victims often cope with their experiences in unhealthy ways (Agnew 2006). And while we might expect victimization to elicit these sorts of responses at any age, there are certain stages of the life course where individuals might be especially susceptible to coping poorly with victimization.

In particular, throughout childhood and adolescence, victimization can have a profound developmental impact (Finkelhor 2008; Turanovic and Pratt 2017; Wright et al. in press). Between the ages of three and sixteen, youth are highly vulnerable to the harms of external stressors, such as violence (Romeo and McEwen 2006). Being victimized during these years can violate an individual's sense of safety, control, and expectations for survival (Cicchetti and Toth 2005) and can lead to distressing flashbacks, problems with insecure attachment, and difficulties with affective and emotional regulation (Heim et al. 2010). Victimization can also influence the development of a "traumatized brain" (Hart and Rubia 2012), where youth experience generalized states of fear, anxiety, and hyperarousal that can affect how they cope (Caffo, Forresi, and Lievers 2005).

Moreover, children and adolescents are less likely to have developed healthy coping techniques in general. Part of that development can be attributed to neurocognitive changes associated with aging. As people move into adulthood and their executive functioning increases, they become better at self-regulation (Smith, Steinberg, and Chein 2014; Pratt 2016). There is evidence that the prefrontal cortex—the part of the brain responsible for decision making, emotional regulation, and inhibitory responses—continues to develop until people are at least twenty years old (Romer 2010). So while most adolescents should be able to understand the risks associated with unhealthy coping behaviors by age fourteen, the inhibitory mechanisms required to resist engaging in these risky behaviors are not really equivalent to that of adults until around age twenty (Pharo et al. 2011).

Thus far, there has not been much empirical research examining how the consequences of victimization vary over the life course. But the few existing studies on the topic seem to suggest that victimization is more strongly linked to negative outcomes earlier in the life course. For example, using data from the Pathways to Desistance Study, Schreck and colleagues (2017) found that victimization was strongly related to offending in adolescence and that this association weakened as people aged into early adulthood. Similarly, using data from the National Longitudinal Study of Adolescent to Adult Health (Add Health), Russell, Vasilenko, and Lanza (2016) found that victimization or exposure to violence was more strongly associated with depressive symptoms and heavy episodic drinking in adolescence relative to early adulthood. And also using data from Add Health, Turanovic (2015) found that victimization during adolescence was linked to a much wider array of psychological, behavioral, and health problems than victimization during adulthood. All told, the various cognitive and social changes that happen over the life course probably have implications for how victims cope with what they have experienced. And even though the literature on this topic isn't very large, the preliminary evidence suggests that the consequences of victimization vary with age—something that a theory of victimization over the life course should consider.

Principle 6: Supportive Social Ties Shape Responses to Victimization over the Life Course

The ways in which victims cope with their experiences over the life course can be also be influenced heavily by their access to coping resources in the form of supportive social ties. Such ties may be formed in the workplace, at school, with friends or family, or through romantic partnerships. These ties often foster the perception of being loved and cared for by others, esteemed and valued, and part of a social network of mutual assistance and obligation. Supportive social ties can facilitate healthy coping via access to emotional, social, and instrumental support and can increase feelings of self-esteem and a sense of control over one's environment (Holtfreter, Reisig, and Turanovic 2016). It can be expected, then, that across the life course, supportive social ties buffer the harms of victimization. This means that individuals with strong social ties are less likely to experience negative outcomes as a result of being victimized (Turanovic and Pratt 2015, 2017).

It is important to remember, however, that social ties are age-graded (Sampson and Laub 1993). Over the life course, they change along with age-specific social roles, and they develop through a process of cumulative continuity (Laub and Sampson 2003). For example, during childhood and adolescence, social ties are primarily formed through family, school, and same-age peers—and thus they typically represent relationships with friends, teachers, and parents. In emerging adulthood, these social ties change, and in addition to parents and friends, they may also come to reflect ties to higher education, a new job, or a romantic partner. Later on in adulthood, as people become more entrenched in their adult roles and responsibilities, social ties might represent a long-term career, a close relationship with a spouse, ties to children, and investment in the community (Umberson, Crosnoe, and Reczek 2010). Even so, not everyone has access to supportive social ties over the life course. In general, social ties are formed through ongoing dynamic transactions between individuals and their support networks. And as people age, they become increasingly more responsible for cultivating and maintaining their own social ties. A person must engage others, develop relationships, and accrue goodwill.

But while supportive social ties should help buffer the consequences of victimization across the life course, at some stages of development it is possible that the protective effects of these ties might be more pronounced, such as in adulthood. More specifically, social ties in adulthood can differ from earlier stages of the life course in a couple of ways. First, these supportive ties likely reflect relationships that individuals formed themselves and put sustained effort into maintaining (Vaux 1988). Earlier in life, such as in childhood and adolescence, it is possible that having supportive social ties does not require as much effort. Most youth attend school where they spend a lot of time with their same-age peers and are watched over by teachers, and they tend to live at home where they interact frequently with their parents or caregivers—people who are obligated to provide them with basic levels of support and care. Adults, on the other hand, typically have to work harder at building their own social ties. And the quality of those ties is typically the result of sustained efforts to keep their relationships healthy.

Second, adult social ties typically have had more time to develop. By the time people reach adulthood, they may have finished college, found a stable job, and spent a length of time in a serious romantic relationship. Thus, adult social ties might be more self-generated, valued, and protective than in previous stages of the life course (Turanovic 2015). They are likely to serve as stronger sources of social control, facilitate the formation of prosocial peer groups, and structure routine activities in conventional ways. This means that adults with strong social ties are less likely to be victimized and that those same social ties can serve as coping resources should adults actually be victimized. Taken together, not only should supportive social ties be protective against the consequences of victimization generally, but also it is possible that the strength and impact of these social ties on the consequences of victimization can vary over the life course. This is something to consider as this area of research continues to develop.

Principle 7: Victimization Influences Social Ties over the Life Course

A person's access to supportive social ties over the life course can be shaped by many factors, not the least of which is victimization. Because victimization is a stressful life event, it can put strain on existing relationships and cause others to break off their social ties to victims (Turanovic and Young 2016). Within certain stages of the life course, such as adolescence, this pattern is particularly pronounced. To be sure, among teens, victimization carries a social stigma that decreases a person's attractiveness as a friend. Studies on peer attitudes have revealed that adolescents often show little concern for their victimized peers, and they generally believe that victims "bring their problems on themselves" (Graham 2001, 504). As a result, youth who are victimized are more likely to lose friends and be avoided by their peers (Turanovic and Young 2016). This also means that adolescent victims might lack strong friendships and the peer support resources that they need to cope effectively with their experiences.

In addition, victimization not only fractures existing relationships, but it also influences selection into the kinds of social ties that are not necessarily supportive or protective. For instance, a study by Kuhl, Warner, and Wilczak (2012) found that violent victimization during adolescence increased the likelihood getting married or cohabitating with a romantic partner at the age of seventeen. And while unions such as marriage or cohabitation might be protective later in life, they are not known to be very healthy or beneficial during the teenage years. What is more, a follow-up study found that youth who had been victimized were more likely to experience intimate partner violence when they entered into these early cohabitating unions (Kuhl, Warner, and Warner 2015). It therefore seems that victimization can propel people into negative social ties that can lead to further harm.

Under some unique circumstances, however, it is possible that victimization can strengthen positive ties to others through the activation of social support. In times of distress, victims may be more likely to elicit support from loved ones, to reach out to friends and coworkers, and to receive advice and guidance from others within their peer networks. Doing so can lead to increased feelings of closeness and can strengthen a person's social ties (Nolen-Hoeksema and Davis 1999)—even if only temporarily. Of course, given the deleterious consequences that victimization often has on people's lives, it is clear that experiencing distress and trauma rarely carries many support benefits for victims. It is thus critical to identify the conditions under which, how, and for whom this happens. The idea that distress can trigger the support process is not a new one (see, e.g., Vaux 1988), but it has yet to be integrated into the study of victimization over the life course.

Principle 8: Victimization Can Be a Turning Point in the Life Course

Turning points are changes in life directions that are accompanied by shifts in emotions, attitudes, and routine activities. They are often thought to represent significant role transitions, like getting married, joining the military, or joining a gang (Sampson and Laub 1993; Melde and Esbensen 2011). They can also stem from traumatic events in the life course, like experiencing the death of a family member, overdosing on drugs, or being shot (Teruya and Hser 2010). And although turning points can sometimes be slow and embody several incremental changes that accumulate over time, abrupt turning points—those sorts of discrete events that "knife off" or "radically separate" individuals from their prior circumstances—provide the greatest potential for changes to occur (Sampson and Laub 1993).

Victimization, particularly when it is violent and unexpected, can represent an abrupt and discrete turning point in the life course. For many, victimization can be a *negative* turning point, where individuals find themselves on a more troubled and disadvantaged life path as a result of being victimized (e.g., by experiencing financial problems, job loss, and school failure; Macmillan 2001). But for others, victimization can be a *positive* turning point that leads people to make prosocial changes to their lives (e.g., by reducing their involvement in risky lifestyles to avoid contact with potential offenders; see Turanovic and Pratt 2014; Turanovic et al. 2018).

Especially for individuals who are criminally involved, victimization can be a "shock" or a "hook for change" that triggers the kinds of cognitive transformations that foster desistance from crime (Giordano, Cernkovich, and Rudolph 2002). Recent research suggests that these cognitive transformations often happen *before* people enter into the kinds of social ties (e.g., marriage and work) that are thought to cause desistance (Skardhamar and Savolainen 2014). Qualitative interviews with offenders support the view that victimization can serve as a catalyst for change (Farrall et al. 2014), especially when victimization is serious and when offenders define the event as the result of their own criminal involvement (Jacques and Wright 2008). More work is certainly needed, however, to identify the conditions under which victimization leads to reductions (rather than increases) in crime over the life course.

WHAT'S THE PROBLEM?

The preceding eight principles were laid out in order to organize a set of ideas on how victimization and its consequences unfold over the life course and to highlight where empirical research is most needed. It is apparent from the above discussion that, while scholarship on victimization has certainly grown, most of this research has focused on victimization during the early and late stages of the life course (i.e., among children and adolescents, and to a lesser extent, the elderly). Studies of the correlates and consequences of victimization during other parts of the life span, such as in early and middle adulthood, are much rarer. This is problematic since, as Laub and Sampson put it, "the adult life course matters" (1993, 320). We need a better understanding of the experiences of victims during all stages of development if we are to put forth a solid theory of victimization over the life course.

That said, there are some real practical constraints to conducting the kind of research that is needed. For one, there are simply not many longitudinal data sets that track individuals beyond adolescence and that capture detailed information on victimization and its key theoretical correlates. Many of the longitudinal data sets that criminologists use to study crime over the life course simply cannot be used to study victimization in the same way. For instance, the National Longitudinal Survey of Youth (NLSY) 1997—an ongoing study that captures a wealth of information on men and women born in the United States between 1980 and 1984—includes detailed and repeated information on offending but not on victimization (with the exception of being a victim of "bullying" between the ages of twelve and eighteen and having been threatened at school; see Connolly and Beaver 2016). In addition, the NLSY 1979—which follows people born between 1957 and 1964 in the United States—also includes limited information on victimization and records only whether respondents were physically harmed by their parents prior to the age of eighteen (see Rehkopf et al. 2016). The Cambridge Study in Delinquent Development is another data source that has tremendously influenced the study of crime over the life course but does not measure victimization (with the exception of whether respondents were injured due to "fighting or horseplay" when they were eighteen to nineteen years old; see Farrington 1999, 309). The reality is that many of the longitudinal data sets that criminologists have access to cannot be used to study victimization with a great deal of rigor.

WHAT'S THE ANSWER?

Making Use of the Data We Have

While there is not necessarily an abundance of life-course data on victimization at our fingertips, there are options. Perhaps the two best available and most easily accessible data sets that can be used to study victimization over time are the Pathways to Desistance Study (Mulvey, Schubert, and Piquero

2014) and the National Longitudinal Study of Adolescent to Adult Health (Add Health; Harris 2013). The Pathways to Desistance Study is a multisite, longitudinal study of serious adolescent offenders that extends into early adulthood. Between November 2000 and January 2003, 1,354 adjudicated youths from the juvenile and adult court systems in Maricopa County (Phoenix), Arizona, and Philadelphia County, Pennsylvania, were enrolled in the study, and all youth were between fourteen to seventeen years old at the time of their committing offense. Data on youth were recorded in six- and twelve-month intervals over the course of seven years and capture a wealth of information on victimization, exposure to violence, social relationships, community conditions, risky lifestyles, and various other psychological and behavioral problems. Although the data are not nationally representative, youth in the Pathways study are serious offenders and, thus, they are more likely than members of the general population to engage in risky lifestyles, reside in structurally disadvantaged communities, and be victims of crime—making the data particularly relevant for policy purposes. Further details on the Pathways to Desistance Study, including participant enrollment, study design, and sample characteristics, can be found in Mulvey et al. (2014).

Alternatively, Add Health is an ongoing, nationally representative study of adolescent and adult health and well-being (Harris 2013). This longitudinal data collection effort started in 1994 by identifying, from a representative sample of high schools and middle or junior high schools, a random subsample of over twenty thousand adolescents enrolled in grades seven to twelve (who were between the ages of eleven and eighteen years old). These youth participated in the Wave I, in-home interview, which took place in 1995. A subset of respondents was interviewed again a year later in 1996 (Wave II). The original Wave I respondents were contacted for another interview during 2001 to 2002 when they were between eighteen and twenty-six years old (Wave III), and again during 2008 to 2009 when they were between the ages of twenty-four and thirty-two (Wave IV). Wave V of data collection is currently underway, and many respondents are now in their mid-thirties. Although there are large stretches of time between each wave of data, the Add Health can be used to provide important snapshots on what is happening at various stages in the life course with respect to victimization—during adolescence (teens), emerging adulthood (early twenties), earliest adulthood (mid- to late twenties), and early adulthood (early to mid-thirties). The Add Health captures many different forms of victimization (e.g., general violence, property victimization, intimate partner violence, child abuse, and sexual assault), and each wave of data contains rich information on a wide variety of social, psychological, behavioral, and health issues that can be assessed in relation to victimization. The availability and accessibility of these data thus provide several opportunities to contribute to research on victimization over several stages of the life course (i.e., between adolescence and early adulthood).

Thinking in Terms of Causal Process

Another way to make the best use of the data we have is to think more clearly about causal processes when we study victimization. Prior research has not always done a great job at specifying theoretically or measuring directly the dynamic causal processes thought to underlie victimization and its consequences over time (e.g., changes to social ties, risky lifestyles, cognitions, and coping strategies). Indeed, the processes by which key variables influence victimization and its consequences are often "black boxed" and are rarely tested explicitly. The typical approach is, instead, to correlate a particular variable with victimization (whether it be self-control, age, sex, race, gender, or marital status), control for other factors statistically, and then see if that variable retains its effect in a multivariate model. If it does, we generally assume that whatever unmeasured causal process we specified is, in fact, responsible for that relationship (see the discussion in Turanovic and Pratt 2014, 46). This strategy, which leaves much to be desired, has been the "norm" in victimization research for decades. This sort of approach is holding us back from developing a much more sound theory of victimization over the life course—one that clearly defines the causal processes responsible for stability and change in victimization and its consequences over time.

In moving toward a stronger emphasis on causal process, part of the challenge will be for scholars to conceptualize both the correlates and consequences of victimization as *dynamic* factors that are subject to considerable change—both situationally and across time. Outside of factors like race, sex, and certain biological characteristics, there are few other traits that are thought to remain fully stable over really long stretches of the life course. We now understand that even traits like low self-control—which were once thought to be formed early on in life and to remain relatively fixed—can vary substantially over time and can influence and be influenced by victimization (Agnew et al. 2011; Burt, Sweeten, and Simons 2014; Pratt 2016). Even the effects of stable traits on victimization (e.g., race, gender, or genetic predispositions) are thought to operate *indirectly* through other more dynamic factors—such as through risky lifestyles and exposure to illicit opportunities (Pratt et al. 2014).

Traditionally, researchers approached the study of victimization by trying to determine if it was the product of "population heterogeneity" or "state-dependent" processes (Lauritsen and Quinet 1995). Population heterogeneity factors refer to those stable, between-person differences that make people more prone to victimization than others; and state-dependent processes refer to within-person changes, events, and actions that can alter a person's future risk of victimization. The working assumption used to be that these processes were somehow competing or that they needed to operate separately from one another—something that may have hindered the advancement of a theory of victimization over the life course. Today, however, lines between population heterogeneity and state dependence perspectives have been blurred and discarded to where categorizing the correlates of victimization is some "either or" sort of fashion no longer makes a lot of sense (Turanovic and Pratt 2013). A better approach is to allow our developmental perspectives to be more of an amalgam of state dependence and population heterogeneity perspectives and recognize that there can be considerable mixing and overlap between these two sets of ideas (Nagin and Paternoster 2000).

CONCLUSION

Victimization is a complicated phenomenon. There is no singular explanation for why it happens, how it changes over the life course, or how it impacts people's lives. A focus on victimization and its consequences over the life span requires using a highly integrative and interdisciplinary approach—one that unifies seemingly divergent conceptions of stability and change in human development. And while the eight principles laid out here can get us closer to delineating a formal theory of victimization over the life course, there is still further to go. This set of guiding principles is still preliminary and, in fact, is intended to be more illustrative than definitive. But it is clear that serious work still needs to be done to unpack the various ways in which victimization and its consequences can unfold across time. From a policy perspective, this research is sorely needed to identify "what works" to prevent victimization and to mitigate its harms across the life course.

REFERENCES

Agnew, R. 2006. *Pressured into Crime: An Overview of General Strain Theory.* New York: Oxford University Press.

Agnew, R., H. Scheuerman, J. Grosholz, D. Isom, L. Watson, and S. Thaxton. 2011. Does victimization reduce self-control? A longitudinal analysis. *Journal of Criminal Justice* 39: 169–174.

Anderson, E. 1999. *Code of the Street: Decency, Violence, and the Moral Life of the Inner City.* New York: W. W. Norton.

Baumeister, R. F., and J. Tierney. 2011. *Willpower: Rediscovering the Greatest Human Strength.* New York: Penguin.

Berg, M. T., E. A. Stewart, C. J. Schreck, and R. L. Simons. 2012. The victim-offender overlap in context: Examining the role of neighborhood street culture. *Criminology* 50: 359–390.

Burt, C. H., G. Sweeten, and R. L. Simons. 2014. Self-control through emerging adulthood: Instability, multidimensionality, and criminological significance. *Criminology* 52: 450–487.

Caffo, E., B. Forresi, and L. Strik Lievers. 2005. Impact, psychological sequelae, and management of trauma affecting children and adolescents. *Current Opinion in Psychiatry* 18: 422–428.

Choi, N. G., and J. Mayer. 2000. Elder abuse, neglect, and exploitation: Risk factors and prevention strategies. *Journal of Gerontological Social Work* 33: 5–25.

Cicchetti, D., and S. L. Toth. 2005. Child maltreatment. *Annual Review of Clinical Psychology* 1: 409–438.

Cohen, L. E., and M. Felson. 1979. Social change and crime rate trends: A routine activity approach. *American Sociological Review* 44: 588–608.

Connolly, E. J., and K. M. Beaver. 2016. Considering the genetic and environmental overlap between bullying victimization, delinquency, and symptoms of depression/anxiety. *Journal of Interpersonal Violence* 31: 1230–1256.

Cooper, C., A. Selwood, and G. Livingston. 2007. The prevalence of elder abuse and neglect: A systematic review. *Age and Ageing* 37: 151–160.

Demers, A., and C. Bourgault. 1996. Changing society, changing drinking: Solitary drinking as a non-pathological behavior. *Addiction* 91: 1505–1516.

Doerner, W. G., and S. P. Lab. 2015. *Victimology*. 7th ed. New York: Routledge.

Elder, G. H. 1975. Age differentiation and the life course. *Annual Review of Sociology* 1: 165–190.

Farrall, S., and A. Calverly. 2006. *Understanding Desistance from Crime: Theoretical Directions in Resettlement and Rehabilitation*. New York: Open University Press.

Farrall, S., B. Hunter, G. Sharpe, and A. Calverley. 2014. *Criminal Careers in Transition: The Social Context of Desistance from Crime*. Oxford: Oxford University Press.

Farrington, D. P. 1999. *Cambridge Study in Delinquent Development [Great Britain]*, 1961–1981. Ann Arbor, MI: Inter-University Consortium for Political and Social Research.

Finkelhor, D. 2008. *Childhood Victimization: Violence, Crime, and Abuse in the Lives of Young People*. New York: Oxford University Press.

Giordano, P. C., S. A. Cernkovich, and J. L. Rudolph. 2002. Gender, crime, and desistance: Toward a theory of cognitive transformation. *American Journal of Sociology* 107: 990–1064.

Graham, S. 2001. Peer victimization in school. In *Adolescence in America: An Encyclopedia*, edited by J. V. Lerner and R. M. Lerner, 449–505. Santa Barbara, CA: ABC-CLIO.

Harris, K. M. 2013. *The Add Health Study: Design and Accomplishments*. Chapel Hill, NC: Carolina Population Center, University of North Carolina at Chapel Hill.

Hart, H., and K. Rubia. 2012. Neuroimaging of child abuse: A critical review. *Frontiers in Human Neuroscience* 6 (52): 1–24.

Heim, C., M. Shugart, W. E. Craighead, and C. B. Nemeroff. 2010. Neurobiological and psychiatric consequences of child abuse and neglect. *Developmental Psychobiology* 52: 671–690.

Hindelang, M. J., M. R. Gottfredson, and J. Garofalo. 1978. *Victims of Personal Crime: An Empirical Foundation for a Theory of Personal Victimization.* Cambridge, MA: Ballinger.

Holtfreter, K., M. D. Reisig, and J. J. Turanovic. 2016. Self-rated poor health and loneliness in late adulthood: Testing the moderating role of familial ties. *Advances in Life Course Research* 27: 61–68.

Jacques, S., and R. Wright. 2008. The victimization–termination link. *Criminology* 46: 1009–1038.

Jeffrey, C. Ray. 1959. The historical development of criminology. *Journal of Criminal Law and Criminology* 50: 3–19.

Kennedy, L. W., and R. A. Silverman. 1990. The elderly victim of homicide. *Sociological Quarterly* 31: 307–319.

Kreager, D. A., K. Rulison, and J. Moody. 2011. Delinquency and the structure of adolescent peer groups. *Criminology* 49: 95–127.

Kuhl, D. C., D. F. Warner, and T. D. Warner. 2015. Intimate partner violence risk among victims of youth violence: Are early unions bad, beneficial, or benign? *Criminology* 53: 427–456.

Kuhl, D. C., D. F. Warner, and A. Wilczak. 2012. Adolescent violent victimization and precocious union formation. *Criminology* 50: 1089–1127.

Laub, J. H., and R. J. Sampson. 1993. Turning points in the life course: Why change matters to the study of crime. *Criminology* 31: 301–325.

———. 2003. *Shared Beginnings, Divergent Lives: Delinquent Boys to Age 70.* Cambridge, MA: Harvard University Press.

Lauritsen, J. L., and K. F. Davis Quinet. 1995. Repeat victimization among adolescents and young adults. *Journal of Quantitative Criminology* 11: 143–166.

Macmillan, R. 2001. Violence and the life course: The consequences of victimization for personal and social development. *Annual Review of Sociology* 27: 1–22.

Mayer, R. R., J. L. Forster, D. M. Murray, and A. C. Wagenaar. 1998. Social settings and situations of underage drinking. *Journal of Studies on Alcohol* 59: 207–215.

Melde, C., and F. Esbensen. 2011. Gang membership as a turning point in the life course. *Criminology* 49: 513–552.

Mulvey, E. P., C. A. Schubert, and A. R. Piquero. 2014. *Pathways to Desistance: Final Technical Report.* Washington, DC: National Institute of Justice.

Nagin, D., and R. Paternoster. 2000. Population heterogeneity and state dependence: State of the evidence and directions for future research. *Journal of Quantitative Criminology* 16: 117–144.

Nolen-Hoeksema, S., and C. G. Davis. 1999. "Thanks for sharing that": Ruminators and their social support networks. *Journal of Personality and Social Psychology* 77: 801–814.

Ong, A. D., C. S. Bergeman, T. L. Bisconti, and K. A. Wallace. 2006. Psychological resilience, positive emotions, and successful adaptation to stress in later life. *Journal of Personality and Social Psychology* 91: 730–749.

Pharo, H., C. Sim, M. Graham, J. Gross, and H. Hayne. 2011. Risky business: Executive function, personality, and reckless behavior during adolescence and emerging adulthood. *Behavioral Neuroscience* 125: 970–978.

Pratt, T. C. 2016. A self-control/life-course theory of criminal behavior. *European Journal of Criminology* 13: 129–146.

Pratt, T. C., and J. J. Turanovic. 2016. Lifestyle and routine activity theories revisited: The importance of "risk" to the study of victimization. *Victims and Offenders* 11: 335–354.

Pratt, T. C., J. J. Turanovic, K. A. Fox, and K. A. Wright. 2014. Self-control and victimization: A meta-analysis. *Criminology* 52: 87–116.

Rehkopf, D. H., I. Headen, A. Hubbard, J. Deardorff, Y. Kesavan, A. K. Cohen, D. Patil, L. D. Ritchie, and B. Abrams. 2016. Adverse childhood experiences and later life adult obesity and smoking in the United States. *Annals of Epidemiology* 26: 488–492.

Romeo, R. D., and B. McEwen. 2006. Stress and the adolescent brain. *Annals of the New York Academy of Sciences* 1094: 202–214.

Romer, D. 2010. Adolescent risk taking, impulsivity, and brain development: Implications for prevention. *Developmental Psychobiology* 52: 263–276.

Russell, M. A., S. A. Vasilenko, and S. T. Lanza. 2016. Age-varying links between violence exposure and behavioral, mental, and physical health. *Journal of Adolescent Health* 59: 189–196.

Sampson, R. J. 2012. *Great American City: Chicago and the Enduring Neighborhood Effect.* Chicago: University of Chicago Press.

Sampson, R. J., and J. H. Laub. 1993. *Crime in the Making: Pathways and Turning Points through Life.* Cambridge, MA: Harvard University Press.

Schreck, C. J., M. T. Berg, G. C. Ousey, E. A. Stewart, and J. M. Miller. 2017. Does the nature of the victimization-offending association fluctuate over the life course? An examination of adolescence and early adulthood. *Crime and Delinquency* 63: 786–813.

Skardhamar, T., and J. Savolainen. 2014. Changes in criminal offending around the time of job entry: A study of employment and desistance. *Criminology* 52: 263–291.

Smith, A. R., L. Steinberg, and J. Chein. 2014. The role of the anterior insula in adolescent decision making. *Developmental Neuroscience* 36: 196–209.

Teruya, C., and Y. Hser. 2010. Turning points in the life course: Current findings and future directions in drug use research. *Current Drug Abuse Reviews* 3: 189–195.

Truman, J. L., and R. E. Morgan. 2016. *Criminal Victimization, 2015.* Washington, DC: Bureau of Justice Statistics.

Turanovic, J. J. 2015. *The Age-Graded Consequences of Victimization.* Doctoral Dissertation, Arizona State University.

Turanovic, J. J., and T. C. Pratt. 2013. The consequences of maladaptive coping: Integrating general strain and self-control theories to specify a causal pathway between victimization and offending. *Journal of Quantitative Criminology* 29: 321–345.

———. 2014. "Can't stop, won't stop": Self-control, risky lifestyles, and repeat victimization. *Journal of Quantitative Criminology* 30: 29–56.

———. 2015. Longitudinal effects of violent victimization during adolescence on adverse outcomes in adulthood: A focus on prosocial attachments. *Journal of Pediatrics* 166: 1062–1069.

———. 2017. Consequences of violent victimization for Native American youth in early adulthood. *Journal of Youth and Adolescence* 46: 1333–1350.

Turanovic, J. J., T. C. Pratt, and A. R. Piquero. 2018. Structural constraints, risky lifestyles, and repeat victimization. *Journal of Quantitative Criminology* 34: 251–274.

Turanovic, J. J., M. D. Reisig, and T. C. Pratt. 2015. Risky lifestyles, low self-control, and violent victimization across gendered pathways to crime. *Journal of Quantitative Criminology* 31: 183–206.

Turanovic, J. J., and J.T.N. Young. 2016. Violent offending and victimization in adolescence: Social network mechanisms and homophily. *Criminology* 54: 487–519.

Umberson, D., R. Crosnoe, and C. Reczek. 2010. Social relationships and health behavior across the life course. *Annual Review of Sociology* 36: 139–157.

U.S. Department of Health and Human Services. 2016. *Child Maltreatment 2014*. Available at http://www.acf.hhs.gov/programs/cb/research-data-technology/statistics-research/child-maltreatment.

Vaux, A. 1988. *Social Support: Theory, Research, and Intervention*. New York: Praeger.

von Hentig, H. 1948. *The Criminal and His Victim*. New Haven, CT: Yale University Press.

Wilson, W. J. 2009. *More Than Just Race: Being Black and Poor in the Inner City*. New York: W. W. Norton.

Wolfgang, M. E. 1958. *Patterns in Criminal Homicide*. Oxford, UK: University of Pennsylvania Press.

Wright, K. A., J. J. Turanovic, E. N. O'Neal, S. J. Morse, and E. T. Booth. In press. The cycle of violence revisited: Childhood victimization, resilience, and future violence. *Journal of Interpersonal Violence*.

6

Translating Theories of Desistance to Policy

MEGAN KURLYCHEK AND
MEGAN DENVER

Researchers increasingly agree that desistance is not simply the sudden termination of involvement in crime or the criminal justice system but is instead a process (Bushway et al. 2001; Laub and Sampson 2001; Maruna 2001).[1] While researchers appear to agree about the concept of desistance as a process, there is less agreement over exactly how the process unfolds over time. For example, scholars have proposed that most people will naturally desist on their own, unless they encounter negative labels and barriers from social interactions that exacerbate their involvement in deviance and crime (Lemert 1951; Matza 1964). Other scholars posit that desistance may not necessarily happen entirely naturally, but that it can be promoted by external social factors that increase an individual's bond to conventional society (e.g., Sampson and Laub 1997). Still other scholars emphasize the role of agency and identity in the desistance process (Giordano, Cernkovich, and Rudolph 2002; Paternoster and Bushway 2009) but propose different motivations and processes through which cognitive transformations or identity changes occur.

There are three key similarities across theoretical perspectives: each considers the role of personal identity, the social environment, and structural barriers and opportunities in the desistance process. Notable differences include the emphasis, timing, and role of each factor in the desistance process. While the similarities lead us to identify key factors that should be addressed from a policy perspective if we hope to encourage desistance from crime, the differences in the theories lead to disjunct notions of how each factor is best addressed.

In this chapter, we review several current prominent theoretical explanations of desistance.[2] We then discuss how their similarities can be used to leverage policy initiatives to reduce crime. We further discuss in detail how variations in the theories might lead to different applications of such policies and propose directions for future research in this area.

THEORETICAL DEPICTIONS OF DESISTANCE

The Labeling Perspective: Barriers to Natural Desistance

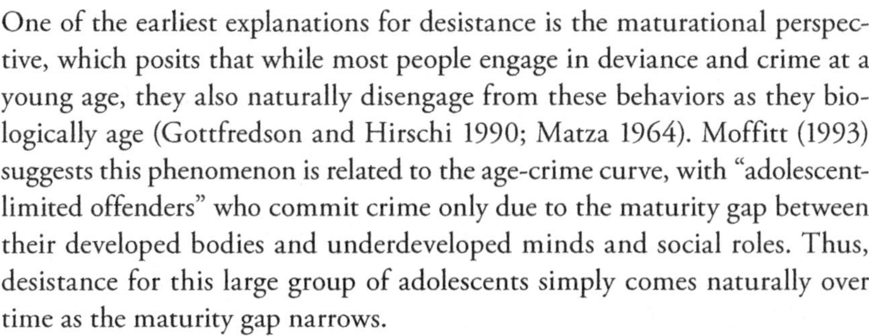

One of the earliest explanations for desistance is the maturational perspective, which posits that while most people engage in deviance and crime at a young age, they also naturally disengage from these behaviors as they biologically age (Gottfredson and Hirschi 1990; Matza 1964). Moffitt (1993) suggests this phenomenon is related to the age-crime curve, with "adolescent-limited offenders" who commit crime only due to the maturity gap between their developed bodies and underdeveloped minds and social roles. Thus, desistance for this large group of adolescents simply comes naturally over time as the maturity gap narrows.

However, social structures and environments can create setbacks in this natural desistance process. Individuals with criminal records are often labeled as "evil" (Tannenbaum 1938) and stigmatized (Goffman 1963). Such labels and negative societal reactions can reduce individuals' opportunities for natural desistance and induce future crime and deviance (Becker 1963; Goffman 1963; Lemert 1951). Labeling theory originated from the symbolic interactionist perspective, which posits that people are constantly creating their own reality through their personal interpretations of interactions and experiences with others (Cooley 1902; Mead 1934). Labeling theorists view deviance as a natural occurrence for most people, particularly during adolescence. What matters then isn't the motivation for the original or early deviance, referred to as "primary deviance" through this theoretical lens, but rather how others react to the behavior and how the individual interprets these reactions. Thus, instead of aging out of crime, those tagged as deviants or delinquents (Tannenbaum 1938) are perceived by others in a negative or unfavorable way, which may lead to differential treatment. In the words of Goffman (1963, 5), individuals without the stigmatizing or discrediting characteristic "exercise varieties of discrimination, through which we effectively, if often unthinkingly, reduce his life chances." Over time the individual may come to accept the definition of himself or herself being communicated by others, and the label of deviant may become part of a self-fulfilling prophecy (Tannenbaum 1938). Therefore, while primary deviance is a common form of social behavior, secondary deviance arises from the perceived deviant identity that the person internalizes due to negative social reactions by others (Lemert 1951).

Labeling theory experienced a severe decline in the mid-1980s due to heavy critiques of the perspective and some perhaps misguided interpretations of the theory's ultimate policy relevance (Gibbs 1966; Tittle 1975, 1980) but has experienced a recent resurgence in both conceptual development (Denver, Pickett, and Bushway 2017; Paternoster and Iovanni 1989) and empirical testing (e.g., Chiricos et al. 2007; Matsueda 1992) over the past few decades. For example, using a national, longitudinal study of self-reported delinquency, youth perceptions, and their parents' perceptions, Matsueda (1992) linked the notion of self-appraisals as a reflection of social reactions (symbolic interactionism) with stigma and secondary deviance (labeling). He found prior delinquency and parental perceptions of the youth to influence the youth's self-appraisals, and in turn, these self-appraisals of being someone who "gets into trouble" and "breaks rules" to increase future delinquency. Similarly, criminal justice system labels appear to influence adult recidivism. Examining a sample of adults convicted of felony crimes in Florida, Chiricos and colleagues (2007) compared cases where judges withheld adjudication of guilt, which prevents individuals from experiencing the collateral consequences associated with a felony conviction, to adjudicated cases. Chiricos et al. (2007) found that those formally labeled as "felons" were more likely to be reconvicted within a two-year period.

When considering the desistance process, the labeling perspective suggests that applying the label of "delinquent" or "criminal" can have significant adverse consequences. Stigmatization and social exclusion can lead to counterproductive public safety outcomes by encouraging individuals to gravitate toward deviant groups (Becker 1963; Bernburg, Krohn, and Rivera 2006) and increasing, rather than reducing, crime. As a result, formal labels and stigma can prevent individuals from entering into what would otherwise be a natural, maturational process of desistance.

Linking Labeling and Social Bonds

Ideas from the labeling perspective have also influenced other criminological theories. One example is Braithwaite's (1989) theory of reintegrative shaming. While not necessarily a theory of desistance, this perspective incorporates the idea that "shaming" can be "disintegrative" and actually increase crime but also suggests that not all punishment is disintegrative or stigmatizing. Therefore, while labeling theory suggests that avoiding criminal justice system contact, penalties, and labels is the best strategy to reduce crime, reintegrative shaming theory embraces the idea that an individual should be held accountable for his or her actions. However, after being held accountable, an individual should also be given a chance to redeem himself or herself and become reintegrated into society. Thus, it is not punishment that causes a re-identification of the self and increased recidivism but rather the consistently blocked opportunities that might follow the shaming are more likely the cause if the label or stigma sticks with the individual beyond the immediate consequences of the criminal act.

Braithwaite's (1989) theory of reintegrative shaming ties nicely to Sampson and Laub's (1997) age-graded theory of crime that integrates social and structural ideas from differential association, social bonding, and labeling theories to propose a life-course approach to studying how delinquency begins, continues, and ultimately ends. Life-course theory starts with the "hallmark" assumption from labeling theory (Matsueda 1992, 1588) that individuals enter society with different statuses that automatically impact their location in the social structure, such as race, gender, birth order in the family, and familial socioeconomic status. Sampson and Laub (1993, 1997) then attribute a person's trajectory toward or away from deviance to early childhood bonds to family, school, and conventional society, an idea that borrows heavily from Hirschi's (1969) social bond theory. As individuals enter late childhood and early adolescence, bonds to peers gain in importance, as suggested by differential association theory (Sutherland 1947). If this set of factors—location in the social structure, bonds to society, connection to peers—aligns in a way that leads one to delinquency, the youth can become labeled as a delinquent and experience resulting stigmatization and increased delinquency.

How then does this youth avoid a lifetime of crime and acceptance of the deviant label? According to Sampson and Laub (1993, 1997), desistance occurs through the formation of new adult social bonds. Specifically, Sampson and Laub (1997: 304) "contend that pathways to both crime and conformity are modified by key institutions of social control in the transition to adulthood (e.g., employment, military service, and marriage)." Just as bonds to parents and school were important for keeping a child out of delinquency, bonds to conventional adult society are important for the desistance process after a person has become involved in delinquency. For example, having a job one does not want to lose or a partner one does not want to leave while in prison can be a convincing factor in the desistance process and can serve as a turning point that changes the trajectory of the life course (Elder 1985). Later revisions to the theory also included "human agency and choice, situational influences, routine activities, local culture, and historical context" (Laub and Sampson 2003, 9) but reiterate that identity changes are not necessary for desistance to occur. Instead, such changes occur in reaction to turning points.

In short, turning points, which Laub, Nagin, and Sampson (1998, 225) refer to as "'triggering events' that are, in part, exogenous," can promote or even "cause" desistance from crime.

Opportunities, Change, and Setbacks

While Sampson and Laub's life-course perspective has become a popular explanation for desistance, some scholars question the temporal ordering of the social bonds–desistance relationship (Skardhamar and Savolainen 2014) or critique the passive role individuals appear to take under a social control perspective. For example, in their theory of cognitive transformation, Giordano, Cernkovich, and Rudolph (2002, 992) pay particular attention to "the 'up front' work accomplished by actors themselves" as transitions in their respondents' lives occur. The authors redefine turning points as "hooks for change." For a hook to be successful it requires more than just the opportunity for change; the person must first be internally open to change and the hook must provide something important and meaningful to the person (Giordano, Cernkovich, and Rudolph 2002). Most adult social bonds, including holding a steady job or maintaining a long-term relationship, are "fundamentally incompatible" with a lifestyle involving crime and deviance (2002, 1001). Giordano and colleagues (2002) also emphasize an individual's agency in pursuing available opportunities while reiterating that any one particular event is a major theme in a broader narrative. In other words, a life event is not an exogenous event that happens to a person, but rather it occurs through an interactive process that involves decisions and actions on the part of the individual. Furthermore, emotions—particularly anger and depression—can help to explain setbacks (or derailments) in the desistance process after a person successfully transitions to a prosocial life-course trajectory (Giordano, Schroeder, and Cernkovich 2007).

Cognitive theorists also promote a deep symbolic interaction foundation similar to that depicted in the early labeling tradition. As Giordano, Cernkovich, and Rudolph (2007, 1607) explain, "thoughts, while located within the individual, are nevertheless deeply social in origin." Individuals may be more receptive to an intervention or opportunity at different points in their life course, and some individuals may more successfully develop hooks at a certain point in time compared to other individuals (Giordano, Cernkovich, and Rudolph 2007). Giordano and colleagues (2007) point to Chris Uggen's (2000) study as an empirical example of differential openness to change. Uggen (2000) reevaluated Supported Work, a transitional job program for individuals returning from prison. Unlike the original evaluation, which found null recidivism effects for the sample of men on average

(Piliavin and Gartner 1981), by exploring a possible moderating effect of age Uggen (2000) found a meaningful reduction in recidivism rates for older men who were provided a work opportunity. Uggen's result is important given existing rigorous evaluations of employment-based programs that typically find null effects for recidivism (Bushway and Apel 2012; Visher, Winterfield, and Coggeshall 2005; Wilson, Gallagher, and MacKenzie 2000).

One potential explanation for Uggen's age-graded employment result is that the older men represented a group that has already initiated the desistance process and were therefore more "motivated" and ready to work when presented with a work opportunity (Bushway and Reuter 2001, 219). One way to tease out the relationship between age and motivation is to change the population under consideration. Transitional job programs, the focus of many of the evaluations referenced above, target individuals returning home from prison. The recently incarcerated population traditionally encounters a variety of serious obstacles to societal integration, including housing, childcare, and transportation, and may not be ready to immediately hold employment. Not participating in the labor market, rather than the inability to find work (i.e., unemployment), is a major source of nonemployment (Apel and Sweeten 2010). Therefore, examining a group of individuals who select into the labor market could allow for age comparisons that are distinct from concepts like motivation or job readiness.

A recent set of studies considered the impact of passing a criminal background check among a group of individuals with criminal convictions who applied for jobs in the healthcare industry in New York State. Bushway, Denver, and Kurlychek (2016) found that individuals with convictions who were cleared to work (relative to those denied) experience large and significant increases in employment levels in both the short term and the long term, and Denver, Siwach, and Bushway (2017) found meaningful impacts on subsequent arrests. In particular, men cleared to work experience large reductions in recidivism, while women cleared to work do not. However, unlike Uggen's (2000) study, this research did not find meaningful age variations for men—both younger and older men benefited (Denver, Siwach, and Bushway 2017). This result provides support for the notion that desistance may involve more than simply maturation, and younger men might also benefit from certain policy strategies.

Shadd Maruna presents another perspective on the role of individual identity and its interaction with the social environment through personal narratives. Instead of social bonds or major life events "knifing off" past lives from the present selves, Maruna (2001) posits that individuals involved in the criminal justice system reconstruct their past to justify their histories and explain the decision to "go straight" (see also Maruna and Roy 2007).

This rewriting of history is particularly important when a person encounters challenges and potential threats to the desistance process. A powerful and convincing story creates an incompatibility between the self-narrative and the negative feelings that accompany engaging in crime (Cressey 1963, cited in Maruna 2001). The individuals engaged in these "willful, cognitive distortion(s)" are "making good" (Maruna 2001, 9) and may be open to and ready for new prosocial opportunities.

Overall these researchers indicate that while turning points are important in the desistance process, the opportunity itself is not enough. The individual must be open to and ready for change, which involves a more complex process. The challenge from a policy perspective is identifying the individuals who are in the process of desisting and are "ready" for such opportunity.

Desistance as a Rational Choice

A recent theory developed by Paternoster and Bushway (2009, 1106) takes the role of human agency one step further than Giordano and colleagues, viewing change as "more cognitive, internal, and individual, at least initially." The identity theory of desistance views desistance as a rational choice, where individuals recognize that the costs of crime outweigh the benefits (Paternoster and Bushway 2009; Paternoster et al. 2015). Individuals make the decision to quit crime because they have simply had enough of their crime-involved lifestyle and its negative consequences. They begin to fear what the future holds and the future version of themselves if they do not make a change (Paternoster and Bushway 2009). Instead of reinterpreting their past lives in reformulated narratives, as do the respondents in Maruna's (2001) study, Paternoster and Bushway's (2009) theory requires deliberate, intentional change from an old identity to a new one. Yet similar to the phenomenological criminology perspective that shapes Maruna's (2001) work, Paternoster and Bushway's theory also focuses on the desired self-images and goals individuals hold to understand how, when, and why they desist from crime. The policy challenge from a rational choice perspective is determining the role programs or interventions should have, if any, for individuals with criminal records, as the "feared self" that provides the impetus for change only comes about after a series of negative consequences stemming from involvement in crime.

THEORETICAL CONCORDANCE AND DISSONANCE

There are several consistent messages that can be taken from popular theories of desistance to create a set of policy choices that can be implemented and empirically tested. First, we believe all of the theoretical perspectives indicate that acceptance of, and adherence to, a criminal identity is a barrier to desistance. The barriers posed by labeling individuals with criminal records, and the associated stigma and discrimination, are the most evident in labeling theory. Yet prohibiting individuals from economic, civic, and social opportunities also creates challenges from a reintegrative shaming perspective, a life-course/social bonds perspective, and a cognitive/identity perspective. Thus, a broad take-away message reiterated across theories is that social policy should be constructed in such a way that it first and foremost helps an individual to avoid accepting a criminal identity to start with, but that it also facilitates readiness and opportunities for change that allow an individual to initiate change and continue along the desistance process.

Second, each theoretical perspective suggests, albeit to varying degrees, that individuals need more than just a willingness to change—they also need true opportunities to desist. While the perspectives presented by Giordano and colleagues, Maruna, and Paternoster and Bushway put more emphasis on internal change being needed before an individual is ready to accept such an opportunity, none of the theories disagrees with the importance of social interactions, adult social bonds, and opportunities for change as originally proposed by Sampson and Laub.[3] Thus, the theories seem to agree that positive social networks and efforts to connect individuals to potential opportunities/hooks for change could be important events along the path to desistance. The difference lies in the timing and emphasis, but not in the basic concept.

Third, to different degrees the various theories also consider the importance of the greater social structure in providing such opportunities. The stigma from a criminal record can influence a person's social status and create barriers to various opportunities at a macro level. If blocked opportunities prevent the individual from acquiring or sustaining change—which theories of desistance predict—people may experience setbacks or "derailments" in the desistance process (Giordano, Schroeder, and Cernkovich 2007). The individual will not be able to develop positive adult social bonds and be fully integrated into society. Moreover, if the person feels blocked at every corner from opportunity with no sign of relief in sight, this may also provide little incentive for the person to restructure his or her identity or interpretation of the past self.

Variations in the Theme

Despite the commonalities across theories, some subtle contrasts and clear divides exist between the perspectives that introduce complications in identifying effective desistance policies. For example, many of the perspectives emphasize the importance of opportunities for integration (Braithwaite 1989; Giordano, Cernkovich, and Rudolph 2002; Sampson and Laub 1993, 1997); however, some theories suggest an opportunity alone will have little impact unless the person has developed a prosocial narrative (Maruna 2001) or is open to change (Giordano, Cernkovich, and Rudolph 2002). Thus, a policy that simply provides an opportunity for change without focusing resources toward certain groups or first helping individuals become ready for change would be folly.

As a more extreme example of divides between theories, at one end of the spectrum labeling theory posits that desistance is typically a natural part of human development. Without social labels and prohibitive barriers, a person simply ages out of youthful behaviors as he or she matures. Thus, a recommended "do nothing" policy should prevail. On the other end of the spectrum, however, the identity theory of desistance posits that individuals need to experience substantial negative consequences to induce change and desistance. Thus, a policy that "did nothing" would actually promote continued crime and not induce desistance. From this perspective systematic and perhaps even harsh responses are required to invoke the feared self and provide a catalyst for change.

To further posit differences between labeling theory and other perspectives, we would also note that labeling theory specifically addresses the early stages of a potential criminal career whereas the other theories all begin at a later stage when an individual is perhaps already more deeply involved in crime and the criminal justice system. Interestingly, though, this particular difference is perhaps not as much of a complication as an insight that raises an important point: one desistance strategy may not fit all. This is a point that we will explore further in the following sections.

PROMOTING THE DESISTANCE PROCESS: INCORPORATING THEORY INTO PRACTICE

In the previous section, we argue that desistance is a process involving the actor, social reactions and opportunities, and the role(s) the actor is permitted to seek in the broader social structure. While the emphasis and timing of these three factors may vary across theoretical perspectives, the themes are consistent. In the following sections we use these themes to direct our discussion of current policies aimed at promoting and identifying desistance and make recommendations for improving, expanding, and altering these policies to better reflect existing empirical knowledge.

Diversion

Here we use the term *diversion* to refer to any policy that provides an individual with the opportunity to avoid continuing on to the next stage of the criminal justice process: that is, if in contact with the police, not to be arrested; if arrested, not to be convicted; and if convicted, not to spend time in a jail or prison. Diversion is not a new idea and is probably a more popular tactic in the juvenile than the adult justice system. However, it is also used in the adult system, particularly for individuals charged with first-time and misdemeanor crimes. Diversion can take many forms, from community service, to payment of restitution to the victim, or to a delayed conviction that is later dismissed if the individual commits no further crimes during a given time period. While a full discussion of all possible diversions is well beyond the scope of this chapter, we introduce the idea here as an example of existing policy that could be effective in promoting desistance if expanded and more systematically applied.

As an example of diversion, we offer here a well-researched diversion program in the adult system: drug courts. According to Gottfredson and colleagues (Gottfredson, Najaka, and Kearley 2003, 172), drug treatment courts are intended to "increase the likelihood that drug addicted offenders will seek and persist longer in drug treatment, which is expected to help these individuals reduce their drug dependency and develop healthier, more productive, and crime-free lifestyles." In these courts, the individual is typically required to undergo treatment for his or her drug addiction and to routinely appear before the judge to report on progress. If the program is successfully completed and the person does not commit any new crimes, the case is dismissed. In a randomized trial of one drug court in Maryland, Gottfredson and colleagues (2003) found that individuals subject to the drug court had a lower recidivism level than those assigned to treatment as usual. Similar findings have been reported in additional evaluations of these programs, with a 2005 Government Accountability Office (GAO) report finding that twenty-three evaluations of drug courts across the country reported that individuals subject to drug courts were less likely to be arrested in the future (U.S. Government Accountability Office, 2005). This report also noted that while such services cost more in the short term, they saved money in the long term due to reductions in crime.

Our focus here is not to promote one diversion program but to (1) show that there are successful diversion programs, and (2) more importantly, indicate that these initiatives are in line with many theories of desistance. From a maturational and labeling perspective, helping an individual who is experiencing a first contact with the criminal justice system to avoid the stigma and criminogenic effects of further system involvement could help the person initiate the desistance process. From a cognitive change perspective, even individuals with many criminal justice system contacts in their past can benefit from diversion, as it can help to promote and maintain a more positive self-identity. Also, from an age-graded perspective that focuses on acquiring adult social bonds, options that let individuals stay in their home community and maintain, or even form, positive prosocial bonds, are also important for desistance.

Sealing/Expunging of Criminal Records

If, however, diversion from arrest or other parts of the criminal justice system is not a viable option, another policy that relieves an individual from the stigmatizing effects of a criminal record is the ability to have that record sealed or expunged. According to a survey conducted by SEARCH in 2012 (a national consortium for justice information and statistics), at least thirty-three states maintain at least some mechanism by which an individual can have a criminal record sealed or expunged under specific circumstances (U.S. Bureau of Justice Statistics 2014). Sealing refers to restricting access to criminal history information to very limited circumstances and may involve the purging of arrest fingerprints,[4] while expungement refers to the complete deletion of the arrest record, fingerprints, and all other associated information.

According to the U.S. Bureau of Justice Statistics (2014) report, however, there was little consistency across states as to how this process worked and to whom and to which types of criminal records it applied. For example, although almost every state allows juvenile records to be sealed, only sixteen states[5] allow for adult records to be sealed under certain circumstances and twenty-seven states allow for the full expungement of criminal records. States also vary greatly in the process for sealing or expungement. In some cases, sealing or expungement is automatic; it is applied after a waiting period in other states; and in some states it is granted only after a formal application, payment of a fee, and review by a judge.

New York State offers one of the most liberal sealing policies in the nation, automatically sealing all arrests that do not lead to conviction, sealing all convictions for minor violations and infractions without any application or review needed, and as of 2017, allowing discretionary sealing for up to two convictions after a ten-year waiting period (one of which can be a felony; see N.Y. Crim. Proc. Law § 160.59). New York also offers a "Youthful Offender" seal that can be granted by the court upon conviction to youth under the age of nineteen at the time of their offense. Thus, a young person is not saddled with the stigma of a criminal record. New York's new sealing policy and other state policies that offer sealing or expungement only after a waiting period and/or with proof of rehabilitation may be more in line with cognitive or identity theories than automatic sealing policies, as the former requires agency on part of the individual to show readiness to be granted such opportunities.

Policies like those in New York that offer up-front sealing seem to be most in line with labeling theory (i.e., avoiding stigma in the first place), while policies that rely on other indicators of rehabilitation to signal change and trigger sealing are more in line with cognitive and identity change theories. Unfortunately, it seems a majority of these policies rely heavily on waiting periods as evidence of change; thus, we note they may be more effective at identifying rather than truly promoting desistance.

Encouraging Individual Change and Readiness for Desistance

While diversion and sealing can help a person to avoid the stigma of a criminal record, some individuals are more engrained in crime and experience heightened social and economic disadvantages before they even come to the attention of the system. More intensive intervention and treatment may be warranted to push these individuals onto a path toward desistance. Assessing individual needs and providing the appropriate response at the correct time are critical to this approach. That is, for the juvenile or young adult with a minor criminal record and few risks and needs, diversion and nonintervention may be the best approach, whereas for an individual with more deeply rooted problems and severe needs, a more intrusive policy may be warranted. The former aligns well with labeling theory, while the latter speaks to both cognitive change and identity theory.

While a discussion of the vast array of treatment programs is far beyond the scope of this chapter, we provide just one example: therapeutic communities (TCs). TCs are typically implemented in a jail or prison setting and, unlike the diversion programs noted above that are reserved for individuals with certain types of low-level criminal records, individuals in TCs may have long conviction histories and intense service needs. Some TCs specifically target individuals with long histories of drug use and dependence for treatment and aim for a "global change in lifestyle involving abstinence from illicit substances, elimination of antisocial activities, and development of employment skills and prosocial attitudes and values" (Wexler and Prendergast 2010, 160). The therapeutic community removes a small group of individuals from the traditional prison setting and has them live and work together as a separate community within the prison that is staffed with clinicians skilled to specifically target their needs. The inmates work to maintain their own community and its rules and to support each other through the treatment process. Research on the use of TCs in Delaware,

California, and Texas has shown that graduates of these programs are more likely to remain both crime free and drug free for years after release (Falkin, Wexler, and Lipton 1992; Inciardi, Martin, and Butzin 2004; Knight, Simpson, and Hiller 1999).

Again, we are not promoting TCs as the only or even the most effective program to help individuals become ready for change, but we use the above example to note (1) that such successful programs do exist and (2) that they are in line with several of the theories of desistance discussed. That is, we cannot assume that everyone who enters the criminal justice system is at a point of individual readiness to change, particularly those who are determined to be in need of incapacitation. Thus, providing opportunities for desistance to these individuals upon release may be futile if we do not first identify and seek to change those problems, risks, and even addictions that led to their incarceration. Promoting readiness for change should be an important component of any comprehensive policy toward desistance. While the foregoing studies track individuals for several years after release and find reduced arrests and drug use, it is important to remember that desistance is a process and not defined simply as recidivism, or the lack of recidivism, in a given time frame. Thus, continued support and encouragement may be needed along the way.

Supporting Progress during Times of Transition

From a life-course perspective we also know that times of transition can be a point when an individual is especially vulnerable to failures (Laub and Sampson 1993) and may be in need of services, particularly to continue any positive change that may have been started while in treatment. Thus, providing additional social supports during transitions, such as returning home from a placement or even at the end of an outpatient treatment program, could be vital steps in turning the individual's life trajectory away from crime.

Aftercare is a term that broadly defines services provided to individuals after a period of placement or incarceration. More popular in the juvenile than the adult system, these programs are designed to specifically help individuals to transition from institutional living back to their new communities. While reintegrative shaming theory focuses on not separating an individual from society, these individuals have already been separated from society—not just physically while incarcerated but also symbolically and literally separated from mainstream culture and normative society. To date, while there is some positive literature on the provision of aftercare services (Hiller, Knight, and Simpson 1999; Josi and Sechrest 1999; Wiebush et al. 2005), the implementation of these programs has been so patchy and diverse that there is not a strong scientific base upon which to move forward. Here, then, rather than a broad scale expansion of such programs, we recommend very targeted practice coupled with empirical evaluations.

While aftercare focuses on continuing positive changes, as previously noted, negative events do happen and should be expected. While recidivism researchers might call these events failures, from a desistance perspective these events may signal the need for additional help toward desistance and not be merely a call for further punishment. An example of a potential place for compromise involves system response to technical violations. The foregoing theories describe desistance as a journey along which the individual can face and be derailed by many obstacles. Criminal justice system agencies can require return to placement for not only the commission of new crimes but also violations of parole conditions, such as moving from an approved residence or missed appointments.[6] Research estimates show that noncrime technical violations account for approximately one in six returns to prison (Glaze and Bonczar 2006). Instead of returning individuals to the criminal justice system, we suggest that such moments are perhaps times when policy should reaffirm and further support positive changes rather than focus on minor setbacks along the way. In addition, encouraging policy makers to consider the institutional and organizational factors that influence parole violations, instead of just individual-level parolee factors, is one way to incorporate a labeling theory perspective (Grattet and Lin 2016) and cognitive identity theories into practice.

Recognizing and Rewarding Change with Opportunity

Just as a person can be derailed from change, a person can also reach out and seize an opportunity as a hook for change. Perhaps most in line with reintegrative shaming theory, some treatment programs, and even jails, now offer graduation ceremonies. A September 2016 article in the *Chicago Post Tribune* offers one such example of seven jail inmates "graduating" from a pilot therapeutic treatment community aimed at addressing drug addiction. At the ceremony the graduates had the opportunity to read good-bye letters to their addiction and receive what one inmate called "saving grace" (Lavalley 2016). In addition to graduation from treatment, some jails and prisons allow inmates to celebrate receiving GEDs or high school diplomas through a formal graduation ceremony. For example, *Utah's Desert News* (Romero 2015) boasts a picture of Utah state prison inmates in caps and gowns walking to receive high school diplomas in a formal ceremony and the *Gaston Gazette* in North Carolina boasts a similar picture of jail inmates in black caps and gowns receiving their GED diplomas (Wildstein 2017).

Ceremonies that help individuals celebrate milestones and promote positive events may be a key feature in helping to affirm a more positive self-identity. There is growing research that suggests that in addition to graduation ceremonies for treatment or educational programs, policy makers can enable individuals to "graduate" from the jail or prison environment itself. Maruna (2001, 162–163) suggests that after being involved in the criminal justice system, an experience that is "almost entirely negative," redemption rituals and ceremonies can provide a "psychological turning point" for individuals with criminal records. For example, Meisenhelder (1977, 329) describes the delabeling process as the "certification" stage of desistance and suggests this is often formalized in a social ritual. This might take the shape of a "status elevation ceremony" that could "serve publicly and formally to announce, sell and spread the fact of the Actor's new kind of being" (Lofland 1969, 227). In such rituals, "Some recognized member(s) of the conventional community must publicly announce and certify that the offender has changed and that he is now to be considered essentially noncriminal" (Meisenhelder 1977, 329). Other research suggests that such delabeling might be even more forceful when rehabilitation is acknowledged from official sources (Wexler 2001), and identifying change can be initiated by not only the criminal justice system or organizations but also by the individuals themselves. This is the topic of the following section.

"Certifying" Desistance

While graduation ceremonies are held by organizations or criminal justice agencies, another policy option allows individuals to signal the decision to "go straight" through the application for and awarding of a certificate of rehabilitation (Maruna 2001). This type of policy could be particularly useful for focusing resources on individuals who are ready for and motivated to accept "hooks for change." Applying Spence's (1973) signaling theory to the prisoner reentry context, Bushway and Apel (2012) note that the signals people send need to be voluntary, relatively uncommon to achieve among the particular population, and more costly for those who are not involved in the desistance process relative to those who are. Prison or community-based program completion and certificates of rehabilitation can theoretically serve as useful signals for desistance (Bushway and Apel 2012).

We are aware of fourteen states[7] that offer certificates of rehabilitation or relief, along with the District of Columbia (Hager 2015). Certificates often require time, resources, and deliberate effort on the part of the individual with a criminal record to successfully secure the document. In return, the documentation offers formal recognition of "rehabilitation," and in most cases, relief from some of the undesired collateral consequences of a criminal record. In some cases, such as Ohio's "Certificates of Qualification for Employment," the employer is also protected from negligent hiring lawsuits if the person holds a certificate (Ohio Justice & Policy Center n.d.).

However, a common requirement for obtaining a certificate of relief involves a waiting period. For example, California Penal Code 4852.01–4852.21 sets forth a certificate of rehabilitation application process that conveys that a criminal record is a "thing of the past" and that the certificate holder is now a law-abiding citizen. If granted, the certificate restores many of the rights that may have been taken away due to the existence of a criminal record and even softens some sex offender registry requirements. Although the application indicates there is an individualized review for such a certificate, the criteria appear to include only a "waiting time" of seven to ten years. Thus, while the idea of the certificate itself is in line with our application of theory, the criteria that consider only "time since last offense" provide little hope for those early on in their journey to desistance.

While perhaps intended to help distinguish between individuals with criminal records, certificates of rehabilitation and formal recognition of change may also be an important part of the desistance process. Access to hooks for change can reaffirm that a person's new identity is inconsistent with past behaviors and actions and help to avoid setbacks in the desistance process (Giordano, Schroeder, and Cernkovich 2007). While granting certificates solely on the basis of a mandatory conviction-free period does technically identify desistance, or the abstinence of crime as measured by an absence of convictions over time (Maruna 2012), this approach is also limited. Even if the goal is to recognize rather than promote desistance, signals can be more versatile than simply waiting for a decade to pass (Bushway and Apel 2012). We focus here on certificates of relief and rehabilitation because they involve a formal certification of the desistance process (Meisenhelder 1977; Wexler 2001) in addition to opening up otherwise blocked social and civic opportunities for individuals with criminal records.

In line with Sampson and Laub's age-graded theory of crime, we must also note that such opportunities themselves are crucial to the desistance process. In the following section we further discuss how these opportunities are situated in, and perhaps limited by, deeper social structures and broader social policy.

LINKING DESISTANCE POLICY TO THE GREATER SOCIAL STRUCTURE

We would be remiss if we did not recognize that the purpose of many existing policies is not necessarily to punish individuals but rather to protect society from what are seen as potentially dangerous individuals. Thus, these policies are trying to strike a balance between what is best for the individual and what is best for society. Employers might have legitimate business reasons for not hiring individuals with certain recent convictions, and society may overall be safer because individuals with certain violent tendencies are restricted from owning firearms. However, we suggest that current policies may overemphasize blanket bans and policies that unnecessarily restrict the rights of many individuals and that in turn do not improve public safety.

With this in mind, we make a broad macro-scale policy recommendation that includes eliminating collateral consequences at the federal, state, and local levels that (1) do not have a direct and empirically supported crime reduction purpose, and (2) have fewer direct and indirect benefits compared to negative consequences. The latter is particularly difficult to measure but is an important area for future research as policy makers are increasingly interested in balancing public safety concerns with opportunities for individuals with criminal records (e.g., Equal Employment Opportunity Commission 2012; New York State Correction Law Article 23-A). For circumstances in which it may not make sense to totally eliminate collateral consequences, policies can also be tailored to only apply to certain individuals with criminal records, to certain types of criminal records, or can have expiration dates (Uggen and Stewart 2014).

There are several current efforts to develop and study programs that attempt to bridge the gap between ensuring public safety and using criminal record information. Federal guidance through the Equal Employment Opportunity Commission (2012) and the U.S. Department of Housing and Urban Development (2016) has provided recommendations to employers and landlords on the factors to consider in the decision-making process rather than blanket banning everyone with a criminal record. The most popular grassroots movement over the past decade is Ban the Box, which aims to remove the "box" inquiring about a criminal history record on applications. The goal is to open up opportunities for individuals with criminal records while still allowing decision makers to reasonably assess the criminal record at a later point (Rodriguez and Avery 2016). However, in the past few years, there has been growing evidence that when the box is removed decision makers use demographic correlates of having a criminal record, particularly being a young black male, to discriminate in lieu of having access to the criminal record information (Agan and Starr 2016; Doleac and Hansen 2016; Vuolo, Lageson, and Uggen 2017). Strategies to reduce such statistical discrimination is an issue of broader discussion and branches far beyond the realms of desistance policy. However, other efforts to restrict the use of a criminal record to address racial disparities are currently gaining national attention.

Another macro-level strategy could be redefining the way people perceive individuals with criminal records. The Department of Justice (DOJ) suggests starting with the language we use to describe individuals with criminal records. The U.S. Assistant Attorney General Karol Mason (2016) proposed replacing terminology such as *felon* or *convict* with descriptions like "person who committed a crime." The reason? In a Guest Post for the *Washington Post*, Mason (2016) explains, "The labels we affix to those who have served time can drain their sense of self-worth and perpetuate a cycle of crime, the very thing reentry programs are designed to prevent." Whether intentionally or not, the DOJ advocated for a policy solution that aligns nicely with labeling theory and connects directly back to the individual identities discussed in the previous section.

Recent research supports the DOJ's concern about stigma and labels. In a study testing the DOJ's language policy with experimental data from a nationally representative sample of U.S. adults, Denver, Pickett, and Bushway (2017) found that using crime-first language ("convicted criminals") relative to person-first language ("people convicted of") can increase public perceptions of recidivism (measured as the likelihood of committing a new crime). Importantly, this differential language finding only applies to violent convictions (i.e., "violent offenders" compared to people convicted of violent crimes)—not property or drug convictions. Furthermore, the public is more supportive of excluding individuals with violent convictions from conventional employment opportunities (Denver, Pickett, and Bushway 2017). The recent employment and housing guidance from two major federal agencies and the DOJ's proposed simple change in terminology bring us full circle back to the undeniable connections between social structure, structured opportunities, and the potential impact such policies can have on individual outcomes and identity.

CONCLUSIONS

In his qualitative study of "persistent thieves" a little over two decades ago, Shover (1996, 121) describes desistance as voluntary. We are inclined to agree. Policy makers cannot force individuals to desist from crime and avert the criminal justice system. However, there are policies—and implementation strategies—that can help individuals to initiate the desistance process and maintain desistance over time. In this chapter we have attempted to draw on some general knowledge and develop overarching themes from major theoretical perspectives related to the desistance process, highlighting both the similarities and the differences across theories. We also apply the themes to examine current policy strategies and make suggestions for the expansion, alteration, and evaluation of such policy in the future.

It is encouraging to see that many policies that might promote desistance are already in place in the criminal justice system. However, it is discouraging to note that these policies are not consistently applied and are not available to all or even to the majority of individuals in the criminal justice system. Whether or not an individual is offered diversion may depend on the resources of the local community and the attending judge, just as the ability to obtain a seal of a criminal record or a certificate or rehabilitation depends on widely varying state policies. Moreover, while the system may offer such a certificate, it is up to others to interpret its meaningfulness. That is, a certificate of rehabilitation may be presented to an employer, but if the employer has formal or even informal rules banning the hire of individuals with criminal records, the certificate may not have the desired meaning or impact for the holder.

We would like to leave the reader with a few thoughts. First, as scholars agree that desistance is a process, it is important for desistance policies to acknowledge and recognize the various stages of this process. Desistance scholars sometimes view change as occurring "along a continuum" (Laub and Sampson 1993, 310); thus, there should be policies in place to address different opportunities to reinforce desistance along this continuum.

Second, this path or continuum is not the same for every individual, and policy makers and practitioners must be aware of and responsive to individual differences. In the same way Risk-Needs-Responsivity (RNR) conducts individualized assessments when people enter the criminal justice system to determine custody placements or supervision levels (Bonta and Andrews 2007), policy makers can target certain policies toward certain individuals to help initiate the desistance process. Such targeting could involve aligning the appropriate individuals with sealing, expungement, diversion programs, and aftercare programs. On the desistance maintenance end, employment interventions may have better success rates for individuals demonstrating a proactive interest in the labor market (Bushway, Denver, and Kurlychek 2016; Denver, Siwach, and Bushway 2017) and individuals can potentially differentiate themselves by acquiring certificates of rehabilitation or other "signals" of desistance (Bushway and Apel 2012).

Third, policies should respect that the desistance path is not without its detours along the way. As Paternoster and Bushway (2009, 1133) note, "In sum, desistance from crime is not easy; in fact, it is exceedingly difficult, and many who embark on the path of self-change fail and do so repeatedly." Thus, policies should recognize positive attempts at change and not quickly label individuals as "failures" for each setback, as is the more traditional approach in recidivism research.

Finally, we recognize that criminal justice system policies that initiate, promote, and support desistance are not enough. The broader social structure of our society must be willing and able to accept and reintegrate individuals with criminal records to help initiate and sustain the desistance process over time. Reducing collateral consequences that are not necessary for public safety, that lack empirical support, or that do not have a net benefit, and considering changes in terminology and labels (Mason 2016) are two potential steps in that direction. To fully support desistance, policy makers need to consider strategies that reach outside the criminal justice system and influence the broader social structure.

NOTES

1. Whether complete and permanent abstinence from crime is necessary for desistance, or possible to detect empirically, has been debated (Farrington 1986; Maruna 2001).

2. Paternoster et al. (2015) discuss the challenges in determining the most prominent theories of desistance. Similar to Paternoster and colleagues, we focus much of the discussion on Sampson and Laub's life-course theory and Giordano's symbolic interactionist perspective, both of which have high citation counts and have influenced the direction of the field. However, we still consider and incorporate an array of theoretical perspectives.

3. Even Paternoster and Bushway (2009, 1106), who take the strongest position on the importance of identity, note that they "are not implying that identity forms without social interaction . . . it is important for the success of the change process that others support the new self or at the very least do not oppose it."

4. For a more detailed discussion of variations in the intent and scope of sealing policies, see Blumstein and Nakamura (2009).

5. Alabama, California, Florida, Georgia, Maine, Michigan, Minnesota, New Mexico, New York, Ohio, Oklahoma, Oregon, South Dakota, Vermont, Virginia, and West Virginia.

6. There is a lot of state variation; see, for example, http://www.pbpp.pa.gov/Understanding%20Parole/Documents/PBPP-347%20VSG.pdf.

7. Arizona, Arkansas, California, Connecticut, Georgia, Illinois, Nevada, New York, New Jersey, North Carolina, Ohio, Rhode Island, Tennessee, and Vermont.

REFERENCES

Agan, A., and S. Starr. 2016. Ban the Box, criminal records, and statistical discrimination: A field experiment. *Law and Economics Research Paper Series.* Paper No. 16-012.

Apel, R., and G. Sweeten. 2010. The impact of incarceration on employment during the transition to adulthood. *Social Problems* 57 (3): 448–479.

Becker, H. S. 1963. *Outsiders: Studies in the Sociology of Deviance.* New York: Free Press.

Bernburg, J. G., M. D. Krohn, and C. J. Rivera. 2006. Official labeling, criminal embeddedness, and subsequent delinquency a longitudinal test of labeling theory. *Journal of Research in Crime and Delinquency* 43 (1): 67–88.

Blumstein, A., and K. Nakamura. 2009. Redemption in the presence of widespread criminal background checks. *Criminology* 47: 327–359.

Bonta, J., and D. A. Andrews. 2007. *Risk-Need-Responsivity Model for Offender Assessment and Treatment* (User Report No. 2007-06). Public Safety Canada, Ottawa, Ontario.

Braithwaite, J. 1989. *Crime, Shame and Reintegration*. Cambridge, UK: Cambridge University Press.

Bushway, S. D., and R. Apel. 2012. A signaling perspective on employment-based reentry programming: Training completion as a desistance signal. *Criminology and Public Policy* 11 (1):21–50.

Bushway, S. D., M. Denver, and M. Kurlychek. 2016. Unpublished manuscript. The Labor Market Impact of Criminal Background Check Decisions for Individuals with Criminal History Records.

Bushway, S. D., A. R. Piquero, L. M. Broidy, E. Cauffman, and P. Mazerolle. 2001. An empirical framework for studying desistance as a process. *Criminology* 39: 491–516.

Bushway, S. D., and P. Reuter. 2001. Labor markets and crime. In *Crime*, edited by J. Q. Wilson and J. Petersilia. Oakland, CA: ICS Press.

Chiricos, T., K. Barrick, W. Bales, and S. Bontrager. 2007. The labeling of convicted felons and its consequences for recidivism. *Criminology* 45: 547–581.

Cooley, C. H. 1902. *Human Nature and the Social Order*. New York: Scribner.

Cressey, D. R. 1963. Social psychological theory for using deviants to control deviation. In *Experiment in Culture Expansion: Proceedings of the Conference on the Use of Products of a Social Problem in Coping with the Problem*, 147–160. Washington, DC: National Institute of Mental Health.

Denver, M., J. Pickett, and S. D. Bushway. 2017. The language of stigmatization and the mark of violence: Experimental evidence on the social construction and use of criminal record stigma. *Criminology* 55: 664–690.

Denver, M., G. Siwach, and S. D. Bushway. 2017. A new look at the employment and recidivism relationship through the lens of a criminal background check. *Criminology* 55: 174–204.

Doleac, J. L., and B. Hansen. 2016. Does "Ban the Box" help or hurt low-skilled workers? Statistical discrimination and employment outcomes when criminal histories are hidden. Presentation to the Institute for Research on Poverty at the University of Wisconsin-Madison, June 22.

Elder, G. H., Jr. 1985. Perspectives on the life course. In *Life Course Dynamics*, edited by G. H. Elder, Jr. Ithaca, NY: Cornell University Press.

Equal Employment Opportunity Commission (EEOC). 2012. *EEOC Enforcement Guidance: Consideration of Arrest and Conviction Records in Employment Decisions under Title VII of the Civil Rights Act of 1964*. Washington, DC: U.S. EEOC. Available at http://www.eeoc.gov/laws/guidance/upload/arrest_conviction.pdf.

Falkin, G. P., H. K. Wexler, and D. S. Lipton. 1992. Drug treatment in state prisons. *Treating Drug Problems* 2: 89–132.

Farrington, D. P. 1986. Age and crime. In *Crime and Justice: An Annual Review of Research*, vol. 7, edited by M. Tonry and N. Morris. Chicago: University of Chicago Press.

Gibbs, J. P. 1966. Conceptions of deviant behavior: The old and the new. *Pacific Sociological Review* 9 (1): 9–14.

Giordano, P. C., S. A. Cernkovich, and J. L. Rudolph. 2002. Gender, crime, and desistance: Toward a theory of cognitive transformation. *American Journal of Sociology* 107: 990–1064.

Giordano, P. C., R. D. Schroeder, and S. A. Cernkovich. 2007. Emotions and crime over the life course: A neo-Meadian perspective on criminal continuity and change. *American Journal of Sociology* 112: 1603–1661.

Glaze, L., and T. Bonczar. 2006. Probation and parole in the United States, 2005. U.S. Department of Justice, Office of Justice Programs, Bureau of Justice Statistics Bulletin.

Goffman, E. 1963. *Stigma: Notes on the Management of Spoiled Identity.* London: Penguin Books.

Gottfredson, D. C., S. S. Najaka, and B. Kearley. 2003. Effectiveness of drug treatment courts: Evidence from a randomized trial. *Criminology & Public Policy* 2 (2): 171–196.

Gottfredson, M. R., and Hirschi, T. 1990. *A General Theory of Crime.* Stanford: Stanford University Press.

Grattet, R., and J. Lin. 2016. Supervision intensity and parole outcomes: A competing risks approach to criminal and technical parole violations. *Justice Quarterly* 33: 565–583.

Hager, E. 2015. *Forgiving vs. Forgetting.* The Marshall Project. Available at https://www.themarshallproject.org/2015/03/17/forgiving-vs-forgetting#.iEKeoIWN5.

Hiller, M. L., K. Knight, and D. D. Simpson. 1999. Prison-based substance abuse treatment, residential aftercare and recidivism. *Addiction* 94 (6): 833–842.

Hirschi, T. 1969. *Causes of Delinquency.* Berkeley: University of California Press.

Inciardi, J. A., S. S. Martin, and C. A. Butzin. 2004. Five-year outcomes of therapeutic community treatment of drug-involved offenders after release from prison. *Crime & Delinquency* 50 (1): 88–107.

Josi, D. A., and D. K. Sechrest. 1999. A pragmatic approach to parole aftercare: Evaluation of a community reintegration program for high-risk youthful offenders. *Justice Quarterly* 16 (1): 51–80.

Knight, K., D. D. Simpson, and M. L. Hiller. 1999. Three-year reincarceration outcomes for in-prison therapeutic community treatment in Texas. *Prison Journal* 79 (3): 337–351.

Laub, J. H., D. S. Nagin, and R. J. Sampson. 1998. Trajectories of change in criminal offending: Good marriages and the desistance process. *American Sociological Review* 63: 225–238.

Laub, J. H., and R. J. Sampson. 1993. Turning points in the life course: Why change matters to study of crime. *Criminology* 31: 301–325.

———. 2001. Understanding desistance from crime. *Crime and Justice* 28: 1–69.

———. 2003. *Shared Beginnings, Divergent Lives: Delinquent Boys to Age 70.* Cambridge: Harvard University Press.

Lavalley, A. 2016. Inmates graduate from jail addictions program. September 1. Available at http://www.chicagotribune.com/suburbs/post-tribune/news/ct-ptb-porter-jail-graduation-st-0901-20160901-story.html.

Lemert, E. 1951. *Social Pathology.* New York: McGraw-Hill.

Lofland, J. 1969. *Deviance and Identity.* Englewood Cliffs, NJ: Prentice Hall.

Maruna, S. 2001. *Defining Desistance.* Washington, DC: American Psychological Association Books.

———. 2012. Elements of successful desistance signaling. *Criminology & Public Policy* 11: 73–86.

Maruna, S., and K. Roy. 2007. Amputation or reconstruction? Notes on the concept of "knifing off" and desistance from crime. *Journal of Contemporary Criminal Justice* 23: 104–124.

Mason, K. 2016. Guest Post: Justice Dept. agency to alter its terminology for released convicts, to ease reentry. *Washington Post.* Available at https://www.washingtonpost.com/news/true-crime/wp/2016/05/04/guest-post-justice-dept-to-alter-its-terminology-for-released-convicts-to-ease-reentry/?tid=a_inl.

Matsueda, R. L. 1992. Reflected appraisals, parental labeling and delinquency: Specifying a symbolic interactionist theory. *American Journal of Sociology* 97: 1577–611.

Matza, D. 1964. *Delinquency and Drift.* New York: Wiley.

Mead, G. H. 1934. *Mind, Self, and Society from the Standpoint of a Social Behaviorist.* Chicago: University of Chicago Press.

Meisenhelder, T. 1977. An exploratory study of exiting from criminal careers. *Criminology* 15: 319–334.

Moffitt, T. E. 1993. Adolescence-limited and life-course-persistent antisocial behavior: A developmental taxonomy. *Psychological Review* 100: 674–701.

Ohio Justice & Policy Center. n.d. *Certificates of Qualification for Employment.* Available at https://drive.google.com/file/d/0B1yt2LRONoS7NFlmS0tZOVFkUUk/edit.

Paternoster, R., R. Bachman, S. Bushway, E. Kerrison, and D. O'Connell. 2015. Human agency and explanations of criminal desistance: Arguments for a rational choice theory. *Journal of Developmental and Life Course Criminology* 1: 209–235.

Paternoster, R., and S. D. Bushway. 2009. Desistance and the "feared self": Toward an identity theory of criminal desistance. *Journal of Criminal Law and Criminology* 99: 1103–56.

Paternoster, R., and L. Iovanni. 1989. The labeling perspective and delinquency: An elaboration of the theory and an assessment of the evidence. *Justice Quarterly* 6: 359–94.

Piliavin, I., and R. Gartner. 1981. *The Impact of Supported Work on Ex-Offenders.* New York: Institute for Research on Poverty and Mathematica Policy Research.

Rodriguez, M. N., and B. Avery. 2016. Ban the Box: U.S. cities, counties, and states adopt fair hiring policies. National Employment Law Project. Available at http://www.nelp.org/publication/ban-the-box-fair-chance-hiring-state-and-local-guide/.

Romero, M. 2015. Prison inmates celebrate graduation, goals with loved ones. *Utah's Desert News,* June 10.

Sampson, R. J., and J. H. Laub. 1993. *Crime in the Making: Pathways and Turning Points through Life.* Cambridge, MA: Harvard University Press.

———. 1997. A life-course theory of cumulative disadvantage and the stability of delinquency. In *Developmental Theories of Crime and Delinquency,* edited by Terence P. Thornberry. New Brunswick, NJ: Transaction.

Shover, N. 1996. *Great Pretenders: Pursuits and Careers of Persistent Thieves.* Boulder, CO: Westview Press.

Skardhamar, T., and J. Savolainen. 2014. Changes in criminal offending around the time of job entry: A study of employment and desistance. *Criminology* 52: 263–291.

Spence, M. 1973. Job market signaling. *Quarterly Journal of Economics* 87: 355–374.

Sutherland, E. H. 1947. *Principles of Criminology*, 4th ed. Philadelphia: Lippincott.

Tannenbaum, F. 1938. *Crime and the Community*. Boston: Ginn.

Tittle, C. R. 1975. Deterrents or labeling? *Social Forces* 53: 399–410.

———. 1980. Labeling and crime: An empirical evaluation. In *The Labeling of Deviance: Evaluating a Perspective*, 2nd ed., edited by W. Gove, 241–263. New York: Wiley.

Uggen, C. 2000. Work as a turning point in the life course of criminals: A duration model of age, employment, and recidivism. *American Sociological Review* 65: 529–546.

Uggen, C., and R. Stewart. 2014. Piling on: Collateral consequences and community supervision. *Minnesota Law Review* 99: 1871–1910.

U.S. Bureau of Justice Statistics. 2014. *Survey of State Criminal History Information Systems*. Washington, DC: U.S. Department of Justice.

U.S. Department of Housing and Urban Development. 2016. *Office of General Counsel Guidance on Application of Fair Housing Act Standards to the Use of Criminal Records by Providers of Housing and Real Estate-Related Transactions*. Washington, DC. Available at https://portal.hud.gov/hudportal/documents/huddoc?id=hud_ogcguidappfhastandcr.pdf.

U.S. Government Accountability Office. 2005. *Adult Drug Courts: Evidence Indicates Recidivism Reductions and Mixed Results for Other Outcomes* [No. GAO-05-219]. Washington, DC.

Visher, C. A., L. Winterfield, and M. B. Coggeshall. 2005. Ex-offender employment programs and recidivism: A meta-analysis. *Journal of Experimental Criminology* 1: 295–316.

Vuolo, M., S. Lageson, and C. Uggen. 2017. Criminal record questions in the era of "Ban the Box." *Criminology & Public Policy* 16: 139–165.

Wexler, D. B. 2001. Robes and rehabilitation: How judges can help offenders "make good." *Court Review* 38: 18–23.

Wexler, H. K., G. Melnick, L. Lowe, and J. Peters. 1999. Three-year reincarceration outcomes for Amity in-prison therapeutic community and aftercare in California. *Prison Journal* 79: 321–336.

Wexler, H. K., and M. L. Prendergast. 2010. Therapeutic communities in United States' prisons: Effectiveness and challenges. *Therapeutic Communities* 31: 157.

Wiebush, R. G., D. Wagner, B. McNulty, Y. Wang, and T. N. Le. 2005. *Implementation and Outcome Evaluation of the Intensive Aftercare Program. Final Report.* Washington, DC: U.S. Department of Justice.

Wildstein, E. 2017. Jail inmate celebrates graduation day. *Gaston Gazette*, January 10.

Wilson, D. B., C. A. Gallagher, and D. L. MacKenzie. 2000. A meta-analysis of corrections-based education, vocation, and work programs for adult offenders. *Journal of Research in Crime and Delinquency* 37: 347–68.

7

From Hot Spots to a Theory of Place

Martin

CODY TELEP AND
DAVID WEISBURD

Criminology has traditionally been focused on answering the question "why do people offend?" (Eck and Weisburd 1995). This has led to an emphasis on individuals in efforts to develop theory and criminal justice practice. Weisburd and Piquero (2008), for example, found that studies published in the journal *Criminology* that sought to predict crime were substantially more likely to focus on individuals than any other units of analysis. They also found that the percentage of variability in crime explained by traditional theories of offending was often quite low. Individual-level theories of criminology frequently have implications for practice that are challenging for police or other criminal justice agencies to implement (e.g., increase informal social control by parents or reduce societal strains). Here we focus on theory, basic research, and evaluation studies that address a different question: "why does crime occur at particular places?" As we discuss in the sections that follow, theoretical perspectives focused on places rather than people offer great promise for advancing our understanding of both the distribution of crime and its control.

This emphasis on places rather than people is not a new one. Criminology has long focused on the relevance of geography in understanding the crime problem and how best to respond to it (Weisburd, Bruinsma, and Bernasco 2009). As we discuss in the next section, the emphasis historically was on larger units of geography, with comparisons of crime rates across jurisdictions or neighborhoods. The last four decades have seen an increased interest in place but with a focus on much smaller units of geography than have traditionally interested criminologists (Weisburd 2015). A large body of research points to the relevance of more micro-units of geography for understanding the distribution and control of crime (see Telep and Weisburd 2018).

In this chapter we first review theoretical perspectives on crime and geography and the relevance of both social disorganization and crime opportunities to understanding the distribution of crime. We then turn to the problem of addressing areas with highly concentrated criminal activity. We review the evidence suggesting that across different contexts crime is highly concentrated at a small number of places (Weisburd 2015). Thus, it makes sense for police and other agencies to focus on these smaller units of geography, commonly known as crime hot spots (Eck 2005), to effectively reduce crime and disorder. We review the strong body of evidence for hot spots policing and focus on a variety of strategies that have been used to target crime hot spots, including more recent work that attempts to integrate what we have learned about why crime concentrates into interventions designed to have long-term effects. We note at the outset that these perspectives do not ignore individuals; offenders and victims obviously cannot be removed from the crime equation. But the emphasis of this line of research is on what matters about specific places and how altering the dynamics of places may reduce crime, regardless of the motivation levels of offenders residing in or visiting such locations.

WHAT'S THE THEORY?

Recent decades have seen a renewed interest in the importance of place in criminology. The emphasis on geographic and community characteristics began in American criminology in the early twentieth century with sociologists at the University of Chicago and the birth of social disorganization theory (see Burgess 1925; Shaw and McKay 1942), although work focusing on community differences in crime dates back to the early nineteenth century in Europe (Weisburd, Bruinsma, and Bernasco 2009). The emphasis in the Chicago School was on examining the dynamics of cities by understanding the characteristics of neighborhoods, with the belief that variability in these characteristics influenced why some places had higher crime than others (Sampson and Groves 1989; Kubrin and Weitzer 2003). Shaw and McKay's work (1942) is the most well-known example from this period. They drew from Burgess's (1925) concentric-zone model of Chicago, which divided the city into five zones of differentiated urban expansion to demonstrate neighborhood differences. Shaw and McKay (1942) not only demonstrated that crime rates varied by neighborhood, with neighborhoods closer to the inner city of Chicago showing higher crime, but they also showed the stability of this variability and correlates of these concentrations. These correlates included economic disadvantage, racial and linguistic heterogeneity, and a lack of residential stability.

Beginning in the 1950s, criticisms of the Chicago School led to a decline in the emphasis of place in criminological work. This partly was a reflection of concerns about the difficulty of mapping crime geographically—without modern computers Shaw and McKay's (1942) early effort to map crime at the neighborhood level was incredibly labor intensive. Additionally, the field moved towards a greater focus on individuals, and skepticism increased regarding models that could not speak to individual propensities to commit crime (Bursik and Grasmick 1993). But social disorganization theories have once again become more prominent since the 1980s, with an increased emphasis on community dynamics to explain neighborhood-level variability in crime (Sampson and Groves 1989; Kubrin and Weitzer 2003). Importantly, the work of Sampson, Raudenbush, and Earls (1997) provided a mechanism by which social disorganization affected crime rates. Collective efficacy refers to a community's level of social cohesion and the extent to which residents are willing to intervene to bring social control to the neighborhood. Neighborhoods high in collective efficacy have higher levels of mutual trust among neighbors, and there is a greater shared sense of the importance of working together to keep the community safe.

Social disorganization theories have traditionally been used to explain variability in crime at communities or other fairly large units of geography. But recent research suggests these concepts may also have relevance to our understanding of the distribution of crime at smaller units of geography. Weisburd, Groff, and Yang (2012) argue that the street segment or street block can be viewed as a micro-community, potentially allowing for a more precise measurement of street-by-street differences in factors associated with social disorganization. They draw on Wicker's (1987, 614) work on "behavior settings" and the idea that small places can be seen as "small-scale social systems." In this context, street segments can be seen as examples of small-scale communities (see Taylor 1997; Smith, Frazee, and Davison 2000).

While social disorganization theory has more recently been applied to smaller units of geography, theories emphasizing the importance of crime opportunities in specific locations have become more prominent in the field in the last four decades. These theories were a reaction, in part, to the failures of traditional criminological theory to provide clear policy implications that could effectively reduce crime. Traditional criminological theory did not ignore opportunity entirely. Cloward and Ohlin, for example, titled their 1960 book *Delinquency and Opportunity* and emphasized that opportunity structures impacted the type of criminal adaptations gangs used to respond to societal strain.

But in a groundbreaking article on routine activities and crime Cohen and Felson (1979) were among the first to suggest that the offender was not the only or even the central part of the crime equation. They suggested that the availability of suitable crime targets and the presence or absence of capable guardians also influence crime events. Cohen and Felson (1979) argued that crime could be prevented by increasing guardianship and decreasing the suitability of targets without changing the motivation levels of potential offenders in society. While they focused on more macro-level factors that affected crime rates, their emphasis on how offenders converged with targets in the absence of guardianship at a specific space and time shifted the emphasis of theory and practice to particular situations and locations.

At about the same time, Clarke's (1983) work on situational crime prevention also challenged the traditional focus on offenders and communities and instead considered the context of criminal events to be critical. At the core of situational prevention is the concept of rational choice and bounded rationality (Clarke 1995). In contrast to offender-based approaches, which usually focus on the dispositions of criminals, situational crime prevention begins with the opportunity structure of the crime situation. Potential offenders use their limited knowledge about victims or guardians in specific situations to consider relative costs and benefits. Clarke and Eck (2005) describe five overarching methods for addressing crime opportunities in particular places and situations to prevent crime: increasing the risk, increasing the effort, reducing rewards, reducing provocations, and removing excuses. Applying these methods can involve interventions as simple and straightforward as target hardening to increase the effort to steal a car or using security cameras to increase the risks for shoplifting.

These new theoretical perspectives thus changed the focus from offender motivation to characteristics of the immediate place and situation that make crime more or less likely to occur. The work of Brantingham and Brantingham (1984) on crime pattern theory brought together ideas from both routine activities theory and situational crime prevention. They focused on the routine activities of potential offenders, who become aware of opportunities to engage in crime in their day-to-day routines when their activity spaces overlap with the activity spaces of targets or victims. These opportunities arise from situations in which guardianship or place management is limited or nonexistent. Changing the opportunity structure of offender activity spaces is thus important in reducing the likelihood of crime. These theoretical perspectives, which we can broadly think of as opportunity theories (Weisburd, Groff, and Yang 2012), all share in common a focus on how particular places and situations make crime possible because of the convergence of a potential offender and an attractive target without a guardian to intervene.

WHAT'S THE PROBLEM?

The theoretical perspectives reviewed in the previous section focus our attention on places. But simply moving the focus from individuals to places does not guarantee crime control benefits. Social disorganization theories have long been used to guide neighborhood crime prevention efforts, beginning with the influence of Shaw and McKay's (1942) work in the creation of the Chicago Area Project to reduce juvenile delinquency. Research on the effects of community-led crime prevention efforts, however, is mixed at best (Bursik and Grasmick 1993; Welsh and Hoshi 2002). Hope (1995, 23) calls this as a "central paradox" in community crime prevention research. While social disorganization and neighborhood structural factors are consistently linked to crime levels, "much of the effort to alter the structure of communities in order to reduce crime has not been noticeably successful or sustainable."

In policing, the most commonly adopted neighborhood-based policing program in recent decades has been community policing. Such efforts to increase community engagement in high-crime areas have been successful in improving perceptions of the police but have not been strongly associated with reduced crime (Gill et al. 2014). There is also little evidence to suggest that the traditional policing tactic of randomly patrolling beats is linked to crime control benefits (Kelling et al. 1974). This is not to say that all neighborhood-based programs in policing have been ineffective. Indeed, the Evidence-Based Policing Matrix, which covers all rigorous policing crime control evaluations, includes a number of effective interventions that use the beat or neighborhood as the unit of analysis (Lum et al. 2011). The most effective of these strategies, however, tend to narrow the focus to particular places or people. McGarrell and colleagues (2001), for example, found directed patrols to reduce gun violence were associated with significant declines in gun violence in one of the two target beats in Indianapolis, Indiana. They argue that the reason for the mixed findings may be the difference in enforcement activities across beats. In the more successful beat, officers focused enforcement activity on the most suspicious individuals (i.e., a targeted offender approach), which seemed to be more successful than a more general strategy of increasing traffic stops in the other beat.

What can explain the mixed evidence for community or police-led prevention efforts at larger units of geography? A number of recent basic research studies suggest that crime is highly concentrated at a small number of micro-places (see Telep and Weisburd 2018). These locations are commonly called hot spots and can vary in size from a single address to a small group of street blocks (Eck 2005). The street segment (both sides of a street between two intersections) has become a commonly used unit for micro-place analyses

(Weisburd, Groff, and Yang 2012). Work on the distribution of crime at micro-places began in the 1980s with Sherman, Gartin, and Buerger's (1989; see also Sherman 1987) analysis of emergency calls for service to addresses over a single year in Minneapolis, Minnesota. They found that only 3.3 percent of the addresses in the city produced just over 50 percent of all emergency calls to the police. Almost 40 percent of addresses did not experience a single call during the year. Pierce and colleagues (1988) found almost identical results when examining crime call concentrations in Boston, Massachusetts.

More recently, studies have found that such concentrations tend to be stable longitudinally. Weisburd et al. (2004) examined crime incidents on street segments in Seattle, Washington, from 1989 to 2002. They found that 50 percent of crime incidents over the fourteen-year period occurred at between 4 and 5 percent of the street segments each year. Group-based trajectory models also suggested a generally stable trend in the majority of street segments over the fourteen-year time series. More than 80 percent of streets were in a trajectory group with generally stable trends longitudinally. Weisburd, Groff, and Yang (2012) updated and expanded these analyses, examining crime incidents at street segments in Seattle from 1989 to 2004. They again found that crime was highly concentrated. The 247 highest-crime street segments, about 1 percent of the total in Seattle, were responsible for over 23 percent of crime incidents across the sixteen-year study period.

The high level of crime concentration as well as the stability of these concentrations has also been found for particular crime types, including gun assaults (Braga, Papachristos, and Hureau 2010) and drug crime (Hibdon, Telep, and Groff 2017). Additionally, concentration levels are fairly similar cross-nationally and in cities of varying sizes (Weisburd 2015). This has led Weisburd (2015, 138) to argue that there is a law of crime concentration that states "for a defined measure of crime at a specific microgeographic unit, the concentration of crime will fall within a narrow bandwidth of percentages for a defined cumulative proportion of crime." When comparing similar measures of crime and similar geographic units, the law of crime concentration predicts a narrow range in the percentage of units containing a particular proportion of crime across jurisdictions.

Not only is crime highly concentrated, but a number of studies also suggest that there is street-by-street variability in crime levels. That is, micro-place concentrations of crime are not simply proxies for neighborhood crime concentrations. This would be the case if high-crime streets were all concentrated in the same neighborhood or community. Instead, crime levels can vary quite dramatically, even within a single neighborhood. In Seattle, Weisburd, Groff, and Yang (2012) found substantial street-by-street variability when examining longitudinal crime patterns by street. The 247 highest-crime street segments showed some level of concentration in the central business district but were scattered throughout the entire city.

Steenbeek and Weisburd (2016) examined crime concentration in The Hague in the Netherlands and found further support for a focus on micro-places rather than just neighborhoods. When partitioning the variance in crime across different-sized geographic units, differences in crime at the street-segment level were responsible for almost two-thirds of the total variance. Neighborhoods, on average, were responsible for a small portion of the total variance, while about one-third of the variance could be attributed to clusters of neighborhoods. This suggests that larger units of geography do play some role in the distribution of crime across a jurisdiction but reinforces the amount of information on crime concentration that would be missed with a focus exclusively on neighborhoods. Schnell, Braga, and Piza (2017) similarly found that the majority of variability in violent crime in Chicago between 2001 and 2014 was at the street-segment level.

The strong evidence that crime is highly concentrated at small units of geography and that, even within high-crime neighborhoods, there is a great deal of street-by-street variability in crime thus provides an explanation for why community-based prevention efforts are less likely to effectively address crime. If high-crime neighborhoods may have many crime-free streets and only a few hot spots driving the neighborhood crime rate, then it makes more sense for the police to narrow their focus to these locations, rather than implement a beat or neighborhood-based intervention.

The importance of micro-places for prevention efforts is reinforced by evidence that the concepts from theories reviewed in the previous section are also highly concentrated at micro-places. Weisburd, Groff, and Yang (2012) drew on both social disorganization theory and opportunity perspectives to examine the concentration of social factors at the street segment in Seattle. Using data from 1989 to 2004, they found tremendous concentration and street-by-street variability in most of the factors they examined. The results showing there were hot spots of crime opportunity were in line with predictions from place-based theories. But social disorganization factors were also concentrated at the street-block level, and as with crime, these concentrations were not just proxies for neighborhood-level effects, suggesting that social disorganization theory indeed has relevance at the street-segment level (see Smith, Frazee, and Davison 2000).

Additionally, these concentrations of opportunity factors and social disorganization were strongly linked in multivariate models predicting whether a street block was in the highest-crime group versus being crime free. The two most important predictors of crime hot spots were drawn from the opportunity perspective. Streets with a larger residential population and more employees were more likely to be hot spots of crime. Arterial roads were also more likely to be high-crime streets. Social disorganization factors also explained a great deal of the variability in crime. The higher the level of physical disorder on a street segment the greater the likelihood of it being a high-crime street segment. High socioeconomic status acted as a protective factor for crime, with crime hot spots much less likely to be found at places with higher property values. Collective efficacy also acted as a protective factor. Street segments with a higher percentage of active voters were much less likely to be crime hot spots. Further evidence of this comes from an ongoing prospective study of high- and low-crime street blocks in Baltimore, Maryland (Weisburd, Ready et al. 2014). Resident survey data suggest lower levels of collective efficacy in crime hot spots compared to low-crime streets (Wooditch et al. 2016).

Weisburd, Groff, and Yang's (2012) findings are not causal but suggest crime is highly predictable at place. Thus, the extent to which police and other agencies can address opportunity and social disorganization factors should have important implications for crime control. The police may not be able to address some of these factors directly. For example, they cannot control the number of employees on a block. But they can allocate resources and focus enforcement activity based on employee levels and can even anticipate changes in crime based on the opening of new businesses. Police may also be able to intervene in efforts to address certain social disorganization factors. This includes a focus on reducing disorder, which is also in line with Wilson and Kelling's (1982) conception of broken windows theory, or working with residents to build collective efficacy. We turn to the evidence on police efforts to intervene in high-crime areas in the next section.

WHAT'S THE ANSWER?

There is strong evidence that police can effectively reduce crime and disorder when they focus on high-crime micro-units of geography. This approach is typically called hot spots policing or place-based policing. The specific tactics involved in hot spots policing projects can vary, but in all cases the police devote extra attention and resources to high-crime locations. This is an especially efficient approach for police, because as we reviewed, crime is highly concentrated, and so police can target a significant proportion of a jurisdiction's crime problem by focusing on a relatively small number of high-crime micro-places (Weisburd and Telep 2010).

Reviews of the policing literature have consistently found for more than a decade that hot spots policing can prevent crime. The National Research Council (NRC) concluded in 2004 that "studies that focused police resources on crime hot spots provide the strongest collective evidence of police effectiveness that is now available" (250). More recently Braga, Papachristos, and Hureau (2014) conducted a systematic review of all experimental and quasi-experimental hot spots policing studies completed between 1989 and 2011, finding an overall significant effect of hot spots policing on crime. They examined twenty-five tests of hot spots policing from nineteen published studies, finding significant crime declines as a result of the intervention in twenty of these tests. Multiple hot spots policing trials suggesting positive results have also been published since the Braga, Papachristos, and Hureau (2014) review (see Telep and Hibdon 2018).

The tactics in hot spots policing can be as simple as increasing officer presence in hot spots. The initial hot spots policing experiment in Minneapolis, Minnesota, focused on increasing patrol presence by up to three hours per day on high-crime street blocks randomly assigned to the intervention (Sherman and Weisburd 1995). On average, patrol presence was doubled in the treatment hot spots during the experimental period relative to control hot spots. Officers were not given specific instructions on what to do while present in hot spots. They simply were told to increase patrol time in the treatment hot spots. The intervention hot spots, as compared with the control hot spots, experienced statistically significant reductions in crime calls and observed disorder. The presumed mechanism at work here was deterrence (see Nagin, Solow, and Lum 2015). The presence of officers was expected to deter criminal activity by increasing the certainty of punishment for offenders who commit crimes in view of officers (see Telep 2018).

Similarly, results from the Philadelphia foot patrol experiment suggested police can reduce violent crime through intensive foot patrols (Ratcliffe et al. 2011). Treatment hot spots were assigned two officers on foot patrol for sixteen hours a day during the summer months. The intervention was especially effective in the highest-crime hot spots, although impacts dissipated fairly quickly once the intervention period ended (Sorg et al. 2013).

There is also evidence that police can prevent crime in hot spots even when they are not physically present. Koper (1995) used data from the Minneapolis study to examine the relationship between time spent by police and how quickly crime recurred once police left. Stops of approximately fifteen minutes in length maximized the residual deterrence of increased police presence. Koper (1995) suggested that police could maximize their effectiveness by using fifteen-minute stops and conducting them at differing times of day to maximize uncertainty in the minds of potential offenders as to when police would be present. A hot spots policing randomized trial in Sacramento guided by these findings showed that police patrols of about fifteen minutes in length conducted in a random sequence approximately every two hours were associated with significant reductions in calls for service and serious crime (Telep, Mitchell, and Weisburd 2014). Thus, police can reduce crime both through their presence for a sustained (but not necessarily constant) period of time and by increasing ambiguity for potential offenders in the certainty of punishment through altering the timing of increased patrols (see Loughran et al. 2011).

Hot spots policing can also take a more complex approach by dealing with the underlying contributors to crime concentrations. This problem-oriented approach to hot spots policing utilizes the SARA model (scanning, analysis, response, assessment; Eck and Spelman 1987). Officers ideally carefully analyze the contributors to the specific problems at each hot spot and then develop a response tailored to the dynamics of each high-crime location. There is evidence from prior studies of problem-oriented policing that officers tend not to engage in the thorough problem analysis originally envisioned by Goldstein (1990) in laying out problem-oriented policing. Nonetheless, even shallow problem solving (Braga and Weisburd 2006) in hot spots is associated with significant crime reductions. Indeed, Braga, Papachristos, and Hureau (2014) found that on average, problem-oriented hot spots studies showed greater crime reduction effects than interventions relying just on increased presence (see Braga and Weisburd 2010) and a number of problem-oriented hot spots policing randomized trials have shown evidence of reducing crime and disorder (e.g., Braga et al. 1999; Taylor, Koper, and Woods 2011).

The specific responses used in problem-oriented hot spots initiatives vary, based on the results of the problem analysis. But such efforts tend to fall into one of the three categories provided by Braga, Hureau, and Papachristos (2011) in their evaluation of the Safe Streets Team hot spots program in Boston. The problem-solving activities in that study were divided into situational and environmental approaches, community outreach or social service interventions, and increased enforcement. Braga and Bond (2008) examined the relative effectiveness of different, similarly categorized responses used in a problem-oriented hot spots intervention in Lowell, Massachusetts. They found that situational strategies that addressed opportunities for crime, such as working with businesses to harden targets, cleaning up graffiti, and improving street lighting, were especially effective in reducing crime. Increases in enforcement, in this case by increasing misdemeanor arrests, were also associated with a crime decline.

As a result of the greater complexity in responses, the particular mechanisms at work in problem-oriented hot spots interventions can also vary more (Eck and Madensen 2017). Deterrence still plays a role, as intensive enforcement is still a commonly used response in problem-oriented hot spots interventions, but police can also address crime through other routes aside from directly sending a deterrent message to potential offenders. These include indirectly impacting offenders through, for example, working with place managers to implement situational crime prevention efforts or building informal social control in handlers who can control the behavior of offenders.

Hot spots policing interventions have thus generally attacked crime opportunities, either in the short term by increasing guardianship and thus making crime more risky or, in the longer term, by using situational prevention to more permanently block opportunities (e.g., by increasing street lighting or razing an abandoned building). While the focus is on increasing police activity in particular places, these approaches do not ignore the importance of offenders. Increased enforcement activity and arrests are often a component of hot spots interventions. In a recent experimental study in Philadelphia, Groff and colleagues (2015) found that an intelligence-led approach focused on identifying and making frequent contact with repeat offenders in hot spots was associated with a reduction in violent crime. The results suggest the benefits of focusing in on "hot people" living in and committing criminal acts in "hot places."

It may also be possible to integrate concepts from social disorganization theory into hot spots interventions. As noted earlier, community crime prevention interventions and community policing have not shown strong evidence of effectiveness in reducing crime. But focusing such interventions on the street-block level could be more successful and would be a more efficient way to deliver such efforts (Weisburd, Groff, and Yang 2014). A current hot spots policing project in Brooklyn Park, Minnesota, for example, focuses on increasing presence but without an enforcement orientation (Weisburd, Davis, and Gill 2015). Instead, officers work to build informal social control in hot spots by building closer relationships to residents and business owners and then using these relationships to encourage groups to take the lead in efforts to reduce crime in hot spots.

This effort to build collective efficacy and reduce crime collaboratively could be a model for future hot spots policing interventions guided by both opportunity and social disorganization theories. More research is needed though, as the Brooklyn Park evaluation remains in progress and Braga and Bond's (2008) analyses did not suggest police-led social service interventions contributed to crime declines in Lowell. Future studies should examine whether hot spots policing interventions that incorporate partnerships to enhance not just formal guardianship but also levels of informal social control can have longer-lasting crime control benefits.

Despite evidence of its effectiveness in reducing crime, hot spots policing has not been without critics. Spatial displacement is a common concern expressed by policy makers and practitioners about place-based interventions

(Clarke and Weisburd 1994). Police, for example, often recognize the benefit of focusing attention on high-crime locations but argue, usually based on anecdotal evidence, that offenders will quickly get the message and simply relocate their criminal activity to a nearby corner. Indeed, Sorg and colleagues (2014) found that officers in the Philadelphia foot patrol experiment frequently left their assigned beat to patrol areas nearby because of a concern that problems had been displaced.

Importantly, hot spots policing does not simply reduce crime by pushing it to areas nearby. The empirical evidence for immediate spatial displacement suggests the phenomenon is not common as a result of hot spots interventions (see Braga, Papachristos, and Hureau 2014). In a review of focused policing interventions, Bowers et al. (2011, 369) concluded that "displacement is far from inevitable" and "the opposite, a diffusion of crime control benefits appears to be a frequent outcome." The Braga, Papachristos, and Hureau (2014) hot spots review also found that, on average, a diffusion of crime control benefits, where areas surrounding the hot spots are likely to also enjoy crime control benefits (Clarke and Weisburd 1994), was more common than immediate spatial displacement. In interviews with offenders in a study of displacement and diffusion in Jersey City, New Jersey, Weisburd and colleagues (2006) found that displacement is not inevitable, because the same opportunities for crime may not exist around the corner. It is also often difficult for drug dealers or prostitutes to relocate their criminal activity to places nearby because of concerns about entering unfamiliar or potentially unsafe turf.

Critics of hot spots policing have also pointed to the tension between the crime prevention effectiveness of focused police efforts and their potentially harmful effects on police-community relations (Rosenbaum 2006; Kochel 2011). That is, if hot spots policing reduces crime in the short term but does so in ways that reduce resident perceptions of police legitimacy, then it could have long-term negative consequences for reducing crime. Evidence, largely from survey-based studies, suggests that when individuals view the police and other authorities as legitimate, they are more likely to obey the law (see Tyler 2004).

But there is limited evidence that hot spots policing has negative impacts on resident views about the police in the areas where police are focusing their attention. Empirical studies to date have found either no impact of hot spots policing tactics on resident perceptions of police legitimacy (Weisburd et al. 2011; Ratcliffe et al. 2015) or only short-term negative impacts that quickly dissipate (Kochel and Weisburd 2017). More attention is needed in future studies, however, on the impacts of hot spots policing on the individuals with whom the police have contact. These people may or may not be the residents of high-crime areas, and so it is important to assess the extent to which they view their interaction with police during hot spots interactions as fair. The New York City Police Department's use of stop, question, and frisk as a primary tactic for hot spots policing, for example, may have contributed to the long-term crime decline in the city, but it also likely led to reductions in citizen perceptions of the police, particularly among young and nonwhite residents (see Weisburd, Telep, and Lawton 2014).

It does not appear that hot spots policing will inevitably be viewed negatively by residents of the areas receiving additional police attention. But could hot spots strategies be designed to actually improve perceptions of police legitimacy? And could doing so also have implications for additional crime control gains? This is the focus of a current multisite study funded by the Laura and John Arnold Foundation that we are working on in collaboration with the Police Foundation. We are testing whether hot spots policing infused with procedural justice through officer training and reinforcement in the field leads to different outcomes in terms of citizen perceptions and crime compared to more standard hot spots policing. The results will have important implications for whether the police can successfully simultaneously increase fairness and effectiveness (see National Research Council 2004).

CONCLUSION

There is strong evidence from basic research that crime is highly concentrated at small units of geography. Theoretical advances in recent decades have put greater attention on micro-places as important units of analysis for the development of both theory and practice. These units are much smaller than the neighborhoods and communities that have traditionally been of interest to criminologists and the police, and the focus is less on offenders than on the spaces within which they operate. Importantly, place-based theories have an emphasis on the practical, and the opportunity structures that help explain why crime is highly concentrated at specific places have been the target of hot spots policing interventions.

Moving forward, we suspect police will expand their toolbox for dealing with hot spots, and we recommend they consider partnering with other agencies to deliver social interventions at small units of geography that can target crime opportunities, as well as social factors operating at the street level. While the evidence base for hot spots policing is strong, there are still a number of questions that should be examined in future studies, including the most appropriate strategies for particular problems and crime types, long-term and jurisdictional impacts, and contextual effects (see Weisburd and Telep 2014; Weisburd et al. 2017). We both authored with several colleagues a recent book reviewing this area of work entitled *Place Matters: Criminology for the Twenty-First Century* (Weisburd et al. 2016). We think this title reflects the importance of crime and place work for the next generation of criminological theory and criminal justice practice. Our review in this chapter makes clear that place does matter for effectively understanding and addressing crime.

REFERENCES

Bowers, K. J., S. D. Johnson, R. T. Guerette, L. Summers, and S. Poynton. 2011. Spatial displacement and diffusion of benefits among geographically focused policing initiatives: A meta-analytical review. *Journal of Experimental Criminology* 7: 347–374.

Braga, A. A., and B. J. Bond. 2008. Policing crime and disorder hot spots: A randomized controlled trial. *Criminology* 46: 577–608.

Braga, A. A., D. M. Hureau, and A. V. Papachristos. 2011. An ex post facto evaluation framework for place-based police interventions. *Evaluation Review* 35: 592–626.

Braga, A. A., A. V. Papachristos, and D. M. Hureau. 2010. The concentration and stability of gun violence at micro places in Boston, 1980–2008. *Journal of Quantitative Criminology* 26: 33–53.

———. 2014. The effects of hot spots policing on crime: An updated systematic review and meta-analysis. *Justice Quarterly* 31: 633–663.

Braga, A. A., and D. Weisburd. 2006. Problem-oriented policing: The disconnect between principles and practice. In *Police innovation: contrasting perspectives*, edited by D. Weisburd and A. A. Braga, 133–154. New York: Cambridge University Press.

———. 2010. *Policing Problem Places: Crime Hot Spots and Effective Prevention*. New York: Oxford University Press.

Braga, A. A., D. Weisburd, E. J. Waring, L. G. Mazerolle, W. Spelman, and F. Gajewski. 1999. Problem-oriented policing in violent crime places: A randomized controlled experiment. *Criminology* 37: 541–580.

Brantingham, P. J., and P. L. Brantingham. 1984. *Patterns in Crime*. New York: Macmillan.

Burgess, E. W. 1925. The growth of a city: An introduction to a research project. In *The City: Suggestions for the Investigation of Human Behavior in the Urban Environment*, edited by R. E. Park and E. W. Burgess, 47–62. Chicago: University of Chicago Press.

Bursik, R. J. Jr., and H. G. Grasmick. 1993. *Neighborhoods and Crime: The Dimensions of Effective Community Control*. New York: Lexington Books.

Clarke, R. V. 1983. Situational crime prevention: Its theoretical basis and practical scope. In *Crime and Justice: A Review of Research*, vol. 14, edited by M. Tonry and N. Morris 225–256. Chicago: University of Chicago Press.

———. 1995. Situational crime prevention. In *Building a Safer Society: Strategic Approaches to Crime Prevention. Crime and Justice: A Review of Research*, vol. 19, edited by M. Tonry and D. Farrington, 91–150. Chicago: University of Chicago Press.

Clarke, R. V., and J. E. Eck. 2005. *Crime Analysis for Problem Solvers in 60 Small Steps*. Washington, DC: Office of Community Oriented Policing Services, U.S. Department of Justice.

Clarke, R. V., and D. L. Weisburd. 1994. Diffusion of crime control benefits: Observations on the reverse of displacement. In *Crime Prevention Studies*, vol. 2, edited by R. V. Clarke, 165–184. Monsey, NY: Criminal Justice Press.

Cloward, R. A., and L. Ohlin. 1960. *Delinquency and Opportunity: A Theory of Delinquent Gangs*. New York: Free Press.

Cohen, L. E., and M. Felson. 1979. Social change and crime rate trends: A routine activity approach. *American Sociological Review* 44: 588–608.

Eck, J. E. 2005. Crime hot spots: What they are, why we have them, and how to map them. In *Mapping Crime: Understanding Hot Spots*, edited by J. E. Eck, S. Chainey, J. G. Cameron, M. Leitner, and R. E. Wilson, 1–14. Washington, DC: National Institute of Justice, U.S. Department of Justice.

Eck, J. E., and T. D. Madensen. 2017. Police and offender choices: A framework. In *The Oxford Handbook of Offender Decision Making*, edited by W. Bernasco, H. Elffers, and J.-L. van Gelder, 374–397. New York: Oxford University Press.

Eck, J. E., and W. Spelman. 1987. *Problem Solving: Problem-Oriented Policing in Newport News*. Washington, DC: Police Executive Research Forum.

Eck, J. E., and D. Weisburd. 1995. Crime places in crime theory. In *Crime and Place. Crime Prevention Studies*, vol. 4, edited by J. E. Eck and D. Weisburd, 1–33. Monsey, NY: Willow Tree Press.

Gill, C. E., D. Weisburd, C. W. Telep, T. Bennett, and Z. Vitter. 2014. Community-oriented policing to reduce crime, disorder, and fear and increase legitimacy and citizen satisfaction in neighborhoods. *Journal of Experimental Criminology* 10: 399–428.

Goldstein, H. 1990. *Problem-Oriented Policing*. New York: McGraw Hill.

Groff, E. R., J. H. Ratcliffe, C. P. Haberman, E. T. Sorg, N. M. Joyce, and R. B. Taylor. 2015. Does what police do at hot spots matter? The Philadelphia policing tactics experiment. *Criminology* 53: 23–53.

Hibdon, J., C. W. Telep, and E. R. Groff. 2017. The concentration and stability of drug activity in Seattle, Washington using police and emergency medical services data. *Journal of Quantitative Criminology* 33: 497–517.

Hope, T. 1995. Community crime prevention. In *Building a Safer Society: Strategic Approaches to Crime Prevention. Crime and Justice: A Review of Research*, vol. 19, edited by M. Tonry and D. Farrington, 21–89. Chicago: University of Chicago Press.

Kelling, G. L., A. M. Pate, D. Dieckman, and C. Brown. 1974. *The Kansas City Preventive Patrol Experiment: Technical Report*. Washington, DC: Police Foundation.

Kochel, T. R. 2011. Constructing hot spots policing: Unexamined consequences for disadvantaged populations and for police legitimacy. *Criminal Justice Policy Review* 22: 350–374.

Kochel, T. R., and D. Weisburd. 2017. Assessing community consequences of implementing hot spots policing in residential areas: Findings from a randomized field trial. *Journal of Experimental Criminology* 13: 143–170.

Koper, C. S. 1995. Just enough police presence: Reducing crime and disorderly behavior by optimizing patrol time in crime hot spots. *Justice Quarterly* 12: 649–672.

Kubrin, C. E., and R. Weitzer. 2003. New directions in social disorganization theory. *Journal of Research in Crime and Delinquency* 40: 374–402.

Loughran, T. A., R. Paternoster, A. Piquero, and G. Pogarsky. 2011. On ambiguity in perceptions of risk: Implications for criminal decision making and deterrence. *Criminology* 49: 1029–1061.

Lum, C., C. Koper, and C. W. Telep. 2011. The Evidence-Based Policing Matrix. *Journal of Experimental Criminology* 7: 3–26.

McGarrell, E. F., S. Chermak, A. Weiss, and J. Wilson. 2001. Reducing firearms violence through directed police patrol. *Criminology and Public Policy* 1: 119–148.

Nagin, D. S., R. M. Solow, and C. Lum. 2015. Deterrence, criminal opportunities, and police. *Criminology* 53: 74–100.

National Research Council. 2004. *Fairness and Effectiveness in Policing: The Evidence*, edited by W. Skogan and K. Frydl. Committee to Review Research on Police Policy and Practices. Committee on Law and Justice, Division of Behavioral and Social Sciences and Education. Washington, DC: National Academies Press.

Pierce, G., S. Spaar, and L. R. Briggs. 1988. *The Character of Police Work: Strategic and Tactical Implications.* Boston: Center for Applied Social Research, Northeastern University.

Ratcliffe, J. H., E. R. Groff, E. T. Sorg, and C. P. Haberman. 2015. Citizens' reactions to hot spots policing: Impacts on perceptions of crime, disorder, safety and police. *Journal of Experimental Criminology* 11: 393–417.

Ratcliffe, J. H., T. Taniguchi, E. R. Groff, and J. D. Wood. 2011. The Philadelphia Foot Patrol experiment: A randomized controlled trial of police patrol effectiveness in violent crime hotspots. *Criminology* 49: 795–831.

Rosenbaum, D. P. 2006. The limits of hot spots policing. In *Police Innovation: Contrasting Perspectives*, edited by D. Weisburd and A. A. Braga, 245–263. New York: Cambridge University Press.

Sampson, R. J., and W. B. Groves. 1989. Community structure and crime: Testing social-disorganization theory. *American Journal of Sociology* 94: 774–802.

Sampson, R. J., S. W. Raudenbush, and F. Earls. 1997. Neighborhoods and violent crime: A multilevel study of collective efficacy. *Science* 277: 918–924.

Schnell, C., A. A. Braga, and E. L. Piza. 2017. The influence of community areas, neighborhood clusters, and street segments on the spatial variability of violent crime in Chicago. *Journal of Quantitative Criminology* 33: 469–496.

Shaw, C. R., and H. D. McKay. 1942. *Juvenile Delinquency and Urban Areas. A Study of Rates of Delinquency in Relation to Differential Characteristics of Local Communities in American Cities.* Chicago: University of Chicago Press.

Sherman, L. W. 1987. *Repeat Calls to the Police in Minneapolis.* Washington, DC: Crime Control Institute.

Sherman, L. W., P. R. Gartin, and M. E. Buerger. 1989. Hot spots of predatory crime: Routine activities and the criminology of place. *Criminology* 27: 27–56.

Sherman, L. W., and D. Weisburd. 1995. General deterrent effects of police patrol in crime hot spots: A randomized controlled trial. *Justice Quarterly* 12: 625–648.

Smith, W. R., S. G. Frazee, and E. L. Davison. 2000. Furthering the integration of routine activity and social disorganization theories: Small units of analysis and the study of street robbery as a diffusion process. *Criminology* 38: 489–523.

Sorg, E. T., C. P. Haberman, J. H. Ratcliffe, and E. R. Groff. 2013. Foot patrol in violent crime hot spots: The longitudinal impact of deterrence and posttreatment effects of displacement. *Criminology* 51: 65–102.

Sorg, E. T., J. D. Wood, E. R. Groff, and J. H. Ratcliffe. 2014. Boundary adherence during place-based policing evaluations: A research note. *Journal of Research in Crime and Delinquency* 51: 377–393.

Steenbeek, W., and D. Weisburd. 2016. Where the action is in crime? An examination of variability of crime across different spatial units in the Hague, 2001–2009. *Journal of Quantitative Criminology* 32: 449–469.

Taylor, B., C. S. Koper, and D. J. Woods. 2011. A randomized controlled trial of different policing strategies at hot spots of violent crime. *Journal of Experimental Criminology* 7: 149–181.

Taylor, R. B. 1997. Social order and disorder of street blocks and neighborhoods: Ecology, microecology, and the systemic model of social disorganization. *Journal of Research in Crime and Delinquency* 34: 13–155.

Telep, C. W. 2018. Not just what works, but *how* it works: Mechanisms and context in the effectiveness of place-based policing. In *Unraveling the Crime-Place Connection: New Directions in Theory and Practice. Advances in Criminological Theory*, edited by D. Weisburd and J. E. Eck, 237–259. Piscataway, NJ: Transaction Publishers.

Telep, C. W., and J. Hibdon. 2018. Understanding and responding to hot spots. In *Problem-Oriented Guides for Police.* Washington, DC: Bureau of Justice Assistance, U.S. Department of Justice.

Telep, C. W., R. J. Mitchell, and D. Weisburd. 2014. How much time should the police spend at crime hot spots? Answers from a police agency directed randomized field trial in Sacramento, California. *Justice Quarterly* 31: 905–933.

Telep, C. W., and D. Weisburd. 2018. The criminology of places. In *Oxford Handbook of Environmental Criminology*, edited by G. Bruinsma and S. Johnson, 583–603. New York: Oxford University Press.

Tyler, T. R. 2004. Enhancing police legitimacy. *Annals of the American Academy of Political and Social Science* 593: 84–99.

Weisburd, D. 2015. The law of crime concentration and the criminology of place. *Criminology* 54: 133–157.

Weisburd, D., A. A. Braga, E. R. Groff, and A. Wooditch. 2017. Can hot spots policing reduce crime in urban areas? An agent-based simulation. *Criminology* 55: 137–173.

Weisburd, D., G.J.N. Bruinsma, and W. Bernasco. 2009. Units of analysis in geographic criminology: Historical development, critical issues, and open questions. In *Putting Crime in Its Place: Units of Analysis in Geographic Criminology*, edited by D. Weisburd, W. Bernasco, and G. J.N. Bruinsma, 3–31. New York: Springer.

Weisburd, D., S. Bushway, C. Lum, and S. M. Yang. 2004. Trajectories of crime at places: A longitudinal study of street segments in the city of Seattle. *Criminology* 42: 283–321.

Weisburd, D., M. Davis, and C. Gill. 2015. Increasing collective efficacy and social capital at crime hot spots: New crime control tools for police. *Policing: A Journal of Policy and Practice* 9: 265–274.

Weisburd, D., J. E. Eck, A. A. Braga, C. W. Telep, B. Cave, et al. 2016. *Place Matters: Criminology for the Twenty-First Century.* New York: Cambridge University Press.

Weisburd, D., E. R. Groff, and S. M. Yang. 2012. *The Criminology of Place: Street Segments and Our Understanding of the Crime Problem.* New York: Oxford University Press.

———. 2014. Understanding and controlling hot spots of crime: The importance of formal and informal social controls. *Prevention Science* 15: 31–43.

Weisburd, D., J. C. Hinkle, C. Famega, and J. Ready. 2011. The possible "backfire" effects of hot spots policing: An experimental assessment of impacts on legitimacy, fear and collective efficacy. *Journal of Experimental Criminology* 7: 297–320.

Weisburd, D., and A. R. Piquero. 2008. How well do criminologists explain crime? Statistical modeling in published studies. In *Crime and Justice: A Review of Research,* vol. 37, edited by M. Tonry, 453–502. Chicago: University of Chicago Press.

Weisburd, D., J. Ready, B. Lawton, B. Cave, M. Nelson, and A. Haviland. 2014. Is living in a hot spot for crime or drugs related to collective efficacy, legitimacy, victimization, deviance and health problems? Presented at the American Society of Criminology Annual Meeting, San Francisco, CA.

Weisburd, D., and C. W. Telep. 2010. The efficiency of place-based policing. In *Evidence-Based Policing. Cahiers Politiestudies,* no. 17, edited by E. De Wree, E. Devroe, W. Broer, and P. Van der Laan, 247–262. Antwerp, Belgium: Maklu Publishers.

———. 2014. Hot spots policing: What we know and what we need to know. *Journal of Contemporary Criminal Justice* 30: 200–220.

Weisburd, D., C. W. Telep, and B. A. Lawton. 2014. Could innovations in policing have contributed to the New York City crime drop even in a period of declining police strength? The case of stop, question and frisk as a hot spots policing strategy. *Justice Quarterly* 31: 129–154.

Weisburd, D., L. A. Wyckoff, J. Ready, J. E. Eck, J. C. Hinkle, and F. Gajewski. 2006. Does crime just move around the corner? A controlled study of spatial displacement and diffusion of crime control benefits. *Criminology* 44: 549–592.

Welsh, B. C., and A. Hoshi. 2002. Communities and crime prevention. In *Evidence-Based Crime Prevention,* edited by L. W. Sherman, D. P. Farrington, B. C. Welsh, and D. L. MacKenzie, 165–197. New York: Routledge.

Wicker, A. W. 1987. Behavior settings reconsidered: Temporal stages, resources, internal dynamics, context. In *Handbook of Environmental Psychology,* edited by D. Stokels and I. Altman, 613–653. New York: Wiley-Interscience.

Wilson, J. Q., and G. L. Kelling. 1982. Broken windows: The police and neighborhood safety. *Atlantic Monthly* 211: 29–38.

Wooditch, A., D. Weisburd, C. White, B. Lawton, and J. Ready. 2016. Collective efficacy in hot spots of crime. Presented at the American Society of Criminology Annual Meeting, New Orleans, LA.

8

Aligning Public Policy, Criminological Theory, and Empirical Findings on the Immigration-Crime Relationship

Glenn Trager and
Charis E. Kubrin

This chapter examines the divergence between political rhetoric and public policy in the United States that demonizes immigrants for their "criminality" and the empirical reality of low crime rates in U.S. immigrant communities. Through a case study that examines a political debate on the propriety of using local police officers to help remove undocumented individuals, we argue that one path toward the tolerance of immigrants as non-harmful and legitimate members of the community is when immigrant groups become, de facto, an acknowledged part of that community and are no longer seen to represent a foreign threat to others. In such a situation, the wholesale rejection of immigrants, including the undocumented, becomes politically costly and undesirable, leading to more nuanced political discourse about the presence of immigrants and local policies related to them. In this chapter, we first examine this divergence. We then present findings from our case study in a Southern California community. Finally, in the conclusion, we argue that recent developments in criminological theory that more accurately account for the empirical reality of the immigration-crime relationship represent a productive step toward delineating those social-ecological factors that help reduce crime rates in immigrant communities and constitute an important part of the national narrative on immigration and crime.

TALKING ABOUT IMMIGRATION AND CRIME: PUBLIC DISCOURSE AND CRIMINOLOGICAL THEORY

Political discourse and mainstream media have long constructed the presence of immigrants in U.S. communities as being problematic and the presence of undocumented persons in particular as presenting an enhanced risk of criminal behavior and social harm (Gilbert 2009; Johnson 2009; Khashu 2009; Romero 2006). Undocumented immigrants are routinely depicted in the media and by politicians as a threat to the very fabric of U.S. society, as hordes of dark bodies running rampant across the border and ruining our communities, and as a foreign "Other" bringing "Americans" into poverty and undermining "American" language and culture (Chavez 2001, 2008; Santa Ana 2002; Schrag 2010).

These depictions have real-world consequences. Indeed, such images and discourse have encouraged political institutions at the federal, state, and local levels to take steps to protect residents against the alleged threats presented by these "illegals" (Eagly 2010; Koulish 2010; Provine et al. 2016). At the federal level, consider recent deportation policy and practices. Deportations of immigrants are the highest they have ever been in U.S. history, leading some to characterize the United States as a "deportation nation" (Kanstroom 2010). In 2015, for example, the Department of Homeland Security (DHS) apprehended 406,595 individuals nationwide and conducted a total of 462,463 removals and returns (DHS 2015), more than two times as many just ten years prior. The irony is that this record deportation comes at a time when the number of undocumented persons in the United States has been dropping substantially for more than half a decade due, in part, to a sluggish economy (Warren 2016).

Evidence of policy at the state level is, perhaps, most telling in recent laws that now criminalize immigrant status, reflecting the intersection of criminal law and immigration law or "crimmigration" (Stumpf 2006). Prior to these laws, being in the United States illegally was not considered a crime but a civil offense. The model of these new laws is found in Arizona's SB 1070, which makes it a misdemeanor for undocumented immigrants to be within Arizona state lines without legal documents; requires authorities to inquire about an individual's immigration status during an arrest when there is "reasonable suspicion" that the individual is undocumented; and allows police to detain anyone they believe is in the country illegally. In recent years, copycat laws have been introduced in Georgia (HB 87), Florida (HB-1C), and Alabama (HB 56). Templates for these laws are found in earlier legislation, such as California's Prop 187 introduced in 1994. Prop 187 called for eliminating benefits to undocumented immigrants, prohibiting their access to healthcare, public education, and other social services in the state. The law also required state authorities to report anyone they suspected might be undocumented. Although Prop 187 was eventually declared unconstitutional, it and related policies paved the way for today's harsher immigration laws.

Finally, as a rubric of risk pervades political discourse about immigrants, many local polities have similarly enacted policies to "manage" this perceived risk through strategies of exclusion, marginalization, and institutionalized control (Danielson 2010; Fleury-Steiner and Longazel 2010; Koulish 2010; Longazel 2014; Provine et al. 2016). In particular, localities have passed ordinances to prohibit the funding of local job centers, to deny licenses to businesses that "aid and abet" undocumented workers, and to make it illegal to rent housing to undocumented workers (Gilbert 2009). Such strategies are designed to make life impossible for undocumented persons and to push them out of the community. Notably, whatever the policy, it is the *perception* of immigrant danger and criminality—rather than reliance on empirical findings—that has captured the public imagination and has pushed the implementation of exclusionary, anti-immigrant policy.

To some degree, these negative images and anti-immigrant rhetoric have a basis in social theory. Sociological and criminological theories have long emphasized a strong connection between immigration and crime (Martinez and Lee 2000). Although the mechanisms linking the two vary considerably, several explanations maintain that increased immigration to an area will result in heightened crime rates. These theories have been discussed at length elsewhere (Kubrin 2013; Martinez and Lee 2000). Given space limitations, we briefly discuss three of the most popular and widely cited explanations: social disorganization theory, local labor market theory, and cultural theory.

Social Disorganization Theory

Social disorganization theory has long theorized a positive association between immigration and neighborhood crime rates (Shaw and McKay [1942] 1969; Thomas and Znaniecki [1920] 1984). According to this perspective, immigration to an area can lead to residential turnover, or the frequent movement of populations in and out of a community (Bankston 1998). Residential turnover can weaken social ties, as residents are unable to create dense networks and friendships in the community are short-lived. A lack of ties can lead to decreases in informal social control, or the capacity of a group to regulate its members according to mutually desired goals such as the desire to live in a crime-free environment. Weak ties and decreased informal social control, in turn, can lead to heightened crime rates.

Immigration is also associated with crime, according to social disorganization theory, because it can generate racial and ethnic heterogeneity, which is similar to residential mobility in that it can undermine the strength and salience of informal social control in communities (Kubrin 2000; Lee and Martinez 2002, 366). Moreover, in areas with diverse racial and ethnic groups living in close proximity, interaction between members will be lower than in racially and ethnically homogeneous communities (Gans 1968). Reasons point to cultural differences between groups, language incompatibility, and the fact that individuals prefer members of their own race or ethnicity to members of different races or ethnicities (Blau and Schwartz 1984). For these reasons, social disorganization theory maintains that residents will be less likely to look out for one another and will not take as great an interest in their neighbors' activities, resulting in less informal social control and, ultimately, more crime (Kubrin 2000).

Local La bor Market Theory

According to another perspective, immigration may increase crime rates in communities by altering the structure of local labor markets (Reid et al. 2005, 761). For example, increased immigration may displace native-born minorities from low-wage occupations (Beck 1996; Waldinger 1997; but see Bean, Lowell, and Taylor 1988), which could lead to an increase in the criminality of the displaced groups (Wilson 1996). Stated alternatively, immigrants may have an adverse effect on crime by crowding natives out of the legal employment sector. If immigrants adversely affect natives' legal alternatives by taking jobs or overburdening the welfare system, low-skilled natives, it is argued, may become more criminally active (Butcher and Piehl 1998b, 459). In this way, immigration may not add to the criminal population but rather "immigration might reshape urban demographic and economic structures in ways that increase the criminality of native-born persons" (Reid et al. 2005, 761).

Cultural Explanations

Cultural explanations also theorize a positive immigration-crime association. Because immigrants, like ethnic minorities, are more likely than native-born whites to reside in areas where "structural conditions have altered the status systems away from idealized middle-class norms and toward a culture of opposition" (Lee, Martinez, and Rosenfeld 2001, 562), cultural theories suggest that immigrant communities should experience high crime rates (Mears 2002, 284; Reid et al. 2005, 760). Indeed, many immigrant communities are segregated from mainstream society and have high rates of poverty, joblessness, and other disadvantages (MacDonald and Saunders

2012, 126; Martinez and Lee 2000; Velez 2009) and as such do not represent "communities of choice" but rather "ghettos of last resort" for immigrants (Glaser, Parker, and Li 2003, 526). As immigrants navigate these disadvantaged communities, they may adopt the tough, aggressive stances common when negotiating the streets (Anderson 1999; Bourgois 2003; Martinez, Lee, and Nielsen 2004; Tonry 1997, 21–22). For these reasons, one might expect a criminogenic street context, or street code (Anderson 1999), to heighten crime rates in areas with high concentrations of immigrants. Moreover, given that immigrants not only settle in disadvantaged neighborhoods but also can face language barriers and experience discrimination in housing and employment markets, cultural perspectives emphasize that immigrants may be denied access to legitimate means to attain culturally prescribed goals of wealth and, therefore, may turn to crime as a way to do so (Lee, Martinez, and Rosenfeld 2001, 561; Mears 2002, 284; Reid et al. 2005, 759).

THE EMPIRICAL REALITY: WHAT RESEARCH REVEALS ABOUT THE IMMIGRATION-CRIME RELATIONSHIP

While political discourse and social theory frequently portray a positive link between immigration and crime, empirical research tells a very different story. In particular, research finds that (1) immigrants are less prone to crime than their native-born counterparts and are also arrested and incarcerated at lower rates (Bersani 2014; Butcher and Piehl 1998a, 1998b, 654; Hagan and Palloni 1999, 629; MacDonald and Saunders 2012; Martinez and Lee 2000; Martinez 2002; McCord 1995; Polczynski Olson et al. 2009; Rumbaut and Ewing 2007, 1; Rumbaut et al. 2006; Sampson, Morenoff, and Raudenbush 2005; Tonry 1997); (2) areas with high concentrations of immigrants have lower rates of crime and violence, all else equal (see discussion below); and (3) increases in immigration are responsible, in part, for the crime decline of last two decades (Martinez, Stowell, and Lee 2010; Ousey and Kubrin 2009, 2018; Stowell et al. 2009; Wadsworth 2010).

The number of studies that examine the immigration-crime relationship across various levels of aggregation has grown immensely. These studies include investigations of metropolitan areas and cities (Butcher and Piehl 1998a; Martinez 2000; Ousey and Kubrin 2009; Reid et al. 2005; Stowell et al. 2009; Wadsworth 2010) as well as neighborhood-level studies that examine the extent to which immigration and crime are associated. As just noted, this literature has produced a fairly robust finding: areas, and especially neighborhoods, with greater concentrations of immigrants have lower rates of crime and violence, all else being equal (Akins, Rumbaut, and Stansfield 2009; Chavez and Griffiths

2009; Desmond and Kubrin 2009; Feldmeyer and Steffensmeier 2009; Graif and Sampson 2009; Kubrin and Ishizawa 2012; Lee and Martinez 2002; Lee, Martinez, and Rosenfeld 2001; MacDonald, Hipp, and Gill 2013; Martinez, Lee, and Nielsen 2004; Martinez, Stowell, and Cancino 2008; Martinez, Stowell, and Lee 2010; Nielsen and Martinez 2009; Nielsen, Lee, and Martinez 2005; Stowell and Martinez 2007, 2009; Velez 2009). The finding that immigrant communities have lower rates of crime holds true for various measures of immigrant concentration (e.g., percent foreign-born, percent recent foreign-born, percent linguistic isolation) as well as for different outcomes (e.g., violent crime, property crime, delinquency) in both cross-sectional as well as longitudinal analyses. In fact, a recent meta-analysis of over fifty immigration-crime studies published between 1994 and 2004 confirms this finding thereby calling into question those theories which advance a strong positive association between immigration and crime, regardless of the mechanism (Ousey and Kubrin 2018).

Despite our earlier discussion about public discourse and social theory, we do not wish to suggest that this empirical reality has gone completely without notice by scholars or members of the public. First, as we discuss in the conclusion to this chapter, these empirical findings are gradually working their way into broader criminological theory. And, second, while many members of the public still find it unfathomable that immigrants could commit less crime than the native-born and that immigrant communities could be some of the safest places around, residents in some localities have resisted efforts to legally (and criminally) target immigrants, including the undocumented, and instead have assisted their integration and acceptance into the community.[1] These efforts remain the exception.

EXPLORING THE (DIS)CONNECTION BETWEEN POLICY, THEORY, AND THE IMMIGRATION-CRIME RELATIONSHIP

In order to more fully explore the factors underlying the limited impact empirical findings have had on political discourse and criminological theory, we examine a political debate about the propriety of using local police officers to help remove undocumented persons from a Southern California community. In December 2005, a group of city council members in Costa Mesa, California, invoked the theme of criminal danger to advocate for a local ordinance that would allow local police to work with Immigration and Customs Enforcement (ICE)[2] to deport undocumented persons who had been detained in the community (the "ICE Proposal"). While this proposal echoed efforts in other communities around the country to exclude unauthorized immigrants through deportation, as well as through ordinances that limit the ability of undocumented persons to rent or work in a locality (Espenshade et al. 2010), the proposal was met with a good deal of public resistance.

In our analysis, we review arguments made by both supporters and opponents of the ICE Proposal at the Costa Mesa City Council meetings in 2005 and 2006 in which the issue of the propriety of the ordinance was considered. This analysis allows us to identify themes and assumptions that were shared by speakers, regardless of their support (or lack thereof) for the proposal. Through analysis we show that, by the time the proposal was introduced, immigrants had become a de facto part of the larger Costa Mesa community and were no longer seen to represent a criminal threat to most residents. This made it politically untenable to criminally target immigrants, including the undocumented, without some additional evidence that they constituted a true danger to the community. In essence, findings from our case study suggest that national (negative) political discourse was trumped by the local political reality of extant diversity in the community.

Study Site: Costa Mesa, California

The site of this study, Costa Mesa, is a small city of just over 100,000 persons situated in Orange County, California, just south of Los Angeles. Despite claims by some scholars that rapid demographic change is a critical factor in local policy making that targets the undocumented (Hopkins 2010), the population of Costa Mesa had remained demographically stable in the period leading up to the ICE Proposal. Costa Mesa's population grew from 108,724 in 2000 to just 114,057 in 2010. With respect to ethnicity, Latinos represented 29.2 percent of the population in 2000 and 28.5 percent in the 2005–2009 time frame. On a political level, the city has been described as fairly conservative, with a three to two advantage in voter registration for the Republican Party.[3]

Our analysis examines efforts taken by a majority on the city council in 2005 to 2006 to enact the ICE Proposal, which would permit the city to negotiate with ICE with the ultimate goal of establishing an agreement that would allow certain Costa Mesa police officers (jail personnel and members of the gang detail) to be able to screen suspects for immigration status. The ICE Proposal was put forward by the mayor of Costa Mesa and one other council member on December 6, 2005 (Costa Mesa City Council Meeting Minutes December 6, 2005). For the next few months, the ICE Proposal remained controversial and was discussed at length by council members as well as by members of the public during monthly city council meetings.

Our case study analyzes comments made about the proposal over the course of these sessions.[4] We organize these comments into three common themes about the propriety of asking local police to help deport undocumented persons in the community: (1) police action is appropriate because the undocumented represent a danger to the community; (2) police action is inappropriate because the undocumented are an integral part of the local community; and (3) police action is appropriate only if undocumented immigrants commit dangerous crimes.

Police Action Is Appropriate Because the Undocumented Represent a Danger to the Community

Initially, a minority of speakers relied on arguments consistent with longstanding negative rhetoric about immigrants in supporting the Costa Mesa measure to allow local police to work with ICE. These speakers adopted a "law and order" approach, one tied closely to images of undocumented persons as criminal and harmful to the community. These speakers forcefully maintained that police intervention against the undocumented was not only logical, but also essential to the health of the community. Comments such as these constituted 30 percent of the total comments made at the city council meetings but only about 16 percent of the comments made by speakers who resided in Costa Mesa. By contrast, over 60 percent of the speakers who traveled to council meetings from outside the boundaries of the city invoked this theme, suggesting that they were more interested in being heard on the generalized "dangers" of immigration than they were on debating the specific threat of immigrants to Costa Mesa itself. For instance, one resident of Mojave, California, a city roughly one hundred miles north of Costa Mesa, declared that, "No one has a right to come into the United States of America illegally, and no true citizen would mind a policeman asking him what his immigration status is" (January 3, 2006). Likewise, a resident from nearby Aliso Viejo, California, similarly emphasized the propriety of police involvement by stating that he was in favor of "preserving this nation's governance by the people under the rule of law, just as our founding fathers envisioned it" (January 3, 2006).

Given the paucity of actual evidence tying immigration to crime in Costa Mesa, such speakers invoked other types of allegedly illicit harms to the community in their arguments about immigrant "criminal danger." For instance, one speaker from nearby Orange, California, discussed the economic harm caused by a "criminal invasion," invoking arguments reminiscent of local labor market theory, discussed earlier:

> When I was their age, one of my first jobs was Jack-in-the-Box. We were all Americans then. You heard American being spoken. Nowadays, you can't go to a Jack-in-the-Box, a McDonald's, a Carl's Jr.,

good luck finding an American. These jobs are being taken from American kids. I'm pretty tired of it. Quite often when I go through Carl's Jr. after I get off work at night, I actually leave a bit depressed. Because I remember when I was a kid, I worked in this job environment. These were Americans working in the job environment. I have nothing against the Spanish language. But what I'm saying is, these were Americans doing this job. These were American kids. What happened? What happened is quite clearly an invasion. Okay? I could go on and on. I'm tired of seeing what has happened to my country. I did not serve in the military to see what has happened to my country. (January 3, 2006)

These arguments demonstrate that a minority of speakers—consistent with long-standing expectations of social theory and political rhetoric—openly blamed the presence of undocumented immigrants for the harms faced by Costa Mesa and argued that such harms should be appropriately dealt with through police intervention. Of perhaps greater interest, however, is that despite the availability of such rhetoric, most speakers, and especially residents of Costa Mesa who attended the city council meetings, explicitly avoided equating immigration with crime.

Police Action Is Inappropriate Because the Undocumented Are an Integral Part of the Local Community

A second group of individuals, representing about 45 percent of all speakers from Costa Mesa, took a different approach when discussing the undocumented in Costa Mesa. Rejecting the expectations of traditional theory and political rhetoric, these speakers implicitly treated the undocumented as a vital part of the community itself, invoking images of immigrants as hard-working, family-oriented residents who have assimilated into the community and have benefited the community. In essence, these individuals asserted that the undocumented were simply like other residents who hoped to get ahead and should be treated just like any other community member. As one Costa Mesa resident explained:

I spent twenty-six years in the air force; I went to Vietnam twice. I only say that because right now, a lot of undocumented immigrants fought with me in Vietnam and are fighting in Iraq today. And, you know, they only get their citizenship if they come home in a body bag. The regular people that had put in for residency and citizenship are waiting five to thirteen years to get their papers. Every good

> Latino that comes here has an objective in mind to take care of his or her family. Jobs. (December 6, 2005)

Other speakers took the presence of immigrant workers in U.S. communities as being inevitable—and not harmful. Such speakers suggested that the undocumented arrived in the United States to meet national labor needs. As one city council member observed:

> [W]e have people working here cooking, and doing the lawns, watching the children, and working in our factories, and people wouldn't be coming here if those jobs weren't available—if people weren't hiring them. (December 6, 2005)

As such, the undocumented were considered an inexorable part of the community in which they worked and lived. They were productive members of the community and were no more criminal than anyone else.

Many opponents of the proposal argued that immigrants were not only inexorably tied to the community but that they also helped to promote family-oriented values. As one Costa Mesa resident noted:

> Mr. Mayor, council members, Senator Foley, I would just like to relate something that happened yesterday, and it touched me. Yesterday, one of my customers who is a Costa Mesa business owner, a father, a husband, suggested he was thinking of moving his family to Mexico. I said, "What the heck are you thinking?" He told me that his wife no longer felt safe here, because she is an undocumented person. Her joys of living here, providing her children a healthy, safe home, education, the opportunity of worthwhile careers, this quality environment to raise their family is now in question. Is this mother just another victim of bigotry or ethnic cleansing? Will this gentle woman live in fear, hiding in her home so her children will have the opportunities? Will she have the strength to stay here with a broken heart? I felt so bad for her that I had to come here tonight and ask, what for and why? What devil amongst us has stolen the soul of Costa Mesa? Who of this council are responsible for tearing this city's heart out? And will this failure to respect every person as an equal member of one human family become the tragedy trophy of Costa Mesa? (October 3, 2006)

The implication of this prosocial construction of the undocumented for opponents of the ICE Proposal was that any effort to permit law enforcement to target such constructive residents would not only undermine the community's value system, but it would also inhibit the ability of police officers to gain the trust of the entire community, a point many speakers voiced. As a Costa Mesa resident explained,

> And I'm just concerned that without a proper education program, [unclear] getting out into the community, if this passes tonight, that this is the perception that's going to be taken up by the community. . . . Because right now, we have a community of citizens, non-citizens and the police; we're on the same side, I think, against the bad guys. And if you do this without the proper education, it'll either polarize the whole community—the citizens and the police on one side, and the non-citizens and the bad guys on the other. (December 6, 2005)

Still other speakers suggested that by being tasked with enforcing immigration priorities, Costa Mesa police would necessarily turn their attention and efforts from curbing "real" crime. A Costa Mesa resident made exactly this point:

> I believe the proposal before you tonight will waste time, waste money, will alter and undermine the priorities of the Costa Mesa police force, and possibly abridge the rights of citizens—my rights and your rights. . . . How much time would be spent in discovering immigration status? Time taken away from officers [unclear] on patrol to protect us, and spent completing paperwork. (December 6, 2005)

In essence, opponents of the measure relied on two arguments to assert that the ICE Proposal would improperly divide residents of Costa Mesa and, ultimately, harm the city. They argued that the proposal would create fear and distrust among residents, thus undermining the capacity of the community to fight crime; they also suggested the proposal would promote distrust of the city's police force, thus undermining community cohesion. These two arguments are nicely summarized in one Costa Mesa resident's statement:

> I think that if I believed that this would actually help law enforcement solve crime, I might believe that this was a good idea. But I haven't heard anything that convinces me that being part of ICE is going to help our police officers solve violent crimes in our community. . . . This proposal is bad fiscally; it's bad philosophically; it's bad for crime prevention; it's bad for community cohesion; and it's bad for the quality of life in the city of Costa Mesa. (December 6, 2005)

Police Action Is Appropriate If the Undocumented Commit Dangerous Crimes

Slightly more than 35 percent of the speakers from Costa Mesa supported the ICE Proposal but did not directly dispute the arguments made by opponents. These supporters legitimized their support in terms of criminality and risk to the community but they equated criminality with harmful criminal acts—not the mere presence of immigrants. Moreover, many of these speakers treated all immigrants, including the undocumented, as part of the class of residents who needed protection from crime.

For instance, the city council members who introduced the proposal consistently denied that they intended to push all undocumented persons out of Costa Mesa, claiming instead that they were focusing their attention on persons who were both unauthorized in legal status *and* represented some criminal threat to the city. As the mayor stated on the night the ICE Proposal was first raised:

> Council Member [name] has suggested, that the—he's pointed out clearly the focus is going to be on aggravated felonies, criminal street gang activity, violent crime. That's going to be the target. . . . The concern I have is that this is being spun the wrong way intentionally. This is not about punishing immigrants, legal or illegal. This is about focusing on major crimes. (December 6, 2005)

While statements such as this do nothing to deny the illegality of undocumented presence, they do shift the focus to the danger of common law crimes like "aggravated felonies, criminal street gang activity, violent crime." This focus on specific, common law harms was made even more explicitly by another council member. He placed the proposal not in the context of the danger presented by immigrants living in the United States without legal status but rather in the context of protecting children from street gang activity:

> Again, we're looking at aggravated felonies, we're looking at street gang activity, we're looking at some pretty nasty stuff: street gang activity. I've got six kids. Some gang banger, or older gang banger comes and beats up on one of my kids, not only do I want to personally wring his neck, string him up, and shoot him myself, but I want him prosecuted, any way and every way. And if he's illegal, and he can be deported, so much the better. If he's not illegal and he's legal, throw him in jail for as long as possible. But I'm very protective of my kids. And anyone who's here legally or illegally, I expect them to

> be just as protective of their kids. And to work just as hard to make a better life for their kids. What my proposal's talking about is strictly crime related. (December 6, 2005)

The council member here distinguishes between immigrants living noncriminal lives in the community and the criminals being targeted by the proposal. Criminals were people who threatened the city's youth: gang bangers and aggravated felons. By contrast, immigrants—legal and illegal—were like all other residents with families who needed to protect their kids. The mayor made this same distinction, identifying the undocumented as part of the class of persons who would benefit from the increased community safety generated by the proposal. In this sense, he treated them as de facto residents of Costa Mesa:

> Again, I'm asking that everyone unites against violent crime. That's what we're all here to focus on this evening. That's the issue that's before us. No matter where you're from, the issue tonight is solving violent crime, and making the community safer for everyone, including those that are here illegally. (December 6, 2005)

Residents from Costa Mesa who spoke at the council meetings reiterated these same themes. The real "law and order" issue was protecting the community, not keeping immigrants out. As one Costa Mesa resident declared, "[i]f you don't want to be deported, don't commit crime in Costa Mesa" (December 6, 2005). Statements such as these clearly distinguish between the illegality of criminal behavior and the legal status of undocumented residents. And it was criminal behavior that worried these speakers, not a class of persons whose presence was illicit. One Costa Mesa resident was blunt in her fears of gang violence and in her belief that implementing the ICE Proposal would reduce the risk of such violence in Costa Mesa. Yet she was also quick to point out that minor legal infractions were not a basis for removing people from the community, thus implicitly acknowledging that many undocumented persons had de facto claims to residential membership in the community:

> That's what I thought this was about, a crime issue. That's what I read in the papers. I don't know if I'm mistaken, but I thought this was about criminals, that do crimes, dangerous crimes. . . . I'm thinking about my family and myself. Now, we're not talking about somebody, who in the privacy of their own house, tore the tag off of their mattress, that ICE is going to storm down their door and drag them off

> somewhere. I think that's what the delusional people in this room is. They're mixing up things. Either you are for crime, and you want to aid that criminals, dangerous, murderers, rapists, people that'll take out a gun and cap you. We all know the gang mentality. I don't know anybody in a gang. I don't want to know anybody in a gang. I don't want to meet up with anybody in a gang. I don't want to be capped. (December 6, 2005)

Some residents took this logic one step further, reinforcing the themes introduced by the city council members. Rather than simply distinguishing between status violations and common law crime in making assertions about criminals, these residents explicitly equated undocumented immigrants with all other Costa Mesa residents. They suggested that the undocumented are no different from anyone else who lives in the community and wants a better life and are just as needy of protection against crime. This logic was voiced most explicitly by one Costa Mesa resident on the day that the ICE Proposal was introduced:

> This is America—a wonderful country where all people, citizens, non-citizens, can discuss any subject. Or should be able to discuss any subject, without fear. I can't fault anyone for wanting to live in the United States. It must be a credit to our system that someone would want to leave their homeland and get here, legally or illegally. I believe all people in our community, be they immigrant, law-abiding illegal immigrant, citizen, or non-citizen would want to rid their community of criminals. If I read this recommendation correctly, this is about criminals: bad guys. This is a public safety issue. (December 6, 2005)

This resident utilized the category of "law-abiding illegal immigrant" to place most undocumented persons inside the ambit of legality. Criminals—the legitimate target of police intervention—are the "bad guys," not the undocumented. They are part of the community and should be protected (and not targeted) by "law and order" efforts, just like all other residents.

CONCLUSION: THE POLITICAL TOLERATION OF IMMIGRANTS AND THE REWORKING OF CRIMINOLOGICAL THEORY

We began this chapter by pointing to a paradox: the long-standing willingness of many to equate immigrants with danger and criminality despite the lack of empirical evidence supporting this link. We propose here that based upon recent research and findings from our case study, this divergence between sociopolitical discourse and empirical reality arises in part from the very strategies immigrant groups have used to successfully navigate life in the United States and keep crime rates low. Recent studies on immigration and crime demonstrate that many immigrant communities have developed social and economic strategies that promote an unexpected degree of intra-group cohesion and economic engagement and, thus, help to reduce criminal activity. While these low crime rates might logically suggest acceptance within the larger community, immigrant neighborhoods in the United States have often developed in relatively segregated portions of larger cities, consistent with the social theory we discussed earlier. In other words, immigrants often live and work in places that make it difficult for them to participate in regularized, sociopolitical activity in the larger community. Our case study indicates, however, that it is the very visibility of immigrants within the normal, political life of that community that may reduce public fear and increase a political toleration of the immigrant presence. In the remainder of this chapter, we briefly reiterate the findings of our case study and discuss the implications of our findings for recent theoretical developments in the field.

In the 2005–2006 time frame, the City of Costa Mesa debated the propriety of using local police officers to help remove undocumented immigrants from the community. Interestingly, while not directly referenced in the debate, the proposed policy was consistent with long-standing social theory on the immigration-crime link. It was not, however, consistent with the empirical evidence regarding the low levels of criminal risk actually posed by immigrants. Yet most supporters of this proposal seemed to accept the fact that (undocumented) immigrants were not inherently dangerous and refused to equate them with the criminal risk to be abated. In fact, as our analysis demonstrates, more than 80 percent of the speakers from Costa Mesa seemed to rely on two shared assumptions about the factors justifying (or not) local police action against immigrants: (1) police use of invasive authority and force is justified—and delimited—by actual threats of harm to the community and its members; and (2) immigrants—usually including the undocumented—are a de facto part of the community, are not inherently harmful, and also deserve protection from crime.

First, the majority of speakers framed their arguments about the intervention of the police, pro and con, in terms of the welfare and safety of the community. This suggests that residents understood law in terms of the health of the community and the legitimacy of police action in terms of the protection of that community. Considerations of law and order, while rhetorically highlighted, became subsumed under the issue of potential dangers to the community. The danger that was most relevant for legitimating police action was the potential of violent crimes. Police authority was about stopping bad guys and hard-core criminals. These are all acts that threaten violence against community residents and the speakers who invoked such images argued that these acts justify invoking police authority and action.

Second, there appeared to be fairly widespread—though not universal—belief that the presence of persons tainted by illegality, by itself, is generally not the type of community harm that justifies invasive police action in the community. This can be seen most clearly in those statements in which speakers first stated that it is improper and illegal for persons to enter the country without proper documentation but then went on to discuss the real threat to the community: dangerous criminal acts. These criminal acts are the ones that necessitate governmental protection and police action.

These shared assumptions suggest that, while far from a universal viewpoint, most people living in Costa Mesa (who cared enough to speak about the issue) recognized the reality of a reasonably settled immigrant community there and were politically unwilling to directly attack that community. This reluctance is best seen in the statements of the two council members who put forward the proposal and hoped to find public support for it. They justified the proposal by saying that it would help remove dangerous immigrants from the community, but they also consistently acknowledged the existence of law-abiding undocumented immigrants who were not dangerous and thus would not be targeted. Immigrants in Costa Mesa had demonstrated a willingness to work with local organizations and with law enforcement to stop the kinds of crimes that most residents considered dangerous. Immigrants were visible to other members of the community and identified by speakers as family-oriented and hardworking. While some residents may have preferred not to have immigrants present in the community, most residents of Costa Mesa seemed to tolerate, or even embrace, the presence of immigrants.

Circling back to the divergence we raised earlier in the chapter and again at the start of our conclusion, the implication here is that empirics on a statistical level may not be particularly salient for residents of communities or for local politics. The rhetoric used in Costa Mesa suggests that what mattered to most residents was the need to protect against true harm. If, as in the case of Costa Mesa, immigrants are generally visible as community members who work, who are part of families, and who cooperate with law enforcement to stop criminal activity, then it becomes problematic to truly demonize them. To residents of Costa Mesa, the issue of immigration, per se, was less important than a sense of community cohesion and safety, and most residents simply did not feel threatened by their immigrant neighbors. In other words, on a policy level, what matters is not just a lack of crime among most immigrants but that immigrants are visible as prosocial and familiar (i.e., living a largely Anglo-American lifestyle) members of the political public.

The findings of this study, oddly enough, both buttress new theoretical insights on the immigration-crime relationship and also suggest some important limits to these insights. In recent years, scholars have begun to challenge claims made in early iterations of social disorganization theory that immigration leads to heightened crime rates because it causes residential turnover and racial/ethnic heterogeneity, weakens social ties, and decreases informal social control in communities. These scholars argue instead that immigration can, in fact, revitalize an area and strengthen informal social control. Lee and Martinez (2002, 376), for example, suggest that "contemporary immigration may encourage new forms of social organization that mediate the potentially crime-producing effects of the deleterious social and economic conditions found in urban neighborhoods. These new forms of social organization may include ethnically situated informal mechanisms of social control and enclave economies that provide stable jobs to co-ethnics." Frequently referred to as the immigration revitalization thesis, this argument emphasizes that far from being a criminogenic force, immigration is an essential ingredient to the continued viability of urban areas, especially those that have experienced population decline and deindustrialization in previous decades (Lee, Martinez, and Rosenfeld 2001, 564).

Along similar lines, other researchers argue that larger immigrant populations in metropolitan areas may invigorate local communities leading to redevelopment of the stagnating economies of the urban core of metropolitan areas (Reid et al. 2005, 762). The causal process by which immigration could lessen crime, it is suggested, is via job growth, both for immigrants and the native-born, business development in previously economically depressed areas, and the repopulation of the urban core. A case in point is found in Portes and Stepick (1993), who discovered that rather than create disorganization in communities, immigration stabilized and revitalized Miami's economic and cultural institutions—due in large part to strong familial and neighborhood institutions and enhanced job opportunities associated with ethnic enclave economies.

These theoretical developments, in contrast to earlier criminological theory, identify causal mechanisms that reduce crime rates in immigrant communities. But only the latter theory suggests that the benefits of lower crime can accrue to the larger urban area of which an immigrant community is a part. In the former case, the benefits of social stability and low crime are likely reserved for immigrants themselves. As Portes and Rumbaut (2006, 41) have pointed out, settlement patterns for contemporary labor migrants are strongly determined by the preexisting presence of "kin and friends who can provide assistance." Newly arrived immigrants tend to congregate in ethnic enclaves where they have family and friends and can more easily find work and a place to live. This neighborhood, in essence, develops largely out of sight of other residents of the broader community.

In Costa Mesa, the residential patterns for immigrants had extended well beyond an ethnic enclave. And, consistent with certain tenants of newer social theory, most speakers identified the immigrant community as noncriminal. But it seemed to be the very visibility of the immigrants in the community as prosocial persons that led to this belief, not any particular empirical findings. Significantly, this level of integration is not universal within the United States, even if low crime rates seem to be. It is therefore the actual social ecology of a community that largely shapes the local political rhetoric about immigration and crime, less so empirical crime rates. This social ecology needs to be fully recognized in the literature.

NOTES

1. The very recent efforts of states such as California and cities such as New York, Chicago, and Los Angeles to resist, for example, efforts to deport undocumented persons in light of the recent presidential election are notable examples (Medina 2016; Medina and Bidgood 2016; Reston 2017). Of course, political efforts to assist immigrants are not new; many date back to the 1980s and even earlier (see, e.g., Brettell 2010; Coutin 2003; Horton 1995; Mitnick and Halpern-Finnerty 2010). These efforts often began as largely subversive political efforts by immigrants themselves to gain social and political recognition (Coutin 2003; Horton 1995) or as efforts by local leaders who recognized the value of immigrant labor to help immigrants (and the community) adjust to life in the United States (Brettel 2010).

2. ICE is Immigration and Customs Enforcement, the immigration enforcement division of the U.S. Department of Homeland Security. As such, it is the federal entity that is charged with removing "undesirable aliens" from the United States.

3. This claim was made by a local newspaper, the *Daily Pilot*, in April 2009.

4. The City of Costa Mesa recorded almost all of its city council meetings since late 2005 and made them publicly available at http://www.costamesaca.gov/index.aspx?page=1958. The first author created transcriptions from these recordings for analysis. No names or key identifying information of the participants are included in the transcriptions other than the city in which the speaker resided, which was information provided by every speaker at the beginning of his or her comments.

REFERENCES

Akins, S., R. G. Rumbaut, and R.Stansfield. 2009. Immigration, economic disadvantage, and homicide: A community-level analysis of Austin, Texas. *Homicide Studies* 13: 307–314.

Anderson, E. 1999. *Code of the Street: Decency, Violence, and the Moral Life of the Inner City*. New York: W. W. Norton.

Bankston, C. L. III. 1998. Youth gangs and the new second generation: A review essay. *Aggression and Violent Behavior* 3: 35–45.

Bean, F. D., L. B. Lowell, and L. J. Taylor. 1988. Undocumented Mexican immigrants and the earnings of other workers in the United States. *Demography* 25 (1): 35–52.

Beck, R. 1996. *The Case against Immigration.* New York: W. W. Norton.

Bersani, B E. 2014. An examination of first and second generation immigrant offending trajectories. *Justice Quarterly* 31 (2): 315–343.

Blau, P. M., and J. E. Schwartz. 1984. *Crosscutting Social Circles.* Orlando, FL: Academic.

Bourgois, P. 2003. *In Search of Respect: Selling Crack in El Barrio.* Cambridge: Cambridge University Press.

Brettell, C. B. 2010. "Big D": Incorporating new immigrants in a sunbelt suburban metropolis. In *Twenty-First-Century Gateways: Immigrant Incorporation in Suburban America,* edited by A. Singer, S. W. Hardwick, and C. B. Brettell. Washington, DC: Brookings Institution Press.

Butcher, K. F., and A. Morrison Piehl. 1998a. Recent immigrants: Unexpected implications for crime and incarceration. *Industrial and Labor Relations Review* 51: 654–679.

———. 1998b. Cross-city evidence on the relationship between immigration and crime. *Journal of Policy Analysis and Management* 17: 457–493.

Chavez, J. M., and E. Griffiths. 2009. Neighborhood dynamics of urban violence: understanding the immigration connection. *Homicide Studies* 13: 261–273.

Chavez, L. R. 2001. *Covering Immigration: Popular Images and the Politics of the Nation.* Berkeley, CA: University of California Press.

———. 2008. *The Latino Threat: Constructing Immigrants, Citizens, and the Nation.* Stanford, CA. Stanford University Press.

Coutin, S. 2003. *Legalizing Moves: Salvadoran Immigrants' Struggle for U.S. Residency.* Ann Arbor: University of Michigan Press.

Danielson, M. S. 2010. All immigration politics is local: The day labor ordinance in Vista, California. In *Taking Local Control: Immigration Policy Activism in U.S. Cities and States,* edited by M. W. Varsanyi. Stanford, CA: Stanford University Press.

Department of Homeland Security. 2015. *DHS Releases End of Fiscal Year 2015 Statistics.* Available at https://www.dhs.gov/news/2015/12/22/dhs-releases-end-fiscal-year-2015-statistics.

Desmond, S. A., and C. E. Kubrin. 2009. The power of place: Immigrant communities and adolescent violence. *The Sociological Quarterly* 50 (4): 581–607.

Eagly, I. V. 2010. Prosecuting immigration. *Northwestern University Law Review* 104 (4): 1281–1359.

Espenshade, J., B. Wright, P. Cortopassi, A. Reed, and J. Flores. 2010. The "Law-and-Order" foundation of local ordinances: A four-locale study of Hazelton, PA, Escondido, CA, Farmers Branch, TX, and Prince William County, VA. In *Taking Local Control: Immigration Policy Activism in U.S. Cities and States,* edited by M. W. Varsanyi. Stanford, CA: Stanford University Press.

Feldmeyer, B., and D. Steffensmeier. 2009. Immigration effects on homicide offending for total and race/ethnicity-disaggregated populations (white, black, and Latino). *Homicide Studies* 13 (3): 211–226.

Fleury-Steiner, B., and J. Longazel. 2010. Neoliberalism, community development, and anti-immigrant backlash in Hazelton, Pennsylvania. In *Taking Local Control: Immigration Policy Activism in U.S. Cities and States,* edited by M. W. Varsanyi. Stanford, CA: Stanford University Press.

Gans, H. 1968. The balanced community: Homogeneity or heterogeneity in residential areas? In *People and Plans: Essays on Urban Problems and Solutions*. New York: Basic Books.

Gilbert, L. 2009. Immigration as local politics: Re-bordering immigration and multiculturalism through deterrence and incapacitation. *International Journal of Urban and Regional Research* 33 (1): 26–42.

Glaser, M. A., L. E. Parker, and H. Li. 2003. Community of choice or ghetto of last resort: Community development and the viability of an African American community. *The Review of Policy Research* 20 (3): 525–548.

Graif, C., and R. J. Sampson. 2009. Spatial heterogeneity in the effects of immigration and diversity on neighborhood homicide rates. *Homicide Studies* 13 (3): 242–260.

Hagan, J., and A. Palloni. 1999. Sociological criminology and the mythology of Hispanic immigration and crime. *Social Problems* 46 (4): 617–632.

Hopkins. D. J. 2010. Politicized places: Explaining where and when immigrants provoke local opposition. *American Political Science Review* 104 (1): 40–60.

Horton, J. 1995. *The Politics of Diversity: Immigration, Resistance, and Change in Monterey Park, California*. Philadelphia: Temple University Press.

Kanstroom, D. 2010. *Deportation Nation: Outsiders in American History*. Boston: Harvard University Press.

Khashu, A. 2009. The role of local police: Striking a balance between immigration enforcement and civil liberties. Washington, DC: Police Foundation. Available at https://www.policefoundation.org/wp-content/uploads/2015/07/Khashu-2009-The-Role-of-Local-Police.pdf.

Koulish, R. 2010. *Immigration and American Democracy: Subverting the Rule of Law*. New York: Routledge.

Kubrin, C. E. 2000. Racial heterogeneity and crime: Measuring static and dynamic effects. *Research in Community Sociology* 10: 189–219.

———. 2013. Immigration and crime. In *Oxford Handbook of Criminological Theory*, edited by F. T. Cullen and P. Wilcox. New York: Oxford University Press.

Kubrin, C. E., and H. Ishizawa. 2012. Why some immigrant neighborhoods are safer than others: Divergent findings from Los Angeles and Chicago. *The Annals of the American Academy of Political and Social Science* 641 (1): 148–173.

Johnson, K. R. 2009. The intersection of race and class in U.S. immigration law and enforcement. *Law and Contemporary Problems* 72 (4): 1–36.

Lee, M. T., and R. Martinez. 2002. Social disorganization revisited: Mapping the recent immigration and black homicide relationship in northern Miami. *Sociological Focus* 35 (4): 363–380.

Lee, M. T., R. Martinez, Jr., and R. Rosenfeld. 2001. Does immigration increase homicide? Negative evidence from three border cities. *Sociological Quarterly* 42 (4): 559–580.

Longazel, J. G. 2014. Rhetorical barriers to mobilizing for immigrant rights: White innocence and Latina/o abstraction. *Law & Social Inquiry* 39 (3): 580–600.

MacDonald, J., and J. Saunders. 2012. Are immigrant youth less violent? Specifying the reasons and mechanisms. *Annals of the American Academy of Political and Social Science* 641 (1): 125–147.

MacDonald, J. M., J. R. Hipp, and C. Gill. 2013. The effects of immigrant concentration on changes in neighborhood crime rates. *Journal of Quantitative Criminology* 29 (2): 191–215.

Martinez, R. 2000. Immigration and urban violence: The link between immigrant Latinos and types of homicide. *Social Science Quarterly* 81 (1): 363–374.

Martinez, R. 2002. *Latino Homicide: Immigration, Violence and Community.* New York: Routledge.

Martinez, R., and M. T. Lee. 2000. On immigration and crime. *Criminal Justice 2000: The Nature of Crime: Continuity and Change,* vol. 1, 485–524. Washington, DC: U.S. Department of Justice.

Martinez, R., M. T. Lee, and A. L. Nielsen. 2004. Segmented assimilation, local context and determinants of drug violence in Miami and San Diego: Do ethnicity and immigration matter? *International Migration Review* 38 (1): 131–57.

Martinez, R., J. I. Stowell, and J. M. Cancino. 2008. A tale of two border cities: Community context, ethnicity, and homicide. *Social Science Quarterly* 89 (1): 1–16.

Martinez, R., J. Stowell, and M. T. Lee. 2010. Immigration and crime in an era of transformation: A longitudinal analysis of homicides in San Diego neighborhoods, 1980–2000. *Criminology* 48 (3): 797–829.

McCord, J. 1995. Ethnicity, acculturation, and opportunities: A study of two generations. In *Ethnicity, Race, and Crime,* edited by Darnell F. Hawkins. Albany: State University of New York Press.

Mears, D. P. 2002. Immigration and crime: What's the connection? *Federal Sentencing Reporter* 14 (5): 284–288.

Medina, J. 2016. California weighs protections for immigrants threatened by Trump policies. *New York Times,* December 4, U.S. Section. Available at https://www.nytimes.com/2016/12/04/us/california-to-consider-laws-to-protect-immigrants-from-trump-policies.html?_r=0.

Medina, J., and J. Bidgood. 2016. Cities vow to fight Trump on immigration, even if they lose millions. *New York Times,* November 27, U.S. Section. Available at https://www.nytimes.com/2016/11/27/us/cities-vow-to-fight-trump-on-immigration-even-if-they-lose-millions.html?action=click&contentCollection=U.S.&module=RelatedCoverage®ion=Marginalia&pgtype=article.

Mitnick, P. A., and J. Halpern-Finnerty. 2010. Immigration and local governments: Inclusionary local policies in the era of state rescaling. *Taking Local Control: Immigration Policy Activism in U.S. Cities and States,* edited by M. W. Varsanyi. Stanford, CA: Stanford University Press.

Nielsen, A. L., M. T. Lee, and R. Martinez. 2005. Integrating race, place and motive in social disorganization theory: Lessons from a comparison of black and Latino homicide types in two immigrant destination cities. *Criminology* 43 (3): 837–872.

Nielsen, A. L., and R. Martinez. 2009. The role of immigration for violent deaths. *Homicide Studies* 13 (3): 274–287.

Ousey, G. C., and C. E. Kubrin. 2009. Exploring the connection between immigration and crime rates in U.S. cities, 1980–2000. *Social Problems* 56: 447–473.

———. 2018. Immigration and crime: Assessing a contentious issue. *Annual Review of Criminology* 1: 63–84.

Polczynski Olson, C., M. K. Laurikkala, L. Huff-Corzine, and J. Corzine. 2009. Immigration and violent crime: Citizenship status and social disorganization. *Homicide Studies* 13 (3): 227–241.

Portes, A., and R. G. Rumbaut. 2006. *Immigrant America: A Portrait.* Berkeley, CA: University of California Press.

Portes, A., and A. Stepick. 1993. *City on the Edge: The Transformation of Miami.* Berkeley, CA: University of California Press.

Provine, M., M. W. Varsanyi, P. G. Lewis, and S. H. Decker. 2016. *Policing Immigrants: Local Law Enforcement on the Front Lines.* Chicago: University of Chicago Press.

Reid, L. W., H. E. Weiss, R. M. Adelman, and C. Jaret. 2005. The immigration-crime relationship: Evidence across US metropolitan areas. *Social Science Research* 34 (4): 757–780.

Reston, M. 2017. Big city mayors confident they'll remain sanctuaries. CNN, January 17. Available at http://www.cnn.com/2017/01/26/politics/donald-trump-sanctuary-cities/index.html.

Romero, M. 2006. Racial profiling and immigration law enforcement: Rounding up of usual suspects in the Latino community. *Critical Sociology* 32: 2–3.

Rumbaut, R. G., and W. A. Ewing. 2007. *The Myth of Immigrant Criminality and the Paradox of Assimilation: Incarceration Rates among Native and Foreign-Born Men.* Washington, DC: Immigration Policy Center, American Immigration Law Foundation.

Rumbaut, R. G., R. G. Gonzales, G. Komaie, C. V. Morgan, and R. Tafoya-Estrada. 2006. Immigration and incarceration: Patterns and predictors of imprisonment among first- and second-generation young adults. In *Immigration and Crime: Race, Ethnicity, and Violence*, edited by R. Martinez and A. Valenzuela. New York: New York University Press.

Sampson, R. J., J. D. Morenoff, and S. Raudenbush. 2005. Social anatomy of racial and ethnic disparities in violence. *American Journal of Public Health* 95 (2): 224–232.

Santa Ana, O. 2002. *Brown Tide Rising: Metaphors of Latinos in Contemporary American Public Discourse.* Austin: University of Texas Press.

Schrag, P. 2010. *Not Fit for Our Society: Immigration and Nativism in America.* Berkeley, CA: University of California Press.

Shaw, C. R., and H. D. McKay. [1942] 1969. *Juvenile Delinquency and Urban Areas.* Chicago: University of Chicago Press.

Stowell, J. I., and R. Martinez. 2007. Displaced, dispossessed, or lawless? Examining the link between ethnicity, immigration, and violence. *Journal of Aggression and Violent Behavior* 5 (12): 564–581.

———. 2009. Incorporating ethnic-specific measures of immigration in the study of lethal violence. *Homicide Studies* 13 (3): 315–324.

Stowell, J. I., S. F. Messner, K. F. McGeever, and L. E. Raffalovich. 2009. Immigration and the recent violent crime drop in the United States: A pooled, cross-sectional time-series analysis of metropolitan areas. *Criminology* 47 (3): 889–928.

Stumpf, J. 2006. The crimmigration crisis: Immigrants, crime, and sovereign power. *American University Law Review* 56 (2): 367–419.

Thomas, W. I., and F. Znaniecki. [1920] 1984. *The Polish Peasant in Europe and America: Edited and Abridged.* Chicago: University of Illinois Press.

Tonry, M. 1997. Ethnicity, crime, and immigration. *Crime & Justice* 21: 1–29.

Velez, M. B. 2009. Contextualizing the immigration and crime effect: An analysis of homicide in Chicago neighborhoods. *Homicide Studies* 13 (3): 325–335.

Wadsworth, T. 2010. Is immigration responsible for the crime drop? An assessment of the influence of immigration on changes in violent crime between 1990 and 2000. *Social Science Quarterly* 91 (2): 531–553.

Waldinger, R. 1997. Black/immigrant competition re-assessed: New evidence from Los Angeles. *Sociological Perspectives* 40 (3): 365–386.

Warren, R. 2016. US undocumented population drops below 11 million in 2014, with continued declines in the Mexican undocumented population. *Journal of Migration and Human Security* 4 (1): 1–15.

Wilson, W. J. 1996. *When Work Disappears: The World of the New Urban Poor.* New York: Alfred A. Knopf.

9

Mass Shootings

Danielle

A New Name for a Familiar Problem

Grant Duwe

WHAT'S THE THEORY?

Unlike the objectivist approach, which defines social problems in terms of their objective conditions, the social constructionist perspective holds that social problems are the product of "the activities of individuals and groups making assertions of grievances and claims with respect to some putative conditions" (Spector and Kitsuse 1977, 75). Child abuse (Pfohl 1977) and wife beating (Tierney 1982), for example, were identified as new social problems during the latter half of the twentieth century, not because they had become more prevalent but because claims makers were successful in bringing these problems to the public's attention. And the news media are the main vehicle through which social problems are constructed, either by making claims directly (i.e., primary claims making) or, more frequently, by reporting the claims made by others (i.e., secondary claims making).

Constructionist research has observed that the "discovery" of a new crime problem is often triggered by the occurrence of a widely publicized event, or landmark narrative, which ultimately comes to define the essence of the problem (Adler 1996; Chermak 2003; Nichols 1997). Indeed, high-profile crimes have been the catalyst for the emergence of social problems such as youth disturbances (Cohen 1972), crimes against the elderly (Fishman 1978), adolescent drug abuse (Ben-Yehuda 1986), missing children (Best 1987), serial murder (Jenkins 1994), and stalking (Lowney and Best 1995). Due to the extensive media coverage they attract, celebrated crimes provide ample opportunities for claims makers to raise public awareness about the problems these crimes purportedly represent. When claims makers construct a social problem, they usually focus on describing the nature of the problem, how prevalent it is, and what can be done to control it.

In describing the nature of a crime problem, claims makers often use typifying examples to characterize the offender, the victim, and the crime itself (Lowney and Best 1995). Previous research has shown that when claims makers typify crime problems, they depict them as random (Adler 1996; Best 1991, 1999), the victims as innocent (Adler 1996; Best 1987; Kappeler, Blumberg, and Potter 1996), and the offenders as monstrous deviants (Jenkins 1994; Kappeler, Blumberg, and Potter 1996). The typification process, which is ongoing and can sometimes change over time, is central to the construction of a crime problem because it shapes perceptions of the problem, which, in turn, shape the policies promoted to control it.

To illustrate the scope and prevalence of the problem, claims makers often rely on statistics. Larger numbers suggest that a problem is serious and demands attention; as a result, claims makers commonly assert that a problem is an "epidemic" (Chiricos 1996; Jacobs and Henry 1995; Jenkins 1994) or that it is increasing and getting worse (Best 1987, 1991; Nichols 1997). But the incidence and growth estimates are often flawed or greatly exaggerated (Ben-Yehuda 1986; Best 1987; Fishman 1978; McCorkle and Miethe 1998) and can occasionally lead to a "moral panic" (Cohen 1972).[1]

Because problems require solutions, claims makers usually prescribe new legislation or policies that would ostensibly reduce the incidence or severity of the problem. The solutions offered are often based not only on the way claims makers have typified a problem (Loseke 1989) but also on their values and interests. When claims makers are able to establish ownership of a problem, which is to say their claims are accepted and viewed as authoritative (Gusfield 1981), their favored solutions are more likely to be implemented.

THE SOCIAL CONSTRUCTION OF MASS MURDER

Drawing on the social constructionist theoretical perspective,[2] I previously examined how and why mass murder—defined as an incident in which four or more victims are killed within a twenty-four-hour period (Duwe 2007; Fox and Levin 2011)—was identified as a new crime problem (Duwe 2005). When claims makers "discovered" mass murder during the 1980s, the high-profile massacres committed by Richard Speck and Charles Whitman in the summer of 1966 (both of which were referred to as "crimes of the century" at the time they were committed) were seen as the beginning of an unprecedented mass murder wave. Prior to 1966, there was a relative scarcity of well-known mass killings in the United States. But from the summer of 1966 to the mid-1980s when claims makers began making claims about mass murder, there had been a fairly steady flow of well-publicized cases. And the Speck and Whitman massacres provided claims makers with highly visible, familiar, and thus credible landmark narratives to support the claim that the mid-1960s marked the onset of the age of mass murder. Research has shown the mass murder rates during the 1920s and 1930s were nearly as high as they were from the mid-1960s through the 1990s (Duwe 2004).

Even though mass murder was, according to claims makers, a historically new crime that emerged in the mid-1960s, the nearly two-decade delay in the identification of mass murder as a novel crime problem was due to the "discovery" of another crime problem—serial murder. Before the 1980s, the term *mass murder* was widely used as a catchall phrase to refer to all incidents in which a number of persons were killed. But in the mid- to late 1960s, there was a dramatic rise in serial killings, or at least in the number publicized by the media (Jenkins 1994), which later gave rise to the creation of the serial murder concept in the late 1970s. The creation of this concept narrowed the meaning of the term *mass murder*. Although popular use of the new, more limited definition was evident as early as 1984, there was still a tendency, especially early on, to conflate the two types of multiple murders. For claims makers, then, it seemed reasonable to assume that mass murder, like serial murder, had increased dramatically since the mid-1960s.

After mass murder was identified as a new crime, claims makers characterized what kind of problem it was by relying on the most heavily publicized cases as typifying examples (Duwe 2005). Existing research has demonstrated that while virtually all mass murders are newsworthy, familicides and felony-related massacres are among the least newsworthy (Duwe 2000). Familicides most often involve a male head of the household killing his partner (i.e., spouse, ex-spouse, or fiancée), their children, relatives, or some combination of these. Familicides almost invariably take place within the privacy of a residential setting, and the offender commits suicide in about two-thirds of these cases. Felony-related massacres, on the other hand, are mass murders committed in connection with other crimes such as robbery, burglary, gang "turf wars," or contract killings (i.e., mob hits). In contrast to familicides, which are almost always carried out by a lone offender, felony-related massacres are more likely to involve multiple offenders (Duwe 2007).

The most newsworthy mass murders are more likely to involve an offender who uses a gun, especially an assault weapon, to shoot a relatively large number of stranger victims in a public location (Duwe 2000). Such cases have been referred to as mass public shootings (Duwe 2007), which are defined as incidents that occur in the absence of other criminal activity (e.g., robberies, drug deals, gang "turf wars," etc.) in which a gun was used to kill four or more victims at a public location within a twenty-four-hour period (Duwe, Kovandzic, and Moody 2002).

Mass public shootings often dominate the news cycle because they involve, on average, a greater number of killed and injured victims than other mass murders (Duwe 2007), and the "body count" is the strongest predictor of the extent to which mass killings get reported by the news media (Duwe 2000). That mass public shooters are more likely than other mass murderers to kill strangers connotes an indiscriminate selection of victims, which increases their newsworthiness by conveying the impression that anyone could be a victim of a mass killing (Duwe 2000). Further, the audience may be more likely to identify with the victims of mass public shootings, who were simply in the wrong place at the wrong time. Mass public shootings are also, by their very definition, highly visible acts of violence. Because publicly occurring mass murders usually involve people who witnessed and survived the attack, these incidents frequently give the news media the means to "deliver a fascinating firsthand account to the audience, allowing them to vicariously experience the horror of the event" (Duwe 2000, 391). More so than other mass murders, mass public shootings tend to be exceptionally newsworthy because they are "riveting, emotionally evocative incidents" that epitomize "news as theater—a morality play involving pure, innocent victims and offenders who seemingly went 'berserk' in a public setting" (Duwe 2000, 391).

Given the reliance on the highest-profile cases as typifying examples, mass public shootings defined the essence of mass murder when it was socially constructed as a new crime problem during the 1980s and 1990s. Indeed, mass murder was widely seen as a gun control, workplace violence, and school shooting problem, due mainly to the fact that mass public shootings involve individuals who use guns to carry out an attack at a public location, such as a school or the workplace. Because perceptions help shape policy recommendations, proposals to reduce mass murder generally focused on reforming gun laws and school and workplace violence policies (Duwe 2005).

Although mass public shootings were seen as the prototypical mass murder, they are rare within the context of mass murder, which is itself a rare form of violence. For example, more than a thousand mass murders have taken place in the United States since 1976, which amounts to an average of twenty-eight per year. During the same period of time in the United States, there have been, on average, a little more than fourteen thousand homicides annually. As a result, mass murders make up a meager 0.2 percent of all homicides (Duwe 2016). Meanwhile, mass public shootings make up only 12 percent of all mass killings (Duwe 2004, 2007) and a mere 0.0003 percent of all homicides annually. In contrast, familicides and felony-related massacres are more common, accounting for nearly 70 percent of mass murders (Duwe 2007). Yet, because familicides and felony-related massacres are less newsworthy and, thus, much less likely to have been used as typifying examples, proposals to curb the incidence and/or severity of mass murder seldom focused on domestic violence, drug policy, or urban crime.

In calling attention to the newly identified mass murder problem in the late 1980s and early 1990s, claims makers asserted it was on the rise. To their credit, however, they also emphasized how rare it was, which may have tempered the urgency to "do something" about mass murder (Duwe 2005). Still, claims makers tasted some success in constructing mass murder. The growing number of high-profile mass public shootings during the 1980s and 1990s not only led to the creation of policies designed to address school and workplace violence, but it also provided gun control proponents with opportunities to advance their claims about the need for a federal assault weapons ban (Duwe 2005; 2007; Koper and Roth 2001). For example, following a 1989 mass murder committed in Louisville, Kentucky, with an AK-47 rifle, California congressman Pete Stark warned, "There will be more and more mindless mass murders until the President and Congress put controls on the sales of assault weapons" (*Los Angeles Times* 1989, 22). In 1994, gun control activists won a major victory with passage of the federal assault weapons ban (AWB). Ten years later, however, the ban was allowed to expire.

WHAT'S THE PROBLEM?

At the dawn of this century, the mass murder problem had largely faded from prominence. Beginning in the mid-2000s, however, a problem bearing a similar, yet slightly different, name emerged to take its place—mass shootings. As Roeder (2016) demonstrates, the news media's use of the phrase "mass shooting" has increased dramatically over the last ten years. In fact, prior to the 2000s, it had hardly been used at all.

Just as mass public shootings were central to the social construction of mass murder in the 1980s and 1990s, the same is true for the mass shooting problem over the last decade. From the 2007 massacre at Virginia Tech to the 2016 attack at the Pulse nightclub in Orlando, it has been the catastrophic, high-profile mass public shootings, as defined here, that have galvanized the public and epitomized the essence of the mass shooting problem. Whereas mass public shootings were generally referred to as mass murders prior to the 2000s, they have, since the mid-2000s, typically been labeled as mass shootings. The term *mass shooting* is therefore a new name for a familiar problem, as it has largely supplanted *mass murder* as the new crime category under which mass public shootings fall.

Given the importance of mass public shootings to the social construction of both problems, mass shootings have, to a large extent, been typified in much the same way that mass murders were in the 1980s and 1990s. Because the typification process influences perceptions, which, in turn, shape the solutions offered for a problem, we see that—like the mass murder problem—the policy proposals to control mass shootings have continued the focus on reforming gun legislation and school and workplace violence policies. This similarity notwithstanding, there have been several notable ways in which the social construction of the mass shooting problem has differed from its predecessor.

First, in the interests of full disclosure, I have been an active participant in the social construction of the mass shooting problem by writing a few op-eds and giving interviews to the news media, usually after the occurrence of a mass public shooting involving a relatively large number of victims. In these interviews, the questions from the news media have mostly centered around three main themes: (1) What type of problem is it? (2) Is the problem getting worse? and (3) What can be done to control it? Although I have generally refrained from offering solutions about what can be done to reduce the incidence and/or severity of mass shootings, I have made claims relating to the nature and prevalence of the mass shooting problem.

There are three sets of claims, in particular, that are worth noting here. First, in my discussions with reporters, I have attempted to clarify—with arguably little success—the definitional distinction between mass shootings and mass public shootings. As mentioned below, while mass public shooting has a single definition that is fairly specific, *mass shooting* has been a broad, somewhat nebulous term that has been defined in a number of different ways. [3] Second, in describing the nature of the problem, I have emphasized the presence of serious mental illness due the relatively high rate observed among mass public shooters (Duwe 2016), which also highlights a difference in how the mass murder and mass shooting problems have been typified. Although generally absent from the social construction of the mass murder problem, mental health reform has been identified as a strategy to help control mass shootings. Third, in response to questions from reporters about whether the incidence of *mass shootings* has increased, I have maintained that *mass public shootings* have not recently been on the rise.

Second, compared to mass murder, there has been much less unanimity in how mass shootings have been defined. With mass murder, the general consensus was that it comprised incidents in which at least three or four victims were murdered within a brief period of time. Yet, as the phrase "mass shooting" has recently grown in popularity (Roeder 2016), so have the efforts to define it. Within the last five years alone, a number of researchers (Krause and Richardson 2015; Lankford 2013; Schildkraut and Elsass 2016) along with entities such as the Gun Violence Archive, Everytown for Gun Safety, Mass Shooting Tracker, *USA Today*, and *Mother Jones* have each developed their own distinct mass shooting definitions. These definitions vary on the basis of the number of victims shot (fatally or nonfatally), the number of victims killed, the location where the shooting took place, the motive for the shooting, whether the manner in which the victims were shot was random or indiscriminate, and whether the offender is included as one of the victims in the event and he or she committed suicide or was killed by police (i.e., suicide by cop). The main purpose behind these efforts at defining mass shootings, of course, has been the collection of data to document their patterns and, more commonly, their prevalence. The methods used to collect data have also varied, as the Congressional Research Service (Krause and Richardson 2015) and *USA Today* (Overberg, Upton, and Hoyer 2013) used both news reports and the FBI's Supplementary Homicide Reports (SHR) as data sources, while the others relied strictly on news coverage.

Finally, and perhaps not surprisingly, the various array of definitions and data collection methods has yielded wildly different findings about the incidence of mass shootings and the trends in their prevalence. Incidence estimates have run the gamut from the single digits to more than several hundred per year, while the conclusions reached about recent trends in the prevalence of mass shootings have ranged from an increase to no increase at all. The proliferation of definitions and prevalence estimates has given way to, as Fox and Levin (2015) aptly put it, "mass confusion" over the phrase "mass shooting."

This confusion has led to considerable debate and uncertainty over the incidence of mass shootings and whether or not they have been on the rise. In an effort to provide some clarity to this debate, I present data on trends in the prevalence and severity of mass shootings in the United States from 1976 to 2014. Prior attempts at estimating the incidence of mass shootings have generally focused on how many cases occur each year and whether the raw number of incidents has recently been increasing. In doing so, however, these attempts have neglected the impact that trends in the severity (i.e., number of victims killed and/or wounded) of mass shootings may have on perceptions about their prevalence. Moreover, when evaluating trends in mass shootings over time, it is necessary—as it is with other types of crime—to adjust for changes in the size of the U.S. population. Accordingly, the prevalence and severity data shown in the following section are calculated on a per capita basis.

WHAT'S THE ANSWER?

Before presenting the results from the analyses of the mass shooting data, it is important to clarify the operational definitions, sources, and methods used to collect the data. As described above, a mass murder is an incident in which four or more victims are killed—with any type of weapon—within a twenty-four-hour period (Duwe 2007; Fox and Levin 2011). A mass shooting, as defined here, is a mass murder carried out with a firearm; in other words, a mass shooting is any gun-related mass murder regardless of whether it occurred in a residential setting or a public location. A mass shooting would thus include incidents such as the 1890 Wounded Knee Massacre, the 1929 St. Valentine's Day Massacre, and the recent mass murder at the Pulse nightclub in Orlando, Florida. A mass public shooting, meanwhile, is a gun-related mass murder that takes place at a public location in the absence of other criminal activity (e.g., robberies, drug deals, gang "turf wars," etc.), military conflict, or collective violence. While the Pulse nightclub massacre would qualify as a mass public shooting, the Wounded Knee and St. Valentine's Day massacres would not. Mass public shootings can thus be seen not only as a type of mass murder but also as a specific type of mass shooting.

The mass shooting definition used here is relatively straightforward, easy to operationalize, and consistent with the definitions used by Fox and Levin (2015), *USA Today* (Overberg, Upton, and Hoyer 2013), and the Congressional Research Service (Krause and Richardson 2015). It is different, however, from other popular mass shooting definitions such as those developed by the Gun Violence Archive, Mass Shooting Tracker, or *Mother Jones*, although it is worth pointing out the "mass shooting" definition used by *Mother Jones* is very similar to the mass public shooting definition described above.

In defining mass shootings, I did not include other criteria found in these definitions, such as wounded victims or victim selection, for a few reasons. First, even though a reasonable case could be made that mass shootings should include incidents in which, say, four victims were wounded and none were murdered, there is no data source currently available that could comprehensively document these types of cases. Although news coverage is a critical source of data on mass shootings, it has several significant limitations, especially when used as the sole data source, which would be magnified for less severe cases. Moreover, these less severe shootings are not the types of cases that have engendered the recent fear and concern over the mass shooting problem. Second, subjective criteria, such as whether victims were indiscriminately targeted, are problematic from an operational standpoint. As noted in the next section, even a relatively objective criterion such as location (e.g., a residence or a public setting) can be challenging to operationalize.

DATA AND METHODS

The data on mass shootings in the United States come from two main sources: the Federal Bureau of Investigation's Supplementary Homicide Reports (SHR) and news coverage. The SHR contain incident, victim, and offender information on most murders committed in the United States. It did not become a valuable source of homicide data, however, until it underwent a major revision in 1976 (Riedel 1999). Therefore, given that 2014 is the most recent year for which SHR data are available, the time frame for this study covers the 1976–2014 period.

While the SHR is the most comprehensive source of U.S. homicide data, it has several notable limitations. First, because the SHR is a voluntary program involving law enforcement agencies across the country, an estimated 8 percent of all homicides are not reported (Fox 2000). Second, the SHR data frequently contain a number of coding errors (Duwe 2000; Wiersema, Loftin, and McDowall 2000). For example, in a previous study (Duwe 2000), I found cases in the SHR data where victims were coded twice for the same incident, wounded victims were counted as fatal victims, more than one law enforcement agency reported the same homicide, and offenders were counted as victims in murder-suicides. Finally, the SHR does not include important information such as the location where the homicide took place or the number of wounded victims.

Compared to the SHR, news accounts usually provide more detailed information, including the location where the homicide occurred (e.g., private residence, school, workplace, etc.) and whether any victims were injured. Moreover, given that some murders are not reported to the SHR, the use of news reports can help minimize the underreporting problem. Still, using news coverage as the sole source of data on mass shootings (or mass murders in general) has its own limitations, too. Even though the vast majority of mass murders, including mass shootings, are reported by the press, many receive limited, mostly local coverage (Duwe 2000; Overberg, Upton, and Hoyer 2013). Successful identification of mass shootings that have taken place is therefore highly dependent on the news media database being used, the news organizations included within the database, and the search terms used. Indeed, not all cases are described by the news media as mass shootings or mass murder, which is why it is necessary to also use search terms such as *quadruple shooting*, *quintuple homicide*, and so on. Moreover, news coverage is generally less accessible for older incidents occurring farther back in time.

The limitations of relying on a single data source, such as news accounts, to identify mass shootings are apparent when we look at two popular, widely cited sources—*Mother Jones* and the Gun Violence Archive. Relying on SHR data and news accounts as sources of data and using a definition of mass shootings similar to the one used by *Mother Jones,* Duwe (2014) reported that the *Mother Jones* list missed more than 40 percent of the mass shootings occurring from 1982 to 2013 that ostensibly met its definitional requirements. Furthermore, the underreporting problem with the *Mother Jones* list was more severe for the older cases that took place in the 1980s and 1990s. Broadly defining a mass shooting as any incident in which a gun was used to kill *and/or* injure four or more victims, the Gun Violence Archive identified 277 incidents that took place in the United States in 2014, of which fourteen would meet the mass shooting definition used here (i.e., four or more victims killed with a gun in a twenty-four-hour period). In comparison, the data used in this study contain twenty mass shootings that occurred in 2014, which means the Gun Violence Archive missed 30 percent of the cases in which four or more victims were killed with a firearm.[4]

To identify mass shootings that took place in the United States between 1976 and 2014, I relied on a triangulated data collection strategy that has been used in prior research on mass murder (Duwe 2000, 2004, 2007; Duwe, Kovandzic, and Moody 2002; Overberg, Upton, and Hoyer 2013) and mass shootings (Krause and Richardson 2015). More specifically, after using the SHR to identify when and where gun-related mass murders took place, I searched online newspaper databases to collect additional information not included within the SHR, such as the number of injured victims and the specific location where the incident occurred. In doing so, I was able to not only identify cases not reported to the SHR but also to correct errors in the SHR data. I also consulted unpublished mass shooting data sets from Brot (2016) and the Congressional Research Service (2014), which added a handful of cases to our data.

Overall, the mass shooting data set contains 752 incidents that occurred between 1976 and 2014. I further examined the 752 cases to determine which ones met the criteria for classification as a mass public shooting. The main issue in classifying mass public shootings centers on how "public location" is operationalized. Measuring public location somewhat broadly, I considered a public place to be any area outside of a residence, which includes single-family dwellings, duplexes, townhouses, apartments, and so on. There were some mass shootings in which victims were shot in both residential and public settings. In these instances, I considered an incident to have taken place in a public location if at least half of the fatal victims were killed outside of a residence.

Of the 752 mass shootings that occurred in the United States between 1976 and 2014, there were 129 (17 percent) mass public shootings, an average of 3.3 per year. As such, a mass public shooting is not only an infrequent form of mass murder, but it is also a rare type of mass shooting. The most common types of mass shootings were familicides and felony-related massacres, which made up nearly three-fourths of the 752 cases.

As indicated earlier, the incidence and severity trend data are expressed on a per capita basis. Rather than using the conventional rate per 100,000,

I used an annual rate of 100 million in the U.S. population due to the rarity of mass shootings. Further, to better illustrate trends over time, I present the rates in terms of three-year, five-year, and ten-year moving averages.

TRENDS IN THE PREVALENCE AND SEVERITY OF MASS SHOOTINGS

In Table 9.1, I present data on the prevalence and severity of mass shootings during the 1976–2014 period. In addition to depicting the raw number of incidents, victims killed, and victims shot each year, Table 9.1 shows the annual rates per 100 million in the U.S. population. For each prevalence and severity measure, I bolded the highest value and bolded and underlined the lowest value. For example, the smallest annual number of mass shootings (9) was observed twice—once in 1979 and one more time in 1985. The "N" value is bolded and underlined for both years. Conversely, the "N" value of 31 is bolded for 1993, which had more mass shootings than any other year during the 39-year period. Therefore, not surprisingly, 1993 had the highest rate (12.02 per 100 million), whereas 1985 had the lowest rate (3.77 per 100 million). The average mass shooting rate for the 1976–2014 period was 7.27.

When we look at trends in the mass shooting rate over time, we see that the highest rates were generally observed during the 1990s. The highest three-year average (11.24) was from 1991 to 1993, the highest five-year average (9.72) from 1989 to 1993, and the highest ten-year average (8.17) from 1990 to 1999 and 1991 to 2000. On the other hand, the lowest three- and five-year averages were observed during the mid-1980s, whereas the 1996–2005 period had the lowest ten-year average (6.73).

Regarding severity, Table 9.1 shows there were 3,606 victims killed in the 752 mass shootings, an average of 92 per year, while the total number of victims shot was 4,470, an annual average of 115. The average annual rate of victims killed per 100 million over the 1976–2014 period was 34.83, and the average annual rate of total victims shot was 43.00.

The trend data indicate the highest rates of victims killed and shot were generally found in the late 1980s and early 1990s. For example, 1991 had the highest annual rates of victims killed and shot, the 1991–1993 and 1989–1991 periods had the highest three-year average rates of victims killed and shot, the 1989–1993 period had the highest five-year average rates, and the 1984–1993 period had the highest ten-year average rates. Meanwhile, the lowest rates of victims killed and shot were mostly observed during the late 1990s and early 2000s. The 1996–2005 period, for example, had the lowest average ten-year rates of victims killed and shot.

TABLE 9.1. TRENDS IN THE PREVALENCE AND SEVERITY OF MASS SHOOTINGS, 1976–2014

Year	Incidence					Victims Killed					Victims Shot				
	N	Rate	3-Yr	5-Yr	10-Yr	N	Rate	3-Yr	5-Yr	10-Yr	N	Rate	3-Yr	5-Yr	10-Yr
1976	17	7.92				76	35.40				79	36.80			
1977	19	8.78				85	39.29				106	49.00			
1978	10	4.59	7.10			44	20.18	31.62			44	20.18	35.33		
1979	**9**	4.09	5.82			39	17.72	**25.73**			39	17.72	28.97		
1980	23	10.21	6.29	7.12		96	42.60	26.83	31.04		113	50.14	**29.35**	34.77	
1981	17	7.42	7.24	7.02		79	34.48	31.60	30.85		104	45.39	37.75	36.49	
1982	26	11.23	9.62	7.51		131	56.58	44.55	34.31		142	61.33	52.29	38.95	
1983	15	6.41	8.35	7.87		76	32.48	41.18	36.77		83	35.47	47.40	42.01	
1984	18	7.62	8.42	8.58		104	44.04	44.37	42.04		137	58.01	51.61	50.07	
1985	**9**	**3.77**	5.93	7.29	7.20	**37**	**15.50**	30.67	36.61	33.83	**38**	**15.92**	36.47	43.22	39.00
1986	15	6.25	5.88	7.06	7.04	76	31.65	30.40	36.05	33.45	86	35.81	36.58	41.31	38.90
1987	17	6.98	**5.67**	6.21	6.86	134	55.05	34.07	35.74	35.03	153	62.86	38.20	41.61	40.28
1988	14	5.70	6.31	**6.06**	6.97	60	24.41	37.04	34.13	35.45	76	30.92	43.20	40.70	41.36
1989	21	8.46	7.05	6.23	7.40	94	37.87	39.11	32.90	37.47	143	57.61	50.46	40.62	45.35
1990	16	6.43	6.86	6.76	7.03	70	28.15	30.14	35.42	36.02	81	32.57	40.36	43.95	43.59
1991	30	11.90	8.93	7.89	7.47	**150**	**59.48**	41.83	40.99	38.52	187	**74.15**	54.78	51.62	46.47
1992	25	9.80	9.38	8.46	7.33	109	42.73	43.45	38.53	37.14	141	55.28	54.00	50.10	45.86
1993	**31**	**12.02**	**11.24**	**9.72**	7.89	144	55.83	**52.68**	**44.81**	**39.47**	187	72.51	**67.31**	**58.42**	**49.56**
1994	15	5.76	9.19	9.18	7.71	62	23.81	40.79	42.00	37.45	92	35.34	54.37	53.97	47.30
1995	20	7.61	8.46	9.42	8.09	91	34.63	38.09	43.30	39.36	103	39.20	49.01	55.30	49.62
1996	16	6.03	6.47	8.25	8.07	69	26.01	28.15	36.60	38.80	78	29.40	34.65	46.34	48.98
1997	18	6.73	6.79	7.63	8.04	76	28.40	29.68	33.74	36.13	89	33.25	33.95	41.94	46.02
1998	17	6.29	6.35	6.48	8.10	74	27.38	27.26	**28.05**	36.43	110	40.70	34.45	35.58	47.00
1999	25	9.17	7.39	7.17	**8.17**	132	48.41	34.73	32.96	37.48	**190**	69.68	47.88	42.45	48.21

	N	Rate	3-Yr	5-Yr	10-Yr	N	Rate	3-Yr	5-Yr	10-Yr	N	Rate	3-Yr	5-Yr	10-Yr
2000	18	6.40	7.28	6.92	**8.17**	86	30.56	35.45	32.15	37.72	94	33.40	47.92	41.29	48.29
2001	13	4.56	6.71	6.63	7.44	53	18.58	32.51	30.66	33.63	60	21.03	41.37	39.61	42.98
2002	22	7.64	6.20	6.81	7.22	97	33.68	27.61	31.72	32.73	107	37.16	30.53	40.39	41.17
2003	29	9.97	7.39	7.55	7.02	125	42.99	31.75	34.84	31.44	154	52.96	37.05	42.84	39.21
2004	15	5.11	7.57	6.73	6.95	69	23.50	33.39	29.86	31.41	80	27.24	39.12	34.36	38.40
2005	16	5.40	6.83	6.53	**6.73**	76	25.63	30.71	28.87	**30.51**	90	30.35	36.85	**33.75**	**37.52**
2006	22	7.35	5.95	7.09	6.86	103	34.40	27.84	32.04	31.35	112	37.41	31.67	37.02	38.32
2007	19	6.30	6.35	6.82	6.82	116	38.46	32.83	33.00	32.36	151	50.06	39.27	39.61	40.00
2008	26	8.55	7.40	6.54	7.04	119	39.14	37.33	32.23	33.53	147	48.35	45.27	38.68	40.76
2009	24	7.82	7.56	7.08	6.91	132	43.00	40.20	36.13	32.99	181	58.96	52.45	45.03	39.69
2010	17	5.50	7.29	7.10	6.82	82	26.51	36.21	36.30	32.59	101	32.65	46.65	45.48	39.62
2011	24	7.70	7.01	7.17	7.13	115	36.91	35.47	36.80	34.42	152	48.78	46.80	47.76	42.39
2012	20	6.37	6.52	7.19	7.01	122	38.86	34.09	36.88	34.94	195	62.12	47.85	50.17	44.89
2013	24	7.59	7.22	7.00	6.77	112	35.43	37.07	36.14	34.18	132	41.76	50.89	48.85	43.77
2014	20	6.27	6.75	6.69	6.88	91	28.54	34.28	33.25	34.69	113	35.44	46.44	44.15	44.59
Total	752					3,606					4,470	4,470			
Avg.	19.28	7.27	7.20	7.31	7.30	92.46	34.83	34.88	35.08	35.02	114.62	43.00	43.20	43.38	43.30

TRENDS IN THE PREVALENCE AND SEVERITY OF MASS PUBLIC SHOOTINGS

As shown in Table 9.2, 129 mass public shootings—a specific type of mass shooting—occurred between 1976 and 2014, which amounts to an average of a little more than three per year and an annual rate of 1.23 per 100 million. Except for 1979, at least one mass public shooting occurred each year during the 39-year period. As such, 1979 had the lowest annual rate. There were three years (1991, 1999, and 2012) in which seven mass public shootings took place in the United States; with a lower population size, 1991 had the highest annual rate (2.78).

The trend data reveal that three periods (1976–1980, 1985–1989, and 1986–1990) shared the lowest five-year average (0.82). Meanwhile, the 1978–1987 period had the smallest ten-year average (1.07). Similar to mass shootings overall, the highest rates were generally observed during the 1990s. The 1991–1993 period had the highest three-year average (2.22), the 1991–1995 period had the highest five-year average (1.72), and the 1991–2000 period had the highest ten-year average (1.52).

Unlike the severity results for mass shootings overall, the trend data in Table 9.2 suggest that mass public shootings have recently increased in severity. A total of 1,484 victims were shot in the 129 mass public shootings, of whom 826 were killed. Due in no small part to the Aurora and Newtown massacres, 2012 had the largest number of victims killed (67) and shot (136). Although 1987 had the highest rate of victims killed (21.77), 2012 had the highest rate of victims shot (43.32). Table 9.2 indicates the 1991–1993 period had the highest three-year averages for victims killed (12.57) and shot (23.42). The 2008–2012 period, on the other hand, had the highest five-year averages for victims killed (11.22) and shot (21.99). The 2003–2012 period had the highest ten-year average rate of victims killed (10.15), whereas the 2005–2014 period had the highest ten-year average rate for the victims shot (18.11). The lowest five-year averages for victims shot (6.35) and killed (4.19), on the other hand, were found for 1976–1980 period.

CONCLUSION

After the rise and fall of the mass murder problem in the late twentieth century, the mass shooting problem has arisen since the mid-2000s to take its place. Despite the differences in how each one has been socially constructed, both have been fueled by mass public shootings, which are rare within the context of either mass shootings or, more broadly, mass murder. When mass murder was constructed as a new crime problem, the height of claims-making activity was during the late 1980s and early 1990s (Duwe 2007), which

TABLE 9.2. TRENDS IN THE PREVALENCE AND SEVERITY OF MASS PUBLIC SHOOTINGS, 1976–2014

Year	Incidence					Victims Killed					Victims Shot				
	N	Rate	3-Yr	5-Yr	10-Yr	N	Rate	3-Yr	5-Yr	10-Yr	N	Rate	3-Yr	5-Yr	10-Yr
1976	1	0.47				7	3.26				9	4.19			
1977	3	1.39				17	7.86				24	11.09			
1978	1	0.46	0.77			4	1.83	4.32			4	1.83	5.71		
1979	**0**	**0.00**	**0.62**			**0**	**0.00**	**3.23**			**0**	**0.00**	**4.31**		
1980	4	1.78	0.74	**0.82**		18	7.99	3.27	**4.19**		33	14.64	5.49	**6.35**	
1981	3	1.31	1.03	0.99		14	6.11	4.70	4.76		36	15.71	10.12	8.66	
1982	5	2.16	1.75	1.14		22	9.50	7.87	5.09		37	15.98	15.44	9.63	
1983	2	0.85	1.44	1.22		12	5.13	6.91	5.75		14	5.98	12.56	10.46	
1984	5	2.12	1.71	1.64		42	17.78	10.81	9.30		66	27.95	16.64	16.05	
1985	1	0.42	1.13	1.37	1.09	4	1.68	8.20	8.04	6.11	5	2.09	12.01	13.54	**9.95**
1986	1	0.42	0.98	1.19	1.09	14	5.83	8.43	7.98	6.37	20	8.33	12.79	12.07	10.36
1987	3	1.23	0.69	1.01	**1.07**	53	**21.77**	9.76	10.44	7.76	65	26.71	12.38	14.21	11.92
1988	3	1.22	0.96	1.08	1.15	15	6.10	11.24	10.63	8.19	27	10.98	15.34	15.21	12.84
1989	2	0.81	1.09	**0.82**	1.23	13	5.24	11.04	8.12	8.71	56	22.56	20.08	14.13	15.09
1990	1	0.40	0.81	**0.82**	1.09	9	3.62	4.99	8.51	8.28	13	5.23	12.92	14.76	14.15
1991	7	**2.78**	1.33	1.29	1.24	47	18.64	9.16	11.07	9.53	82	32.52	20.10	19.60	15.83
1992	4	1.57	1.58	1.35	1.18	18	7.06	9.77	8.13	9.28	29	11.37	16.37	16.53	15.37
1993	6	2.33	**2.22**	1.58	1.33	31	12.02	**12.57**	9.31	9.97	68	26.37	**23.42**	19.61	17.41
1994	2	0.77	1.55	1.57	1.19	8	3.07	7.38	8.88	8.50	32	12.29	16.68	17.55	15.84
1995	3	1.14	1.41	**1.72**	1.27	14	5.33	6.81	9.22	8.87	18	6.85	15.17	17.88	16.32
1996	2	0.75	0.89	1.31	1.30	10	3.77	4.06	6.25	8.66	14	5.28	8.14	12.43	16.01
1997	3	1.12	1.01	1.22	1.29	12	4.48	4.53	5.73	6.93	21	7.85	6.66	11.73	14.13
1998	3	1.11	0.99	0.98	1.28	13	4.81	4.35	4.29	6.80	48	17.76	10.29	10.00	14.81
1999	7	2.57	1.60	1.34	1.45	52	19.07	9.45	7.49	8.19	104	38.14	21.25	15.17	16.36

Continued

TABLE 9.2. CONTINUED

Year	Incidence					Victims Killed					Victims Shot				
2000	3	1.07	1.58	1.32	**1.52**	17	6.04	9.97	7.63	8.43	18	6.40	20.76	15.08	16.48
2001	3	1.05	1.56	1.38	1.35	12	4.21	9.77	7.72	6.99	19	6.66	17.06	15.36	13.90
2002	1	0.35	0.82	1.23	1.23	4	1.39	3.88	7.10	6.42	9	3.13	5.39	14.42	13.07
2003	4	1.38	0.92	1.28	1.13	20	6.88	4.16	7.52	**5.90**	29	9.97	6.59	12.86	11.43
2004	3	1.02	0.91	0.97	1.16	15	5.11	4.46	4.72	6.11	26	8.85	7.32	7.00	11.09
2005	4	1.35	1.25	1.03	1.18	24	8.09	6.69	5.13	6.38	36	12.14	10.32	8.15	11.62
2006	5	1.67	1.35	1.15	1.27	27	9.02	7.41	6.10	6.91	36	12.02	11.01	9.22	12.29
2007	4	1.33	1.45	1.35	1.29	49	16.25	11.12	9.07	8.09	81	26.85	17.01	13.97	14.19
2008	5	1.64	1.55	1.40	1.34	26	8.55	11.27	9.40	8.46	48	15.79	18.22	15.13	14.00
2009	4	1.30	1.42	1.46	1.22	38	12.38	12.39	10.86	7.79	78	25.41	22.68	18.44	12.72
2010	4	1.29	1.41	1.45	1.24	20	6.47	9.13	10.53	7.83	31	10.02	17.07	18.02	13.08
2011	4	1.28	1.29	1.37	1.26	23	7.38	8.74	10.20	8.15	48	15.40	16.94	18.69	13.96
2012	7	2.23	1.60	1.55	1.45	**67**	21.34	11.73	**11.22**	**10.15**	**136**	**43.32**	22.92	**21.99**	17.98
2013	3	0.95	1.49	1.41	1.41	21	6.64	11.79	10.84	10.12	34	10.76	23.16	20.98	18.06
2014	3	0.94	1.37	1.34	1.40	14	4.39	10.79	9.24	10.05	30	9.41	21.16	17.78	**18.11**
Total	129					826					1,484				
Avg.	3.31	1.23	1.25	1.26	1.26	21.18	7.85	8.00	8.01	8.00	38.05	14.05	14.36	14.36	14.28

coincides with the highest incidence rates observed for mass public shootings since the mid-1970s. Likewise, the mass shooting problem has emerged during a time when the severity of mass public shootings has increased. Recall that the numbers of victims killed and wounded are the strongest predictors of the extent to which a mass killing gets reported by the news media (Duwe 2000). Therefore, even though the per capita prevalence of mass public shootings has not increased over the last ten years, it may nevertheless seem they are now more commonplace due to the recent growth in their severity and the extensive news coverage that accompanies catastrophic mass public shootings.

While this conclusion may help answer the question of why mass shootings have been perceived to be on the rise, it also raises a number of other questions. Why has the severity of mass public shootings increased since the mid-2000s? Why were the highest incidence rates, for both mass shootings and mass public shootings, observed during the late 1980s and early 1990s? Conversely, why were the lowest incidence and severity rates, at least for mass shootings, observed during the late 1990s and early 2000s? Addressing these issues is, to be sure, beyond the scope of this chapter. Yet these questions also signal that there remains much to be learned about mass killings involving the use of firearms.

NOTES

1. It is worth noting, however, that social constructionist research is not synonymous with debunking. Just because crime problems are socially constructed does not mean that claims made about a problem are at odds with the empirical evidence. For example, as noted later in this chapter, claims makers correctly asserted that mass murder was rare when it was constructed as a new crime problem in the 1980s and 1990s.

2. To be more precise, I relied on a contextual constructionist approach, which assumes we can attain a sufficient knowledge of objective conditions. The strict constructionist approach, on the other hand, avoids making any assumptions about the objective conditions of a problem because it is presumed these are unknowable.

3. The confusion arising from the application of the nebulous, overly broad phrase "mass shooting" to incidents that fit the more specific definition of mass public shooting was on full display after the Orlando massacre. In the aftermath of this atrocity, many news organizations labeled it the worst mass shooting in U.S. history. Some segments within social media took umbrage with this assertion, pointing out that there have been more catastrophic massacres in which guns have been used (in terms of the number of victims killed), such as the 1890 Wounded Knee Massacre and the 1921 Tulsa Race Riot.

4. The extent of the underreporting problem for the overall Gun Violence Archive (GVA) data is likely worse than 30 percent. Like our data, the GVA data follow a heavy-tail distribution in which most of the incidents have smaller numbers of victims, while only 5 percent had four or more fatal victims. Previous research has shown that the

number of victims killed has a significant positive effect on the newsworthiness of a homicide (Duwe 2000; Johnstone, Hawkins, and Michener 1994; Wilbanks 1984). What this means is that cases falling in the flat tail of the distribution (i.e., those with four or more fatal victims) are more likely to get reported by the news media than those with fewer fatal (or no fatal) victims, which make up the bulk of the cases in the GVA data set. Therefore, if the GVA data missed 30 percent of the most newsworthy cases, the percentage of missing cases is likely higher for the less severe shootings, either because they received minimal news coverage or were never reported at all.

REFERENCES

Adler, J. S. 1996. The making of a moral panic in 19th-century America: The Boston garroting hysteria. *Deviant Behavior: An Interdisciplinary Journal* 17: 259–278.

Ben-Yehuda, N. 1986. The sociology of moral panics: Toward a new synthesis. *Sociological Quarterly* 27: 495–513.

Best, J. 1987. Rhetoric in claims-making: Constructing the missing children problem. *Social Problems* 34: 101–121.

———. 1991. "Road warriors" on "hair-trigger highways": Cultural resources and the media's construction of the 1987 freeway shooting problem. *Sociological Inquiry* 61: 327–345.

———. 1999. *Random Violence: How We Talk About New Crimes and New Victims.* Los Angeles: University of California Press.

Brot, R. 2016. Unpublished mass shooting data set.

Chermak, S. M. 2003. *Searching for a Demon: The Media Construction of the Militia Movement.* Boston: Northeastern University Press.

Chiricos, T. G. 1996. Moral panic as ideology: Drugs, violence, race and punishment in America. In *Justice with Prejudice: Race and Criminal Justice in America*, edited by Michael J. Lynch and E. Britt Patterson, 19–48. Guilderland, NY: Harrow and Heston.

Cohen, S. 1972. *Folk Devils and Moral Panics.* London: McGibbon and Kee.

Congressional Research Service. 2014. Unpublished mass public shooting data set.

Duwe, G. 2000. Body-count journalism: The presentation of mass murder in the news media. *Homicide Studies* 4: 364–399.

———. 2004. The patterns and prevalence of mass murder in twentieth-century America. *Justice Quarterly* 21: 729–761.

———. 2005. A circle of distortion: The social construction of mass murder in the United States. *Western Criminology Review* 6: 59–78.

———. 2007. *Mass Murder in the United States: A History.* Jefferson, NC: McFarland and Company, Inc.

———. 2014. The truth about mass public shootings. Reason.com, October 28. Available at http://reason.com/archives/2014/10/28/the-truth-about-mass-public-shootings.

———. 2016. The patterns and prevalence of mass public shootings in the United States, 1915–2013. In *Handbook of the Psychology of Mass Shootings*, edited by L. Wilson. New York: Wiley.

Duwe, G., T. Kovandzic, and C. Moody. 2002. The impact of right-to-carry concealed firearms laws on mass public shootings. *Homicide Studies* 6: 271–296.

Fishman, M. 1978. Crime waves as ideology. *Social Problems* 25: 531–543.

Fox, J. A. 2000. Demographics and U.S. homicide. In *The Crime Drop in America*, edited by A. Blumstein and J. Wallman, 288–317. New York: Cambridge University Press.

Fox, J. A., and J. Levin. 2011. *Extreme Killing: Understanding Serial and Mass Murder*. Thousand Oaks, CA: Sage.

———. 2015. Mass confusion concerning mass murder. *Criminologist* 40 (1): 8–11.

Gusfield, J. R. 1981. *The Culture of Public Problems*. Chicago: University of Chicago Press.

Jacobs, J. B., and J. S. Henry. 1995. The social construction of a hate crime epidemic. *Journal of Criminal Law and Criminology* 86: 366–391.

Jenkins, P. 1994. *Using Murder: The Social Construction of Serial Homicide*. Hawthorne, NY: Aldine De Gruyter.

Johnstone, J.W.C., D. F. Hawkins, and A. Michener. 1994. Homicide reporting in Chicago dailies. *Journalism Quarterly* 71: 860–872.

Kappeler, V., M. Blumberg, and G. W. Potter. 1996. *The Mythology of Crime and Criminal Justice*. Prospect Heights, IL: Waveland Press.

Koper, C. S., and J. A. Roth. 2001. The impact of the 1994 Federal Assault Weapon Ban on gun violence outcomes: An assessment of multiple outcome measures and some lessons for policy evaluation. *Journal of Quantitative Criminology* 17: 33–74.

Krause, W. J., and D. J. Richardson. 2015. *Mass Murder with Firearms: Incidents and Victims, 1999–2013*. Washington, DC: Congressional Research Service.

Lankford, A. 2013. *The Myth of Martyrdom: What Really Drives Suicide Bombers, Rampage Shooters, and Other Self-Destructive Killers*. New York: Palgrave Macmillan.

Los Angeles Times. 1989. Louisville mayhem seen spurring gun debate; activists on both sides expect new drive to widen curbs on assault weapons. September 15.

Loseke, D. R. 1989. Violence is "violence" . . . or is it? The social construction of "wife abuse" and public policy. In *Images of Issues: Typifying Contemporary Social Problems*, edited by J. Best, 191–205. New York: Aldine de Gruyter.

Lowney, K. S., and J. Best. 1995. Stalking strangers and lovers: Changing media typifications of a new crime problem. In *Images of Issues: Typifying Contemporary Social Problems*, edited by J. Best, 33–57. New York: Aldine DeGruyter.

McCorkle, R. C., and T. D. Miethe. 1998. The political and organizational response to gangs: An examination of a "moral panic" in Nevada. *Justice Quarterly* 15.

Nichols, L. T. 1997. Social problems as landmark narratives: Bank of Boston, mass media and "money laundering" *Social Problems* 44: 324–341.

Overberg, P., J. Upton, and M. Hoyer. 2013, December 3. USA Today research reveals flaws in mass-killing data. *USA Today*. Available at http://www.usatoday.com/story/news/nation/2013/12/03/fbi-mass-killing-data-inaccurate/3666953/.

Pfohl, S. J. 1977. The "discovery" of child abuse. *Social Problems* 24: 310–323.

Riedel, M. 1999. Sources of homicide data. In *Studying and Preventing Homicide: Issues and Challenges*, edited by M. D. Smith and M. A. Zahn, 31–48. Thousand Oaks, CA: Sage.

Roeder, O. 2016. The phrase "mass shooting" belongs to the 21st century. Available at http://fivethirtyeight.com/features/we-didnt-call-them-mass-shootings-until-the-21st-century/.

Schildkraut, J., and H. J. Elsass. 2016. *Mass Shootings: Media, Myths, and Realities*. Santa Barbara, CA: Praeger Books.

Spector, M., and J. I. Kitsuse. 1977. *Constructing Social Problems.* Menlo Park, CA: Cummings Publishing Co.

Tierney, K. J. 1982. The battered women movement and the creation of the wife beating problem. *Social Problems* 29: 207–219.

Wiersema, B., C. Loftin, and D. McDowall. 2001. A comparison of Supplementary Homicide Reports and National Vital Statistics System homicide estimates for U.S. counties. *Homicide Studies* 4: 317–340.

Wilbanks, W. 1984. *Murder in Miami: An Analysis of Homicide Patterns and Trends in Dade County (Miami) Florida, 1917–1983.* Lanham, MD: University Press of America.

PART II

Theories of the Criminal Justice System

Introduction to Part II

The chapters in Part II of this book remind us that social reality can often be too complex for our existing understandings of human behavior and the response to that behavior. They take an inductive method of reasoning by beginning with a specific problem and identifying the empirical facts that surround that problem to create a more abstract theory of criminology or criminal justice to then suggest an answer to the problem. Thus, many authors organize their chapters by answering the questions: "What's the problem?" "What's the theory?" and "What's the answer?" An inductive method often starts with crime or some form of it and works backward to end in an abstract theory. For example, pushpins indicating home addresses of delinquents on a map of Chicago by Clifford Shaw and Henry McKay showed that delinquency was concentrated in certain areas, thereby contributing to social disorganization theory and the Chicago Area Project as an answer. Characteristics of effective rehabilitation programs as seen firsthand by Don Andrews, James Bonta, and friends showing that something does work to reduce recidivism contributed to the theory of effective intervention and a variety of evidence-based correctional programs as an answer. The nature of crime, as described by Michael Gottfredson and Travis Hirschi, showing that criminal acts were impulsive, gratifying, and took little effort, meaning criminals were likely impulsive, seeking gratification, and lazy, contributed to self-control theory and prevention efforts in early childhood as an answer. These classic examples make clear that criminological theory often originates as a function of the behavior it seeks to explain.

Daniel Mears and Jillian Turanovic begin Part II by exploring the usefulness of creating a theory of offender recidivism in Chapter 10. They start by identifying the problem in that over three-fourths of individuals sent to prison are rearrested within five years of release. They then judiciously work through a critical conceptual question: would a theory of recidivism be any different than a theory of offending? Mears and Turanovic suggest that existing theories provide a solid foundation for understanding recidivism, but they also leave the door open for the idea that recidivism may be different in that system-involved individuals may have causes of offending that differ in number, intensity, and effect. Further, they suggest that the actual system involvement of these individuals may decrease or increase recidivism, and they argue that this experience should be central to any theory of recidivism. They cautiously conclude that a theory of recidivism may be warranted and they lay out a series of recommendations for what that theory might address. In doing so, it becomes clear that the answer to the problem of recidivism will need to be informed by an integrated theory in which the many theories of offending are tested to see how well they hold up in explaining the reoffending of individuals who have been caught or sanctioned.

The problem of police misconduct is due in part to a lack of theory to guide policies and disciplinary structures designed to prevent misbehavior, according to Natalie Todak and Michael White in Chapter 11. They suggest that police misconduct—including excessive force, corruption, and discriminatory policing—is inadequately explained by existing theories that often focus on one level of explanation and fail to distinguish between purposeful forms of misconduct such as brutality and tacit forms of misconduct such as unnecessary force. They propose an integrated, reflexive theory of police misconduct that addresses each of these concerns by including organizational, sociological, and individual antecedents of both deliberate and passive forms of misconduct. Todak and White conclude by providing answers in the form of accountability mechanisms at the individual level for deliberate misconduct and effective training and auditing procedures at the organizational level for passive forms of misconduct.

Cassia Spohn addresses the problem of racial disparity in punishment by presenting a number of compelling statistics followed by an even more compelling review of the multiple waves of race and sentencing research in Chapter 12. Eight decades of increasingly sophisticated research have documented that racial and ethnic disparities in punishment cannot be explained away completely by racial and ethnic differences in offending. Thus, the problem of race "infecting" the sentencing process persists and, according to Spohn, the critical determinations today are in identifying the circumstances under which race and ethnicity influence sentencing and the ways in which disparities accumulate over the life course of a criminal case. She provides three complementary theoretical perspectives that can help to sort out these critical issues (critical race theory, conflict theory, and attribution theory), and she contends that the answers lie not within policies that eliminate discretion by criminal justice system actors but rather in legislative reform to modify or repeal policies such as mandatory minimum sentences that ensnared disproportionately large numbers of racial minorities in the imprisonment boom.

Chapter 13 begins to demonstrate the effects of this imprisonment boom as Kathleen Powell and Sara Wakefield tackle the problem of intergenerational effects of crime and punishment. They begin by acknowledging the modest but consistent overlap between parents and children in levels of involvement in criminal behavior. Powell and Wakefield add to this understanding by suggesting that parental incarceration itself has transformed this problem such that "youth are indirectly embedded within the criminal justice system through the incarceration of their parents." This problem produces the need for theory that distinguishes between the effects of parental crime and the effects of parental punishment and calls into question research that finds a "clean incarceration effect" without teasing apart the combined effects of parental crime, contact with the system, and separation through incarceration. The answers therefore require policy interventions that match the actual mechanisms behind the intergenerational effects of both crime and punishment.

Rod Brunson and Michelle Block present the problem of distressed police–minority community relations as seen through a historical lens in Chapter 14. In doing so, they show the complementing value of an inductive approach that starts on the ground level as compared to the deductive approach to this issue taken by Farrell and colleagues in Chapter 2. Brunson and Block trace conflict between police and minority citizens from the informal watch systems of northern states and slave patrols in southern states to modern day, resulting in the "place" effect of disadvantaged communities. They argue that these communities are policed in such a way that the criminalization of black youth endures and that relations between police and minority residents suffer when disrespectful police treatment results in a cynical view of the law. Brunson and Block identify focused deterrence strategies as part of the answer, and they echo Farrell and colleagues (and Telep and Weisburd) by also calling for community engagement to be incorporated into crime control strategies.

The difficulty of implementing change within criminal justice organizations is addressed by Danielle Rudes and Shannon Magnuson in Chapter 15. They begin by identifying the murky concept of "organizational culture" as the typical scapegoat for failed reform efforts and suggest that existing knowledge of the concept suffers from a number of critical shortcomings. Rudes and Magnuson address these gaps by invoking additional organizational theory to help facilitate a culture of change: organizational communication, organizational learning, and anticipation of organizational resistance. They focus on corrections specifically to illustrate the value in thinking about organizational change from the macro- through the meso- to the micro-level, and they provide a detailed blueprint for scholars to follow change through this pathway instead of waiting for reform to fail at the end with organizational culture to blame.

Jennifer Carlson writes about the contentious issue of gun policy in America in Chapter 16. She unpacks the issue to show that there are multiple gun policy approaches and multiple gun publics in the United States. This complicates the understanding of American gun policy quite a bit—and Carlson astutely moves beyond the gun control–gun rights dichotomy to examine three different paradigms with regard to gun policy: targeted enforcement approach, preventive approach, and self-defense approach. These approaches take shape in various forms at the federal, state, and local policy levels, as well as in the existing criminological research, and lead Carlson to argue that cultural perceptions of risk must play a role alongside empirical evidence when it comes to support for or against policies. Part of the answer, she writes, is through "creatively and conscientiously bridging divides" to evaluate gun policy on both its practical impact and political feasibility.

Kevin Wright and Cheryl Jonson address the familiar problem of how to punish individuals convicted of a crime while ensuring that the punishment does not increase their likelihood of continued criminal behavior in Chapter 17. They begin by suggesting that those released from prison today are serving longer sentences than ever before, which likely means that the deck is stacked against them in securing affordable and stable housing, obtaining gainful employment, and establishing supportive relationships. Wright and Jonson borrow from theories surrounding place-based pedagogic techniques, social support, and desistance to suggest that prison programming in the form of correctional education can serve to build the skills of people who are incarcerated while keeping them in contact with the outside world. They suggest that a particular type of correctional education, the Inside-Out Prison Exchange Program, is an especially appealing answer to this problem—yet they also acknowledge that program evaluations are needed before it can be anointed as evidence-based programming.

In Chapter 18, Robert Morgan and Robert Ax conclude Part II by writing about the problem of overrepresentation of persons with mental illness in the criminal justice system. They diligently unpack the relationship between mental illness and crime to demonstrate how existing theoretical knowledge regarding thinking styles that support a criminal lifestyle (i.e., antisocial attitudes) should be integrated with knowledge regarding psychiatric disorders. Specifically, they provide empirical support for the idea that it is rare for people to end up in the jail or prison system due to complications from mental illness alone. Instead, they argue that the evidence suggests these individuals have both psychiatric and criminal risk concerns, which requires an answer that is different than the problem posed by persons with mental illness in the general population or persons without mental illness in the correctional population. This answer comes in the form of programs that recognize the reciprocal relationship between criminal behavior and mental illness, and Morgan and Ax recommend interventions such as Changing Lives and Changing Outcomes that focus on addressing the co-occurring issues of mental illness and criminal proclivity.

10

A Theory of Offender Recidivism

DANIEL P. MEARS AND
JILLIAN J. TURANOVIC

Recidivism constitutes a central policy challenge for the criminal justice system. Over three-fourths (77 percent) of individuals sent to prison, for example, are rearrested within five years of release (Durose, Cooper, and Snyder 2014). From 1980 to the present, the correctional system—including individuals on probation or parole or in jails or prisons—grew from approximately two million individuals to seven million individuals (Mears and Cochran 2015). One contributing factor was the widespread adoption of get-tough policies and practices by law enforcement, the courts, probation and parole departments, and jails and prisons (Petersilia 2003; Garland 2013; Gottschalk 2013; Cullen, Jonson, and Mears 2017). Tougher sentencing laws and funding to support their implementation provided the foundation for this growth.

For scholars, the emergence of prisoner reentry as a focal area of inquiry provided the impetus for a rich line of research on desistance from offending (Travis and Visher 2005; Petersilia and Reitz 2012; Travis, Western, and Redburn 2014). This work raised questions about crime across the life course and how criminal justice system involvement might contribute to trajectories of offending (Laub and Sampson 2003; Mears, Cochran, and Siennick 2013; Schubert, Mulvey, and Pitzer 2016).

One critical question that the get-tough era and this interest in desistance raise is whether we need a theory of offender recidivism. They raise, too, the question of how any such theory might differ from a theory of offending or reoffending. In this chapter, we suggest that a theory of recidivism may be helpful, but we do not present one. Rather, we present the contours of what such a theory must entail and, in so doing, delineate the challenges associated with theorizing recidivism in a way that both explains reoffending and provides useful guidance for policy and practice. We begin first with a series of observations and considerations and then distill them down to a set of dimensions that we argue should feature prominently in a theory of recidivism. The chapter concludes with a discussion of the implications of this argument for scholarship and for policy and practice.

WHAT'S THE PROBLEM?

Any theory of recidivism must confront the question of what exactly differentiates recidivism from offending in general and how the causes of one may differ from the other. For society, any crime poses a problem. Here, however, our concern centers on recidivism.

Recidivism Is Reoffending That a Subgroup of "Offenders" Commits

Recidivism is reoffending committed by individuals who have been caught or sanctioned (Nagin, Cullen, and Jonson 2009). It differs only from repeated offending in that it entails offending that occurs after an individual has been (1) caught or (2) sanctioned.

One might refer to individuals who have been caught or sanctioned as *offenders*. However, if we accept this terminology, the question arises of what term to use for individuals who break the law, and perhaps do so frequently, but never are caught or sanctioned. The fact remains that typically we think of offenders as individuals who get caught or sanctioned. Researchers often refer to these individuals as offenders. Yet the fact is that all individuals who commit crime might reasonably be termed *offenders*. If we include delinquency, then that means nearly everyone—except a small percentage of individuals—are offenders, given that the vast majority of youth engage in some form of delinquency during adolescence (Moffitt 1993; Mears 2012).

Offender, as a descriptive label, then, conveys perhaps more than it should. For example, it suggests that offenders somehow differ from others. The fact that almost everyone commits some type of delinquency belies that idea. Even so, here we will assume that offenders are individuals who have committed a crime and have been caught or sanctioned.

The term *recidivism* presents additional confusion. Scholars and policy makers employ the term *recidivism* frequently, as if the term has a clear meaning. It does not. The commonsense idea is that recidivism amounts to reoffending that occurs after contact with or sanction by the criminal justice system. What, though, about offending when the person is not caught? In this case, offending occurred, but it simply did not come to the attention of law enforcement or the courts—possibly because of random luck or because the offense was not especially serious.

What, too, about offending where the individual is caught but not sanctioned? A probation officer, for example, might learn that someone on his or her caseload committed what could be viewed as a crime. Perhaps the individual had a physical altercation with someone else. Charges could have been pursued but were dropped, and the probation officer might seek to work with the probationer informally, perhaps through greater supervision and referral for services (Mears 2012). Does this situation involve recidivism? No correct answer exists. Clearly, offending occurred. Yet offending is not really "criminal" until it is so labeled (Matza 2010). Perhaps, then, we should not use the term *recidivism* unless some formal social control agent has characterized a given behavior as criminal.

What about offending that occurs many years after completion of a sanction? If we studied offending among a population of individuals who were never caught or sanctioned, we would characterize our study as an investigation into the causes of crime. Why, then, call a study of individuals who completed sanctions a study of recidivism? Again, no correct answer exists.

These observations lead to the idea that recidivism might more accurately be viewed as an event, one that entails or reflects a cluster of considerations—the commission of a possible crime, the severity of the crime, the likelihood of being caught or sanctioned, and the philosophy of the law enforcement or court community where an individual resides. From this perspective, recidivism tells us something about each of these considerations. It is not simply a statement about an individual and his or her propensity to commit crime.

The latter meaning, however, prevails in discussions about recidivism. In many scholarly and policy-maker accounts, the meaning seems to be self-evident in the way the term is used. Somehow we must be talking about a "true" criminal, one who has a "propensity" to offend and who will reoffend unless we do something. That position is, in fact, illogical and counter to empirical research. Virtually all individuals have some nonzero probability of offending. And all individuals who have committed a crime once have a nonzero probability of offending a second time, regardless of whether they are caught or sanctioned, and regardless of the severity of the prior offense.

The term *recidivism* thus necessarily implicates both offending and labeling processes that themselves are intertwined with notions of "us" (the "normal" people) and "them" (the criminals). They also are intertwined with conceptualizations of criminality as being located "in" individuals rather than in the social, political, and criminal justice system contexts in which these individuals reside or are embedded. Accordingly, a theory of recidivism likely should entail simultaneously a theory of offending among those who are caught or sanctioned and a theory of social context and the processes that contribute to offending—how it is perceived, classified, and addressed (Mears and Bacon 2009; Matza 2010; Mears and Jonson 2017).

That said, below we proceed from the standpoint that our sole interest is in explaining reoffending (recidivism) among individuals who commit crime and are caught or sanctioned. In so doing, we identify several dimensions that should be part of a theory of recidivism, that is, a theory about offending that occurs among the subset of individuals who commit crime and get caught or sanctioned. This subset of individuals may differ from the general population—in their characteristics, the crime causation factors to which they are exposed, and the sequelae of being caught and sanctioned—in ways that contribute to their offending and that may not apply to members of the general population. After discussing the different considerations and dimensions below, we outline the contours of a theory of recidivism.

The Causes of Offending Presumptively Are the Causes of Recidivism

Criminology is an established discipline, one that has many well-supported theories of offending (Agnew 2005; Akers and Sellers 2013; Lilly, Cullen, and Ball 2015). Presumptively, we can anticipate that the causes of crime identified by these theories—low self-control, strain, weak social bonds, social learning processes that teach or promote criminal conduct, labeling processes that lead to the acquisition of criminal thinking and identity, and so on—apply as well to recidivism. Indeed, there exists little theoretical or empirical basis to expect otherwise.

That observation does not mean that extant theories exhaust the possibilities. Nor does it mean that there may not be unique factors that contribute to recidivism—that is, offending among caught or sanctioned individuals. It simply means that existing criminological theories provide a strong foundation for predicting and explaining recidivism.

The Causes of Offending May Be Greater in Number for Caught or Sanctioned Individuals

Individuals who commit crime and are caught or sanctioned likely have more exposure to various causes of crime. A comprehensive theory of recidivism thus should not focus on just one cause or another but instead should focus on a wide range of possible causes.

This approach differs from traditional theoretical approaches in criminology. Most theories of offending typically focus on one causal dimension (e.g., self-control, strain, social learning, social bonds, or labeling) rather than on many at once (Stafford and Mears 2015). Although exceptions exist and integrated theories have been proposed (Akers and Sellers 2013; Lilly, Cullen, and Ball 2015), they usually only include a small handful of known correlates of crime.

The relevance for explaining recidivism lies in the fact that if we wish to understand and address offending among the caught or sanctioned, we need to consider multiple causes of crime and draw on multiple criminological theories. At the same time, we should not rely on extant integrated theories because of their narrow scope.

The Causes of Offending May Be Greater in Intensity for Caught or Sanctioned Individuals

Individuals who are caught or sanctioned for offending likely have greater levels of various causes of offending. For example, low self-control may contribute to offending, but caught or sanctioned offenders may be lower in self-control than individuals who commit crime but do not get caught or sanctioned. Among those who engage in more frequent offending—or who are caught or sanctioned more than once—the causes of offending may be even greater.

This possibility can be seen by considering the prison population. The profile of this group points to individuals who, on average, tend to come from marked social disadvantage, to have a spotty employment history, and to have lower intelligence, a learning disability, a mental illness, and/or a substance abuse problem (Mears and Cochran 2015). These individuals vary so greatly from the general population that, at the very least, the range and intensity of criminogenic factors should be considered simultaneously in attempting to explain recidivism.

The Causes of Offending May Be Greater in Effect for Caught or Sanctioned Individuals

Individuals who are caught for offending or sanctioned for it may be affected more strongly by the causes of offending. Why? For this group of offenders, they are at once likely to be exposed to more causes of crime, and these causes may well interact with one another (Agnew 2005; Mears and Cochran 2015). In addition, at higher (crime-causing) levels of a given criminogenic variable, there may be disproportionately greater effects on offending than at lower levels (Agnew 2005; Mears and Cochran 2013; Mears, Cochran, and Beaver 2013).

The possibility of interactions bears special emphasis. When any of us are tired, we may be more likely to react harshly to a rude person. When we are hungry, the same may be true. However, when we are both tired and hungry, we may be much more likely to respond negatively. Hunger may amplify the effect of fatigue or, conversely, fatigue may amplify the effect of hunger. All of us understand this possibility intuitively—that is, forces may interact to create more pernicious effects than the mere addition of causal forces would suggest.

For those who are caught or sanctioned, the likelihood increases greatly that multiple causal factors may be present and thus that interactions may occur (Agnew 2005; Mears, Cochran, and Beaver 2013). In addition, the likelihood is greater that some criminogenic factors are present at a high level, thereby creating the possibility for strong interaction effects. A typical two-way interaction between causal force X1 (e.g., self-control) and causal force X2 (strain), for example, does not have to imply a strong effect. However, if the two-way interaction between X1 and X2 is leveraged at high values of one or the other causal force, the resulting effect can be dramatic. If higher-order interactions (e.g., three-way or four-way interactions) exist, the effect in escalating the risk of further offending may be appreciable.

Being Caught or Sanctioned May Decrease or Increase Recidivism

The very act of being caught for a crime, or of being caught and sanctioned, may either decrease or increase the probability of reoffending. Much depends on the nature of the law enforcement and sanctioning experience, as well as the conditions that attach to a particular sanction (Cochran, Mears, and Bales 2014; Cochran et al. 2014; Latessa, Listwan, and Koetzle 2014; Mears and Cochran 2015; Mears, Cochran, and Cullen 2015). Unfair law enforcement and sanctioning, punishments that entail little to no programming or services, supervision that entails policing rather than assisting offenders, sanctioning that ignores the factors that contributed to an individual engaging in crime, sanctioning that closes off opportunities to connect with families or obtain housing or employment—these and other such factors may increase the likelihood of offending. The opposite emphasis in each instance might decrease the likelihood of offending.

This unique dimension—the crime-causing potential of the sanctioning process, the sanctions, and the collateral consequences of convictions—assumes special relevance in contemporary America because of the punitive turn in criminal justice (Gottschalk 2013; Latessa, Listwan, and

Koetzle 2014; Mears and Cochran 2015). The dramatic growth in all aspects of the criminal justice system created case processing pressures. It also limited access to programming and services, increased exposure to policing-focused supervision rather than social welfare–focused supervision, and introduced convicted felons to a wide array of restrictions (e.g., the right to vote, access to public housing, opportunities to work in a range of occupations). As a result, offenders today face a different and potentially more criminogenic formal social control experience than did offenders prior to the emergence of the get-tough era.

This situation is relevant to our focus given that recidivism is nothing more than reoffending that occurs among individuals who were caught or sanctioned. These individuals may differ in their characteristics or social contexts, as compared to those who are not caught or sanctioned. *In addition, they experience being caught or sanctioned and the sequelae of that experience.* This unique experience should be considered as part of attempts to explain and predict recidivism, and it likely should be central to any theory of recidivism in contemporary America.

Recidivism Risk Prediction Is Helpful but Has Limitations

Traditional as well as more recent advances in recidivism prediction tend to be atheoretical and so provide little explanation about the causes of reoffending (Mears and Cochran 2015). Even so, recidivism prediction efforts can be useful for helping to understand, explain, and reduce recidivism (Latessa, Listwan, and Koetzle 2014). They can help to identify individuals who are at high risk of recidivating and point to potential areas of need that might be targeted for intervention.

Yet prediction efforts typically fall short of what we want. Even the best recidivism risk prediction efforts have several limitations. For example, risk prediction yields many false positives and false negatives; it typically fails to tell us which factors most contribute to recidivism risk and how; it does not, by and large, identify how we might best intervene to help reduce risk (exceptions exist—see Latessa, Listwan, and Koetzle 2014); it locates most criminality within individuals rather than the contexts in which they reside; it frequently ignores criminological theory; it frequently ignores, too, recent changes in an individual's life; and it misses the potential for risk factors to interact or to involve threshold effects (Mears and Cochran 2015).

These limitations aside, if we wish to understand recidivism, the risk prediction literature provides a critical platform for insights. For example, it highlights that many individuals in the criminal justice system have or are exposed to multiple criminogenic conditions. Accordingly, explanation and reduction of reoffending for these individuals likely require a comprehensive approach to understanding their behavior and how to change it.

Recidivism Risk Likely Varies According to Sanction Experiences and Social Contexts

Recidivism risk is not likely a constant phenomenon. Rather, it may vary depending on a multitude of factors. It may vary, for example, based on the nature of the punishment experience, including the time served, level of supervision, how individuals are treated by probation or prison officers, and the types of services and programming received. It may vary, too, based on peer, family, school, or community contexts within which an individual resides (see, generally, Bales and Mears 2008; Mears et al. 2008; Mears et al. 2011; Mears et al. 2012; Mears and Mestre 2012; Cochran et al. 2014; Mears et al. 2016; Wright, Turanovic, and Rodriguez 2016).

Risk prediction efforts have not typically in a systematic manner incorporated information about the sanction experience or social context (Mears and Cochran 2015). These dimensions may matter enormously. For example, prisons that rely on effective interventions may produce lower recidivism rates than prisons that do not (Latessa, Listwan, and Koetzle 2014). Individuals who return to areas with high crime rates and few employment opportunities may be more likely to recidivate (Wang, Mears, and Bales 2010; Mears, Wang, and Bales 2014). Similarly, individuals who return to supportive families and social networks may be less likely to recidivate, while those who return to dysfunctional families and networks of active offenders may be more likely to recidivate (Maruna 2001; Cochran and Mears 2013; Cochran 2014).

Individuals who commit crimes and have been caught or sanctioned may well come from and return to areas, families, and social networks that differ markedly from those of one-time or never-caught offenders (see, generally, Maruna 2001; Turanovic, Rodriguez, and Pratt 2012; Travis, Western, and Redburn 2014). Accordingly, any attempt to predict and explain recidivism likely should systematically incorporate information about these areas, families, and social networks as well as the varying aspects of the sanctioning experience.

Recidivism Risk Likely Varies over Time

Recidivism risk is not a constant phenomenon. Rather, individuals change over time in ways that contribute to desistance, that is, a lower probability of reoffending (Laub and Sampson 2003; Mears, Cochran, and Siennick 2013; Ridgeway 2013; Latessa, Listwan, and Koetzle 2014; Cullen, Jonson, and Mears 2017). Successful attempts to improve recidivism risk prediction and explanation therefore likely need to be updated on a frequent basis. For example, inmates may have changed during the course of their incarceration stay. Thus, risk prediction efforts should tap such change (Bushway and Apel 2012; Mears and Mestre 2012). Similarly, if individuals on probation or parole obtain housing or employment, then we can anticipate that their risk of recidivism may decline. Alternatively, if they lose their housing or employment, then this risk may increase. Identifying such a change provides an opportunity to intervene and potentially reduce recidivism. The first step, however, entails the development of a comprehensive recidivism risk prediction model that is updated, monitored, and acted upon on a regular basis.

How might that occur? Many approaches exist. Prison officers, for example, might enter into a database their perceptions about inmate change in the months prior to release. Inmates, too, might complete questionnaires that ask questions about a range of factors reflecting the main causal forces identified by leading theories of crime. Individuals on probation or parole, and their officers, might be tasked with a similar undertaking. Real-time risk prediction then could be undertaken using algorithms that assign weights to levels and changes in the different risk factors and to combinations of such factors (Mears and Cochran 2015).

WHAT'S THE THEORY?

Individuals who come into repeated contact with the criminal justice system likely differ along a range of dimensions from individuals who commit crime only one time or who commit crime and do not get caught. Accordingly, a theory of offender recidivism may be warranted. Drawing on the above discussion, we argue that a useful theory of recidivism—one that explains recidivism and provides guidance on how to effectively reduce it—should include or address the following dimensions.

First, it should be able to explain *how and why the term recidivism is used* and what it means. This approach means that the theory likely must explain multiple outcomes. In addition, it should explain not only reoffending among caught or sanctioned individuals but also labeling and sanctioning processes and how these affect the classification and treatment of individuals.

Second, it should draw on *extant theories of offending*. There is no need to reinvent the wheel. Any starting point for a theory of recidivism should begin with systematic incorporation of existing, well-supported theories of crime.

Third, it should include consideration of *all relevant crime-causing factors* identified by criminological theories that seek to explain individual-level offending. Focusing in a delimited manner on one or another causal factor

may advance testing of established theories of offending, but it will do little to explain much of the variation in recidivism.

Fourth, it should consider *how these causal factors may be present at high doses*, how they may *accrete* into an overall effect, and how they may *interact* to create even greater risks of offending than would be suggested by an additive model of offending. The individuals who come into contact with the criminal justice system, especially those who are sanctioned to probation or prison, likely have or are exposed to multiple criminogenic factors. That likelihood suggests the need to consider potential additive and interactive effects of various causal factors.

Fifth, it should *go beyond risk prediction that is too narrow theoretically*. Considerable advances in recidivism prediction have occurred in recent decades. However, most prediction efforts provide little guidance about how exactly various causal factors contribute to an individual's risk of recidivism. A central starting point begins with relying on established theories of offending and research on effective correctional interventions (Latessa, Listwan, and Koetzle 2014).

Sixth, it should include consideration of *individual characteristics and contextual factors* that may contribute to recidivism. Many theories of offending, and even more risk prediction efforts, ignore social context, including communities, families, and social networks. The prediction and explanation of recidivism can be improved by considering individual and contextual effects (Wright and Cesar 2013; Mears and Cochran 2015). Prediction efforts may be improved, too, by considering victimization experiences, additional life stressors, and access to coping resources (Turanovic and Pratt 2013; Turanovic, Reisig, and Pratt 2015).

Seventh, it should consider how *individuals may change* from day to day, week to week, and year to year, and how such changes may affect the likelihood of reoffending. Many theories of crime and risk prediction efforts proceed from the premise that individuals only have "levels" of a given causal factor. Yet individuals can and do change over time (Laub and Sampson 2003). Even individuals' more stable traits, such as low self-control, can vary markedly over the life course (Burt, Sweeten, and Simons 2014; Pratt 2016). Assessment of recidivism risk should therefore include information about changes in criminogenic factors among offenders.

At present, no single criminological theory combines or addresses these different considerations (see, however, Agnew 2005; Mears and Cochran 2015). Any attempt to do so would run into the challenge that confronts integrated theories (Akers and Sellers 2013; Lilly, Cullen, and Ball 2015). Such theories tend to entail internally contradictory assumptions and lack coherent and consistent rules or criteria for identifying how different sets of factors affect or interact with one another. They also tend to be untestable. Parts of them may be amendable to empirical evaluation, but the overall theories themselves cannot be (Gibbs 1997).

There exists no simple resolution to this situation. Escaping into atheoretical empiricism results in less predictive accuracy and offers no guidance about how to reduce recidivism. Escaping into single-factor theories also results in only limited predictive accuracy as well as limited guidance about prevention or intervention. Accepting an integrated theory at face value, too, is problematic because its validity may be suspect.

From our perspective, the middle ground consists of applying what might be termed a checklist approach to predicting and explaining recidivism. Apply all, or the major, crime theories to individuals who have been caught or sanctioned. Measure the level of and changes in these factors. Ensure that family, community, and, more generally, social context measures are included. Investigate how these levels and changes may affect recidivism and, in so doing, systematically test for threshold and interaction effects (Berk and Bleich 2013; Ridgeway 2013; Wright and Cesar 2013; Mears and Cochran 2015; Mears 2016).

This middle ground effort should ensure that the measures include information about criminogenic experiences during and after contact or sanctioning, with an emphasis on criminogenic factors that accord with established theories of offending (e.g., experiences during prison that weaken or strengthen self-control or social bonds). At the same time, the models of recidivism should be tested through intervention. If an individual's risk of recidivism appears to be driven primarily by strain, address that strain. Unless a situation of irreversible causation is present (Lieberson 1985), recidivism risk then should decline. If it does not, perhaps strain for this particular individual is not as salient as some other potentially crime-causing factor. Perhaps the simultaneous presence of strain and low self-control elevates an individual's recidivism risk. Addressing both might greatly reduce the probability of recidivism. If the intervention to address each exerts a much greater reduction in recidivism than anticipated from an additive model, it would lend support to a theoretical model of recidivism that contemplates an interaction between self-control and strain.

Not least, this middle ground effort should be flexible. Theories tend to be rigid, where a core idea is expressed about some causal force. Here, though, we advocate no allegiance to a particular theory or set of theories. Rather, the goal through a checklist approach is to continuously improve recidivism prediction and explanation by systematically applying theories of offending to offenders and by continuously assessing and updating the many dynamic factors that may influence the risk of recidivism.

WHAT'S THE ANSWER?

We have argued that offenders and recidivism are inherently complicated concepts. Each suggests that some concrete, discernible difference exists. Offenders differ somehow from nonoffenders, even though all individuals have a nonzero probability of offending. Recidivism differs somehow from offending, even though it requires reoffending to be so classified, and even though offenders who do not get caught or sanctioned reoffend. Such observations led us to suggest that any theory of recidivism likely should be focused both on criminal behavior and on social control processes. The latter include many dimensions, such as the laws that define criminal behavior, the application of these laws, and the framing of criminality as something that inheres in individuals rather than in society and labeling activities.

Turning to recidivism proper—that is, reoffending among caught or sanctioned individuals—we argued that a wide range of considerations points to the need for a theoretical approach that builds on prior criminological theory. Indeed, we see no need to reinvent the wheel. No new theories are needed, per se, because so many well-established theories of offending exist. Although a formally articulated integrated theory will encounter substantial resistance and be difficult if not impossible to test empirically, what nonetheless is needed is a theoretical approach that draws on criminological theories, recognizes the multicausal nature of recidivism, and considers the unique contribution of sanctioning processes and experiences to offending.

Accordingly, we suggest that one fruitful avenue by which to improve the understanding and prediction of recidivism and efforts to reduce it entails a checklist approach. This approach would involve the application of all, or most, well-established criminological theories to predict and explain the reoffending of individuals who have been caught or sanctioned. In applying this checklist, the systematic incorporation of information about the criminogenic experiences that individuals experience during and after contact or sanctioning—as well as the community, family, and social network contexts to which they are exposed—should be included. These experiences and contexts in particular distinguish offenders from nonoffenders (i.e., individuals who committed offenses but were not caught or sanctioned).

Methodological tools exist to monitor and assess the predictive utility of a range of factors, including changes in and interactions among them (see, e.g., Berk 2012; Ridgeway 2013). When coupled with criminological theory, they provide a potentially powerful conduit through which to advance our understanding of offending among individuals in general and of offending among caught or sanctioned individuals in particular. From a policy perspective, the use of theoretically informed and empirically based recidivism risk monitoring and intervention constitutes a central foundation for promoting government accountability and effective improvements in public safety (MacKenzie 2006; Mears 2007, 2010; Welsh and Pfeffer 2013). Reliance on offending theory, advances in database systems, and improvements in statistical modeling would provide a powerful foundation for achieving these goals.

For criminological theory, a focus on recidivism affords an opportunity to create greater understanding about offending in general. Extant theories either focus on specific forces (e.g., self-control, social bonds, strain) that may affect offending or rely on integration of a subset of such theories. Few take a comprehensive view of the range of causal factors that may add up or interact to affect a given individual's probability of engaging in criminal behavior (Agnew 2005). They also tend to ignore the potential salience of turning points, including sanctions, for desistance from offending (Mears, Cochran, and Siennick 2013). Extant theory, too, tends to adopt a static view of offending. For example, levels of a given causal variable are viewed as varying in tandem with the likelihood of offending. A focus on recidivism can lead to efforts to find ways to provide more comprehensive explanations of offending. It can lead, too, to a focus on turning points and the effects of changes in one or more causal forces.

It may well be that new modes of integrating theories and of including information about individual and contextual change will be needed if we are to provide more complete and accurate accounts of offending. For scholars, such an undertaking should be intrinsically interesting and important; for policy makers and practitioners, it is essential for efforts to promote public safety. → Agree?

REFERENCES

Agnew, R. 2005. *Why Do Criminals Offend? A General Theory of Crime and Delinquency.* Los Angeles, CA: Roxbury.

Akers, R. L., and C. S. Sellers. 2013. *Criminological Theories: Introduction, Evaluation, and Application,* 6th ed. New York: Oxford.

Bales, W. D., and D. P. Mears. 2008. Inmate social ties and the transition to society: Does visitation reduce recidivism? *Journal of Research in Crime and Delinquency* 45: 287–321.

Berk, R. 2012. *Criminal Justice Forecasts of Risk: A Machine Learning Approach.* New York: Springer.

Berk, R. A., and J. Bleich. 2013. Statistical procedures for forecasting criminal behavior: A comparative assessment. *Criminology and Public Policy* 12: 513–544.

Burt, C. H., G. Sweeten, and R. L. Simons. 2014. Self-control through emerging adulthood: Instability, multidimensionality, and criminological significance. *Criminology* 52: 450–487.

Bushway, S. D., and R. Apel. 2012. A signaling perspective on employment-based reentry programming. *Criminology and Public Policy* 11: 21–50.

Cochran, J. C. 2014. Breaches in the wall: Imprisonment, social support, and recidivism. *Journal of Research in Crime and Delinquency* 51: 200–228.

Cochran, J. C., and D. P. Mears. 2013. Social isolation and inmate behavior: A conceptual framework for theorizing prison visitation and guiding and assessing research. *Journal of Criminal Justice* 41: 252–261.

Cochran, J. C., D. P. Mears, and W. D. Bales. 2014. Assessing the effectiveness of correctional sanctions. *Journal of Quantitative Criminology* 30: 317–347.

Cochran, J. C., D. P. Mears, W. D. Bales, and E. A. Stewart. 2014. Does inmate behavior affect post-release offending? Investigating the misconduct-recidivism relationship among youth and adults. *Justice Quarterly* 31: 1044–1073.

Cullen, F. T., C. L. Jonson, and D. P. Mears. 2017. Reinventing community corrections: Ten recommendations. *Crime and Justice* 46 (1): 27–93.

Durose, M. R., A. D. Cooper, and H. N. Snyder. 2014. Recidivism of prisoners released in 30 states in 2005: Patterns from 2005 to 2010. Washington, DC: Bureau of Justice Statistics.

Garland, D. 2013. The 2012 Sutherland Address: Penality and the penal state. *Criminology* 51: 475–517.

Gibbs, J. P. 1997. Seven dimensions of the predictive power of sociological theories. *National Journal of Sociology* 11: 1–28.

Gottschalk, M. 2013. The carceral state and the politics of punishment. In *Sage Handbook of Punishment and Society*, edited by J. Simon and R. Sparks, 205–241. Thousand Oaks, CA: Sage.

Latessa, E. J., S. J. Listwan, and D. Koetzle. 2014. *What Works (and Doesn't) in Reducing Recidivism*. Waltham, MA: Anderson Publishing.

Laub, J. H., and R. J. Sampson. 2003. *Shared Beginnings, Divergent Lives: Delinquent Boys to Age 70*. Boston: Harvard University Press.

Lieberson, S. 1985. *Making It Count*. Berkeley: University of California Press.

Lilly, J. R., F. T. Cullen, and R. A. Ball. 2015. *Criminological Theory: Context and Consequences*, 6th ed. Thousand Oaks, CA: Sage.

MacKenzie, D. L. 2006. *What Works in Corrections: Reducing the Criminal Activities of Offenders and Delinquents*. New York: Cambridge University Press.

Maruna, S. 2001. *Making Good: How Ex-Convicts Reform and Rebuild Their Lives*. Washington, DC: American Psychological Association.

Matza, D. 2010. [1969.] *Becoming Deviant*. Revised ed. New Brunswick, NJ: Transaction.

Mears, D. P. 2007. Towards rational and evidence-based crime policy. *Journal of Criminal Justice* 35: 667–682.

———. 2010. *American Criminal Justice Policy: An Evaluation Approach to Increasing Accountability and Effectiveness*. New York: Cambridge University Press.

———. 2012. The front end of the juvenile court: Intake and informal vs. formal processing. In *Oxford Handbook of Juvenile Crime and Juvenile Justice*, edited by B. C. Feld and D. M. Bishop, 573–605. New York: Oxford University Press.

———. 2016. Policy evaluation and assessment. In *Advancing Criminology and Criminal Justice Policy*, edited by T. G. Blomberg, J. M. Brancale, K. M. Beaver, and W. D. Bales, 26–39. New York: Routledge.

Mears, D. P., and S. Bacon. 2009. Improving criminal justice through better decision making: Lessons from the medical system. *Journal of Criminal Justice* 37: 142–154.

Mears, D. P., and J. C. Cochran. 2013. What is the effect of IQ on offending? *Criminal Justice and Behavior* 40: 1280–1300.

———. 2015. *Prisoner Reentry in the Era of Mass Incarceration.* Thousand Oaks, CA: Sage.

Mears, D. P., J. C. Cochran, W. D. Bales, and A. S. Bhati. 2016. Recidivism and time served in prison. *Journal of Criminal Law and Criminology* 106 (1): 81–122.

Mears, D. P., J. C. Cochran, and K. M. Beaver. 2013. Self-control theory and nonlinear effects on offending. *Journal of Quantitative Criminology* 29: 447–476.

Mears, D. P., J. C. Cochran, and F. T. Cullen. 2015. Incarceration heterogeneity and its implications for assessing the effectiveness of imprisonment on recidivism. *Criminal Justice Policy Review* 26: 691–712.

Mears, D. P., J. C. Cochran, S. J. Greenman, A. S. Bhati, and M. A. Greenwald. 2011. Evidence on the effectiveness of juvenile court sanctions. *Journal of Criminal Justice* 39: 509–520.

Mears, D. P., J. C. Cochran, and S. E. Siennick. 2013. Life-course perspectives and prisoner reentry. In *Handbook of Life-Course Criminology: Emerging Trends and Directions for Future Research*, edited by Marvin D. Krohn and Chris L. Gibson, 317–333. New York: Springer-Verlag.

Mears, D. P., J. C. Cochran, S. E. Siennick, and W. D. Bales. 2012. Prison visitation and recidivism. *Justice Quarterly* 29: 888–918.

Mears, D. P., and C. L. Jonson. 2017. Signification: The state as a cause of crime. In *Delinquency and Drift Revisited: The Criminology of David Matza and Beyond*, edited by T. G. Blomberg, F. T. Cullen, C. Carlsson, and C. L. Jonson, 199–218. New Brunswick, NJ: Transaction Publishers.

Mears, D. P., and J. Mestre. 2012. Prisoner reentry, employment, signaling, and the better identification of desisters: Introduction to the special issue. *Criminology and Public Policy* 11: 5–15.

Mears, D. P., X. Wang, and W. D. Bales. 2014. Does a rising tide lift all boats? Labor market changes and their effects on the recidivism of released prisoners. *Justice Quarterly* 31: 822–851.

Mears, D. P., X. Wang, C. Hay, and W. D. Bales. 2008. Social ecology and recidivism: Implications for prisoner reentry. *Criminology* 46: 301–340.

Moffitt, T. E. 1993. Adolescence-limited and life-course-persistent antisocial behavior: A developmental taxonomy. *Psychological Review* 100: 674–701.

Nagin, D. S., F. T. Cullen, and C. L. Jonson. 2009. Imprisonment and reoffending. *Crime and Justice* 38: 115–200.

Petersilia, J. 2003. *When Prisoners Come Home: Parole and Prisoner Reentry.* New York: Oxford University Press.

Petersilia, J., and K. R. Reitz, eds. 2012. *Oxford Handbook of Sentencing and Corrections.* New York: Oxford University Press.

Pratt, T. C. 2016. A self-control/life-course theory of criminal behavior. *European Journal of Criminology* 13: 129–146.

Ridgeway, G. 2013. Linking prediction and prevention. *Criminology and Public Policy* 12: 545–550.

Schubert, C. A., E. P. Mulvey, and L. Pitzer. 2016. Differentiating serious adolescent offenders who exit the justice system from those who do not. *Criminology* 54: 56–85.

Stafford, M. C., and D. P. Mears. 2015. Causation, theory, and policy in the social sciences. In *Emerging Trends in the Behavioral and Social Sciences: An Interdisciplinary, Searchable, and Linkable Resource*, edited by R. A. Scott and S. M. Kosslyn, 1–14. Hoboken, NJ: Wiley.

Travis, J., and C. Visher, eds. 2005. *Prisoner Reentry and Crime in America*. New York: Cambridge University Press.

Travis, J., B. Western, and S. Redburn, eds. 2014. *The Growth of Incarceration in the United States*. Washington, DC: National Academies Press.

Turanovic, J. J., and T. C. Pratt. 2013. The consequences of maladaptive coping: Integrating general strain and self-control theories to specify a causal pathway between victimization and offending. *Journal of Quantitative Criminology* 29: 321–345.

Turanovic, J. J., M. D. Reisig, and T. C. Pratt. 2015. Risky lifestyles, low self-control, and violent victimization across gendered pathways to crime. *Journal of Quantitative Criminology* 31: 183–206.

Turanovic, J. J., N. Rodriguez, and T. C. Pratt. 2012. The collateral consequences of incarceration revisited: A qualitative analysis of the effects on caregivers of children of incarcerated parents. *Criminology* 50: 913–959.

Wang, X., D. P. Mears, and W. D. Bales. 2010. Race-specific employment contexts and recidivism. *Criminology* 48: 201–241.

Welsh, B. C., and R. D. Pfeffer. 2013. Reclaiming crime prevention in an age of punishment: An American history. *Punishment and Society* 15: 534–553.

Wright, K. A., and G. T. Cesar. 2013. Toward a more complete model of offender reintegration: Linking the individual-, community-, and system-level components of recidivism. *Victims and Offenders* 8: 373–398.

Wright, K. A., J. J. Turanovic, and N. Rodriguez. 2016. Racial inequality, ethnic inequality, and the system involvement of at-risk youth: Implications for the racial invariance and Latino paradox theses. *Justice Quarterly* 33 (5): 863–889.

11

An Integrated, Reflexive Theory of Police Misconduct

Natalie Todak and
Michael D. White

WHAT'S THE PROBLEM?

Two contradictory themes tell the story of twenty-first-century policing. On one hand, there have been tremendous innovations in police strategies and tools. Problem-oriented policing, hot spots, and evidence-based policing, as well as crime analysis and mapping, DNA testing, and body cameras, have exponentially improved the efficiency and effectiveness of law enforcement (White and Fradella 2016). At the same time, tales of police misconduct permeate the media. In the last two years, the discriminatory use of "stop, question, and frisk" (White and Fradella 2016), federal investigations of systemic agency problems (see, e.g., U.S. Department of Justice 2015), and numerous police shootings of unarmed black citizens are constant reminders of the undercurrent of racial injustice in policing. Further, they highlight the devastating impact of misconduct on communities, police, and the relationship between the two. For example, a 2016 task force investigating the Chicago Police Department concluded that citizens of color were regularly "stopped without justification, verbally and physically abused, and in some instances arrested, and then detained without counsel" (Police Accountability Task Force 2016). It is difficult to understand how both innovation and victimization of minorities have come to define modern policing.

Unfortunately, current theories of police misconduct insufficiently explain this problem (Kane and White 2013). The absence of a strong theory base has led to ineffective policies and disciplinary structures designed to prevent misconduct: "Absent theory, police administrators are left to blindly apply policies that target a 'significant' correlate of misconduct with no idea *why* the variable has an impact or… whether the variable even has a logical causal relationship with misconduct" (Wolfe and Piquero 2011, 334). Accordingly, with this chapter we seek to improve our understanding of misconduct by presenting an integrated and reflexive theory, which builds on the limitations of existing theories and explains multiple forms of behavior. We first review definitions of misconduct, existing theories, and their limitations. Then we elucidate our new theory and apply it to the current state of American policing.

Defining Police Misconduct

The term *police misconduct* has been used to describe a wide range of behaviors. This conceptual ambiguity contributes to its weak theory base. Kappeler, Sluder, and Alpert (1998) situated the concept of police deviance in terms of both an organization's policies and external laws. Deviance occurs when one or both of these standards are violated, so officers who are not implicated in a crime by legal standards can still be reprimanded internally. Misconduct is included in this larger category but applies more specifically to use of an officer's *employment* to engage in *job-specific* malpractice (Kane 2002). For brevity, this chapter concentrates on three forms of misconduct that threaten democratic freedoms in twenty-first-century policing: excessive force, corruption, and discriminatory policing.

Excessive Force

The police are authorized to apply force to overcome resistance to legitimate use of their authority and to defend public safety. Bittner (1970) argues that the legitimate use of coercive force distinguishes the police officer from all other social roles. At the same time, it is expected this authority is used competently, minimally, and in good faith (Reiman 1985). Legally, excessive force is defined by the Supreme Court's decision in *Graham v. Connor* (1989), which ruled that force is lawful if the officer's actions were "objectively reasonable"; that is, a reasonable officer would have perceived a legitimate threat and employed similar force under those same circumstances (a few years earlier the Supreme Court had set a specific legal standard for deadly force in *Tennessee v. Garner*).

Fyfe (1996) distinguished between two types of excessive force: extralegal and unnecessary. *Extralegal force* is the intentional physical abuse of citizens driven by an officer's malice (i.e., brutality). In contrast, *unnecessary force* is excessive force perpetrated through carelessness or incompetence (i.e., it is committed unintentionally without malice). This behavior occurs in situations that could have otherwise been resolved peacefully by a more skilled or properly trained police officer. Fyfe (1996) argued that unnecessary force is the bigger problem because it occurs more often. It is also more difficult to identify because of the shortsighted review traditionally applied to officer behavior—what he called the "split second syndrome" (Fyfe 1986, 207). According to Fyfe and others (Binder and Scharf 1980; Terrill 2005), police-citizen encounters are complex evolving transactions in which earlier decisions carry consequences that impact the final outcome. As such, evaluations of force should assess the full range of decisions an officer made, from start to finish, not just the split second before force is applied. This distinction between unnecessary and extralegal force is critically important for understanding excessive force and, as we argue in this chapter, other forms of police misconduct as well.

Corruption

Experts define corruption as the use of authority for personal gain (e.g., for a profit, sex, or drugs; Goldstein 1977; Sherman 1978). In policing, most cases involve low-level behaviors such as accepting meals or gifts (Alpert and Dunham 1992). While citizens may offer gifts to express gratitude, most agree it is unjust when they expect something in return, such as protection from criminal culpability. To ensure services are distributed equally and legitimately, many departments prohibit officers from accepting gratuities of any kind.

Sherman (1974) categorized departments based on the extent to which corruption is organized within the agency. In Type I departments, only a few officers are involved, evidencing true patterns of rotten apples (individual officers) and rotten pockets (small groups that act alone). Type II departments display more pervasive corruption, but actions are decentralized and disorganized. In Type III departments, corruption is pervasive, organized, and hierarchical, involving line officers, higher-level department officials, and external authority figures. In a famous example of a Type III department, the Knapp Commission (1972) uncovered corruption in the New York Police Department that was both rampant and highly organized. It was estimated that over one-half of the NYPD was engaged in some form of profit-motivated misconduct. The commission's report drew an important distinction between two categories of officers involved. *Grass eaters* were those who passively engaged in minor corruption or accepted bribes for keeping quiet. This group was identified as the most significant problem since they represented the engrained culture of the NYPD and enabled the corruption to continue and spread. *Meat eaters* were a much smaller group in terms of numbers but were actively involved in aggressive, orchestrated corruption.

In this chapter we draw a theoretical distinction between meat eater and grass eater corruption that parallels Fyfe's unnecessary-extralegal force dichotomy.

Discriminatory Policing

Discriminatory policing involves any action or inaction that differentially affects a constituent based on extralegal characteristics such as race, ethnicity, gender, language, religion, sexuality, and economic status (Rice and White 2010). Discrimination has a long history in American law enforcement, though court decisions, political pressure, social progress, and public interest groups have succeeded in reducing its prevalence. Perhaps the most notorious form of discriminatory policing is racial profiling (Fridell et al. 2001), which involves the temporary detention of a person based on race or ethnicity. Hard profiling uses race or ethnicity as the sole factor in assessing suspicion, while soft profiling uses race or ethnicity in combination with other factors, such as the state of the car being driven, the neighborhood, and the time of day.

Profiling has been linked to officers' reliance on suspicion heuristics—schemas used in split seconds to assess whether someone poses a threat (Richardson and Goff 2012). Given that a majority of Americans hold an implicit (unconscious) bias linking darker skin tones with danger, suspicion heuristics carry significant negative consequences for minority citizens (Fradella, Morrow, and White 2016). For example, District Court Judge Shira A. Scheindlin held that the disproportionate stop, question, and frisks of black and Hispanic citizens by the New York Police Department demonstrated that officers were using implicit biases to make assessments about whether citizens' behaviors were furtive and then citing this assessment as a basis for reasonable suspicion to make a stop (Fridell 2013). Explicit bias, on the other hand, involves animus toward members of other social groups of which the biased person is consciously aware (what Fridell 2013 refers to as "your grandparents' prejudice"). We argue there is a distinction between unintentional forms of discriminatory policing (resulting from implicit bias) and direct, intentional forms (explicit bias), offering a third application of Fyfe's unnecessary-extralegal dichotomy to police misconduct.

WHAT'S THE THEORY?

Theories of police misconduct have focused on officer characteristics, the police socialization process, the organizational structure of the agency, and the larger community. Unfortunately, very few studies have integrated two or more of these factors, though the research that follows suggests each is related to misconduct. This section reviews existing theories of misconduct and identifies two major shortcomings of this body of work.

Individual Theories

The psychological paradigm of misconduct views the behavior at the individual level, in light of the tendency for policing to attract people with common traits, such as aggression, authoritarianism, and cynicism (Kappeler, Sluder, and Alpert 1998). This trait-based paradigm is linked to the rotten apple theory, which asserts that misconduct results when "bad apples" slip through the screening process. Other scholars have applied individual-level theories of crime to the study of police misconduct. For example, according to self-control theory, low self-control is a predisposition that increases the likelihood an individual will take advantage of criminal opportunities (Gottfredson and Hirschi 1990). The theory is useful for understanding misconduct, since officers are often confronted with deviant opportunities (Kane and White 2013). Further, the theory suggests individuals who experience high arousal and fatigue are more vulnerable to self-control depletion, and these stressors are very familiar to those in police work. Testing this hypothesis, Donner and Jennings (2014) found that officers who exhibited lower self-control were more likely to receive complaints for abuse, to be the subject of an internal investigation, and to engage in misconduct.

Life-course theory focuses on individual factors that influence deviant behavior over the course of a lifetime (or career) while taking into consideration the person's unique circumstances and turning points. The theory accounts for the relationship between how each of these circumstances interacts and changes over time and influences deviant behavior. Studies applying the theory to misconduct have found that officers who exhibit earlier onset into problematic behavior tend to have longer and more serious involvement over their careers and are more likely to be involuntarily separated from their job as a result (Harris 2010, 2012, 2014; Kane and White 2013).

Sociological and Anthropological Theories

Officers endure a professionalization process in the academy, field and in-service training, and through the demands of police work. The sociological and anthropological perspectives view misconduct as a result of how these processes shape an officer's cognitive properties and cultural values (Kappeler, Sluder, and Alpert 1998). Chappell and Piquero (2004) explored misconduct through social learning theory, which posits that individuals learn deviant or conforming behaviors through differential associations with social groups (Akers 1998). The authors found support for a social learning perspective in a policing context—peer associations with deviant others, reinforcement, and the officer's own moral definitions were related to whether an officer received a citizen complaint (Chappell and Piquero 2004).

Further, the unique, demanding nature of police work fosters a distinct occupational culture (Paoline 2003) and working personality (Skolnick 1966). Through the professionalization process, officers learn to distinguish between the in-group (other officers) and the out-group (everyone else) and to value bravery, autonomy, and secrecy. Police also hold a unique authority position, allowing them to engage in activities that would be against the law if committed by a citizen (e.g., speeding, trespassing, and physically detaining individuals against their will). Because police are permitted to perform these behaviors, they do not generally arouse suspicion; their authority provides a justification (Chappell and Piquero 2004). Kappeler, Sluder, and Alpert's (1998) anthropological theory views police misconduct through this cultural lens, while positing that officers' misbehavior is explained by how officers cope with their unique occupational and opportunity structures. Similarly, Kane and White (2013) describe how strain theory is useful for understanding misconduct, given the stressors associated with police work. Strain theory's central tenets are that individuals who are blocked from achieving valuable goals may use innovative (and perhaps illegal) means to achieve them. Kane and White (2013) highlight that police officers may feel blocked from achieving their law enforcement goals by an ambiguous mandate, exposure to appalling human behavior, bureaucratic frustrations of the criminal justice system, and lack of praise for good work. General strain theory would predict that some officers cope with these numerous and significant strains through deviant means.

Organizational Theories

A few studies have adopted an organizational approach to study police misconduct. Wolfe and Piquero (2011) examined whether perceptions of organizational justice (the perceived fairness of punishments and the methods by which they are distributed) are related to misconduct. They found officers who perceived higher organizational justice in their department were less likely to adhere to the "code of silence" when other officers committed misconduct. They were also less likely to agree that corruption is justified and engage in actual misconduct. Klockars et al. (2000) examined how the culture of a department shapes officer behavior, finding the extent to which an organization promoted integrity influenced officers' misconduct. Applying control balance theory, Hickman and colleagues (2001) found the level of control exerted on an officer by the agency was related to the willingness to report colleagues for misconduct. Finally, applying a deterrence perspective, Pogarsky and Piquero (2004) tested whether sanctions designed to prevent misconduct influenced officer behavior. The authors found that deterrence concerns indeed factored into officers' decisions to engage in police misconduct, though impulsivity (a psychological trait) lessoned the deterrent effects of these sanctions. Each of these studies suggests organizational structure influences police officer (mis)behavior.

Ecological Theories

Ecological theories acknowledge the importance of the external environment within which the police officer works in shaping his or her behavior. These theories draw on studies demonstrating that officers use more force in neighborhoods with higher levels of disadvantage and violent crime (Terrill and Reisig 2003) and, more generally, highlighting the influence of neighborhood context on crime and deviance (Bursik and Grasmick 1999; Sampson and Groves 1989; Shaw and McKay 1942). Applying social disorganization theory, Kane (2002) found officers were more likely to engage in misconduct in neighborhoods characterized by structural disadvantage, high levels of population mobility, and changes in the Latino population.

Limitations to Existing Theories

There are two important limitations to existing theories of police misconduct. First, the literature suggests rather conclusively that numerous factors—psychological, sociological, anthropological, organizational, and ecological—are involved in the production of police misconduct. Therefore, the traditional "silo-based" theoretical approach, which fails to account for causes at multiple levels, provides an incomplete explanation of the problem. Second, existing theories have failed to distinguish between malicious/intentional and passive/unnecessary misconduct. We call this the "reflexivity problem" and argue that Fyfe's (1996) dichotomy of extralegal and unnecessary police violence applies equally well to other forms of misconduct, including corruption and discriminatory policing. On one hand, we have extralegal force (brutality), meat eater corruption, and hard racial profiling—all purposeful and direct forms of officer misconduct. One the other hand, there is unnecessary force, grass eater corruption, and implicit bias—all tacit forms of misconduct. We argue that the causes, correlates, and methods for preventing these distinct forms of misconduct are varied. Theories that fail to account for the reflexivity problem will also be insufficient for understanding and preventing misconduct.

WHAT'S THE ANSWER?

We propose an integrated, reflexive theory of police misconduct (see Figure 11.1). Our theory does not jettison prior theories of misconduct; rather, it jettisons

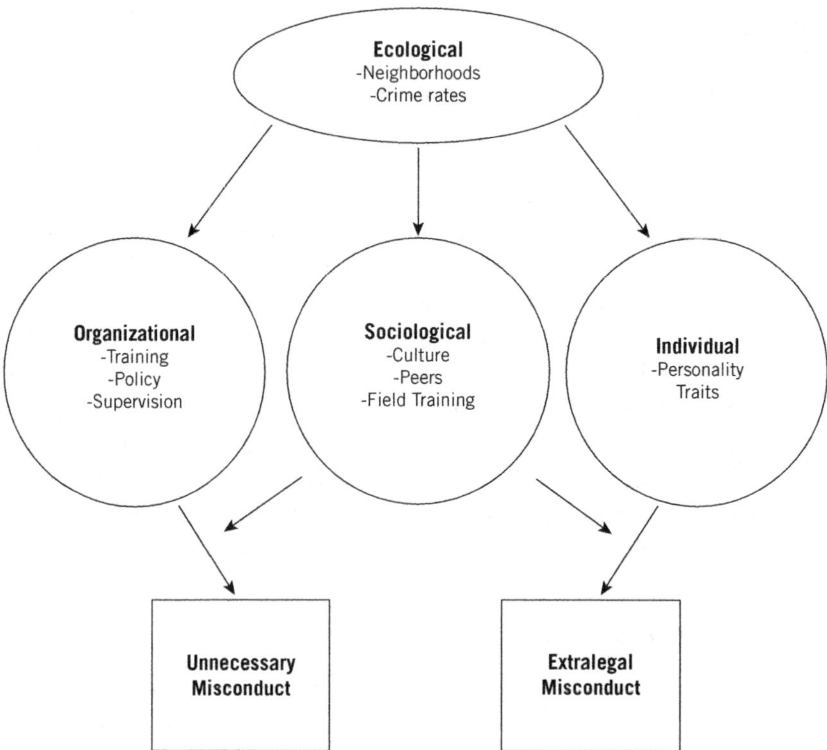

Figure 11.1 An integrated, reflexive theory of police misconduct.

the idea that individual, sociological, organizational, and ecological theories represent competing explanations of the phenomena. We acknowledge that each framework offers value, and we capitalize on that value. However, we also recognize that each framework by itself is insufficient. For example, individual-level or rotten apple theories do not account for widespread pattern or practice forms of misconduct that are clearly tied to the organization. Further, the code of silence that so frequently accompanies misconduct scandals is not sufficiently explained by ecological features—it is a consequence of a culture that is transmitted through a learned socialization process. Our theory incorporates each of these frameworks. We also see an important role for the effects of ecology on officer behavior but argue that organizational, sociological, and individual-level antecedents play more direct roles.

Drawing on Fyfe's (1996) distinction between unnecessary and extralegal force, our theory also highlights the reflexivity of police misconduct. This is conveyed in the separation of misbehaviors into those that are passive/unnecessary and those that are deliberate/extralegal. Table 11.1 provides examples of this distinction for three forms of misconduct—corruption, discriminatory

TABLE 11.1 MISCONDUCT TYPE BY REFLEXIVITY

	Passive/Unnecessary	Deliberate/Extralegal
Corruption	Grass eaters	Meat eaters
Discriminatory Policing	Implicit bias	Hard profiling/Explicit bias
Excessive Force	Unnecessary force	Brutality

policing, and excessive force. We recognize that each type of misconduct can be caused by any combination of the causal antecedents, but there are more prominent and likely pathways that should garner our attention. In twenty-first-century policing, the meat eater, the hard profiler, and the brutal cop are more likely to have their origins at the individual level, and in Sherman's (1974) terms, they are more likely to operate as rotten apples or in rotten pockets. Grass eater corruption, implicit bias, and unnecessary force tend to have causes originating in the organization, resulting from poor training, supervision, or policy.

As depicted in Figure 11.1, our theory further combines Fyfe's (1996) model of excessive force with Kappeler, Sluder, and Alpert's (1998) anthropological theory of police deviance. That is, we identify sociological factors such as police culture, peer associations, and mentorship received through field training as crucial in understanding both unnecessary and extralegal misconduct. The sociological environment can either exacerbate or temper the effects of the organizational and individual-level factors on misconduct, depending on the behaviors, values, and attitudes supported by that culture. For example, a department that receives harsh criticism from its citizenry may be more likely to close ranks and adhere to a code of silence. Through continual reinforcement, a department's culture can also value certain behaviors over others, such as aggressively taking charge in dangerous encounters rather than standing back and taking time to assess a situation (Paoline 2003). Likewise, a department's culture can place higher values on preventing certain crimes, such as getting gang members, illicit drugs, or weapons off the streets. Respectively, these cultural emphases can result in the use of excessive force or pretext stops and racial profiling. We argue that, in such a cultural environment, both unnecessary and extralegal forms of misconduct are more likely to occur.

Corruption

The Oakland (California) police scandal in 2016 is an example of deliberate extralegal (meat eater) corruption. A female sex worker from the Oakland area alleged she had sex with nearly two dozen police officers from the

Oakland Police Department and surrounding agencies (Artz and DeBolt 2016). The accusations include that she had sex with several officers while she was a minor, she exchanged sex for money, and officers forewarned her about upcoming prostitution stings, compromising the safety of other officers. Multiple officers have been criminally charged, the chief has been fired, and several command staff have been demoted. Our integrated, reflexive theory suggests the roots of this corruption scandal can be found at the individual level, by examining characteristics of the small number of police officers who were actively involved in intentional behavior that was both criminal and violated agency policies (command staff were disciplined or fired for failure to identify the misconduct of their subordinates).

The U.S. Department of Justice's investigation of the Ferguson (Missouri) Police Department (FPD) is an example of passive (grass eater) corruption. This investigation revealed that the city's revenue goals permeated law enforcement activities across the city:

> Patrol assignments and schedules are geared toward aggressive enforcement of Ferguson's municipal code, with insufficient thought given to whether enforcement strategies promote public safety or unnecessarily undermine community trust and cooperation. Officer evaluations and promotions depend to an inordinate degree on "productivity," meaning the number of citations issued. Partly as a consequence of City and FPD priorities, many officers appear to see some residents, especially those who live in Ferguson's predominantly African-American neighborhoods, less as constituents to be protected than as potential offenders and sources of revenue. (U.S. Department of Justice 2015, 2)

FPD officers continually engaged in grass eater corruption (and discrimination) for the benefit of the city and department. Based on the investigation's final report, the roots of the problem appear to lie at the organizational level, resulting from a law enforcement program that disregarded the interests and rights of citizens, supervisory practices that explicitly encouraged officers to engage in the corrupt behavior, and a lack of accountability structures. These behaviors also represent unnecessary misconduct by Fyfe's definition—those that have the potential to be fixed via training, supervision, and policy.

Discrimination

Examples from the New York Police Department's (NYPD) stop, question, and frisk (SQF) program demonstrate how both deliberate/extralegal and passive/unnecessary discriminatory policing can emerge in the same context.

At the individual level, officers engaged in intentional, discriminatory SQF activities. NYPD Officer Michael Daragjati was charged in October 2011 with federal civil rights violations resulting from an unconstitutional stop and frisk (Secret 2011). When the citizen objected to the stop and asked for his badge number, the officer arrested the man and charged him with resisting arrest. The next day, the NYPD and federal authorities recorded Daragjati bragging about the arrest and saying that he had "fried another nigger" (Secret 2011). This is a clear example of extralegal discriminatory police misconduct.

In August 2013, a federal judge ruled in *Floyd v. City of New York* that the NYPD's entire SQF program was unconstitutional (White and Fradella 2016). Testimony from officers during the trial described internal pressures to generate stops, along with a tacit acceptance of stopping minorities. NYPD Officer Adhyl Polanco testified that officers in his precinct were expected to issue twenty summonses and make at least one arrest per month.

> Polanco claimed it was not uncommon for patrol officers who were not making quotas to be forced to "drive the sergeant" or "drive the supervisor," which meant driving around with a senior officer who would find individuals for the patrol officer to arrest or issue a summons to, at times for infractions the junior officer did not observe. (Devereaux 2013)

Similarly, NYPD Officer Pedro Serrano recorded a supervisor instructing him to stop "the right people, the right time, the right location" (Devereaux 2013). Other officers' testimony during the trial demonstrated a general lack of understanding of the legal standards required for a constitutionally valid SQF. Overall, testimony revealed a large-scale acceptance of discriminatory policing fed largely not only by organizational demands (unnecessary misconduct) but also by individual-level explicit biases toward minority citizens (extralegal misconduct).

Excessive Force

Since 2014, citizen deaths at the hands of the police have prompted public and sometimes violent protest. On April 4, 2015, Walter Scott, an unarmed black man, was shot by North Charleston (South Carolina) Police Officer Michael Slager (Melvin 2015). A recording of the incident captured by a bystander shows Scott pushing away from Slager and fleeing. Next, the officer shoots Scott eight times in the back as he runs away. The officer claimed the man was reaching for his TASER and therefore posing a safety threat, but a federal grand jury later indicted Slager on murder charges (Berman and Lowery 2016; McLaughlin 2016). In September 2016, Tulsa Police Officer Betty Shelby shot and killed an unarmed black man who was walking along the side of the road with his arms raised in the air. Some have argued the officer was justified in her decision to use deadly force because the man was reportedly acting strange, high on PCP, refusing to comply with officers' commands, and moving toward his vehicle where officers believed him to have a weapon. Others argue the man was simply having car trouble and was clearly unthreatening, given that he had his hands in the air to demonstrate he was unarmed. In July 2016, a police officer shot a mental health caregiver in North Miami. At the time of the shooting, the caregiver had his hands up and was not a threat.

Unless outwardly stated (as in the Daragjati case), it is often difficult to prove that an officer's actions were intentional and driven by malice or prejudice. Nevertheless, in each of these cases police officers used force that was excessive for the situation. At a minimum, we argue that each of these situations involved the use of unnecessary force by Fyfe's (1996) standard—more force than a highly skilled and trained officer would have used given the same facts and circumstances (see also Klockars 1996). It is also possible that these fatal events could represent deliberate/extralegal misconduct. Though the evidence is not clear in two of the incidents, the grand jury in the Slager case certainly drew that conclusion.

IMPLICATIONS OF AN INTEGRATED, REFLEXIVE THEORY

Our integrated, reflexive theory carries implications for preventing and responding to both forms of misconduct displayed at the bottom of Figure 11.1. We advocate for the new model of accountability outlined by Walker and Archbold (2014), which includes elements for specifically targeting both unnecessary and extralegal misconduct.

Extralegal Misconduct

For cases of deliberate/extralegal misconduct, the causal antecedents tend to occur at the individual level and so should the accountability mechanisms. Kane and White (2009, 765) argued for continued restrictive applicant screening that identifies and removes candidates who are ill-suited for the job: "[P]olice departments should continue to exclude people from policing who have demonstrated records of criminal involvement and employee disciplinary problems." After hiring, certain accountability mechanisms are especially appropriate for "rooting out" officers who engage in deliberate/extralegal misconduct, such as early intervention systems, integrity tests, and peer officer comparisons (Walker and Archbold 2014). An early intervention or warning system consists of real-time data that identify officers who may be engaged in questionable conduct and relies on a series of predetermined red flags that represent threshold levels of risky outcomes (e.g., more than three citizen complaints in a six-month period; more than two automobile accidents in a one-year period). When an officer is flagged, a supervisor investigates the incidents to determine if there is a reasonable explanation or if the officer is indeed engaged in problematic activities. The system then delivers a nonpunitive intervention to address the behavior, such as training, peer mentoring, or referral (e.g., counseling). Continued monitoring by the supervisor ensures that the problematic behavior has stopped.

Integrity tests are a proactive response by the Internal Affairs (IA) unit to investigate misconduct. Typically, IA is reactive: an investigation begins only after a complaint has been lodged. An integrity test provides an officer who is suspected of misbehavior with a staged opportunity to engage in misconduct (Morrow 2015). For example, if an officer is suspected of accepting bribes to allow drug dealing on his or her beat, the integrity test could involve a staged encounter where undercover officers engage in a "drug transaction" in view of the officer. The key outcome is the officer's response to the staged crime.

Peer comparisons are also useful in the investigation of deliberate/extralegal misconduct. The idea is to examine the range of behaviors among officers working in similar areas, on similar shifts, with the same assignment. An analysis of use of force, resisting arrest charges, stops of minority drivers, and so on among peer officers should identify outliers—those who are far above the group average for the activity of interest. Supervisors can then further investigate an outlier officer to determine whether the officer has a legitimate reason for being an outlier or if there is problematic behavior occurring. This peer comparison could also lead to the identification of a "rotten pocket."

Unnecessary Misconduct

There are numerous accountability mechanisms available that are well-suited for identifying passive/unintentional misbehavior. Kane and White (2009) argue for the screening in of applicants who have skills, qualities, and personality traits that will make the organization as a whole better behaved. Just as certain characteristics serve as risk factors for misconduct, others serve as protective factors, such as leadership skills, empathy, patience, and independent thinking. These traits could provide officers with a natural resistance to passive forms of misconduct (and deliberate forms), and they could also break down the code of silence that permeates policing and inhibits accountability (Reuss-Ianni 1983).

Despite the fact that individual officers or even groups of officers can engage in isolated forms of passive/unintentional misconduct, this type of misbehavior can often be traced back to deficiencies at the organizational level. Fyfe (1996) identified training principles that could reduce unnecessary force, and White and Fradella (2016) extended those same principles to racially discriminatory policing: effective training must be realistic; training should be tailored to the officers' and community's needs; training must be continuous; and incident review should concentrate on officers' conduct throughout the encounter rather than incident outcomes. Fyfe (1996) concluded:

> The development of successful boxers, diplomats, combat soldiers, and trial lawyers demonstrates that maintaining one's temper under stressful and confrontational conditions is a skill that can be taught. At the broadest level, police training designed to do so may involve providing students with what Muir (1977) called understanding—a nonjudgmental sense that people's behavior, no matter how bizarre or provocative, may usually be explained by factors that go beyond the dichotomy of good and evil...Even if genuine understanding, as defined by Muir, cannot be imparted to individuals who bring extremely narrow views to policing, officers can be made to know in training that they simply will not be permitted to act out their prejudices through violent or even discourteous conduct. (165–166)

Fyfe's statements on training from twenty years ago are entirely consistent with the current focus on de-escalation. The President's Task Force on 21st Century Policing (2015) highlighted the importance of training officers in de-escalation and alternatives to arrest, especially in encounters with the mentally ill (e.g., crisis intervention training; Dupont, Cochran, and Pillsbury 2007).

Training can also reduce misconduct resulting from implicit bias. According to Fridell (2016), research demonstrates that even well-intentioned people who outwardly reject prejudice have biases. This evidence provides the foundation for her "fair and impartial" police training programs that teach officers about the prevalence of implicit bias and how it can affect their behavior outside their conscious awareness. The goal of the training is to encourage controlled, fact-based, effective policing through increased awareness—directly addressing Fyfe's (1996) argument that unnecessary force can occur through ignorance and lack of training rather than through deliberate acts of misconduct. Fridell's (2016) training program also offers specialized programs for first-line supervisors, managers, and command staff as well as a program to train in-house trainers. These programs and others (see, e.g., James and James 2016) are grounded in a belief that discriminatory policing resulting from a lack of awareness of an individual's implicit biases is vastly different than the deliberate/extralegal targeting of minority citizens.

Because the causes of passive/unintentional misconduct tend to rest at the organizational level, external mechanisms should be in place to provide ongoing monitoring of an agency. Walker and Archbold (2014) highlighted the auditor model, in which one individual with legal and/or policing expertise serves as a full-time monitor. The auditor generally does not investigate individual complaints but rather provides a broader level of oversight focused on systems and practices (e.g., the entire complaint process). There are currently more than a dozen police auditors in the United States (Walker and Archbold 2014), and they provide a valuable accountability mechanism that is especially well-suited to address organizational deficiencies that can lead to passive/unintentional misconduct. Likewise, federal oversight can also play a role in police accountability. As part of the Violent Crime Control and Law Enforcement Act of 1994, Section §14141 authorizes the U.S. attorney general to initiate structural reform litigation (SRL) against local police departments displaying systemic misconduct. The Special Litigation Section of the Civil Rights Division investigates agencies suspected of a "pattern or practice" of unconstitutional conduct, and if found, the Civil Rights Division and agency negotiate the terms of a consent decree that incudes remedies to address the misconduct, as well as federal oversight through a court-appointed monitor. Section §14141 consent decrees are a promising mechanism for addressing widespread organizational failures in training, policy, supervision, culture, and management that lead to passive/unintentional misconduct (Chanin 2014; Rushin 2014).

CONCLUSION

Our theory of police misconduct integrates causal mechanisms at multiple levels of analysis and acknowledges the reflexivity problem that complicates our understanding of the major forms of police officer misbehavior. The integrated, reflexive theory draws a critical distinction between deliberate/extralegal misconduct (meat eater corruption, hard profiling, brutality) and passive/unnecessary misconduct (grass eater corruption, implicit bias, unnecessary force). We argue there are distinct, prominent pathways for each form of misconduct, and as a consequence, the most promising accountability mechanisms vary by misconduct type and should target the appropriate causal antecedents.

REFERENCES

Akers, R. L.1998. *Social Learning and Social Structure: A General Theory of Crime and Deviance.* New Brunswick, NJ: Transaction.

Alpert, G. P., and R. G. Dunham. 1992. *Policing Urban America.* Prospect Heights, IL: Waveland Press.

Artz, M., and D. DeBolt. 2016. Oakland police scandal spreads: Teen claims sex with dozens of officers. *Mercury News,* June 12. Available at http://www.mercurynews.com/bay-area-news/ci_30005624/oakland-police-scandal-spreads-other-east-bay-departments.

Berman, M., and W. Lowery. 2016. Former South Carolina police officer who fatally shot Walter Scott indicted on federal civil rights violation. *Washington Post,* May 11. Available at https://www.washingtonpost.com/news/post-nation/wp/2016/05/11/former-north-charleston-officer-who-shot-walter-scott-indicted-on-federal-civil-rights-violation/.

Binder, A., and P. Scharf. 1980. The violent police-citizen encounter. *Annals of the American Academy of Political and Social Science* 452 (1): 111–121.

Bittner, E. 1970. *The Functions of Police in Modern Society.* Bethesda, MD: National Institute of Mental Health.

Bursik, R. J., and H. G. Grasmick. 1999. *Neighborhoods & Crime: The Dimensions of Effective Community Control.* New York: Lexington Books.

Chanin, J. M. 2014. Examining the sustainability of pattern or practice police misconduct reform. *Police Quarterly* 18 (2): 163–192.

Chappell, A. T., and A. R. Piquero. 2004. Applying social learning theory to police misconduct. *Deviant Behavior* 25: 89–108.

Devereaux, R. 2013. NYPD officers testify stop-and-frisk policy driven by quota system and race. March 22, The Guardian. Available at: https://www.theguardian.com/world/2013/mar/22/nypd-stop-frisk-quota-race.

Donner, C. M., and W. G. Jennings. 2014. Low self-control and police deviance: Applying Gottfredson and Hirschi's general theory to officer misconduct. *Police Quarterly* 17 (3): 203–225.

Dupont, R., S. Cochran, and S. Pillsbury. 2007. Crisis Intervention Team core elements. The University of Memphis, School of Urban Affairs and Public Policy, Department of Criminology and Criminal Justice, CIT Center.

Fradella, H. F., W. J. Morrow, and M. D. White. 2016. Terry and SQF viewed through the lens of the suspicion heuristic. *Criminal Law Bulletin* 52 (4): 871–922.

Fridell, L. 2013. This is not your grandparents' prejudice: The implications of the modern science of bias for police training. *Translational Criminology* 10–11.

———. 2016. Training. Available at http://www.fairimpartialpolicing.com/training-programs.

Fridell, L., R. Lunney, D. Diamond, and B. Kubu. 2001. *Racially Biased Policing: A Principled Response.* Washington, DC: Police Executive Research Forum.

Fyfe, J. J. 1986. The split-second syndrome and other determinants of police violence. In *Violent Transactions,* edited by A. T. Campbell and J. J. Gibbs, 207–225. Oxford, UK: Basil Blackwell.

———. 1996. Training to reduce police-citizen violence. In *Police Violence: Understanding and Controlling Police Abuse of Force,* edited by W. A. Geller and H. Toch. New Haven, CT: Yale University Press.

Goldstein, H. 1977. *Policing a Free Society*. Cambridge, MA: Ballinger Press. Available at http://papers.ssrn.com/sol3/Papers.cfm?abstract_id=2596883.

Gottfredson, M. R., and T. Hirschi. 1990. *A General Theory of Crime*. Stanford, CA: Stanford University Press.

Harris, C. J. 2010. Problem officers? Analyzing problem behavior patterns from a large cohort. *Journal of Criminal Justice* 38 (2): 216–225.

———. 2012. The residual career patterns of police misconduct. *Journal of Criminal Justice* 40 (4): 323–332.

———. 2014. The onset of police misconduct. *Policing: An International Journal of Police Strategies & Management* 37 (2): 285–304.

Hickman, M. J., A. R. Piquero, B. A. Lawton, and J. R. Greene. 2001. Applying Tittle's control balance theory to police deviance. *Policing: An International Journal of Police Strategies & Management* 24 (4): 497–519.

James, L., and S. M. James. 2016. Counter bias training simulation. Available at http://www.cbtsim.com.

Kane, R. J. 2002. The social ecology of police misconduct. *Criminology* 40 (4): 867–896.

Kane, R. J., and M. D. White. 2009. Bad cops: A study of career-ending misconduct among New York City police officers. *Criminology & Public Policy* 8 (4): 737–769.

———. 2013. *Jammed Up: An Examination of Career-Ending Police Misconduct*. New York: New York University Press.

Kappeler, V. E., R. D. Sluder, and G. P. Alpert. 1998. *Forces of Deviance: Understanding the Dark Side of Policing*, 2nd ed. Long Grove, IL: Waveland Press.

Klockars, C. B. 1996. A theory of excessive force and its control. In *Police Violence: Understanding and Controlling Police Abuse of Force*, edited by W. A. Geller and H. Toch, 1–22. New Haven: Yale University Press.

Klockars, C. B., S. K. Ivkovich, W. E. Harver, and M. R. Haberfeld. 2000. *Measurement of Police Integrity: Executive Summary*. Washington, DC: U.S. Department of Justice, Office of Justice Programs, National Institute of Justice.

Knapp Commission. 1972. *Report of the New York City Commission to Investigate Allegations of Police Corruption and the City's Anti-Corruption Procedures*. New York: Bar Press.

McLaughlin, E. C. 2016. Ex-North Charleston officer indicted on federal charges in Walter Scott death. May 11, CNN. Available at http://www.cnn.com/2016/05/11/us/north-charleston-police-michael-slager-indicted-walter-scott-shooting/.

Melvin, C. 2015. Michael Slager, cop who killed Walter Scott, says he felt threatened. September 8, NBC News. Available at http://www.nbcnews.com/storyline/walter-scott-shooting/lawyer-michael-slager-cop-who-killed-walter-scott-says-he-n423672.

Morrow, W. 2015. Examining the potential for racial/ethnic disparities in use of force during NYPD stop and frisk activities (Dissertation). Phoenix: Arizona State University. Available at https://repository.asu.edu/attachments/157948/content/Morrow_asu_0010E_15162.pdf.

Muir, W. K. 1977. *Police: Streetcorner Politicians*. Chicago: University of Chicago Press.

Paoline, E. A. 2003. Taking stock: Toward a richer understanding of police culture. *Journal of Criminal Justice* 31 (3): 199–214.

Pogarsky, G., and A. R. Piquero. 2004. Studying the reach of deterrence: Can deterrence theory help explain police misconduct? *Journal of Criminal Justice* 32 (4): 371–386.

Police Accountability Task Force. 2016. *Recommendations for Reform: Restoring Trust between the Chicago Police and the Communities They Serve*. Chicago: Police Accountability Task Force. Available at http://www.chicagotribune.com/news/local/breaking/ct-chicago-police-accountability-task-force-final-report-20160413-htmlstory.html.

President's Task Force on 21st Century Policing. 2015. Final Report of the President's Task Force on 21st Century Policing. Washington, DC: Office of Community Oriented Policing Services.

Reiman, J. 1985. The social contract and the police use of deadly force. In *Moral Issues in Police Work*, edited by F. A. Ellison and M. Feldberg. Savage, MD: Rowman & Littlefield.

Reuss-Ianni, E. 1983. *Two Cultures of Policing: Street Cops and Management Cops*. New Brunswick, NJ: Transaction.

Rice, S. K., and M. D. White, eds. 2010. *Race, Ethnicity, and Policing: New and Essential Readings*. New York: New York University Press.

Richardson, L. S., and P. A. Goff. 2012. Self-defense and the suspicion heuristic. *Iowa Law Review* 98: 293.

Rushin, S. 2014. Federal enforcement of police reform (82 *Fordham Law Review* 3189 No. Illinois Public Law Research Paper No. 14–38).

Sampson, R. J., and W. B. Groves. 1989. Community structure and crime: Testing social-disorganization theory. *American Journal of Sociology* 94 (4): 774–802.

Secret, M. 2011. Officer held in civil rights case after frisking. October 17, New York Times. Available at: http://www.nytimes.com/2011/10/18/nyregion/officer-accused-of-civil-rights-violation-in-false-arrest.html.

Shaw, C. R., and H. D. McKay. 1942. *Juvenile Delinquency and Urban Areas*. Chicago: University of Chicago Press.

Sherman, L. W. 1974. *Police Corruption: A Sociological Perspective*. Garden City, NY: Doubleday-Anchor.

———. 1978. *Scandal and Reform: Controlling Police Corruption*. Berkeley: University of California Press.

Skolnick, J. H. 1966. *Justice Without Trial: Law Enforcement in a Democratic Society*. New York: John Wiley and Sons.

Terrill, W. 2005. Police use of force: A transactional approach. *Justice Quarterly* 22 (1): 107–138.

Terrill, W., E. A. Paoline, and P. K. Manning. 2003. Police culture and coercion. *Criminology* 41 (4): 1003–1034.

Terrill, W., and M. D. Reisig. 2003. Neighborhood context and police use of force. *Journal of Research in Crime and Delinquency* 40 (3): 291–321.

U.S. Department of Justice. 2015. Investigation of the Ferguson Police Department. U.S. Department of Justice, Civil Rights Division.

Walker, S., and C. A. Archbold. 2014. *The New World of Police Accountability*. Thousand Oaks, CA: Sage.

White, M. D., and H. F. Fradella. 2016. *Stop and Frisk: The Use and Abuse of a Controversial Policing Tactic*. New York: New York University Press.

Wolfe, S. E., and A. R. Piquero. 2011. Organizational justice and police misconduct. *Criminal Justice and Behavior* 38 (4): 332–353.

12

Sentencing Disparity

A Focus on Race and Ethnicity

Cassia Spohn

In the late 1930s, Dr. Gunnar Myrdal, an economics professor at the University of Stockholm, was invited by the Carnegie Corporation of New York to undertake a "comprehensive study of the Negro in the United States" (Myrdal 1944, ix). Myrdal's examination of "courts, sentences and prisons," which relied primarily on anecdotal accounts of differential treatment of black and white people in southern court systems, documented widespread racial discrimination in court processing and sentencing. Myrdal noted that southern courts failed to provide black defendants with competent lawyers to represent them, imposed prohibitively high bail on black defendants, and engaged in quasi-legal machinations to preserve the all-white jury. He also observed that black defendants were handled informally and with a lack of dignity and stated that convictions often were obtained with less than convincing evidence.

Myrdal reserved his harshest criticism for the differences in punishment imposed on similarly situated black and white defendants. He noted that grand juries routinely refused to indict white people for crimes against black people, that white people who were indicted for crimes against black people were rarely convicted, and that those who were convicted received only the mildest punishment. He also pointed out that crimes by black people against other black people were not regarded as serious and, as a result, also were unlikely to result in indictment, conviction, or appropriate punishment. By contrast, black people convicted of, or even suspected of, crimes against white people were subject to the harshest treatment. Myrdal concluded that "[t]he whole judicial system of courts, sentences, and prisons in the South is overripe for fundamental reforms" (555).

WHAT'S THE PROBLEM?

Myrdal's conclusion was based on his assessment of the situation regarding race and punishment in the early part of the twentieth century. It is clear that much has changed since then. Legislative reforms and Supreme Court decisions protecting the rights of criminal defendants, coupled with changing attitudes toward race and race relations, have made it less likely that criminal justice officials will treat defendants of different races differently. Black defendants are no longer routinely denied bail, tried by all-white juries without attorneys to assist them in their defense, or convicted on scanty evidence. The level of opprobrium assigned to crimes and the severity of punishment imposed on those convicted of crimes no longer reflect overt discrimination based on the race of the defendant and the race of the victim. Thus, white people who commit crimes against black people are not beyond the reach of the criminal justice system, black people who victimize other black people are not immune from punishment, and black people suspected of crimes against white people do not receive "justice" at the hands of white lynching mobs. As the twenty-first century unfolds, there is little evidence of widespread and systematic overt racial discrimination in punishment.

Although most commentators would agree that the flagrant racism described in *An American Dilemma* (Myrdal 1944) has been eliminated, most also would argue that significant inequities persist (Tonry, 2011). As evidence of this, consider that in 2004 the United States celebrated the fiftieth anniversary of *Brown v. Board of Education,* the landmark Supreme Court case that ordered desegregation of public schools. Also in 2004 the Sentencing Project issued a report entitled "Schools and Prisons: Fifty Years after *Brown v. Board of Education"* (Sentencing Project 2004). The report noted that, whereas many institutions in society had become more diverse and more responsive to people of color in the wake of the *Brown* decision, the American criminal justice system had taken "a giant step back-ward" (5). To illustrate this, the report pointed out that in 2004 there were *nine times* as many black Americans in prison or jail as on the day the *Brown* decision was handed down—the number increased from 98,000 to 884,500. The authors of the report concluded that "such an outcome should be shocking to all Americans" (5).

Other statistics confirm that racial minorities—and especially young black and Hispanic men—are substantially more likely than white people to be serving time in prison. In 2014, black people comprised about 13 percent of the U.S. population but 39 percent of all state and federal prison inmates.

Hispanics were 17 percent of the U.S. population but 24 percent of prison inmates. By contrast, non-Hispanic white people made up 63 percent of the total population but only 37 percent of the prison population (U.S. Department of Justice, Bureau of Justice Statistics 2015). Stated another way, people of color comprised only 30 percent of the U.S. population but more than three-quarters of all prison inmates. There also is evidence that blacks and Hispanics are more likely than white people to be serving life (and life without the possibility of parole) sentences. A Sentencing Project report (Sentencing Project 2013) on the expansion of life sentences revealed that black people comprised 47.2 percent of those serving life sentences and 58 percent of those serving life sentences with no possibility of parole in state and federal prisons in 2012. The proportion of black people among those serving life sentences was even higher in states such as Maryland (77.4 percent), Georgia (72 percent), and Mississippi (62.3 percent). Hispanics made up 16.4 percent of those serving life sentences nationwide, with the largest proportions in New Mexico (44.1 percent), California (35.7 percent), and Arizona (30.9 percent). According to Garland (2001, 2), statistics such as those reported above suggest the "systematic imprisonment of whole groups of the population."

Another indicator of racial/ethnic disparity in punishment is the lifetime likelihood of imprisonment, which shows that black males have the highest likelihood of incarceration and have experienced the most rapid increase in that likelihood since 1974. In 2001, the chances of ever going to prison were highest among black males (32.2 percent) and Hispanic males (17.2 percent); by contrast, the odds of lifetime imprisonment were 5.9 percent for white males, 5.6 percent for black females, 2.2 percent for Hispanic females, and 0.9 percent for white females (U.S. Department of Justice, Bureau of Justice Statistics 2003). For black men, the lifetime chances of going to prison increased from 13.2 percent in 1974 to 32.2 percent in 2001, compared to an increase from 2.2 percent to 5.9 percent for white males. Among black men born in the late 1960s who dropped out of high school, the cumulative risk of imprisonment was an astonishing 58.9 percent; in comparison, it was 11.2 percent for white male high school dropouts (Western 2006, 26). According to Western (2006, 31), "The criminal justice system has become so pervasive that we should count prisons and jails among the key institutions that shape the life course of recent birth cohorts of African American men."

There is also clear and convincing evidence of racial disparity in the application of the death penalty (NAACP Legal Defense and Educational Fund 2016). In 2016, there were 2,905 prisoners under sentence of death in the United States. Of these, 42.3 percent were white, 41.8 percent were black, and 13.1 percent were Hispanic. Similar disparities are found in statistics regarding those executed by the states and by the federal government. Of the

1,419 prisoners executed from 1977 through 2016, 55.6 percent were white, 34.5 percent were black, 8.3 percent were Hispanic, and 1.6 percent were Native American or Asian. There also is compelling evidence that those who murder white people are sentenced to death and executed at disproportionately high rates. From 1977 through 2016, 75.6 percent of the persons executed were convicted of killing white people, 15.3 percent were convicted of killing black people, and 6.9 percent were convicted of killing Hispanics (NAACP Legal Defense and Educational Fund 2016). These disparities were particularly pronounced for the crime of rape (use of the death penalty for rape was ruled unconstitutional in 1977 in *Coker v. Georgia* [486 U.S. 584]). Among those executed for rape from 1930 through 1972, 89 percent (405 of the 455 who were executed) were black men (U.S. Department of Justice, Bureau of Justice Statistics 1992, 8). During this time period, Louisiana, Mississippi, Oklahoma, Virginia, West Virginia, and the District of Columbia executed 66 black men, but not a single white man, for the crime of rape (Wolfgang and Riedel 1975).

The statistics presented above provide compelling historical and contemporary evidence of racial *disparity* in punishment. They indicate that the sentences imposed on black and Hispanic offenders have been and continue to be different—that is, harsher—than the sentences imposed on white offenders. These statistics, however, do not tell us *why* this occurs. They do not tell us whether the racial disparities in imprisonment and use of the death penalty reflect racial discrimination and, if so, whether that discrimination is institutional or contextual, overt or implicit.

Explanations for the disproportionate number of blacks and Hispanics under the control of the criminal justice system are complex. A number of studies determined that a large portion of the racial disparity in incarceration rates can be attributed to racial differences in offending patterns and criminal histories (Blumstein 1982, 1993). As the National Research Council's Panel on Sentencing Research concluded in 1983, "Factors other than racial discrimination in the sentencing process account for most of the disproportionate representation of black males in U.S. prisons" (Blumstein et al. 1983, 92). Although there is recent evidence that the proportion of the racial disparity in incarceration unexplained by racial differences in arrest rates is increasing (Baumer 2013; Tonry and Melewski 2008; Western 2006), as well as evidence that racial differences in offending patterns cannot account for racial differences in incarceration for drug offenses (Beckett et al. 2005; Tonry 1995), most scholars would contend that the conclusion proffered by the Panel on Sentencing Research in 1983 is still valid today.

Not all of the racial disparity, however, can be explained away in this fashion. Critics contend that at least some of the overincarceration of racial minorities is a result of criminal justice policies and practices with racially disparate effects (Alexander 2010; Tonry and Melewski 2008; Wacquant 2002). As one commentator noted, "A conclusion that black overrepresentation among prisoners is not primarily the result of racial bias does not mean that there is no racism in the system" (Tonry 1995, 49). Alexander's critique is even more pointed. As she put it, "The fact that more than half of the young black men in any large American city are currently under the control of the criminal justice system (or saddled with criminal records) is not—as many argue—just a symptom of poverty or poor choices, but rather evidence of a new racial caste system at work" (Alexander 2010, 16).

Researchers have conducted dozens of studies designed to untangle the complex relationship between race and punishment and to determine if racial disparities result from overt or unconscious racial bias and/or the implementation of policies and practices with racially disparate effects. Over this time period, the research questions became more theoretically sophisticated and the methodologies used to answer those questions more analytically rigorous; the answers to these questions also changed over time. A comprehensive review of this body of research is beyond the scope of this chapter. Instead, I focus on the noncapital sentencing process and the conclusions emanating from five waves of research published over the past eight decades.

Studies conducted during the first two waves of sentencing research—which began during the 1930s and continued through the 1970s—often concluded that racial disparities in sentencing reflected racial discrimination and that "equality before the law is a social fiction" (Sellin 1935, 217). Reviews of these early studies, however, found that most of them were methodologically flawed (Hagan 1974; Kleck 1981). Many—including the somewhat more methodologically sophisticated studies from the 1960s and 1970s—employed inadequate or no controls for crime seriousness and prior criminal record, and most used inappropriate statistical techniques to isolate the effect of race. Kleck's evaluation of forty noncapital sentencing studies revealed that many of them found no evidence that race affected sentence outcomes and most that did find such evidence either did not control for prior record or used a crude measure that simply distinguished between offenders with some type of criminal history and those with no criminal history. According to Kleck (1981, 792), "the more adequate the control for prior record, the less likely it is that a study will produce findings supporting a discrimination hypothesis."

The conclusions proffered by Hagan (1974) and Kleck (1981), coupled with the findings of its own review of sentencing research (Hagan and Bumiller 1983), led the National Research Council's Panel on Sentencing Research to claim that the sentencing process, although not racially neutral, was not characterized by systematic and widespread racial discrimination.

Rather, "some pockets of discrimination are found for particular judges, particular crime types, and in particular settings" (Blumstein et al. 1983, 93). The panel echoed the concerns voiced by Hagan and Kleck regarding the absence of controls for prior criminal record in many of the early studies. Members of the panel also noted that even more recent and methodologically rigorous studies (i.e., those published in the late 1970s and early 1980s) suffered from measurement error and sample selection problems that raised "the threat of serious biases in the estimates of discrimination effects" (Blumstein et al. 1983, 109).

The findings of studies published during the third wave of sentencing disparity research suggested that these conclusions might have been premature (for a review of this research, see Zatz 1987). Social scientists conducting research in the 1970s and 1980s challenged the no- discrimination thesis and suggested that racial disparities in sentencing had not declined or disappeared but had become more subtle and difficult to detect. They contended that testing only for direct race effects was insufficient and asserted that disentangling the effects of race and other predictors of sentence severity required tests for indirect race effects and the use of interactive, as well as additive, models. Methodological refinements and the availability of more complete data enabled third-wave researchers to test hypotheses regarding these indirect and interactive effects of race on sentencing. Although some researchers uncovered evidence of direct racial bias, others demonstrated that race affected sentence severity indirectly through its effect on variables such as pretrial status or type of attorney, or that race interacted with other variables to produce harsher sentences for racial minorities for some types of crimes (e.g., less serious crimes), in some types of settings (e.g., the South), or for some types of offenders (e.g., the unemployed). Research conducted during this third wave also revealed that black people who victimized white people were sentenced much more harshly than either black people who victimized other black people or white people who victimized black people. According to Zatz (1987, 70), these third-wave studies indicated "that overt and more subtle forms of bias against minority defendants *did* occur, at least in some social contexts."

During the fourth wave of race and sentencing research, researchers began to investigate the effect of race on sentencing severity using data from jurisdictions—including the federal district courts—with determinate sentencing and sentencing guidelines (for reviews of this research, see Chiricos and Crawford 1995; Mitchell 2005; Spohn 2000). Research conducted during this era, which was published from the mid-1980s through the mid-2000s, improved on research from the earlier eras in a number of important ways. Although the studies varied in terms of their analytical rigor, most did not suffer from the serious methodological deficiencies that characterized the early research. The research conducted during this era used appropriate multivariate statistical techniques and controlled for relevant legal and extralegal variables; most studies also included a wide variety of offenses rather than only one or two types of offenses, and many of them tested interactive as well as additive models. Finally, many of these fourth-wave studies, particularly those conducted using federal data, examined the effect of ethnicity as well as race.

Spohn's (2000) review of state and federal sentencing studies that used data from the 1980s and 1990s highlighted the importance of attempting to identify "the structural and contextual conditions that are most likely to result in racial discrimination" (Hagan and Bumiller 1983, 21). Spohn reported that many of the forty studies she examined found a direct race effect. At both the state and federal levels, there was evidence that blacks and Hispanics were more likely than whites to be sentenced to prison; at the federal level, there also was evidence that black people received longer sentences than white people. Noting that "evidence concerning direct racial effects . . . provides few clues to the circumstances under which race matters," Spohn (2000, 458) also evaluated the research for evidence of indirect or contextual discrimination. She concluded that the studies revealed four themes or patterns of contextual effects: (1) the combination of race and ethnicity and other legally irrelevant offender characteristics (e.g., age, sex, education, and employment status) produced greater sentence disparity than race or ethnicity alone; (2) process-related factors such as pretrial detention, pleading guilty, hiring an attorney, and providing evidence or testimony in other cases moderated the effect of race and ethnicity on sentence severity; (3) the severity of punishment was contingent on the race of the victim as well as the race of the offender; and (4) the effects of race and ethnicity were conditioned by the nature of the crime. Spohn (2000, 478) concluded that the sentencing reforms implemented during the last quarter of the twentieth century had not achieved their goal of eliminating racial disparity and discrimination in sentencing.

The studies conducted during the fourth wave of race and sentencing research improved on earlier work in a number of important ways. Nonetheless, as Baumer (2013; see also Piehl and Bushway 2007; Ulmer 2012) argued recently, even this fourth wave of research left a number of questions unanswered. Of particular importance is that the typical race and sentencing study from this era, which relied on what Baumer (2013) refers to as "the modal approach" involving regression-based analysis of the final sentencing outcome, could not identify the mechanisms that led to racially disparate sentencing. Stated differently, even these more theoretically and methodologically sophisticated fourth-wave studies were unable to explain *why* racial minorities were sentenced more harshly than white people, whether disparate treatment was found only at sentencing or accumulated as cases moved through the court process, or whether the disparities that appeared reflected decisions made by prosecutors as well as judges. These criticisms of research on racial justice are not new. Forty years ago Hagan (1974, 379) called for studies that better captured "transit through the criminal justice system" especially as it operates "cumulatively to the disadvantage of minority group defendants." Four decades later, Baumer (2013, 240) reiterated this concern, arguing that "it would be highly beneficial if the next generation of scholars delved deeper into the various ways that 'race'" matters "across multiple stages of the criminal justice process."

Researchers are just beginning to address these issues. During this fifth wave of research on race/ethnicity and sentencing, the focus has begun to shift from the final sentencing outcome to the life course of a criminal case and the ways in which disparities accumulate as the case progresses through the criminal justice process. Arguing that a key limitation of extant sentencing research is its failure to consider the conditioning effects of the many consequential case processing decisions that precede the final punishment decision (Baumer 2013; Piehl and Bushway 2007; Starr and Rehavi 2013; Ulmer 2012), these wave five scholars point out that focusing on a single decision-making stage (i.e., sentencing) may mask disparities originating at other discretionary points in the system.

Although select work demonstrates that early charging decisions (Shermer and Johnson 2010; Starr and Rehavi 2013) or intermediate bail and pretrial detention decisions (Spohn 2009a) can affect final sentencing outcomes, only a handful of studies address the issue of cumulative disparity in the prosecution and sentencing of criminal defendants (Kutateladze et al. 2014; Schlesinger 2007; Stolzenberg, D'Alessio, and Eitle 2013; Sutton 2013). Together, these studies reveal the importance of examining decisions that precede the final sentencing decision and of attempting to tease out the ways in which these earlier decisions affect sentencing. For example, Sutton (2013) found that blacks and Latinos were substantially more likely than whites to be detained prior to trial; that pretrial detention had differential effects on the likelihood of a guilty plea for whites, blacks, and Latinos; and that both pretrial detention and guilty pleas affected sentence outcomes. Sutton also found that "once prior events are fully taken into account, Latinos and blacks experience about the same rather large cumulative disadvantage," but that the mechanisms that produced this cumulative disadvantage varied for defendants in the two racial groups (Sutton 2013, 1217). Kutateladze and colleagues (2014), who used data on a large sample of white, black, Latino, and Asian defendants charged with misdemeanors and felonies in New York City, similarly found strong evidence of disparity in pretrial detention, plea offers, and use of incarceration: for each of these outcomes, blacks and Latinos were treated more harshly and Asians were treated more leniently than whites. Moreover, pretrial detention had a large and statistically significant effect on subsequent outcomes. They also found that blacks, and to a lesser extent Latinos, were more likely than whites to suffer from cumulative disadvantage; for both felonies and misdemeanors, the most disadvantaged combination of outcomes (pretrial detention; case not dismissed; custodial plea offer, misdemeanors only; and incarceration) was most likely for blacks and Latinos and least likely for Asians.

As this review demonstrates, research examining the relationship between race/ethnicity and sentencing has evolved both theoretically and methodologically over the past eight decades. Of particular importance is the fact that the questions asked have changed dramatically. Most researchers now acknowledge that it is overly simplistic to ask whether race and ethnicity matter at sentencing. The more interesting questions—and those whose answers will help us understand the mechanisms underlying the harsher punishment imposed on blacks and Hispanics—revolve around the contexts in which or the circumstances under which race and ethnicity influence sentencing and the ways in which disparities accumulate over the life course of a criminal case. The statistical techniques used to answer these questions also have changed; researchers have moved from bivariate comparisons of outcomes for members of different racial groups to multivariate and multilevel models incorporating relevant control variables, to propensity score matching methods designed to ensure that offenders in each racial group are equivalent, to structural equation models that identify direct, indirect, and total racial effects, and to use of techniques that allow the calculation of cumulative effects. As the fifth wave of race and sentencing research continues to unfold, more definitive answers to questions regarding race, ethnicity, and punishment should be forthcoming.

WHAT'S THE THEORY?

Criminologists and legal scholars use three complementary perspectives to explain the persistence of racial disparities in criminal justice outcomes. Critical race theorists (Crenshaw et al. 1995; Delgado and Stefancic 2001) contend that racism (and sexism) are ubiquitous and deeply embedded in laws and criminal justice policies and that the criminal justice system is an institution that reinforces hierarchies in society based on race, class, gender, and other sociodemographic characteristics. These theorists further contend that the substance and procedures of American law are structured to maintain the privilege of white people (white males in particular) to the detriment of people of color. Similarly, conflict theorists (Chambliss and Seidman 1971;

Quinney 1970) emphasize the salience of race and class in explanations of social control. They argue that society is made up of groups with competing norms and values and maintain that the authority of the state is used to protect the interests of those in power. Central to conflict theory is the premise that the law is applied to maintain the power of the dominant group to control the behavior of those who threaten that power; thus, criminal justice agencies wield their considerable power to control and subjugate those—especially racial minorities—who threaten the political and economic elite.

In contrast to critical race theory and conflict theory—both of which contend that law and the criminal justice system are used to maintain white privilege and power and which focus on systemic factors and macro-level processes—attribution theory posits that race-linked perceptions and stereotypes shape decisions. This theory also focuses on the micro-level processes through which decision makers assess and evaluate offenders and their crimes. A number of scholars, for example, argue that the decisions made by judges, probation officers, and other criminal justice officials reflect race-linked—as well as gender- and class-linked—beliefs about an offender's dangerousness, threat, and potential for rehabilitation (Albonetti 1991; Bridges and Steen 1998; Hawkins 1980; Steffensmeier, Ulmer, and Kramer 1998). According to this perspective, criminal justice officials typically do not have the information needed to make accurate assessments of an offender's culpability, dangerousness, and likelihood of reoffending; as a result, they develop a "perceptual shorthand" (Hawkins 1980) based on stereotypes and attributions that are themselves linked to offender characteristics such as race, ethnicity, gender, and age. Thus, race, age, and gender interact to influence criminal justice outcomes "because of images or attributions relating these statuses to membership in social groups thought to be dangerous and crime prone" (Steffensmeier, Ulmer, and Kramer 1998, 768).

These complementary theoretical perspectives provide a cogent and convincing explanation of the persistence of racial and ethnic disparity in punishment. Although it may no longer be true, as W.E.B. DuBois (1903) asserted more than a hundred years ago, that the central problem facing the United States is "the problem of the color line," race nonetheless remains a salient feature of American society. Criminal justice officials—whether consciously or unconsciously, overtly or implicitly—use race "as a proxy for an increased likelihood of criminal misconduct" (Kennedy 1997, 137), with the result that blacks and Hispanics are subject to more formal social control than whites. Viewed in this way, racial profiling, whether on the streets or in the courtroom, is an institutionalized practice that is firmly embedded in the agencies of the criminal justice system and that is widely regarded as a legitimate and effective weapon in the war on crime.

WHAT'S THE ANSWER?

Concerns about disparity, discrimination, and unfairness in sentencing are not new. In 1918, the Bureau of the Census published a report on the "Negro Population." The authors of the report noted that blacks made up only 11 percent of the population but constituted 22 percent of the inmates of prisons, jails, reform schools, and workhouses. The authors then posed a question that would spark debate and generate controversy for the next hundred years:

> While these figures . . . will probably be generally accepted as indicating that there is more criminality and lawbreaking among Negroes than among whites and while that conclusion is probably justified by the facts . . . it is a question whether the difference . . . may not be to some extent the result of discrimination in the treatment of white and Negro offenders on the part of the community and the courts. (U.S. Department of Commerce, Bureau of the Census 1918, 438)

This question—whether the disproportionate number of racial minorities incarcerated in state and federal prisons might be "to some extent the result of discrimination"—is a question that is still being asked today. That it is reflects the fact that the racial disparity in imprisonment documented by the Bureau of the Census has worsened over time, to the point that blacks and Hispanics now make up three-quarters of all persons locked up in our nation's prisons.

What can be done to remedy the situation and to ensure that imprisonment will no longer be a "common life event" for young black and Hispanic men (Western 2006, 31)? In the 1970s, critics of the sentencing process lobbied for reforms designed to curb discretion, reduce disparity and discrimination, and achieve proportionality and parsimony in sentencing. The initial focus of reform efforts was the indeterminate sentence, in which the judge imposed a minimum and maximum sentence and the parole board determined the date of release. Under indeterminate sentencing, sentences were tailored to the individual offender, and discretion was distributed not only to the criminal justice officials who determined the sentence but also to corrections officials and the parole board. The result of this process was "a system of sentencing in which there was little understanding or predictability as to who would be imprisoned and for how long" (U.S. Department of Justice, Bureau of Justice Assistance 1996, 6).

Both liberal and conservative reformers challenged the principles underlying the indeterminate sentence. Liberals and civil rights activists argued that indeterminate sentencing was arbitrary and capricious and therefore violated defendants' rights to equal protection and due process of law (Davis 1969; Frankel 1972). Liberal critics were also apprehensive about the potential for racial bias under indeterminate sentencing. They asserted that "racial discrimination in the criminal justice system was epidemic, that judges, parole boards, and corrections officials could not be trusted, and that tight controls on officials' discretion offered the only way to limit racial disparities" (Tonry 1995, 164). Political conservatives, on the other hand, argued that the emphasis on rehabilitation too often resulted in excessively lenient treatment of offenders who had committed serious crimes or had serious criminal histories (Wilson 1975). They also charged that sentences that were not linked to crime seriousness and offender culpability were unjust.

After a few initial "missteps," in which jurisdictions attempted to *eliminate* discretion altogether through flat-time sentencing, states and the federal government adopted structured sentencing proposals designed to *control* the discretion of sentencing judges. A number of states adopted determinate sentencing policies that offered judges a limited number of sentencing options and included enhancements for use of a weapon, presence of a prior criminal record, or infliction of serious injury. Other states and the federal government adopted sentence guidelines that incorporated crime seriousness and prior criminal record into a sentencing "grid" that judges were to use in determining the appropriate sentence. Other reforms enacted at both the federal and state levels included mandatory minimum penalties for certain types of offenses (especially drug and weapons offenses), "three-strikes-and-you're-out" laws that mandated long prison sentences for repeat offenders, and truth-in-sentencing statutes that required offenders to serve a larger portion of the sentence before being released.

Advocates of these policy changes believed that their enactment would result in fairer—that is, less disparate and discriminatory—sentence outcomes. Although there is evidence that sentences are more uniform and less disparate in jurisdictions with sentencing guidelines, there is little evidence that the reforms reduced or eliminated the racial and ethnic disparities that were the focus of the sentencing reform movement (Spohn 2009b). Studies of sentences imposed under federal and state guidelines reveal that blacks and Hispanics continue to receive harsher outcomes than whites and research focusing on mandatory minimum sentences, three-strikes provision, and habitual offender laws also find that the application of these provisions disadvantages racial minorities. These findings imply that prosecutors and judges are reluctant to base sentences on only crime seriousness and prior criminal record and that statutorily irrelevant factors such as race and ethnicity (as well as sex, age, and social class) may be factually relevant to criminal justice officials' assessments of dangerousness, threat, and culpability. They attest to the validity of Tonry's (1996, 180) assertion that "there is, unfortunately, no way around the dilemma that sentencing is inherently discretionary and that discretion leads to disparities."

This suggests that the problem of racial and ethnic disparities in sentencing and punishment requires something more than the passage of legislation designed to reduce the discretion of prosecutors, judges, and corrections officials. The most obvious solution—decarceration—may also be the most politically unpalatable, as releasing large numbers of offenders before they have served most of their sentences or reducing the incarceration rate will inevitably trigger charges that those who advocate these solutions are "soft on crime." Nonetheless, as Tonry and Melewski (2008) convincingly demonstrate, it is the only solution that will significantly reduce the prison population and, in so doing, reduce the number of imprisoned black Americans. Although reducing racial bias and discrimination in the criminal justice system is important and should continue to be a goal of policy efforts, doing so will not appreciably affect the number of blacks and Hispanics behind bars. By contrast, if imprisonment rates were returned to 1980 levels, the black incarceration rate would fall from 2,661 to 827 per 100,000 and there would be 702,400 fewer black Americans locked up in our nation's prisons (Tonry and Melewski 2008, 36). According to Tonry and Melewski (2008, 37), "To attempt to limit damage done to people now entangled in the arms of the criminal justice system, devices need to be created for reducing the lengths of current prison sentences and releasing hundreds of thousands of people from prison."

Assuming that large-scale decarceration is unlikely, what is to be done? A number of policy reforms would reduce the likelihood that those convicted of crimes will go to prison and the severity of sentences imposed on those who are incarcerated. These reforms include the elimination of mandatory minimum sentences, restrictions on the use of life without parole sentences, and the repeal or modification of three-strikes and truth-in-sentencing laws. Each of these sentencing "reforms" played a role in the imprisonment boom that ensnared disproportionately large numbers of racial minorities. Modifying or repealing them will reduce the punitive bite of conviction for nonserious crimes, help to bring the U.S. incarceration rate more in line with the rates of other Western democracies, and reduce the racial disparities that result from implementation of these policies.

A final area of reform concerns the death penalty. Following the Supreme Court's decision in *McCleskey v. Kemp*, in which the justices ruled against McCleskey's claim of racial discrimination in the application of the death penalty, the U.S. House of Representatives added the Racial Justice Act to the Omnibus Crime Bill of 1994. A slim majority of the House voted for the provision, which would have allowed condemned offenders to challenge their death sentences using statistical evidence showing a pattern of racial discrimination in the capital sentencing process in their jurisdictions. Under this provision, the offender would not have had to show that criminal justice officials acted with discriminatory purpose in his or her case. Opponents of the Racial Justice Act argued that it would effectively abolish the death penalty in the United States and the provision eventually was eliminated from the crime bill. Although racial justice acts were enacted in Kentucky in 1998 and in North Carolina in 2009, the North Carolina legislature repealed the act in 2013; no other states have enacted racial justice acts.

The defeat of the Racial Justice Act in Congress and the failure of the issue to gain traction in the states, coupled with persuasive evidence of racial disparity in the application of the death penalty, suggest that the remedy for racial bias in the capital sentencing process is abolition of the death penalty. Advocates for reforming the process contend that the capital sentencing process can be fixed through the enactment of reforms (e.g., access to postconviction DNA testing, funding to pay for DNA tests requested by indigent offenders, and establishing standards on qualifications and experience for defense attorneys in capital cases) designed to ensure that innocent persons are not convicted and sentenced to death. Those who advocate abolishing the death penalty contend that the system is fatally flawed. To support their position, these "new abolitionists" (Sarat 1998a) cite mounting evidence of wrongful conviction of those on death row, as well as evidence that the death penalty is administered in an arbitrary and racially discriminatory manner. They also contend that the implementation of the proposed procedural rules cannot solve the problems inherent in the capital sentencing process. According to Sarat (1998b, 256), the underlying problem is that "[p]articipants in the legal system—whether white or black—demonize young black males, seeing them as more deserving of death as a punishment because of their perceived danger. These cultural effects are not remediable in the near term."

Reducing the racial disproportionality in our nation's prisons and eliminating racial bias in the noncapital and capital sentencing processes should be highly prioritized goals of policy makers and politicians. The mass imprisonment of young black (and Hispanic) men has altered their life-course trajectories, which, in turn, has had dire consequences for their families, children, and communities. Evidence that race infects the sentencing process undermines respect for the law and casts doubt on the ability of the criminal justice system to ensure due process for all and equal protection under the law. The policy changes needed to accomplish these goals and to erase the legacy of several decades of insensitivity to the plight of racial minorities in this country are straightforward. Policy makers must significantly reduce, through decarceration, the number of men and women locked up in our nation's prisons and must modify or repeal sentencing laws and practices that make imprisonment for decades the rule rather than the exception to the rule and that lead to racially tainted death sentences and execution.

REFERENCES

Albonetti, C. 1991. Integration of theories to explain judicial discretion. *Social Problems* 38: 247–266.

Alexander, M. 2010. *The New Jim Crow: Incarceration in the Age of Colorblindness.* New York: The New Press.

Baumer, E. P. 2013. Reassessing and redirecting research on race and sentencing. *Justice Quarterly* 30: 231–261.

Beckett, K., K. Nyrop, L. Pfingst, and M. Bowe. 2005. Drug use, drug possession arrests, and the question of race: Lessons from Seattle. *Social Problems* 52: 419–441.

Blumstein, A. 1982. On the racial disproportionality of United States' prison populations. *Journal of Criminal Law and Criminology* 73: 1259–1281.

———. 1993. Racial disproportionality of U.S. prison populations revisited. *University of Colorado Law Review* 64: 743–760.

Blumstein, A., J. Cohen, S. E. Martin, and M. H. Tonry, eds. 1983. *Research on Sentencing: The Search for Reform,* vol. I. Washington, DC: National Academy Press.

Bridges, G. S., and S. Steen. 1998. Racial disparities in official assessments of juvenile offending: Attributional stereotypes as mediating mechanisms. *American Sociological Review* 65: 554–570.

Chambliss, W. J., and R. B. Seidman. 1971. *Law, Order and Power.* Reading, MA: Addison-Wesley.

Chiricos, T. G., and C. Crawford. 1995. Race and imprisonment: A contextual assessment of the evidence. In *Ethnicity, Race, and Crime,* edited by Darnell Hawkins. Albany: State University of New York Press.

Crenshaw, K., N. Gotanda, G. Peller, and K. Thomas. 1995. *Critical Race Theory: The Key Writings That Formed the Movement.* New York: The New Press.

Davis, K. C. 1969. *Discretionary Justice: A Preliminary Inquiry.* Baton Rouge, LA: Louisiana State University Press.

Delgado, R., and J. Stefancic. 2001. *Critical Race Theory: An Introduction.* New York: New York University Press.

Du Bois, W.E.B. 1903. *The Souls of Black Folk.* Chicago: McClurg.

Frankel, M. 1972. *Criminal Sentences: Law without Order.* New York: Hall & Wang.

Garland, D. 2001. Introduction: The meaning of mass imprisonment. *Punishment and Society* 3: 5–7.

Hagan, J. 1974. Extra-legal attributes and criminal sentencing: An assessment of a sociological viewpoint. *Law and Society Review* 8: 357–383.

Hagan, J., and K. Bumiller. 1983. Making sense of sentencing: A review and critique of sentencing research. In *Research on Sentencing: The Search for Reform,* vol. I, edited by A. Blumstein, J. Cohen, S. E. Martin, and M. H. Tonry. Washington, DC: National Academy Press.

Hawkins, D. 1980. Perceptions of punishment for crime. *Deviant Behavior* 1: 193–215.

Kennedy, R. 1997. *Race, Crime, and the Law.* New York: Vintage Books.

Kleck, G. 1981. Racial discrimination in sentencing: A critical evaluation of the evidence with additional evidence on the death penalty. *American Sociological Review* 43: 783–805.

Kutateladze, B., N. Andiloro, B. Johnson, and C. Spohn. 2014. Cumulative disparity: Examining racial and ethnic disparity in prosecution and sentencing. *Criminology* 52 (3): 514–551.

Mitchell, O. 2005. A meta-analysis of race and sentencing research: Explaining the inconsistencies. *Journal of Quantitative Criminology* 21: 439–466.

Myrdal, G. 1944. *An American Dilemma: The Negro Problem and American Democracy.* New York: Harper and Row.

NAACP Legal Defense and Educational Fund. 2016. *Death Row USA*. Washington, DC: Author.

Piehl, A. M. and S. D. Bushway. 2007. Measuring and explaining charge bargaining. Journal of Quantitative Criminology, 23 (2): 105-125.

Quinney, R. 1970. *The Society Reality of Crime.* Boston: Little Brown.

Sarat, A. 1998a. Recapturing the spirit of Furman: The American Bar Association and the New Abolitionist politics. *Law and Contemporary Problems* 61: 5–28.

———. 1998b. *When the State Kills: Capital Punishment and the American Condition.* Princeton, NJ: Princeton University Press.

Schlesinger, T. 2007. Racial and ethnic disparity in pretrial criminal processing. *Justice Quarterly* 22: 170–192.

Sellin, T. 1935. Race prejudice in the administration of justice. *American Journal of Sociology* 41: 212–217.

Sentencing Project. 2004. Schools and prisons: Fifty years after *Brown v. Board of Education*. Washington, DC: Author.

———. 2013. *Life Goes On: The Historic Rise in Life Sentences in America*. Washington, DC: Author.

Shermer, L. O., and B. D. Johnson. 2010. Criminal prosecutions: Examining prosecutorial discretion and charge reductions in U.S. federal district courts. *Justice Quarterly* 27: 394–430.

Spohn, C. 2000. Thirty years of sentencing reform: The quest for a racially neutral sentencing process. In *Criminal Justice 2000: Policies, Process, and Decisions of the Criminal Justice System*, 427–480. Washington, DC: U.S. Department of Justice.

———. 2009a. *How Do Judges Decide? The Search for Fairness and Justice in Punishment.* Los Angeles: Sage.

———. 2009b. Race, sex and pretrial detention in federal court: Indirect effects and cumulative disadvantage. *University of Kansas Law Review* 57: 879–902.

Starr, S., and M. M. Rehavi. 2013. Mandatory sentencing and racial disparity, assessing the role of prosecutors and the effects of *Booker. Yale Law Journal* 123: 2–80.

Steffensmeier, D., J. Ulmer, and J. Kramer. 1998. The interaction of race, gender and age in criminal sentencing: The punishment cost of being young, black, and male. *Criminology* 36: 363–397.

Stolzenberg, L., S. J. D'Alessio, and D. Eitle. 2013. Race and cumulative discrimination in the prosecution of criminal defendants. *Race and Justice* 3: 275–299.

Sutton, J. R. 2013. Structural bias in the sentencing of felony defendants. *Social Science Research* 42: 1207–1221.

Tonry, M. 1995. *Malign Neglect: Race, Crime, and Punishment in America.* New York: Oxford University Press.

———. 1996. *Sentencing Matters.* New York: Oxford University Press.

———. 2011. *Punishing Race: A Continuing American Dilemma.* New York: Oxford University Press.

Tonry, M., and M. Melewski. 2008. The malign effects of drug and crime control policies on black Americans. *Crime and Justice* 37: 1–44.

Ulmer, J. T. 2012. Recent developments and new directions in sentencing research. *Justice Quarterly* 29: 1–40.

U.S. Department of Commerce, Bureau of the Census. 1918. *Negro Population: 1700–1915.* Washington, DC: U.S. Government Printing Office.

U.S. Department of Justice, Bureau of Justice Assistance. 1996. *National Assessment of Structured Sentencing.* Washington, DC: Author.

U.S. Department of Justice, Bureau of Justice Statistics. 1992. *Capital Punishment, 1991.* Washington, DC: Author.

———. 2003. *Lifetime Likelihood of Going to State or Federal Prison.* Washington, DC: Author.

———. 2015. *Prisoners in 2014.* Washington, DC: Author.

Wacquant, L. 2002. From slavery to mass incarceration. *New Left Review* 13: 41–60.

Western, B. 2006. *Punishment and Inequality in America.* New York: Russell Sage.

Wilson, J. Q. 1975. *Thinking about Crime.* New York: Basic Books.

Wolfgang, M. E., and M. Reidel. 1975. Rape, race, and the death penalty in Georgia. *American Journal of Orthopsychiatry* 45: 658–668.

Zatz, M. 1987. The changing forms of racial/ethnic biases in sentencing. *Journal of Research in Crime and Delinquency* 25: 69–92.

What about the sentence for the crime? Would swift, certain + severe punishment deter future criminality?

Can severe punishment be short sentences with highly concentrated behavioral modification classes/therapy?

13

Intergenerational Effects of Crime and Punishment

Kathleen Powell and
Sara Wakefield

The insight that crime tends to run in families is not new. The intergenerational transmission of status attainment and disadvantage is a core area of interest in several social scientific disciplines, given that parents and children tend to look more similar than different across a host of outcomes. In criminology, theories must account for the co-occurrence of crime in parents and children. What is new, however, are recent sweeping changes in the practice of punishment in both the adult and juvenile justice systems that have generated new research questions and have broadened the scope of outcomes of interest. Consequently, researchers have been challenged to draw finer distinctions between crime and punishment in order to more clearly describe their influence on child and family well-being in the mass incarceration era.

The essay to follow proceeds in four parts: We first describe the substantial overlap between parents and children with regard to crime and introduce several perspectives to explain this connection. We then suggest that extensive changes in the practice of criminal justice in the United States have modified the intergenerational transmission of crime and punishment in two main ways. First, children who have no direct criminal justice contact are at heightened risk of indirect harm from the system through parental criminality and punishment in the era of mass incarceration. Experiencing parental incarceration during childhood has emerged as a new and consequential form of contact with the criminal justice system. Second, among children who *do* have direct contact with the criminal justice system as a result of their own offending, mass incarceration has changed the character and scope of that experience and the degree to which it confers long-term disadvantage. We then use several theories of crime to delineate important distinctions between parental crime and parental incarceration. Finally, we reflect on the policy and research challenges raised by our discussion and suggest several fruitful paths to pursue in future work.

WHAT'S THE PROBLEM?

The modest but consistent overlap between parents and children in levels of involvement in criminal behavior is evident across a variety of studies and in a number of countries (Farrington, Coid, and Murray 2009; Farrington et al. 2001; Glueck and Glueck 1950; Gottfredson and Hirschi 1990; Lipsey and Derzon 1998; Roettger and Swisher 2009; Smith and Farrington 2004; Thornberry et al. 2003; van de Rakt, Nieubeerta, and de Graaf 2008). The mechanisms that explain this overlap are less clear, however. Farrington (2011) describes a variety of potential mechanisms that link parents and children in their levels of criminal involvement, including shared risk and exposure to disadvantage (Farrington, Coid, and Murray 2009; Thornberry et al. 2003), co-offending and role modeling (Gottfredson and Hirschi 1990), genetic transmission and assortative mating (Beaver 2013; Junger et al. 2013; Wilson and Herrnstein 1985), and exposure to police or justice system surveillance (Besemer, Farrington, and Bijleveld 2013; Hagan and Palloni 1990). In earlier work, Hagan and Palloni (1990) bluntly distinguish between two competing theoretical explanations of the mechanisms driving this relationship. "Cultural or characterological process" focuses on family processes and child-rearing while "structural or imputational process" focuses on how formal social control agents interact with children of criminally active parents (Hagan and Palloni 1990: 266).

We suggest that a new factor, the experience of parental incarceration, represents a need to both broaden and refine our existing understanding of the causes and effects of the intergenerational transmission of crime *and* punishment. Unprecedented shifts in the practice of criminal punishment in the United States (and elsewhere) have complicated the parent-to-child criminal involvement relationship. Most observers focus on the phenomenon of mass incarceration. The adult incarceration rate in the United States, for example, grew from a relatively stable 100 per 100,000 in the early 1970s to 612 per 100,000 in 2015 (Carson 2015). An exclusive emphasis on the incarceration rate, however, masks broad growth in the scope of criminal justice processing with respect to types of sanctions. By 2012, about one in every thirty-six adults in the United States was serving a sentence in a prison or jail, on probation, or on parole (Kaebel et al. 2016). However, even these numbers imperfectly capture the sheer volume of people who have contact with the criminal justice system, through their reliance on average daily population counts. To take the most obvious example, on any given day, the daily jail population is about one-half the size of the prison population—yet more than eleven million people in total pass through local jails every year (Minton and Zeng 2015). The expansion of the criminal justice system is further evidenced at earlier, less invasive stages of system contact. There has been considerable growth in the likelihood of experiencing an arrest (Brame et al. 2011), petty misdemeanor justice (Kohler-Hausmann 2013), and mass surveillance via probation (Phelps 2017). Taken together, such expansions have profoundly increased the number of people who have criminal justice contact and, most importantly, have measurably changed their family life, parenting, and childhood experiences. These effects are not randomly distributed across the population but are concentrated among specific demographic groups (Wakefield and Wildeman 2013).

The mass incarceration era is also characterized by a transformed juvenile justice system. While different in operationalization, recent policy changes in the practice of youth justice are nonetheless indicative of a national trend toward punitive justice policy and a growing culture of control (Garland 2001). Most interestingly, the scope of the juvenile system did not experience a parallel sustained growth: as adult incarceration rates continued to rise in the mid-1990s, juvenile court caseloads and confinement rates actually began a period of steady decline (Furdella and Puzzanchera 2015; Hockenberry 2016). Instead, the punitive system changes during this time sought to increase delinquents' accountability and institute harsher punishments (Feld 1999). While the intergenerational transmission of criminal behavior is relatively well established, conclusions about the transmission of system contact are less definitive (but see Besemer et al. 2013; Hagan and Palloni 1990) but nonetheless concerning in this era of increasingly expansive and retributive system contact for both adults and juveniles.

Punitive reforms to the practice of juvenile justice demonstrate a deviation from its guiding principles of rehabilitation and treatment, a philosophical orientation adopted by the system since its creation in the early twentieth century. Starting in the 1960s, policy changes reflect a changing perception of the system's purpose and function. During this time, several landmark cases decided by the Supreme Court formalized juvenile court proceedings by awarding youth limited due process protections, creating a "second class criminal court for young people" (Feld 1999, 3). More recent changes strongly signal a shift toward retributive responses to delinquency through expanded provisions for the waiver of youth to adult court (Bishop 2000), reduced judicial discretion to individualize sentences and treatment (Tannenhaus 2000), the opening of juvenile proceedings and records (National Research Council

2001), and net-widening of system involvement from increased use of diversionary programs (Mears et al. 2016). In a variety of ways, then, punishment, rather than rehabilitation, came to be the modal response in delinquency proceedings. While some signs point to a shift back toward rehabilitation—for example, recent SCOTUS rulings rejecting the constitutionality of the juvenile death penalty and life without parole sentences—progress is slow, and many states maintain laws that continue to administer harsh punishments to delinquent youth.

Contemporary juvenile justice contact thus constitutes a radically different experience, in both character and scope, relative to that of prior eras—generating additional risks of disadvantage and inequality for formally processed delinquents. Research has shown that even the most superficial forms of contact with the juvenile justice system can be harmful and disruptive to normative development (Gatti, Tremblay, and Vitaro 2009; Wiley 2015; Wiley, Slocum, and Esbensen 2013;), especially in the areas of educational achievement (Hirschfield 2009; Hjalmarsson 2008; Kirk and Sampson 2013; Sweeten 2006). As transfer became a more common experience, it has been associated with more severe sentences (Johnson and Kurlychek 2012; Kurlychek and Johnson 2004, 2010) and worsened outcomes (Augustyn and Loughran 2017; Bishop et al. 1996; Podkopacz and Feld 1996) for waived youth, relative to similarly situated peers remaining in juvenile court. Official system intervention during adolescence diminishes well-being into adulthood, with reductions in education attainment, welfare receipt, and human capital development (Augustyn and Loughran 2017; Lopes et al. 2012).

While a relatively small proportion of youth directly experience punishment in childhood—6.6 percent of all juvenile arrests in 2010 were for youth thirteen years of age or younger (Sickmund and Puzzanchera 2014)—a far greater number of youth are indirectly embedded within the criminal justice system through the incarceration of their parents. About 1.9 million children have a parent currently incarcerated (Glaze and Maruschak 2008) and a recent estimate suggests that more than 5 million children (~7 percent of all children) experienced the incarceration of a residential parent during childhood (Murphey and Cooper 2015). These estimates are surely undercounts because they are necessarily limited to parents who are currently incarcerated or cohabiting with their children, omitting parents with incarceration histories or separated families. As is true of incarceration generally, parental incarceration is highly concentrated among the most disadvantaged children and minority racial groups (Sykes and Pettit 2014; Wildeman 2009).

Studies of parental incarceration tend to examine a broader range of outcomes than studies of parental crime, with the latter typically placing a sole focus on criminal behavior. This diversity in outcomes studied in conjunction with parental incarceration is likely reflective of the interests of the diverse set of involved disciplines, including criminology, sociology and family demography, developmental psychology, and economics. In accordance with findings on parental crime, parental incarceration (especially paternal) is modestly but consistently associated with a variety of attainment outcomes for children. Children of incarcerated parents have higher rates of mental health and behavioral problems (Geller et al. 2012; Wakefield and Wildeman 2013), increased BMI (Roettger and Boardman 2012), homelessness (Wildeman 2014), grade retention and educational outcomes (Haskins 2014; Murray, Farrington, and Sekol 2012; Turney and Haskins 2014), material hardship (Schwartz-Soicher, Geller, and Garfinkel 2011; Sugie 2012), and delinquency (Porter and King 2015; Roettger and Swisher 2011). With regard to institutional contact, children of incarcerated parents involved in the justice system are more likely to face confinement, partially due to negative assessments about familial welfare associated with the parent's imprisonment (Rodriguez et. al. 2009). The effects of parental incarceration on children are also evident in other Western democracies (Murray et al. 2014). Notably, many of the disadvantages caused by (or at least associated with) parental incarceration are also strong predictors of later criminal involvement.

WHAT'S THE THEORY?

We have thus far hinted at a central issue concerning the intergenerational transmission of crime and punishment: the challenge of distinguishing the effects of parental crime from that of parental punishment. Criminologists have historically made little empirical or theoretical distinction between criminal involvement and criminal punishment insofar as it relates to the intergenerational transmission of crime. On the other hand, a nontrivial number of studies on parental incarceration in other fields could be faulted for omitting the role of crime in the study of punishment. The studies reviewed above measure criminal behavior using either official conviction or self-reported involvement—thus, crime and punishment are treated as interchangeable. Conceptual imprecision of this sort may have had few consequences for the state of knowledge when incarceration was much less common and collateral consequences far less severe. At today's high levels of incarceration and justice involvement, however, the distinction is important—even if we assume that the official criminal histories of the incarcerated are a complete and unbiased measure of their underlying criminal involvement (which, of course, they are not).

Why should this distinction matter? Classic debates between control and learning theories of crime offer a useful example. Classic and contemporary social learning theories (Burgess and Akers 1966; Sutherland 1939) posit that all criminal behavior is the by-product of a learning process through which behavioral norms are continually communicated and reinforced. Individuals are more likely to be deviant if they have been continually exposed to positive or rationalizing messages about law violations through an operant conditioning process (Akers et al. 1979). While this communication can be direct or indirect, the messages received from families or peer groups are most salient (Akers et al. 1979). Children of criminally active parents may be more likely to engage in delinquency through a social learning process if imitation of parental behavior is continually unpunished or positively reinforced (Akers and Jensen 2006). Thus, learning theories offer a clear link to intergenerational crime by proposing social mechanisms that translate parent behaviors to the child.

These views of initiation into deviance contrast with those of early social bonding theories of crime. Control or bonding theories envision family processes as one of many elements of control that constrain an individual's innate tendency to engage in crime. Those with stronger social bonds have a stronger connection to surrounding social institutions and effectively will be tied down to conventional, law-abiding behavior to avoid harming these relationships (Hindelang 1973; Hirschi 1969). Conversely, those with weakened bonds will be more "free" to act on natural predispositions toward crime and have a higher propensity toward criminal behavior. Parents are one of the strongest socializing forces in their children's lives, shaping perceptions of conventional behavior and the nature of their connection to the social world. One can infer that parents who have been involved in criminal behavior have attenuated social bonds that may be passed on to their children—effectively raising their risk of deviance through an intergenerational developmental process.

Learning and control theories clearly depart from one another in fundamental ways, yet they both assign central roles to parents in the prevention of crime in their children. Learning perspectives connect the intergenerational transmission of criminal behavior through visible and apparent parental criminality, not simply associated instability. Along the same lines, classic control theory (e.g., Hirschi 1969) assigns a central role to parents in the inhibition of crime in their children—but makes it less clear how much parental crime is, on average, visible to or consequential for children. Moreover, even when crime and associated instability are visible to children, early control theories were clear that criminally involved parents rarely endorsed crime or criminal lifestyles for their children (see, for example, Hirschi 1969; Nye 1958). While such distinctions are less important in more contemporary versions of control theories (e.g., Gottfredson and Hirschi 1990), it is nonetheless useful to draw a theoretical distinction between criminally involved parents and criminally *punished* parents when thinking about how the experience affects children (see Wakefield and Apel 2017 for an extended discussion of criminological perspectives on parental incarceration).

One perspective that explicitly distinguishes between parental criminality and parental punishment is labeling theory. Early formations of labeling theory propose that an individual's behavior and habits—both conforming and nonconforming—are influenced and formed by societal reactions from surrounding family, friends, and institutions (Becker 1963). Secondary deviance, or repeated deviance, becomes more likely following an initial act of deviance through a multistep process rooted in symbolic interactionalism (Lemert 1951; Mead 1934). If initial actions are met with negative responses, individuals are at a heightened risk of being stigmatized as an outsider by their social group or officially labeled by a formal social control institution (Becker 1963). These individuals may associate with others who have also been rejected from their conventional social groups to form new groups, adopting behavioral norms that justify continued deviance and a modified self-concept (Becker 1963). Classic work by Hagan and Palloni (1990) and more recent work by Besemer and colleagues (Besemer et al. 2013) offer compelling evidence of an intergenerational labeling effect, whereby formal conviction of parents is the vehicle by which children come to the attention of police or other criminal justice agencies.

There are other closely related examples of institutional spillover that do not explicitly leverage a labeling mechanism, contrary to the research described above, but are nonetheless instructive. Berger and colleagues (2016) show substantial overlap between parental involvement in the criminal justice system and the child welfare system, echoing the findings of others (Edwards 2016; Johnson and Waldfogel 2004). These finding suggests that official responses from institutions of social control and social welfare may have an enduring and intergenerational impact on children and families, increasing the child's likelihood of contact with the justice system net of his or her actual behaviors. Importantly, all are contingent on a parent's formal punishment, not on a parent's level of criminal involvement per se.

We raise these examples not to prioritize a focus on either parental crime or parental incarceration. Indeed, much of the research on parental incarceration can be faulted for claiming to have demonstrated a clean incarceration effect, when in reality findings likely reflect the combined effects of parental crime, contact with police and courts, separation from a parent due to incarceration, and a host of other experiences. The reverse is also the case. Studies that purport to measure parental crime are also often capturing the additional effect of engagement with bureaucratic, irrational, and often hostile institutions. We raise these examples to demonstrate the utility of paying attention to the processes that drive outcomes for children and youth who experience some combination of parental criminality (with varying degrees of visibility) and parental punishment (with varying degrees of severity) to derive effective policy interventions and criminal justice reforms.

WHAT'S THE ANSWER?

Criminologists and those in related fields (often in parallel but nonoverlapping research streams) have amassed an impressive array of evidence linking parental crime and punishment to outcomes for children—not just for their delinquent behavior but also for a host of factors that largely determines overall life chances. We thus argue that research has stumbled not in its scope of outcomes but in detailing the mechanisms responsible for these effects. Consequently, policy interventions designed to break the link are often ineffective. We suggest here that the answer lies in greater attention to treatment heterogeneity across parents, children, and contexts, increased conceptual clarity, and leveraging criminological strengths in policy intervention to better understand the processes behind intergenerational transmission.

With respect to heterogeneity, that the intergenerational transmission of crime/punishment is evident in places as different as the United States (Wakefield and Wildeman 2013), Denmark (Andersen 2016), or the United Kingdom (Murray et al. 2014) is important and suggestive of a general (though complicated) process that may be based in family processes, genetic transmission, labeling, and institutional attributions—or some combination of these mechanisms. However, this knowledge is not new: it has been evident for quite some time but has produced little actionable policy guidance. It may be more useful to understand, for example, how children's experiences might differ if growing up with a parent sporadically involved in crime relative to a parent sporadically incarcerated. We take no position here on which is more harmful or consequential, on average, but suggest the effects of each may be very different and require different policy interventions. Importantly, few contemporary data sets would allow for such a study.

Greater conceptual clarity with respect to crime and punishment would allow for more integration between criminology's traditional fields of study. For example, heightened levels of parental incarceration may affect perceptions of criminal justice legitimacy among the large and growing population of children of incarcerated parents in much the same way that aggressive policing tactics decrease the legitimacy of the police. Such a relationship might be interrogated through the mechanisms of social learning theories. Similarly, the finding of Hagan and Palloni (1990) of an intergenerational labeling effect of criminal justice contact might be further explored for any additional implications on perceived system legitimacy or experienced trauma. These types of inquiries may highlight additional avenues through which parental punishment influences children's behaviors and promote a more comprehensive understanding of the impact of mass incarceration.

With respect to the juvenile justice system, limited signs suggest that the system may be shifting gears back toward a (predominantly) rehabilitative approach. While it is early, these changes are encouraging given that numerous studies document negative consequences of formal contact with the juvenile justice system. We encourage continued research into both delinquency and formal system contact that explicitly accounts for theoretical processes through which parental criminality and punishment might be consequential to youth, akin to Rodriguez and colleagues informative study of detrimental attributions of parental incarceration and children's' experiences in the justice system (Rodriguez et. al. 2009). Such research might inform appropriate policies and practices that hold youth accountable for their behavior in a rehabilitative, rather than punitive, fashion without conferring additional penalties predicated on their parents' criminal histories.

Finally, the study of parental incarceration, like criminology itself, is interdisciplinary in nature. Though it should not be surprising that criminologists have historically focused on crime as the outcome of interest, investment from other fields—including sociology, psychology, family demography, and economics—in the study of parental incarceration has considerably broadened the scope of knowledge of associated outcomes, documenting declines in child well-being, school readiness, material deprivation, political engagement, and child homelessness. We suggest that increased attention to the distinction between crime and punishment when estimating collateral consequences may help to inform policy interventions by identifying the most consequential forms of justice system contact.

REFERENCES

Akers, R. L., and G. F. Jensen. 2006. The empirical status of social learning theory of crime and deviance: The past, present, and future. In *Advances in Criminological Theory: Vol. 15. Taking Stock: The Status of Criminological Theory* edited by F. T. Cullen, J. P. Wright, and K. R. Blevins, 37–76. Piscataway, NJ: Transaction.

Akers, R. L., M. D. Krohn., L. Lanza-Kaduce, and M. Radosevich. 1979. Social learning and deviant behavior: A specific test of a general theory. *American Sociological Review* 44 (4): 636–655.

Andersen, L. H. 2016. How children's educational outcomes and crimininality vary by duration and frequency of paternal incarceration. *Annals of the American Academy of Political and Social Science* 665 (1): 149–170.

Augustyn, M. B., and T. A. Loughran. 2017. Juvenile waiver as a mechanism of social stratification: A focus on human capital. *Criminology* 55 (2): 405–437.

Beaver, K. 2013. The familial concentration and transmission of crime. *Criminal Justice and Behavior* 40 (2): 139–155.

Becker, H. 1963. *Outsiders: Studies in the Sociology of Deviance.* New York: The Free Press.

Berger, L. M., M. Cancian, L. Cuesta, and J. L. Noyes. 2016. Families at the intersection of the criminal justice and child protective services systems. *The Annals of the American Academy of Political and Social Science* 665 (1): 171–194.

Bernard, T. J., and M. C. Kurlychek. 2010. *The Cycle of Juvenile Justice.* New York: Oxford University Press.

Besemer, S., D. P. Farrington, and C.C.J.H. Bijleveld. 2013. Official bias in intergenerational transmission of criminal behavior. *British Journal of Criminology* 53 (3): 438–455.

Bishop, D. M. 2000. Juvenile offenders in the adult criminal justice system. *Crime and Justice* 27: 81–167.

Bishop, D. M., C. E. Frazier, L. Lanza-Kaduce, and L. Winner. 1996. The transfer of juveniles to criminal court: Does it make a difference? *Crime & Delinquency* 42 (2): 171–191.

Brame, R., M. G. Turner, R. Paternoster, and S. D. Bushway. 2011. Cumulative prevalence of arrest from ages 8 to 23 in a national sample. *Pediatrics* 129 (1): 21–27.

Burgess, R. L., and R. L. Akers. 1966. A differential association-reinforcement theory of criminal behavior. *Social Problems* 14 (2): 128–147.

Carson, E. A. 2015. *Prisoners in 2014.* Washington, DC: U.S. Government Printing Office.

Edwards, F. 2016. Saving children, controlling families: punishment, redistribution, and child protection. *American Sociological Review* 81 (3): 75–595.

Farrington, D. P. 2011. Families and crime. In *Crime and Public Policy,* edited by J. Q. Wilson and J. Petersilia. Oxford, UK: University of Oxford Press.

Farrington, D. P., J. W. Coid, and J. Murray. 2009. Family factors in the intergenerational transmission of offending. *Criminal Behavior and Mental Health* 19 (2): 109–124.

Farrington, D. P., D. Jolliffe, R. Loeber, M. Stouthamer-Loeber, and L. M. Kalb. 2001. The concentration of offenders in families, and family criminality in the prediction of boys' delinquency. *Journal of Adolescence* 24: 579–596.

Feld, B. C. 1999. *Bad Kids: Race and the Transformation of the Juvenile Court.* Oxford: Oxford University Press.

Furdella, J., and C. Puzzanchera. 2015. *Delinquency Cases in Juvenile Court, 2013.* Washington, DC: Department of Justice, Office of Justice Programs, Office of Juvenile Justice and Delinquency Prevention.

Garland, D. 2001. *The Culture of Control.* Oxford: Oxford University Press.

Gatti, U., R. E. Tremblay, and F. Vitaro. 2009. Iatrogenic effect of juvenile justice. *Journal of Child Psychology and Psychiatry* 50 (8): 991–998.

Geller, A., C. E. Cooper, I. Garfinkel, O. Schwartz-Soicher, and R. B. Mincy. 2012. Beyond absenteeism: Father incarceration and child development. *Demography* 49 (1): 49–76.

Glaze, L. E., and L. M. Maruschak. 2008. *Parents in Prison and Their Minor Children.* Washington, DC: U.S. Government Printing Office.

Glueck, S., and E. Glueck. 1950. *Unraveling Juvenile Delinquency.* Cambridge, MA: Harvard University Press.

Gottfredson, M. R., and T. Hirschi. 1990. *A General Theory of Crime.* Stanford: Stanford University Press.

Hagan, J., and A. Palloni. 1990. The social reproduction of a criminal class in working class London, circa 1950–1980. *American Journal of Socioloy* 96 (2): 265–299.

Haskins, A. R. 2014. Unintended consequences: Effects of paternal incarceration on school readiness and later special education placement. *Sociological Science* 1: 141–158.

Hindelang, M. J. 1973. Causes of delinquency: A partial replication and extension. *Social Problems* 20 (4): 471–487.

Hirschfield, P. 2009. Another way out: The impact of juvenile arrests on high school dropout. *Sociology of Education* 82 (4): 368–393.

Hirschi, T. 1969. *Causes of Delinquency.* Berkeley: University of California Press.

Hjalmarsson, R. 2008. Criminal justice involvement and high school completion. *Journal of Urban Economics* 63 (2): 613–630.

Hockenberry, S. (2016). *Juveniles in Residential Placement, 2013.* Washington, DC: U.S. Department of Justice, Office of Justice Programs, Office of Juvenile Justice and Delinquency Programs.

Johnson, B. D., and M. C. Kurlychek. 2012. Transferred juveniles in the era of sentencing guidelines: Examining judicial departures for juvenile offenders in adult criminal court. *Criminology* 50 (2): 525–564.

Johnson, E., and J. Waldfogel. 2004. Children of incarcerated parents: multiple risks and children's living arrangements. In *Imprisoning America: The Social Effects of Mass Incarceration,* edited by M. E. Patillo, D. F. Weiman, and B. Western, 97–131. New York: Russell Sage Foundation.

Junger, M., J. Greene, R. Schipper, F. Hesper, and V. Estourgie, V. 2013. Parental criminality, family violence, and the intergenerational transmission of crime within a birth cohort. *European Journal on Criminal Policy and Research* 19 (2): 117–133.

Kaebel, D., L. E. Glaze, A. Tsoutis, and T. Minton. 2016. *Correctional Populations in the United States, 2014.* Washington, DC: U.S. Government Printing Office.

Kirk, D. S., and R. J. Sampson. 2013. Juvenile arrest and collateral educational damage in the transition to adulthood. *Sociology of Education* 86 (1): 36–62.

Kohler-Hausmann, I. 2013. Misdemeanor justice: Control without conviction. *American Journal of Sociology* 119 (2): 351–393.

Kurlychek, M. C., and B. D. Johnson. 2004. The juvenile penalty: A comparison of juvenile and young adult sentencing outcomes in criminal court. *Criminology* 42 (2): 485–517.

———. 2010. Juvenility and punishment: Sentencing juveniles in adult criminal court. *Criminology* 48 (3): 725–758.

Lemert, E. M. 1951. *Social Pathology: A Systematic Approach to the Theory of Sociopathic Behavior.* New York: McGraw Hill.

Lipsey, M. W., and J. H. Derzon. 1998. Predictors of violent or serious delinquency in adolescence and early adulthood: A synthesis of longitudinal research. In *Serious and Violent Juvenile Offenders: Risk Factors and Successful Interventions,* edited by R. Loeber and D. P. Farrington. Thousand Oaks, CA: Sage Publications.

Lopes, G., M. D. Krohn, A. J. Lizotte, N. M. Schmidt, B. E. Vasquez, and J. G. Bernburg. 2012. Labeling and cumulative disadvantage: The impact of formal police intervention on life chances and crime during emerging adulthood. *Crime and Delinquency* 58 (3): 456–488.

Mead, G. H. 1934. *Mind, Self, and Society.* Chicago: University of Chicago Press.

Mears, D. P., J. J. Kuch, A. M. Lindsey, S. E. Siennick, G. B. Pesta, M. A. Greenwald, and T. G. Blomberg. 2016. Juvenile court and contemporary diversion. *Criminology & Public Policy* 15 (3): 953–981.

Minton, T. D., and Z. Zeng. 2015. *Jail Inmates at Midyear 2014.* Washginton, DC: U.S. Department of Justice.

Murphey, D., and P. M. Cooper. 2015. Parents behind bars: What happens to their children? Available at http://www.childtrends.org/wp-content/uploads/2015/10/2015-42ParentsBehindBars.pdf.

Murray, J., C.C.J.H. Bijleveld, D. P. Farrington, and R. Loeber. 2014. *Effects of Parental Incarceration on Children: Cross-National Comparative Studies.* Washington, DC: American Psychological Association.

Murray, J., D. P. Farrington, and I. Sekol. 2012. Children's anti-social behavior, mental health, drug use, and educational performance after parental incarceration: A systematic review and meta-analysis. *Psychological Bulletin* 138 (2): 175–210.

National Research Council. 2001. *Juvenile Crime, Juvenile Justice.* Washington, DC: National Academies Press.

Nye, I. 1958. *Family Relationships and Delinquency.* New York: John Wiley and Sons.

Phelps, M. S. 2017. Mass probation: Toward a more robust theory of state variation in punishment. *Punishment and Society* 19 (1): 53–73.

Podkopacz, M. R., and B. C. Feld. 1996. The end of the line: An empirical study of judicial waiver. *Journal of Criminal Law and Criminology* 86 (2): 449–492.

Porter, L. C., and R. King. 2015. Absent fathers or absent variables? A new look at paternal incarceration and delinquency. *Journal of Crime and Delinquency* 52 (3): 414–443.

Rodriguez, N., H. Smith, and M. S. Zatz. 2009. "Youth is emmeshed in a highly dysfunctional family system": Exploring the relationship among dysfunctional families, parental incarceration, and juvenile court decision making. *Criminology* 47: 177-208.

Roettger, M. E., and J. D. Boardman. 2012. Parental incarceration and gender-based risks for increased BMI: Evidence from a longitudinal study of adolescents and young adults in the United States. *American Journal of Epidemiology* 175 (7): 636–644.

Roettger, M. E., and R. Swisher. 2009. *Examining Racial Variations in the Associations of Father's History of Incarceration with Son's Delinquency and Arrest in Contemporary U.S. Society.* National Center for Marriage Research. Bowling Green State University. Bowling Green.

———. 2011. Associations of father's history of incarceration with delinquency and arrest among black, white, and Hispanic males in the U.S. *Criminology* 49 (4): 1109–1147.

Schwartz-Soicher, O., A. Geller, and I. Garfinkel. 2011. The effect of paternal incarceration on material hardship. *Social Service Review* (3): 447–473.

Sickmund, M., and C. Puzzanchera, eds. 2014. *Juvenile Offenders and Victims: 2014 National Report.* Pittsburgh, PA: National Center for Juvenile Justice.

Smith, C. A., and D. Farrington. 2004. Continuities in antisocial behavior and parenting across three generations. *Journal of Child Psychology and Psychiatry* 45 (2): 230–247.

Sugie, N. 2012. Punishment and welfare: Paternal incarceration and families' receipt of public assistance. *Social Forces* 90 (4): 1403–1427.

Sutherland, E. H. 1939. *Principles of Criminology*. Philadelphia: J. B. Lippincott Company.

Sweeten, G. 2006. Who will graduate? Disruption of high school education by arrest and court involvement. *Justice Quarterly* 23 (4): 462–480.

Sykes, B. L., and B. Pettit. 2014. Mass incarceration, family complexity, and the reproduction of childhood disadvantage. *Annals of the American Academy of Political and Social Science* 654 (1): 127–149.

Tannenhaus, D. S. 2000. The evolution of transfer out of the juvenile court. In *The Changing Borders of Juvenile Justice: Transfer of Adolescents to the Criminal Court,* edited by J. Fagan and F. E. Zimring, 13–43. Chicago: University of Chicago Press.

Thornberry, T. P., A. Freeman-Gallant, A. J. Lizotte, M. D. Krohn, and C. A. Smith. 2003. Linked lives: the intergenerational transmission of antisocial behavior. *Journal of Abnormal Psychology* 31 (2): 171–184.

Turney, K., and A. R. Haskins. 2014. Falling behind? Children's early grade retention after paternal incarceration. *Sociology of Education* 87 (4): 241–258.

van de Rakt, M., P. Nieubeerta, and N. D. de Graaf. 2008. Life father, like son: The relationship between conviction trajectories of fathers and their sons and daughters. *British Journal of Criminology* 48: 538–556.

Wakefield, S., and R. Apel. 2017. Criminological perspectives on parental incarceration. In *When Parents Are Incarcerated: Interdisciplinary Research and Interventions to Support Children.* Edited by Christopher Wildeman, Anna R. Haskins, and Julie Tynan-Poehlmann. Washington, D.C.: American Psychological Association.

Wakefield, S., and C. Wildeman. 2013. *Children of the Prison Boom: Mass Incarceration and the Future of American Inequality.* New York: Oxford University Press.

Wildeman, C. 2009. Parental imprisonment, the prison boom, and the concentration of childhood advantage. *Demography* 46: 265–280.

———. 2014. Parental incarceration, child homelessness, and the invisible consequences of mass imprisonment. *Annals of the American Academy of Political and Social Science* 651 (1): 74–96.

Wiley, S. A. 2015. Arrested development: Does the grade level at which juveniles experience arrest matter? *Journal of Developmental and Life Course Criminology* 1: 411–433.

Wiley, S. A., L. A. Slocum, and F. A. Esbensen. 2013. The unintended consequences of being stopped or arrested: An exploration of the labeling mechanisms through which police contact leads to subsequent delinquency. *Criminology* 5: 927–966.

Wilson, J. Q., and R. Herrnstein. 1985. *Crime and Human Nature.* New York: Simon and Schuster.

14

R-e-s-p-e-c-t

Communities of Color and the Criminal Justice System

Rod K. Brunson and
Michelle N. Block

Recent clashes between protestors and the police eerily resemble violent images captured decades ago during the civil rights era. Similarly, the latest wave of collective community action reflects unrealized optimism concerning ending police violence. Moreover, renewed urban unrest reflects marginalized citizens' distrust of officers and a legal system that is often silent and/or complicit concerning police wrongdoing.

The acquittal of George Zimmerman following his killing of seventeen-year-old Trayvon Martin marked a tipping point for those concerned with the pervasive and long-standing criminalization of black men and boys (Muhammad 2010). Furthermore, in the summer of 2014, the fatal shooting of yet another unarmed black teenager, Michael Brown, led to fervent calls for criminal prosecution and several days of intense protests. The militaristic police response to the protests in Ferguson, mostly against peaceful demonstrators, fueled tensions and provoked riots. In the following weeks, the nation watched several businesses looted and burned. Police sweepingly responded to offenders, bystanders, clergy, and even national reporters with tear gas, rubber bullets, and unwarranted use of force. Unfortunately, the subsequent deaths of Tamir Rice, Eric Harris, Walter Scott, Jonathan Ferrel, Sandra Bland, Laquan McDonald, Freddie Gray, Alton Sterling, Philando Castile, and Terence Crutcher, all black suspects thought to have died by either direct police action or while in police custody, further called into question whether black lives *truly* matter.

Overall, the nation's heightened awareness about the continuing crisis of tenuous police-minority community relations has been met with responsive action (e.g., President's Task Force on 21st Century Policing [COPS Office 2015]), empathy, and yet also considerable naiveté from public and academic audiences alike. For many individuals, the deteriorating relationship between people of color and the U.S. criminal justice system is merely the result of minority citizens' persistent overrepresentation among violent offenders. Persistently frayed police-minority community relations, however, stem from decades of disparate treatment of black people by various government institutions. In this chapter, we (1) use a historical lens to situate contemporary police-minority community relations, (2) identify sources of strife between people of color and law enforcement, and (3) illuminate evidence-based initiatives in the hope of ameliorating entrenched mutual hostilities.

THROUGH A HISTORICAL LENS

In order to fully understand current tensions between police and minority citizens requires recognition that law enforcement has historically played a critical role in the formal subjugation of marginalized groups. The undeniable reality is that the policing profession is rooted in oppression and cruelty against Native Americans, poorer immigrants, and enslaved Africans. Descendants of these populations continue to view police through this historical lens and may struggle to consider police as viable sources of protection with moral authority.

Modern-day police organizations have emerged from the informal watch systems of northern states and also slave patrols within southern states, tasked with providing organized terror to deter runaway and revolting slaves (Bass 2001; Websdale 2001). In this context, those sanctioned to secure public order and safety were actually responsible for enforcing a racial caste system. For instance, when first drafted, the Constitution reified the notion that people of color should be denied the full rights afforded to white people. Furthermore, the Thirteenth Amendment, which abolished slavery, failed to protect minorities from the reign of white supremacy that followed the Civil War. In addition to withstanding racial violence from individuals, black people were also routinely victimized by organized hate groups (i.e., the Ku Klux Klan) that incessantly used public lynching as a key form of violence, intimidation, and control. However, rather than providing protection, many police departments incited if not knowingly participated in state-sponsored violence.

Similar to black Americans, other racial groups have experienced unsettling mistreatment while supposedly under the watchful eye of government agencies. For instance, the Bureau of Indian Affairs was responsible for the subjugation of many Indigenous peoples of the Americas. As European-American expansion efforts were prioritized, native inhabitants' humanity was routinely usurped. From the perspective of many Native American tribes, the aforementioned agency, originally responsible for fostering positive relations between the United States and Native American/Alaskan communities, eventually transformed into a device for untold negligence and cultural devastation (O'Brien 1996).

Following the abolition of slavery and until 1965, the Jim Crow system of laws enforced racial segregation and discrimination. This was especially the case in the South where the criminal justice system and its agents consistently controlled black people through discriminatory practices in housing, occupation, and voting rights (Bass 2001). More broadly, people of color were routinely denied protections through social, economic, and legal means. By 1954, however, the Supreme Court's ruling in *Brown v. Board of Education*, which outlawed segregation, as well as the subsequent civil rights movement, reshaped the oppression of minorities and black people in particular. Unfortunately, these strides to improve black people's societal position were also met by extreme violence, often at the hands of local police. At best, officers used water hoses, clubs, hoses, and canines and, at worst, bullets.

Following the civil rights era, within major parts of American society, overtly racist acts were replaced with economic, political, and social assaults along racial lines. Recognizing the importance of geographic location, federal policies, political leaders, and law enforcement officials all played a significant role in maintaining "white neighborhoods" and restricting black people to inner-city areas with scarce resources, including limited employment opportunities (Bass 2001). It was during this time that economic stratification by race and place first took the nation by hold.

Scholars have devoted considerable attention to investigating how geographic location helps to shape local crime control initiatives, highlighting that physical characteristics of areas largely determine the type and quality of policing services available to residents (Klinger 1997). In fact, this line of inquiry has consistently shown that "place matters," extolling the benefits of focusing crime prevention efforts on criminogenic places rather than individuals (Braga, Papachristos, and Hureau 2014). Law enforcement strategies benefitting from improved understandings of social ecology, if properly leveraged, have the potential to strengthen police-minority community relations.

Social disorganization theory asserts that certain neighborhood characteristics, such as extreme poverty, high resident turnover, and ethnic heterogeneity, lead to increased crime rates through their adverse effect on informal social control (Shaw and McKay 1942). In sum, socially disorganized communities are limited in their ability to establish strongly held conventions and regulate residents' and visitors' undesirable public behaviors. Sampson, Raudenbush, and Earls (1997) emphasize the importance of collective efficacy, defined as social cohesion and mutual trust among residents. Collective efficacy, when combined with residents' willingness to intervene in the best interest of the community, mediates much of the relationship between neighborhood structural factors and crime (Sampson, Raudenbush, and Earls 1997).

Although social disorganization theory has yielded advanced knowledge regarding crime and disorder, it can also help to sensitize policy makers to unintended consequences arising from heavy-handed law enforcement approaches. For example, research demonstrates that aggressive policing tactics are disproportionately underway in highly disadvantaged neighborhoods and help to shape residents' widespread distrust of officers' motives (Anderson 1999; Fagan and Davies 2000; Sampson and Bartusch 1998; Sampson, Raudenbush, and Earls 1997). On the other hand, rather than indiscriminately targeting entire neighborhoods for enhanced enforcement, hot spots policing (HSP) confines officers to small geographic areas where persistent crime clusters (Lawton, Taylor, and Luongo 2005; Ratcliffe et al. 2011; Sherman and Rogan 1995; Sherman and Weisburd 1995). Despite this innovation in deployment, research examining HSP's impact on police-community relations is mixed (Braga, Papachristos, and Hureau 2014). Moreover, there is concern that concentrating large numbers of hard-charging officers within small geographical spaces may unwittingly lead to unchecked discretion and increased abuse (Kochel 2010).

By emphasizing the relationship between economic disadvantage and crime as suggested by theory, police face the difficult task of disentangling race from place as people of color predominantly reside in such ecological contexts. Places can easily become typified and regulated by race, thereby exposing people of color to patterns of disparate treatment by law enforcement, further damaging their relationship with the legal system. For example, the 1991 videotaped beating of Rodney King by LAPD police officers reignited debates surrounding injustices faced by black people at the hands of police. Today, these discussions resonate even more vividly given black people's collective experiences of police abuse and vivid accounts often shared across the nation (Brunson 2007; Brunson and Miller 2006). Among people of color, these powerful narratives suggest police seeking to control crime have consistently demonstrated themselves as simply another menace plaguing public safety (see also the National Advisory Commission on Civil Disorders 1968 [Kerner Commission Report]).

Minority citizens' unfavorable assessments of the police represent a substantial threat to public safety, potentially reinforcing residents' legal cynicism toward the overall criminal justice system and lack of confidence regarding officers' ability to ensure their well-being (Anderson 1999; Sampson and Bartusch 1998). Most often reported in high-crime contexts, legal cynicism acts as a cultural mechanism, influencing individuals' behaviors, thereby contributing to trends in violence (Kirk and Papachristos 2011; Sampson and Bartusch 1998). Thus, with social disorganization theory in mind, not only do the nature and extent of police-citizen interactions help to shape neighborhood residents' beliefs about the legitimacy of the law but also their understandings regarding their own social status.

Over the past fifty years, policing efforts have perpetuated a relationship between the legal system and minority communities that is defined by authoritarianism rather than collaboration. Through discriminatory practices and policies, racial segregation and discrimination are preserved, and criminalization of black youth endures. While not all police participate in wrongdoing, the unsettling, undeniable reality is that people of color face a disproportionate amount of police harassment and misconduct. Thus, residents of minority communities frequently report experiencing the cumulative effects of racially biased policing practices, shaped through the frequent use of law enforcement to administer unjust laws (Brunson 2007; Brunson and Miller 2006; Weitzer 2000). A recent string of police shootings of unarmed black citizens serves as a stark reminder of an unfair justice system. The long-standing practice of racially biased policing may explain why the intense acrimony between the police and minority communities cannot be easily remedied. Moreover, it is through this historical framework that many people of color view contemporary policing, regardless of whether they have had firsthand negative encounters. Finally, it is worth noting that the ecological contexts conducive to over-policing also engender black citizens' complaints about under-policing, instances where officers trivialize residents' calls for service or decline to take action in distressed communities for conduct that would not be permitted in well-to-do neighborhoods.

THREATS TO POSITIVE POLICE-MINORITY COMMUNITY RELATIONS

Policing Strategies in Urban Contexts

Communities differ on several important dimensions, including their capacity for informal social control as well as the amount of crime and disorder (Bursik and Grasmick 1993). As a result, policing strategies in distressed areas are vastly different from those underway in more affluent neighborhoods (Kenney and McNamara 1999). Despite variations in responses to crime, officers' primary role requires that they remain focused on ensuring public safety. Notwithstanding, citizen assessments of the police are shaped by race with minorities, on average, expressing less favorable views when compared to white people (Brunson 2007; Weitzer and Tuch 1999, 2002). Racial differences concerning attitudes toward police should not be surprising given that aggressive policing efforts are more pervasive in disadvantaged communities where people of color disproportionately reside (Bass 2001; Howell 2009).

Precarious police-minority citizen relations largely stem from aggressive crime control tactics, creating an atmosphere where even law-abiding citizens have involuntary police contacts. In comparison to other locales, residents of high-crime communities experience greater police presence, unwelcomed police attention, and constant surveillance (Fagan and Davies 2000). Although some public officials argue that higher crime rates within urban communities warrant aggressive strategies, the nature of these efforts also engender greater opportunities for disrespectful treatment, abuses of authority, and corruption (Fagan and Davies 2000; Gau and Brunson 2015). For instance, research consistently demonstrates that residents exposed to heavy-handed policing are vulnerable to excessive use of force, arrests, pedestrian and vehicle stops, slow response times, and fewer police protections (Klinger 1997). Minority citizens' frequent experiences with proactive and aggressive crime control strategies cumulatively shape their understandings of the police as unreceptive and distrustful. More importantly, these negative effects also influence the collective sentiment among many communities of color.

Fragile police-community relations disproportionately affect minorities and are often further damaged by racially biased policing practices. Police focus on ecological conditions often departs from the original postulations of social disorganization theory. Instead, it can transform into unwarranted attention to the individual characteristics of those residing in places characterized by high crime. When officers broadly characterize neighborhoods with high levels of crime, disadvantage, and disorder as inherently dangerous, they may inadvertently do the same regarding its residents. Individuals residing or visiting such areas are frequently met with unilateral suspicion from police officers (Brunson and Miller 2006). The majority of persons within these contexts, especially, young black men, report proactive policing methods as often being comprised of degrading and aggressive speech, frequent street stops, or neighborhood sweep activities (Brunson and Miller 2006).

In an examination of three racially different but socioeconomically similar neighborhoods, Brunson and Weitzer (2009) concluded that differences in police treatment were largely attributed to citizen race. For example, white youth and those located within white neighborhoods of disadvantage reported having positive police relationships and held more positive views of officers compared to their black counterparts. In addition, white youths' police contacts were less confrontational and aggressive (Brunson and Weitzer 2009). This finding suggests that citizen race has the potential to become synonymous with being labeled suspicious, criminally inclined, and/or violent in the eyes of officers.

Relating these findings back to theory allows for negative perceptions and injustices of the past to be seen as a part of a neighborhood's legacy. Police behaviors and initiatives help to shape the community heritage that is transmitted to future generations. Residents' frequent and salient negative police encounters have the potential to influence how victims of police abuse weigh future decisions and behaviors (Kirk and Papachristos 2011).

Citizen trust in law enforcement is also potentially undermined when city leaders cite disputed official data in an attempt to defend against allegations of racially biased policing. For instance, New York City's crime drop in the 1990s received national acclaim and was widely celebrated among policy makers who attributed this feat to the adoption of order maintenance policing (OMP). This strategy, however, called for aggressive targeting of low-level offenses, through stop-and-frisk activities, primarily within disadvantaged communities of color. In fact, several scholars assert that policing strategies linking disorder to crime focus simply on policing poor people in distressed places (Fagan and Davies 2000; Harcourt 2001; Howell 2009; Rosenfeld, Fornango, and Rengifo 2007). Finally, numerous researchers challenge the notion that OMP contributed to New York City's crime decline, noting other likely influences and highlighting methodological inconsistencies (Harcourt 2001; Rosenfeld, Fornango, and Rengifo 2007).

Police Culture

In addition to the manner in which crime control initiatives are executed, officers' shared beliefs concerning specific places and individuals whom they might encounter there have a profound effect on police-minority community relations. For example, already strained relationships between police and residents of high-crime neighborhoods may be worsened if officers treat everyone as especially menacing. Through socialization processes, patrol officers develop and share an understanding that, when performing even routine tasks, there is always potential for danger. It makes perfect sense that this awareness is heightened within disadvantaged settings, given that police culture, in terms of widely held attitudes, values, and behavioral norms, reflects officers' reasonable and unreasonable responses to their occupational environments (Paoline 2003). Unfortunately, however, such shared understandings can also allow for fear to drive officers' attitudes and behaviors toward minority communities. This can result in enforcement patterns that fixate on both proactively identifying evidence of prior or ensuing criminal behavior and expanding the range of acceptable police behaviors.

Due to elevated safety concerns, officers patrolling impoverished, high-crime areas might be susceptible to assuming that the majority of people they encounter are involved in crime (Kenney and McNamara 1999; Klinger 1997). Officers working in distressed urban contexts are exposed to greater violent crime rates compared to officers working in more affluent areas. Thus, due to structural disadvantage, inner-city officers are also more likely to encounter people of color. Even officers assigned to more tranquil beats may be influenced by colleagues' vivid descriptions of dangerous settings and/or people, helping to shape how officers collectively view minority citizens and enforce the law (Kenney and McNamara 1999).

When communities of color are policed with insensitivity and as though residents are inherently dangerous, officers may inadvertently foster contexts where law enforcement mistrust can flourish. Confronted with negative police interactions, residents' suspicions about law enforcement may affect their capacity for trust and engagement, thereby increasing crime and additional negative police responses. If the development of a community culture where residents share common values depends on contextual factors, it is likely that modern policing tactics and police culture thwart opportunities for positive relations.

Irrespective of community context, the police must be mindful that each day they will encounter victims and perpetrators. This acknowledgment requires that officers resist the urge to make assumptions about all individuals within a community who fit a certain demographic profile. Generally, officers do not aggressively scrutinize, stop, disrespect, or use excessive force simply because they are racist. To the contrary, police culture suggests that aggression is acceptable and expected, given the level of perceived danger that characterizes disadvantaged communities. As a consequence, people of color live daily with the realization of increased scrutiny and greater likelihood of police abuse.

Legal Cynicism

In addition to the effect of social-structural processes on crime put forth by ecological theories, Tyler (1990) highlights the importance of process-based judgements for obtaining improved understandings of fragile police-minority community relations. Tyler and colleagues' collection of work has helped to shape contemporary discourse regarding applications of legal authority, emphasizing the benefits of public compliance and cooperation. In particular, community reactions to law enforcement are strongly determined by their judgments of the fairness in which "legal authorities make decisions and treat members of the public" (Tyler 2003, 284).

An abundant body of research has established that assessments of procedural justice and legitimacy are determined by police behavior as they go about enforcing the law (Tyler and Huo 2002). For instance, procedural justice, the perceived neutrality and consistency of law enforcement agents' decision making, encourages perceptions of legitimacy (Sunshine and Tyler 2003; Tyler 1990). Legitimacy is a property of an authority or institution that in turn leads people to view legal authorities as deserving of their cooperation, resulting in voluntary compliance (Engel 2005; Jonathan-Zamir, Weisburd, and Hasisi 2014; Sunshine and Tyler 2003; Tankebe 2013). Taken together, research asserts individuals' assessments of procedural justice and legitimacy help determine their willingness to comply with the law (Kirk and Matsuda 2011; Reisig, Wolfe, and Holtfreter 2011; Sunshine and Tyler 2003; Tyler 1990).

Widespread concerns about the lack of police legitimacy plague minority communities (Brunson et al. 2015; National Advisory Commission on Civil Disorders 1968; Pegram, Brunson, and Braga 2016). Disrespectful police treatment routinely exhibited in disadvantaged neighborhoods can erode citizens' trust and their willingness to comply with the law (Fagan and Davies 2000; Gau and Brunson 2015; Howell 2009; Kirk and Papachristos 2011). Citizen perceptions of procedural justice, legitimacy, and effectiveness have largely been studied as part of a broader concept—legal cynicism.

Beyond considerations of race or ethnicity, research indicates that legal cynicism acts as a compelling narrative framework. Individually held cynicism toward the police and the application of legal norms is viscerally shared between residents' kinship and friendship networks, generating a shared culture where conventional social norms (including legal norms) lack relevance (Sampson and Bartusch 1998). Specifically, legal cynicism can act as common beliefs about the functioning of police to the extent that people observe, perceive, and interpret situations through this frame (Kirk and Papachristos 2011).

Drakulich and Crutchfield (2013) reported that perceptions of procedural injustice are strongly related to individual race and neighborhood racial composition. Due to perceptions of an unsupportive legal institution, a community's capacity and motivation for informal social control may be seriously threatened (Kirk and Matsuda 2011). Kirk and Matsuda (2011) found that perceptions of police as biased and ineffective allow people to view any potential informal social control efforts as largely useless, thereby undermining both formal and informal control efforts. In addition, legal cynicism has a strong negative relationship with collective efficacy in that those who maintain attitudes of mistrust toward the police will be less likely to participate in local crime control efforts (Kirk and Matsuda 2011). As a result of residents' constrained decisions regarding whether to participate in informal social control, neighborhoods are vulnerable to increased criminal activity and, in response, more of the very police tactics that erode police legitimacy and increase citizen mistrust.

Individuals' rejection of police assistance has the potential to increase their reliance on personal methods of conflict resolution. Gau and Brunson's (2015) research involving young men residing in disadvantaged neighborhoods revealed that policing tactics were largely seen as arbitrary, biased, and harassing. Furthermore, their study participants described the demeanor of police during encounters as unnecessarily rough, rude, and disrespectful (Gau and Brunson 2015). In response, the majority of youths lacked trust in the genuine motives of police officers and instead relied on self-help means for securing their personal safety, such as establishing networks of neighborhood peers for protection. Gau and Brunson (2015) noted that as a result of study participants relying on their peers for safety, officers viewed them as potential dangers, most likely because personal methods of resolution have been reported to increase the likelihood of neighborhood violence in instances where victims solicit informal assistance from a friend or family member to resolve disputes (Anderson 1999). Officers as a result responded to those they perceived as rejecting their role of legal authority and assistance with greater surveillance and aggressive arrest practices (Gau and Brunson 2015).

Aside from reducing the ability of police to sanction criminal behavior, Kirk and Matsuda (2011) found that legal cynicism potentially leads to increased offending because it lowers the controlling influence of the law among individuals who question the legitimacy of those representing and upholding the law. Communities that view the police as an occupying force may reject the notion that laws should be regarded with sanctity. As a result, individuals' behavior options are expanded to also include illegal activity as such behavior may be perceived as justified given the level of alleged police misconduct or ineffectiveness.

IMPROVING THE CURRENT STATE OF AFFAIRS THROUGH EVIDENCE-BASED SOLUTIONS

A recent upsurge in media attention regarding dubious police killings of black males has made it difficult for most Americans to claim ignorance regarding frayed relations between law enforcement and blacks, and more importantly, the role that aggressive policing strategies play in worsening tensions. While general and reactive policing strategies were once preferred crime prevention methods, scholars have recently called for policing practices based on rigorous scientific evaluation. For example, "evidenced-based policing" (EBP) approaches benefit from systematic research informing the implementation of effective crime reduction policies (Sherman 1998, 2). Lum, Koper, and Telep (2011) reported that policing initiatives that are place based, proactive, and specific (such as focused deterrence) are more likely to offer larger crime reduction benefits than those that are individual based, reactive, and general.

Moreover, the growing body of EBP research demonstrates that criminal justice policies have much to gain in terms of crime reduction when they consider improving citizens' perceptions of police legitimacy, collective efficacy, and overall police-community relations. This requires police responses guided by principles of fairness and respect. Focused deterrence approaches are especially important given their demonstrated promise for reducing crime and strengthening police-community relations (Brunson 2015). While there is no shortage of contemporary crime reduction strategies, focused deterrence is recognized for its clear implementation structure and use of effective crime control principles (Lum, Koper, and Telep 2010). In the next section, we detail the breadth, underlying mechanisms, and overall societal benefits of focused deterrence.

Overview of Intervention

"Pulling-levers" strategies, set within the focused deterrence framework, are distinguished from other approaches because they emphasize tailored solutions to specific recurring crime problems while incorporating community engagement. Rather than casting a wide net across entire neighborhoods, potentially entangling both law-abiding and law-violating residents, this approach focuses on a small number of chronic offenders (Braga and Weisburd 2012). In addition, this intervention offers an added benefit compared to heavy-handed policing strategies commonly used in disadvantaged neighborhoods. Specifically, offenders are confronted by representatives of the criminal justice system and community members. They are sternly advised of the severe sanctions to come if criminal involvement continues. The warnings are then accompanied by compassionate offers of help, providing opportunities for improved police legitimacy in the eyes of community residents.

Papachristos, Mears, and Fagan (2007) examined the impact of four related focused deterrence interventions targeting gun violence in Chicago. Offender notification meetings were utilized as a way to encourage offenders to "buy in" and voluntarily comply with community members' efforts to curtail violence. Throughout the implementation phase, leaders encouraged compliance and cooperation by interacting and communicating with offenders in ways that enhanced procedural justice, treating targeted individuals with "respect and dignity" (Papachristos, Mears, and Fagan 2007, 18). At the conclusion of the quasi-experimental evaluation, Papachristos, Mears, and Fagan (2007) found that homicide rates in targeted police districts were significantly reduced by 37 percent when compared to homicide trends in matched precincts. In addition, Papachristos and colleagues observed significant reductions in gun homicides and aggravated assaults. These results are promising, as the referenced intervention heavily relied on not only altering the perceived likelihood and costs of illegal gun trafficking and gun use but also "changing the perceived legitimacy of law and legal institutions" (Papachristos, Mears, and Fagan 2007, 2).

Like most crime control approaches, focused deterrence has potential drawbacks. For example, during offender notification meetings, officers must emphasize that they are engaged in lawful and fair means to inspire compliance. If law enforcement representatives are perceived as implementing the strategy in a hostile manner, police legitimacy could be further reduced. Fortunately, there are several examples of successful pulling-levers efforts that can prove instructive for police administrators and other public officials (Braga and Weisburd 2012).

Focused deterrence has been consistently touted as an effective means of reducing criminal incidents, victimizations, and calls for service at both the city and neighborhood levels (Braga and Weisburd 2012). In a recent meta-analysis of focused deterrence strategies, Braga and Weisburd (2012) determined that the approach was associated with a significant overall effect size of 0.617, consistent with a medium standardized effect size. Although these findings were generated from primarily weaker quasi-experimental designs, they align with existing research supporting strategies, such as focused deterrence, as an effective means to reduce crime when compared to other policing strategies.

Moreover, well-coordinated, data-driven strategies allow for multi-agency collaborations, increasing the prospects for implementing interventions with consistency and transparency. Focused deterrence strategies have been successfully launched in several jurisdictions, addressing a wide range of serious crime problems (Braga et al. 2001; Braga et al. 2008; Braga and Weisburd 2012; Corsaro, Brunson, and McGarrell 2009; Corsaro and Engel 2015; Papachristos, Mears, and Fagan 2007). A growing body of literature highlights its promise for strengthening police-community relations by enhancing mutual trust between citizens and officers (Brunson et al. 2015; Corsaro, Brunson, and McGarrell 2009; Pegram, Brunson, and Braga 2016).

R-E-S-P-E-C-T: FINDING OUT WHAT IT MEANS: INTERVENTION'S MECHANISMS AND SOCIETAL BENEFITS

To improve trust of the police in minority communities, the manner in which officers enforce the law must be reconsidered. Equally important, law enforcement executives must be receptive to empirical findings informing their decisions and willing to implement new tactics. Focused deterrence interventions influence crime through several methods that can simultaneously function to enhance police legitimacy: utilizing problem-oriented frameworks, delivering proactive deterrence messages and incorporating social intervention, and community engagement messages. Put simply, this intervention encourages positive perceptions of police by employing community engagement, data-driven law enforcement tactics, fairness, and respectful treatment.

Pulling levers is situated within the problem-oriented policing framework and provides agencies with a detailed mechanism for achieving effective crime control. As such, authorities rely on public safety efforts that are both concentrated and collaborative. The best-known application of focused deterrence was conducted in Boston as part of the Operation Ceasefire Strategy (Braga et al. 1999). Rather than uniformly increasing sanctions and subjecting community residents to unwarranted, increased scrutiny, Ceasefire identified and targeted the underlying sources of persistent community crime.

Problem-oriented strategies rely on "data intelligence gathering" (Brunson 2015, 507) to diagnose crime problems, conduct comprehensive problem analysis, and develop tools for responding to and implementing customized responses (Braga, McDevitt, and Pierce 2006). Crime statistics, incident reports, offense data, and in-depth interviews with residents direct the identification of key patterns in local crime problems. These methods allow for the range and quality of criminal justice punishments to be greatly improved upon. More importantly, the initiative benefits from partnerships between law enforcement officials, community-based groups, and academic researchers.

Moreover, this initiative provides targeted crime prevention and social service delivery. Policing strategies guided by deterrence principles have been considered effective toward altering offenders' perceived benefits. Advocates of deterrence theory suggest that offenders' decisions to commit crime are influenced by the risk of punishment related to certainty, swiftness, and severity (Zimring and Hawkins 1973). Empirical evidence demonstrates, however, that the greatest deterrent effects are linked to crime reduction initiatives focused on increasing the certainty rather than the severity of punishment (Nagin 2013).

Unfortunately, severity-based deterrent approaches form the bedrock of policing tactics underway in many high-crime contexts. On the other hand, focused deterrence strategies incorporate specificity, creativity, engagement, and fairness. For instance, Braga and Weisburd (2012) suggest that this crime reduction strategy, in addition to increasing the risks of offending, strengthens the perceived legitimacy of police actions. Police legitimacy is improved in the eyes of community residents because public call-in meetings offer a fair-minded reaction to persistent crime while law enforcement officials respond to those demonstrating commitment to maintaining criminal lifestyles with the full weight of the criminal justice system.

Furthermore, by incorporating community engagement and social intervention within the crime control approach, focused deterrence has the potential to enhance community collective efficacy (Braga and Weisburd 2012). As such, the strategy aligns well with social disorganization theory, addressing weak controls in disadvantaged communities by allowing residents to develop cohesiveness as they participate in crime control efforts. Overall, implementing crime reduction strategies grounded in procedurally just methods potentially results in strengthened police-community relations.

Focused deterrence programming is geared toward providing long-term crime prevention. Police do not inspire voluntary compliance with the law when individuals are routinely accosted or victimized but do when individuals receive lawful and respectful treatment at the hands of officers. Persons at high risk of interpersonal violence consistently report being involved in fewer incidents of gun violence and overall crime after receiving the focused deterrence message delivered during call-in sessions (Braga, Papachristos, and Hureau 2014). Notably, the content of communications to offenders emphasizes the legal consequences for failing to comply, community support, as well as the availability of social services with equal weight (Papachristos, Mears, and Fagan 2007). In addition, this intervention's meticulous use of data to issue responses protects the majority of citizens within high-crime areas from insensitive officer behaviors that are commonly perceived as thoughtless, harassing, and largely ineffective. Ideas reflective of procedural justice are promoted when these tactics are combined with the working group's concern regarding how messages are delivered to offenders.

This strategy's ability to gain cooperation relates not only to offender compliance but also to community engagement and receptivity. Braga and Weisburd (2012) contend that collective efficacy is enhanced as a result of enlisting neighborhood residents in the crime control effort. Sampson, Raudenbush, and Earls (1997) explain that neighborhood crime rates are determined by a community's capacity to exert informal social control through shared expectations of normative behavior. Focused deterrence achieves a similar outcome as a result of improved citizen trust and confidence. Community support of focused deterrence initiatives increases the likelihood that crime control tactics appear more impartial and humane. In a mixed-methods evaluation of focused deterrence strategies implemented in an open-air drug market, in-depth interviews with residents of Rockford, Illinois, revealed respondents' improved confidence and support of police (Corsaro, Brunson, and McGarrell 2009).

In addition, research consistently highlights community engagement, community group partnership, and local political support as critical elements in developing successful crime reduction strategies (Braga, McDevitt, and Pierce 2006; Brunson 2015; Corsaro and Engel 2015). Police agencies must be committed to establishing collaborations because some local organizations are well positioned to lend their credibility to otherwise unpopular law enforcement efforts (Brunson 2015). Furthermore, involving community partners in the planning process can help to guide implementation strategies and promote policing that provides justice for those who need it most.

Neighborhood residents are more likely to support law enforcement operations when they understand the rationale for particular responses, their method of application, and who will be targeted. This crime reduction approach increases the likelihood that citizens will perceive police treatment as respectful and police processes as fair.

CONCLUSION

Focused deterrence strategies provide a mechanism for addressing the shortcomings of proactive crime control strategies underway in many communities of color across the United States. The intervention includes both targeted sanctions and pathways to desistence, resulting in a novel public safety approach. As police agencies seek to reduce crime in disadvantaged contexts, they must acknowledge the historical disparate treatment faced by people of color, especially at the hands of law enforcement officials. Numerous video recordings of incidents depicting police brutality, police misconduct, and police-involved shootings do well in providing visual evidence of what people of color have asserted for many decades. In addition, to ensure that the policing method fosters positive outcomes, research partners should work toward improving officers' understanding of evidenced-based policies. In developing effective crime control responses, police should be reminded that successful crime reduction desperately depends on strong relationships with the communities they serve. Interventions should be evaluated not only in terms of reducing crime but also regarding whether they foster public support and mutual respect. This requires an understanding that citizen cooperation and compliance are strongly influenced by rank-and-file officers' actions. Simply put, police officers themselves can improve relations with the public by simply adhering to principles of fairness and respect.

The notion that disadvantaged community contexts, where minorities disproportionately reside, warrants heavy-handed policing tactics will continue to worsen fragile police-minority community relations. Public discourse calling for black citizens challenging racially discriminatory policing practices to first "stop killing one another" is polarizing and detrimental. For instance, Braga and Brunson (2015, 1) explain, "The term 'black-on-black' violence, while statistically correct, is a simplistic and emotionally charged definition of urban violence that can be problematic when used by political commentators, politicians and police executives. To the vast majority of urban black residents who are not involved in violence or criminal behavior, the term invokes visions of indiscriminate and aggressive police enforcement responses applied to a broad range of black people." Police must be willing to engage with individuals who are distrustful and express concerns about the fairness of crime strategies. In a just society, individuals who are perceived as suspicious and/or dangerous should not forfeit their civil liberties. Focused deterrence interventions strive to make this expectation an attainable reality by enhancing public safety and promoting principles of fairness.

REFERENCES

Anderson, E. 1999. *Code of the Street: Decency, Violence, and the Moral Life of the Inner City*. New York: W. W. Norton.

Bass, S. 2001. Policing space, policing race: Social control imperatives and police discretionary decisions. *Social Justice* 28 (1): 156–176.

Braga, A. A., and R. K. Brunson. 2015. The police and public discourse on "black on black" violence. *New Perspectives on Policing*. Washington, DC: U.S. Department of Justice, National Institute of Justice, 2015. NCJ 248588.

Braga, A. A., D. M. Hureau, and C. Winship. 2008. Losing faith? Police, black churches, and the resurgence of youth violence in Boston. *Ohio State Journal of Criminal Law* 6 (1): 141–172.

Braga, A. A., D. M. Kennedy, E. J. Waring, and A. M. Piehl. 2001. Problem-oriented policing, deterrence, and youth violence: An evaluation of Boston's Operation Ceasefire. *Journal of Research in Crime and Delinquency* 38 (3): 195–225.

Braga, A. A., J. McDevitt, and G. L. Pierce. 2006. Understanding and preventing gang violence: Problem analysis and response development in Lowell, Massachusetts. *Police Quarterly* 9 (1): 20–46.

Braga, A. A., A. V. Papachristos, and D. M. Hureau. 2014. The effects of hot spots policing on crime: An updated systematic review and meta-analysis. *Justice Quarterly* 31 (4): 633–663.

Braga, A. A., and D. L. Weisburd. 2012. The effects of pulling levers' focused deterrence strategies on crime. *Campbell Systematic Reviews* 6.

Braga, A. A., D. L. Weisburd, E. J. Waring, L. G. Mazerolle, W. Spelman, and F. Gajewski. 1999. Problem-oriented policing in violent crime places: A randomized controlled experiment. *Criminology* 37 (3): 541–580.

Brunson, R. K. 2007. "Police don't like black people": African-American young men's accumulated police experiences. *Criminology and Public Policy* 6 (1): 71–101.

———. 2015. Focused deterrence and improved police–community relations. *Criminology and Public Policy* 14 (3): 507–514.

Brunson, R. K., A. A. Braga, D. Hureau, and K. Pegram. 2015. We trust you, but not *that* much: Examining police-black clergy partnerships to reduce youth violence. *Justice Quarterly* 32: 1006–1036.

Brunson, R. K., and J. Miller. 2006. Young black men and urban policing in the United States. *British Journal of Criminology* 46 (4): 613–640.

Brunson, R. K., and R. Weitzer. 2009. Police relations with black and white youths in different urban neighborhoods. *Urban Affairs Review* 44 (6): 858–885.

Bursik, R. J., and H. G. Grasmick. 1993. *Neighborhoods and Crime: The Dimensions of Effective Community Control.* Lanham, MD: Lexington Books.

COPS Office. 2015. *President's Task Force on 21st Century Policing Implementation Guide: Moving from Recommendations to Action.* Washington, DC: Office of Community Oriented Policing Services.

Corsaro, N., R. K. Brunson, and E. F. McGarrell. 2009. Problem-oriented policing and open-air drug markets: Examining the Rockford pulling levers deterrence strategy. *Crime & Delinquency* 59 (7): 1085–1107.

Corsaro, N., and R. S. Engel. 2015. Most challenging of contexts. *Criminology & Public Policy* 14 (3): 471–505.

Drakulich, K. M., and R. D. Crutchfield. 2013. The role of perceptions of the police in informal social control: Implications for the racial stratification of crime and control. *Social Problems* 60 (3): 383–407.

Engel, R. S. 2005. Citizens' perceptions of distributive and procedural injustice during traffic stops with police. *Journal of Research in Crime and Delinquency* 42: 445–481.

Fagan, J., and G. Davies. 2000. Street stops and broken windows: Terry, race and disorder in New York City. *Fordham Urban Law Journal* 28: 457.

Gau, J. M., and R. K. Brunson. 2015. Procedural injustice, lost legitimacy, and self-help young males' adaptations to perceived unfairness in urban policing tactics. *Journal of Contemporary Criminal Justice* 31 (2): 132–150.

Harcourt, B. E. 2001. *Illusion of Order: The False Promise of Broken Windows Policing.* Cambridge, MA: Harvard University Press.

Howell, K. B. 2009. Broken lives from broken windows: The hidden costs of aggressive order maintenance policing. *New York University Review of Law & Social Change* (3): 271.

Jonathan-Zamir, T., D. Weisburd, and B. Hasisi. 2014. The effects of security threats on antecedents of police legitimacy. In *Policing Terrorism, Crime Control, and Police-Community Relations,* 79–97. New York: Springer International Publishing.

Kenney, D. J., and R. P. McNamara. 1999. *Police and Policing: Contemporary Issues.* Westport, CT: Praeger.

Kirk, D. S., and M. Matsuda. 2011. Legal cynicism, collective efficacy, and the ecology of arrest. *Criminology* 49 (2): 443–472.

Kirk, D. S., and A. V. Papachristos. 2011. Cultural mechanisms and the persistence of neighborhood violence. *American Journal of Sociology* 116 (4): 1190–1233.

Klinger, D. A. 1997. Negotiating order in patrol work: An ecological theory of police response to deviance. *Criminology* 35 (2): 277–306.

Kochel, T. R. 2010. Constructing hot spots policing: Unexamined consequences for disadvantaged populations and for police legitimacy. *Criminal Justice Policy Review* 22 (3): 350–374.

Lawton, B. A., R. B. Taylor, and A. J. Luongo. 2005. Police officers on drug corners in Philadelphia, drug crime, and violent crime: Intended, diffusion, and displacement impacts. *Justice Quarterly* 22 (4): 427–451.

Lum, C., C. S. Koper, and C. W. Telep. 2011. The evidence-based policing matrix. *Journal of Experimental Criminology* 7 (1): 3–26.

Muhammed, K. G. 2010. The condemnation of blackness: Race, crime and the making of modern urban America. Cambridge, MA: Harvard University Press.

Nagin, D. S. 2013. Deterrence in the twenty-first century: A review of the evidence. *Crime and Justice* 42 (1): 199–263.

National Advisory Commission on Civil Disorders. 1968. *Report of the National Advisory Commission on Civil Disorders*. Washington, DC: U.S. Government Printing Office.

O'Brien, S. 1996. Bureau of Indian Affairs. In *Encyclopedia of North American Indians*, 85–88. New York: Houghton Mifflin Harcourt Publishing Company.

Paoline, E. A. 2003. Taking stock: Toward a richer understanding of police culture. *Journal of Criminal Justice* 31 (3): 199–214.

Papachristos, A. V., T. L. Mears, and J. Fagan. 2007. Attention felons: Evaluating project safe neighborhoods in Chicago. *Journal of Empirical Legal Studies* 4 (2): 223–272.

Pegram, K., R. K. Brunson, and A. A. Braga. 2016. The doors of the church are now open: Black clergy, collective efficacy, and neighborhood violence. *City & Community* 15 (3): 289–314.

Ratcliffe, J. H., T. Taniguchi, E. R. Groff, and J. D. Wood. 2011. The Philadelphia foot patrol experiment: A randomized controlled trial of police patrol effectiveness in violent crime hotspots. *Criminology* 49 (3): 795–831.

Reisig, M. D., S. E. Wolfe, and K. Holtfreter. 2011. Legal cynicism, legitimacy, and criminal offending the nonconfounding effect of low self-control. *Criminal Justice and Behavior* 38 (12): 1265–1279.

Rosenfeld, R., R. Fornango, and A. F. Rengifo. 2007. The impact of order-maintenance policing on New York City homicide and robbery rates: 1988–2001. *Criminology* 45 (2): 355–384.

Sampson, R. J., and D. J. Bartusch. 1998. Legal cynicism and (subcultural?) tolerance of deviance: The neighborhood context of racial differences. *Law and Society Review* 777–804.

Sampson, R. J., S. W. Raudenbush, and F. Earls. 1997. Neighborhoods and violent crime: A multilevel study of collective efficacy. *Science* 277 (5328): 918–924.

Shaw, C., and H. McKay. 1942. *Juvenile Delinquency and Urban Areas*. Chicago: University of Chicago Press.

Sherman, L. W. 1998. Evidence-based policing. Ideas in American policing. July. Washington DC, Police Foundation. Available at https://www.policefoundation.org/publication/evidence-based-policing/.

Sherman, L. W., and D. P. Rogan. 1995. Effects of gun seizures on gun violence: "Hot spots" patrol in Kansas City. *Justice Quarterly* 12 (4): 673–693.

Sherman, L. W., and D. Weisburd. 1995. General deterrent effects of police patrol in crime "hot spots": A randomized, controlled trial. *Justice Quarterly* 12 (4): 625–648.

Sunshine, J., and T. R. Tyler. 2003. The role of procedural justice and legitimacy in shaping public support for policing. *Law & Society Review* 37 (3): 513–548.

Tankebe, J. 2013. Viewing things differently: The dimensions of public perceptions of police legitimacy. *Criminology* 51 (1): 103–135.

Tyler, T. R. 1990. *Why People Obey the Law: Procedural Justice, Legitimacy, and Compliance.* New Haven, CT: Yale University Press.

———. 2003. Procedural justice, legitimacy, and the effective rule of law. *Crime and Justice* 283–357.

Tyler, T. R., and Y. Huo. 2002. *Trust in the Law: Encouraging Public Cooperation with the Police and Courts.* New York: Russell Sage Foundation.

Websdale, N. 2001. *Policing the Poor: From Slave Plantation to Public Housing.* Boston: Northeastern University Press.

Weitzer, R. 2000. Racialized policing: Residents' perceptions in three neighborhoods. *Law and Society Review* 34 (1): 129–155.

Weitzer, R., and S. A. Tuch. 1999. Race, class, and perceptions of discrimination by the police. *Crime & Delinquency* 45 (4): 494–507.

———. 2002. Perceptions of racial profiling: Race, class, and personal experience. *Criminology* 40 (2): 435–456.

Zimring, F. E., and G. Hawkins. 1973. *Deterrence: The Legal Threat in Crime Control.* Chicago: University of Chicago Press.

15

Organizational Change and Criminal Justice

Working within the Iron Cage

Danielle Rudes and
Shannon Magnuson

Walk the halls of any criminal justice organization and you are sure to hear this sentiment at least once: "Things around here never change." While it is true that the external environment often moves quickly as new laws, policies, regulations, and technological advances dramatically insert change into criminal justice organizations, life inside justice organizations traditionally moves at a glacial pace. Due in part to a largely mechanistic (Burns and Stalker 1961) structural design that includes an overwhelmingly top-down, quasi-militaristic, bureaucratic framework, implementing change or reform inside today's prisons, courts, and parole/probation units is challenging at best. When change does not occur, or does not occur as planned, organizational culture commonly receives the blame. An amorphous concept, organizational culture (and its sister concept, climate), collectively form an ever present "catchall" repository for excuses regarding why and how reform and change did not implement as designed or failed completely. Although frequently named and studied, organizational culture is poorly understood and research seldom emphasizes the mechanisms and contexts of particular cultures and knowledge of the amalgamation of culture broadly. That is, although it is a common topic of study in criminal justice research, knowledge of organizational culture suffers from four primary failures: (1) culture/climate studies largely focus on the macro-organizational level, leaving the contextual nuance of particular organizations or units/departments within organizations virtually unexamined; (2) culture/climate studies primarily rely on survey methodology that limits the answer pool and aggregates findings up, again neglecting the meso- and micro-organizational levels; (3) scholars studying organizational culture/climate make numerous assumptions about how culture in other fields or disciplines may operate similarly in criminal justice organizations, but without much empirical data to support these hypotheses, and (4) culture/climate studies do not regularly explore related concepts known to organizational scholars that hold promise for unpacking the culture/climate black box. These include (1) organizational learning, (2) organizational communication (specifically framing), and (3) resistance to change.

In this chapter, we consider the extant scholarship on organizational culture as it conceptually relates to these three areas. We offer a review of existing scholarship, recommendations, and suggestions for how and why organizational culture is under- or mis-studied and how and why improving our knowledge in the areas of organizational learning, communication, and resistance may potentially improve change processes and outcomes within organizations broadly and within criminal justice organizations (e.g., corrections organizations) specifically.

WHAT'S THE PROBLEM?

Macro-understanding

Max Weber's *iron cage* metaphor represents a conceptual and ideological prison that is akin to an organizational self-fulfilling prophecy. As Weber imagined it, organizations—once they develop a bureaucratic structure—surrender to that structure in perpetuity. In essence, organizations continually reify and recreate their own bureaucratic structural components as they conduct their work, leaving no pathway for broad structural change. Over the years, the iron cage idea gained tremendous traction in organizational studies as an inertial force stagnating organizational form and impeding or blocking organizational change. As a "black box" of organizational lore, the iron cage regularly represents a common excuse for failed reform and yet remains a relatively misunderstood feature of organizations.

Likewise, organizational culture—another commonly used, yet largely misunderstood, organizational concept—is regularly conceptualized to encompass the iron cage, that is, a collection of lived experiences projecting from an organization's structural inertia. Organizational culture permeates in the halls and resides in the nooks and crannies of the cage, where over time, as workers accomplish tasks and jobs, the cloud of culture exudes into the organizational environment, controlling the ways business is done (Ouchi and Wilkins 1985). The seemingly homogenous cloud permeates the organization, developing under conditions of long, stable membership, hierarchical boundaries, and an absence of institutional alternatives (Ouchi and Wilkins 1985), reaffirming its broad and nebulous conceptualization by scholars.

The macro-analytic approach details organizational culture generally as evolving from patterned formal and informal practices, beliefs, languages, symbols, and other functions needed to maintain social structure and order. Particularly, in correctional agencies, culture facilitates normative control (Kunda 1992) and resistance to explicit attempts toward manipulation and change. This does not suggest organizational actors passively operate within the iron cage. To the contrary, they at times accept, deny, react to, and reshape their occupational environment (Goffman 1961). Their responses reflect their organization with the structural components of a mechanistic environment infused by the ways people work within it.

Despite much research in this area, this macro-organizational sum of ideas remains abstract at this level, leaving the contextual nuance within organizations inexplicit. As organizations proffer culture as the force undermining change efforts, the unexamined and unexplored nature of culture lends little to understanding specific conditions facilitating or halting change. Highly mechanistic and bureaucratic organizations, like correctional agencies, remain stagnant, stale, and unresponsive to the outer environmental demands for change without the guidance of theoretical developments at a meso-level, where the most variability and least understanding exists.

Methodology

Organizational culture as a descriptive extension of Weber's iron cage traces its roots from research observations of how groups routinize practices and beliefs through explicit and implicit rituals. As such, early developments relied on ethnographic and observational methodologies, leading to some generalizations of organizational culture from determinations of individual people. Efforts to develop defined constructs of culture led scholars to move away from qualitative methods and primarily to surveying individuals within organizations. Using actors within an organization as the unit of analysis elicits responses about potential new constructs of culture by the population responsible for its development. For example, in a survey of transportation managers, Odom, Boxx, and Dunn (1990) use a twenty-four-item scale measured on a four-point Likert scale with responses describing three umbrella dimensions of organizational culture: *bureaucratic* (measured as hierarchical, procedural, structured, orderly, established, cautious, power oriented, and internally regulated), *innovative* (measured as risk taking, results oriented, creative, pressure oriented, stimulating, challenging, enterprising, and driving), and *supportive* (measured as collaborative, people oriented, encouraging, sociable, equitable, safe, and trusting). Other measures also operationalize additional concepts relating to culture, such as the relational aspects of culture where scholars measure *respect for people* (measured as fairness, respect for individual rights, and praise for contribution; O'Reilley, Chatman, and Caldwell 1991; Erdogan, Liden, and Kraimer 2006), *aggressiveness* (measured as competitiveness and lack of supportiveness; O'Reilley, Chatman, and Caldwell 1991; Erdogan, Liden, and Kraimer 2006), and *team orientation* (measured as development of friends and low conflict; Uhl-Bien, Graen, and Scandura 2000; Erdogan, Liden, and Kraimer 2006).

Despite these meaningful contributions to understanding culture, Hofstede and colleagues (1990, 289) note organizations include several culturally varied units/departments consisting of "culturally different work groups." This is particularly true for corrections agencies with various departments and staff roles. They further add, "Determining units [of analysis] sufficiently homogenous for comparing cultures is both a theoretical and empirical problem" (289). Simply relying on the individual as the unit of analysis without additional meso-level identifiers (work groups/departments) reinforces aggregation and macro-knowledge despite contributions of new discrete and independent constructs. This results in few practical suggestions for organizations undergoing change or assessing organizational capacity/readiness to change.

Broad Assumptions

Without practical suggestions and meso- and micro-level findings, scholars studying correctional agencies can only report broad implications and posit assumptions regarding antecedents or cultural proxies as indicators of organizational change. For example, research suggests haphazardly articulated goals or competing ideologies increase role conflict (staff working without purpose unsure of tasks, deadlines, and how their work contributes to the organizational mission; Hepburn and Albonetti 1980; Morill 1998) or role ambiguity (Rizzo, House, and Lirtzman 1970), thus leading to decreased job satisfaction (Getahun, Sims, and Hummer 2008; Simmons, Cochran, and Blount 1997) and organizational commitment (Lambert, Kelley, and Hogan 2013). These structural inadequacies then invite burnout (Whitehead and Lindquist 1986)—among other challenges—and staff turnover (Camp 1994), potentially complicating change efforts.

Intuitively, these cultural dimensions and consequences may explain the difficulty in implementing change. However, they do not prescribe a theoretical framework for a culture of change. Further, as scholars continue studying change in correctional agencies, their conclusions imply a need for theoretical development. For example, following an initiative to change business practices within the California Department of Corrections, Battalino, Beutler, and Shani (1996) suggest linking change to operational goals, removing rigid role definitions, and developing a learning structure fostering staff ability to learn, adopt, and adapt change for the setting.

This call for a framework infused with communication and learning continues in studies years later. In corrections-specific studies, Farrell, Young, and Taxman (2011) and Steiner, Travis, and Makarios (2011) urge agencies to clarify their mission, connect it to anticipated outcomes of change innovations, and include this link in training programs. Explanatory inclusion of how change will improve the organization and staff roles might mitigate staff precontemplation following introduction of reform (Rogers 2003), particularly when staff do not immediately identify with new goals. Scholars emphasizing the need to assess prechange context (Rudes, Lerch, and Taxman 2011) highlight the absence of a theoretical framework to do so.

Studies, particularly correctional studies, emphasizing the role of culture in organizational change do not regularly explore related concepts known to organizational scholars that hold promise for facilitating a culture of change. These include (1) organizational communication (i.e., framing), (2) organizational learning, and (3) resistance to change. These are imperative for guiding correctional agencies through their own metaphorical and literal iron cage during change.

WHAT'S THE THEORY?

Organizational Communication (and Framing)

In highly bureaucratic and quasi-militaristic environments such as correctional agencies, change often emerges via top-down administrative mandates with little regard for how this and other micro-processes of communication directly or indirectly impact change and performance. Drawing from extensive sociological and political science literature regarding mobilizing social movements and collective action, institutional framing or constructing a purposeful distinction between the old process and the new process provides a viable framework for communicating change (Ybema 2010).

Borrowing from collective action frames, the process denotes a bidirectional "schemata of interpretation" where individuals with their own frames—organized collections of experiences, assumptions, and beliefs driving action—consume institutional information simplified to appeal to the institution's interpretation of how these individual frames interact with mobilizing and legitimizing change (Goffman 1974; Snow and Benford 1988). That is, an institutional strategy of change-selling rhetoric is presented to strike the most responsive chord to mobilize the greatest number of people (Dutton, O'Neill, and Lawrence 2001). This micro-process of organizational communication is foundational for achieving "mobilizing potency" (Benford and Snow 2000) where organizational actors outside the inner circle of selecting the change are the initiators of the change.

However, the degree of frame resonance and subsequent action are contingent upon issues of consistency, credibility, and reliability (Benford 1993; Benford and Snow 2000). Consistency refers to the degree of congruence between messages over time, where frames containing dissonance and contradictions undermine earlier successfully delivered frames (Benford 1993). Maintaining clear messages facilitates credibility or the fit/alignment between frame and change (Snow and Benford 1988; Benford 1993). Issues of credibility not only include fit of change itself but also the change messenger; institutional status and respect of communicator influence plausibility of claims (Benford 1993). Secured credibility then guides reliability or concordance between empirical validity of change and the change's frame (Benford 1993; Benford and Snow 2000).

Achieving resonance in bureaucratic agencies suggests aggregation of individuals but also requires meso-alignment as measured by either departmental alliance or managerial alliance (Bacharach, Bamberger, and Sonnenstuhl 1996). This meso-level can also be responsible for framing logics on the ground (McPherson and Sauder 2013) or repeating the institutional frame downward and subjected to equal emphasis of consistency, credibility, and reliability by the micro-level or front line. Not only are meso-level actors responsible for digesting and translating decision-making messages, but they are also responsible for knowing how best to present these logics both in order and in form (Dutton, O'Neill, and Lawrence 2001). These micro-processes of frame alignment between each functional node within a hierarchical environment (Bacharach, Bamberger, and Sonnenstuhl 1996) provide implications for adopting and facilitating change while also highlighting communication channels and processes easily vulnerable to misalignment, thus impeding the possibility of change.

Not surprisingly, studies detailing links between positive perceptions of communication and increased job performance occur in the private sector (Lull, Frank, and Piersol 1955; Pincus 1986). However, Garnett, Marlowe, and Panday (2008) find communication mediates positive effects on performance in mission-oriented cultures but not in rule-oriented cultures. Latessa (2004) notes the importance of managerial communication of change to individual workers as a way of helping improve connections between how they understand the change and their roles and responsibilities within the changing environment. Further, Rudes and colleagues (2011), during a period of transitioning at a detention facility (to a reentry facility), found the absence of change explanations reinforced change adversity and undermined reform efforts. Although typically bound by rigid rules and structure, correctional agencies are typically mission-oriented organizations with goals of improving public safety and reducing recidivism. Taken together, framing change in the context of the mission and as perceptive of meso- or micro-audience needs provides the potential for redirecting structural inertia and begins providing a theoretical framework for facilitating effective change processes.

Organizational Learning

Despite consistency, credibility, and reliability of change and the presence of frame alignment between hierarchical nodes, the change promised is not always the change delivered. This paradox creates a gulf between perceptions and knowledge. Although individual learning informs an organization's capacity for learning, organizational learning is not the total of individual learning. Organizational learning refers to improving organizational actions through the development and maintenance of supportive structures facilitating on-going collective learning and routines (Levitt and March 1988). For mechanistic organizations such as correctional agencies, this seems to imply an existing structure. Although intense routinization exemplifies correctional agencies, in its current form, routines do not enhance the cognitive development of members. Change guided by organizational learning is not a process to adjust change within the structure (Hedberg 1981). Rather, it is a process for redefining norms, values, and views and establishing a knowledge market economy with both supply and demand for new information and learning (Ardichvili, Page, and Wentlin 2003).

More specifically, Crossan, Lane, and White (1999) suggest four related processes of organizational learning during stages of strategic renewal or change. These include: (1) intuiting, (2) interpreting, (3) integrating, and (4) institutionalizing. These processes occur within individual, group, and organizational levels. Intuiting and interpreting occur at individual levels and refer to observing new experiences from change and refining and developing meaning (Crossan, Lane, and White 1999). This process of sense making occurs at the individual level but fosters robustness when it occurs by interacting with peers. As groups make sense of change in tandem with coordinated actions with colleagues, interpreting then naturally transitions to the integrating process. Collective actions perceived as effective are repeated, suggesting group-level dynamics make determinations about the parts of change worthy of replication and routinization. Formal rules and procedures, or institutionalization, embed change and occur at the organizational level.

This dynamic process continues to resemble features of bureaucratic processes but separates itself by promoting a bottom-up learning process instead of a traditional process of institutionalization occurring first.

Reversing the process of diffusion through an organization's network and structure relates positively to job satisfaction (Jurik and Winn 1987). Interestingly, job satisfaction and its sister indicator, organizational commitment, positively influence knowledge building and, more specifically, knowledge donating—communication of knowledge capital (Van Den Hooff and de Ridder 2004), suggesting a cyclical and on-going learning process. This is especially useful in mission-driven organizations where knowledge donating (supply) and knowledge collecting (demand) are not bound by rigid structure but are instead perceived as necessary processes for outcomes.

In correctional settings, to secure correctional officer use of social learning and behavioral management techniques with offenders, one statewide community corrections agency implemented an organizational learning environment within a subset of its units (Taxman 2008). Officers received technical training and an opportunity to offer feedback on both the training and the feedback they received from use of the skills learned in training. Additionally, supervisors received empirical evidence supporting use of the new behavioral management practice and suggesting processes for transporting evidence into supervision strategies. Lastly, the agency promoted opportunities for learning by electronically sharing journal articles and fostering reading clubs (Taxman 2008). Ultimately, the change model focused on improving skills and enhancing cognitive development of officers to create an environment focused on offender achievements and resulted in improvements to change goals of reduced technical violations and new arrests (Taxman 2008).

In contrast, in her evaluation of a cognitive skills development program, aimed to provide problem-solving and reasoning skills to juvenile offenders, Pullen (1996) found the structure and implementation of the learning experience for probation officers undermined the effectiveness of teaching the skills necessary for officers to run the program themselves, particularly because they were not held accountable for understanding the information at trainings or translating manual language to a conversational tone. Coupled with a lack of enthusiasm for training and the absence of removing workload in exchange for participation, Pullen (1996) concludes the lack of an open and constructive learning environment undermined the quality and effectiveness of the training program and ultimate use of the development program.

Despite scant literature regarding the presence and impact of organizational learning cultures on correctional agencies, it nonetheless provides another theoretical framework considering three measures of analysis: individual, group, and organizational processes as part of unpacking mechanisms facilitating change.

Organizational Resistance

Together, organizational communication/framing and organizational learning theories offer frameworks facilitating iterative and contextually responsive strategies for introducing change. These frameworks consider staff experiences and their intellectual development as a necessary condition for achieving outcomes. However, individual interpretations of organizational or meso-level frames may misalign or individual sense-making processes may not receive support from group-level interpretations, creating a tension for change that leads either individuals or meso-units to resist change.

In overt and formal meso/group action, resistance constitutes strikes, work stalls, grievances, and departmental interest in maintaining the status quo (Griener 1967). In most cases, however, displays of resistance are far more informal, pervasive (Kolb and Putnam 1992), and often undetected, including taking unauthorized breaks, purposefully reducing outputs, noncooperation, absenteeism/lateness, social sabotage, employee theft, or resignation (Leibowitz and Tollison 1980; Jones 1984; Scott 1985; Tucker 1993, LaNeuz and Jernier 1994; Rosigno and Hodson 2004; Lawrence and Robinson 2007). These actions serve as coping mechanisms or "small wins" of professional autonomy (Morill 1998, 249) and may be the result of ideological alignment or self-interest (Cheliotis 2006).

In the context of change, ideological reasoning and self-interest are commonly confused with and interconnected to individual sense making of the organization's framing or failure to provide learning opportunities. Persson and Svensson (2011), following new protocols of using a risk assessment as part of presentence reports, found officers dismayed by a new report formula (to include risk assessment results) because they perceived it to limit discretion in the writing process. However, under closer examination, Persson and Svensson (2011) discover that officers did not understand the use of risk assessment results as part of the final report submitted. As a result, noncompliance was not necessarily the result of resisting inclusion of risk results or the tool itself but misconceptions of why the report formula changed and how it improved processes.

As part of introducing change, organizations must make explicit connections between change efforts and workload impact and job effectiveness. Although some organizations responded to staff concerns and needs by integrating these topics into initial trainings (Ferguson 2002), failure to do so can result in staff not trusting or believing in the change or tool (Viglione, Rudes, and Taxman 2014), thereby impacting its usefulness in practice (Turpin-Petrisio 1999; Viglione, Rudes, and Taxman 2014).

Resistance as a common response to misaligned frames, lack of knowledge, or a reflection of individual or department feelings toward change (fear, distrust, self-interest, etc.) can impede or ultimately disallow change from diffusing as the new way "things are done." Considering organizational resistance as part of a framework for understanding change not only provides information as to what change is morphing into but also why this process is occurring. This is fundamental for providing practical guidance to correctional agencies where pockets of resistance at either the individual- or meso-level suggest the strongest indicators of structural inertia and the places where plugging these holes may allow the organization to leverage momentum in a constructive and change-oriented direction.

WHAT'S THE SOLUTION?

As corrections organizations continue instituting change in a turbulent environment consistently demanding implementation of "what works" strategies, they face implementation processes rich with challenges and without a framework for understanding why these challenges exist and how best to tackle them. Reliance on existing scholarship about organizational change only provides broad generalizations to a field desperate for practical guidance. However, changing how scholars study change demands tackling another iron cage of structural inertia, or a misguided and consistently reifying academic perception that the all-encompassing "culture" is to blame. This perception is clouding the ways correctional scholars study culture within the proverbial and actual iron cage and demands a movement from macro- *through meso-level* to micro-level understandings from both a theoretical and methodological point of view.

To initiate this momentum, scholars must resist reliance on broad-scale organizational theories and move toward studying the minutia of change theory. This may require a synthesis of traditional approaches with implementation theory. Gendreau, Goggin, and Smith (1999, 184) argue that frontline staff need to "participate directly in designing" new programming and are an untapped resource in most processes as their knowledge regarding the needs of the population and the situational work contexts contribute to a greater understanding of the practicality of translating and transporting reform into practice (Maynard-Moody, Musheno, and Palumbo 1990). Thus, as scholars continue to outline new constructs of culture hampering change, they must consider appropriate methods where meso-level (departments or middle management) and micro-level (individuals, small working groups, or small units) units of analysis are standard practice and necessities of influential research. This is particularly crucial because these subunits do not merely exist within the iron cage but are also part of accepting, interpreting, reacting, and reshaping the ongoing streams of routine in which they work

(Goffman 1961; Cheloitis 2006). They are true implementers of ground-level change (Rudes, Lerch, and Taxman 2012) and, without considering these valuable points of view, a more narrowly focused and implementation science-infused framework offers little room for knowledge growth and practical guidance.

Further, scholars must consider using an implementation framework to understand the tenets of organizational culture(s) rather than relying on individual- or staff-level actions/reactions to change as key indicators of culture. To do this, correctional scholars must (1) consider agency framing logics during introductory periods of change alongside the roles of meso-units (e.g., management) for interpreting and translating organizational frames to staff within the context of individual logics. Then, after considering alignment/misalignment between organizational nodes, scholars must (2) consider organizational learning processes or capacity-building strategies, including the content, quality, and delivery of all training. Once organizations provide the necessary resources and skills to staff, (3) correctional scholars must then assess how organizations continue to use framing logics to set expectations and discuss change efforts within the context of direct workload and efficiency impacts. As the change meets line staff on the ground, (4) traditional questions and forms of understanding alignment and sense making should continue but with layers or meaningful subsets of the organization up for consideration in addition to individual interpretations. The limited research discussed above suggests that (5) scholars must continue investigating nuanced resistant and discretionary efforts by various units. This will provide a crucial next step toward developing practical suggestions for discussing localizing practices as well as (6) studying the process of change before, during, and after implementation. As research builds in each of these areas scholars can (7) ask meaningful change sustainability questions and propose constructive fidelity measures and guidelines for facilitating a culture systematically measuring its own change efforts.

Improving knowledge regarding organizational culture, particularly via organizational communication/framing, learning and resistance may improve change processes and outcomes within organizations broadly and within criminal justice (e.g., corrections organizations) specifically. It may not only clarify the nebulous cloud of culture living within the black box of Weber's iron cage, but it also may provide constructive guidance to organizational leaders suffering from the mechanistic and bureaucratic framework characterizing the more literal iron cage. "Culture" may continue serving as the catchall excuse for slow or stalled organizational change, but armed with new knowledge of its nuance, it may no longer be in response to why change does not happen, but instead it may provide answers to *why and how change occurs.*

REFERENCES

Ardichvili, A., V. Page, and T. Wentlin. 2003. Motivation and barriers to participation in virtual knowledge-sharing communities of practice. *Journal of Knowledge Management* 7 (1): 64–77.

Bacharach, S., P. Bamberger, and W. J. Sonnenstuhl. 1996. The organizational transformation process: The micropolitics of dissonance reduction and the alignment of logics in action. *Administrative Science Quarterly* 41 (3): 477–506.

Battalino, J., L. Beutler, and A. B. (Rami) Shani. 1996. Large-system change initiative: Transformation in progress at the California Department of Corrections. *Public Productivity & Management Review* 20 (1): 24–44.

Benford, R. 1993. Frame disputes within the nuclear disarmament movement. *Social Forces* 71 (3): 677–701.

Benford, R., and D. Snow. 2000. Framing processes and social movements: An overview and assessment. *Annual Review of Sociology* 26: 611–639.

Burns, T., and G. M. Stalker. 1961. *The Management of Innovation*. 2nd ed. London: Tavistock Publications.

Camp, S. D. 1994. Assessing the effects of organizational commitment and job satisfaction on turnover: An event history approach. *Prison Journal* 74: 279–305.

Cheloitis, L. 2006. How iron is the iron cage of new penology? *Punishment and Society* 8 (3): 313–340.

Crossan, M. M., H. W. Lane, and R. E. White. 1999. An organizational learning framework: From intuition to institution. *Academy of Management Review* 24 (3): 22–537.

Dutton, J., R. O'Neill, and K. Lawrence. 2001. Moves that matter: Issue selling and organizational change. *Academy of Management Journal* 44 (4): 716–736.

Erdogen, B., R. Liden, and M. Kraimer. 2006. Justice and leader-member exchange: The moderating role of organizational culture. *Academy of Management Journal* 49 (2): 395–406.

Farrell, J., D. W. Young, and F. S. Taxman. 2011. The effects of organizational factors on use of juvenile justice supervision practices. *Criminal Justice & Behavior* 38: 565–583.

Ferguson, J. 2002. Putting the "what works" research into practice. *Criminal Justice and Behavior* 29 (4): 472–492.

Garnett, J. L, J. Marlowe, and S. K. Panday. 2008. Penetrating the performance predicament: Communication as a mediator or moderator of organizational culture's impact on public organizational performance. *Public Administrative Review* 68 (2): 266–281.

Gendreau, P., C. Goggin, and P. Smith. 1999. The forgotten issue in effective correctional treatment: Program implementation. *International Journal of Offender Therapy and Comparative Criminology* 43: 180–187.

Getahun, S., B. Sims, and D. Hummer. 2008. Job satisfaction and organizational commitment among probation and parole officers: A case study. *Professional Issues in Criminal Justice* 3 (1): 1–16.

Goffman, E. 1961. *Asylums: Essays on the Social Situation of Mental Patients and other Inmates*. London: Penguin.

———. 1974. *Frame Analysis*. New York: Harper & Row.

Greiner, L. E. 1967. Patterns of organizational change. *Harvard Business Review* 45 (3): 119–130.

Hedberg, B. 1981. How organizations learn and unlearn? In *Handbook of Organizational Design*, edited by P. C. Nystrom and W. H. Starbuck, 8–27. London: Oxford University Press.

Hepburn, J. R., and C. Albonetti. 1980. Role conflict in correctional institutions. *Criminology* 17 (4): 445–459.

Hofstede, G., B. Neuijen, D. Ohayv, and G. Sanderes. 1990. Measuring organizational cultures: A qualitative and quantitative study across twenty cases. *Administrative Science Quarterly* 35 (2): 286–316.

Jones, G. R. 1984. Task visibility, free riding, and shirking: Explaining the effect of structure and technology on employee behavior. *Academy of Management Review* 9 (4): 684–695.

Jurik, N. C., and R. Winn. 1987. Describing correctional-security dropouts and rejects: An individual or organizational profile? *Criminal Justice and Behavior* 14: 5–25.

Kolb, D., and L. Putnam. 1992. Introduction: The dialectics of disputing. In *Hidden Conflict: Uncovering the Behind-the-Scenes Disputes,* 1–31. Thousand Oaks, CA: Sage.

Kunda, G. 1992. *Engineering Culture: Control and Commitment in a High Tech Corporation*, 8–22, 88–91, 108–113, 154–159. Philadelphia: Temple University Press.

Lambert, E. G., T. Kelley, and N. L. Hogan. 2013. Hanging on too long: The relationship between different forms of organizational commitment and emotional burnout among correctional staff. *American Journal of Criminal Justice* 38 (1): 51–66.

LaNeuz, D., and J. M. Jermier. 1994. Sabotage by managers and technocrats: Neglected patterns of resistance at work. In *Resistance and Power in Organizations*, edited by J. J. Jermier, D. Knights, and W. R. Nord. London: Routledge.

Latessa, E. J. 2004. The challenge of change: Correctional programs and evidence-based practices. *Crime and Public Policy* 3 (4): 547–560.

Lawrence, T. B., and S. L. Robinson. 2007. Ain't misbehavin: Workplace deviance as organizational resistance. *Journal of Management* 33 (3): 378–394.

Leibowitz, A., and R. Tollison. 1980. A theory of legislative organization: Making the most of your majority. *Quarterly Journal of Economics* 94 (2): 261–277.

Levitt, B., and J. March. 1988. Organizational learning. *Annual Review of Sociology* 14: 319–340.

Lull, P. E., E. F. Frank, and D. T. Piersol. 1955. What communication means to the corporation president. *Advanced Management* 20: 17–20.

Maynard-Moody, S., M. Musheno, and D. Palumbo. 1990. Street-wise social policy: Resolving the dilemma of street-level influence and successful implementation. *Western Political Quarterly* 43 (4): 833–848.

McPherson, C. M., and M. Sauder. 2013. Logics in action: Managing institutional complexity in a drug court. *Administrative Science Quarterly* 58: 1–32.

Morrill, C. 1998. Honor and conflict management in corporate life. In *The New American Cultural Sociology*, edited by Philip Smith, 230–259. Cambridge: Cambridge University Press.

Odom, R., R. Boxx, and M. Dunn. 1990. Organizational cultures, commitment, satisfaction, and cohesion. *Public Productivity & Management Review* 14 (2): 157–169.

O'Reilly, C., J. Chatman, and D. Caldwell. 1991. People and organizational culture: A profile comparison approach to assessing person-organization fit. *Academy of Management Journal* 34 (3): 487–516.

Ouchi, W., and A. Wilkins. 1985. Organizational culture. *Annual Review of Sociology* 11: 457–483.

Persson, A., and K. Svensson. 2011. Signs of resistance? Swedish probation officers' attitudes towards risk assessments. *European Journal of Probation* 3 (3): 95–107.

Pincus, J. D. 1986. Communication satisfaction, job satisfaction, and job performance. *Human Communication Research* 12 (3): 395–419.

Pullen, S. 1996. Evaluation of the reasoning and rehabilitation cognitive skills development program as implemented in juvenile ISP in Colorado. Colorado Division of Criminal Justice. NIJ 93-IJ-CX-K017.

Rizzo, J. R., R. J. House, and S. I. Lirtzman. 1970. Role conflict and ambiguity in complex organizations. *Administrative Science Quarterly* 15 (2): 150–163.

Rogers, E. M. 2003. *Diffusion of Innovations.* 5th ed. New York: Free Press.

Roscigno, V., and R. Hodson. 2004. The organizational and social foundations of worker resistance. *American Sociological Review* 69: 14–39.

Rudes, D. S., J. Lerch, and F. S. Taxman. 2012. Implementing a reentry framework at a correctional facility: Challenges to the culture. *Journal of Offender Rehabilitation* 50 (8): 467–491.

Scott, J. C. 1985. *Weapons of the Weak.* New Haven, CT: Yale University Press.

Simmons, C., J. K. Cochran, and W. R. Blount. 1997. The effects of job-related stress and job satisfaction on probation officers' inclinations to quit. *American Journal of Criminal Justice* 21 (2): 213–229.

Snow, D. A., and R. D. Benford. 1988. Ideology, frame resonance and participant mobilization. *International Social Movement Research* 1: 197–217.

Steiner, B., L. F. Travis, and M. D. Makarios. 2011. Understanding parole officers' responses to sanctioning reform. *Crime and Delinquency* 57 (2): 222–246.

Taxman, F. S. 2008. No illusions: Offender and organizational change in Maryland's proactive community supervision efforts. *Crime and Public Policy* 7 (2): 275–302.

Tucker, J. 1993. Everyday forms of employee resistance. *Sociological Forum* 8 (1): 25–45.

Turpin-Petrisio, C. 1999. Are limiting enactments effective? An experimental test of decision making in a presumptive parole state. *Journal of Criminal Justice* 27 (4): 321–332.

Uhl-Bien, M., G. B. Graen, and T. Scandura. 2000. Implications of leader-member exchange LMX for strategic human resource management systems: Relationships as social capital for competitive advantage. In *Research in Personnel and Human Resource Management*, edited by G. Ferris. Greenwich, CT: JAI Press.

Van Den Hooff, B., and J. A. de Ridder. 2004. Knowledge sharing in context: The influence of organizational commitment, communication, climate and CMC use on knowledge sharing. *Journal of Knowledge Management* 8 (6): 117–130.

Viglione, J., D. S. Rudes, and F. S. Taxman. 2014. Misalignment in supervision implementing risk/needs assessment instruments in probation. *Criminal Justice and Behavior* 42 (3): 263–285.

Whitehead, J. T., and C. A. Lindquist. 1986. Correctional officer job burnout: A path model. *Journal of Research in Crime and Delinquency* 23: 23–42.

Ybema, S. 2010. Talk of change: Temporal contrasts and collective identities. *Organizational Studies* 31: 481–501.

16

Gun Policy

Jennifer Carlson

The American gun debate is often treated as one of the most intractable and divisive culture wars in the contemporary political context. Galvanized by the clarion calls like "What part of 'shall not be infringed' do you not understand?" and "I don't dial 911!" on the gun rights side and "Gun sense voter" and "Disarm hate" on the gun control side, these two factions often present the debate as one of clear choices between diametrically opposed policy proposals.

Simplifying the complexities of policy work—that is, after all, what politicians do. Yet peeling back the layers of American gun policy reveals that this debate is anything but simple. Gun regulation occupies a crowded policy arena with hundreds of laws operating at times together but oftentimes at odds—at the local, state, and federal levels (Spitzer 2015a, 2015b). This means that there is no single American gun policy; rather, the policies Americans experience are vastly divergent.

To understand this complexity, consider the regulations necessary to purchase a firearm in the two bordering states of Arizona and California. Each state is, of course, part of the United States of America, bound by the U.S. Supreme Court decisions in *Heller v. District of Columbia* and *McDonald v. Chicago*. These 2008 and 2010 decisions, respectively, affirmed an individual-rights interpretation of the Second Amendment (Winkler 2011). Yet consider how this individual right is regulated in practice across the two states:

- In Arizona, gun purchasers may buy a firearm from a private seller or a federally licensed firearms dealer. Arizona does not require private sellers to conduct background checks on purchasers, although it does require that gun sellers do not knowingly sell to a prohibited person or sell a long gun to a person under the age of eighteen or a handgun to a person under the age of twenty-one. By law, all federally licensed firearms dealers must conduct a background check with the FBI's National Instant Criminal Background Check System (NICS) based on the buyer's government-issued identification; a check is usually completed within minutes, at which point the buyer can take possession of the firearm. There are no restrictions on the purchase of ammunition.

- In California, gun sales and transfers must be completed through a licensed California dealer, who will conduct a background check on all purchases against both the California Department of Justice database of prohibited persons and the federal NICS. A government-issued identification is required to establish proof of identity, residency, and age (eighteen for long guns; twenty-one for handguns). As of January 1, 2015, the California Office of the Attorney General requires that all firearms purchases include a Firearms Safety Certificate (FSC; previously Handgun Safety Certificate) and successful safety demonstration with the purchased handgun (*or* an FSC exemption) as well as proof of California residency (such as a utility bill, a property deed, or a government-issued identification other than the Department of Motor Vehicles identification required to establish identification). Previously, these requirements applied only to handguns. In 2016, Governor Jerry Brown signed into law new ammunition regulations that restrict ammunition sales by licensed vendors and that require purchasers to undergo a background check.

This example of the stunning divergence in gun-purchase regulation across the United States is matched by equally stark differences in other arenas of gun regulation. Indeed, far from a coherent gun-policy framework, the United States exhibits multiple gun-policy approaches and multiple gun publics. The goal of this chapter is to contextualize American gun policy in its unique gun-rich, high-crime, and politically divisive setting, to introduce the intricacies of American gun policy, and to evaluate the impacts—both intended and unintended—of these policies.

The chapter starts by mapping out the broad context of guns in America, including gun violence, gun availability, and gun attitudes. It examines the great variation in approaches—both conceptually and practically—to gun policy, including *what* can be regulated and *how* at the federal, state, and local levels. It then considers the impacts of different gun policies, exploring both their intended and unintended consequences. The chapter concludes by offering some thoughts on how to address both the pragmatics and politics of gun-policy making by taking stock of how gun cultures and gun policies intertwine.

THE CONTEMPORARY GUN CONTEXT

To understand American gun policy requires understanding the American gun context. Three aspects distinguish it: first, the scope and magnitude of gun-related injury and death; second, the supply of guns in circulation and the proportion of Americans who own them; and, third, the complex state of public opinion on guns, which is hotly divided on some issues but broadly united on others.

Gun Violence

According to the Centers for Disease Control and Prevention (CDC), more than 30,000 gun deaths occur every year in the United States; about one-third of these are homicides, and the other two-thirds are suicides. CDC figures reveal that a small but meaningful number of gun deaths—about 600—occur every year because of "accidental" or "negligent" discharges of firearms. This is a little greater than the number of deaths resulting from "mass shootings": although there is no universal agreement on what constitutes a mass shooting (thus, debate about whether such shootings are increasing in frequency persists), shootings involving at least four people killed or wounded (other than the shooter) resulted in 475 deaths in 2015 according to the crowd-sourced wiki Mass Shootings (Kelly 2015).[1]

According to FBI data, gun homicides and negligent firearms deaths have significantly decreased since the 1990s, while gun suicides have increased along with other suicides, according to the National Center for Health Statistics. As Mark Shields observed on *PBS NewsHour* (Jacobson 2013), more Americans have died at the barrel of a gun since 1968 than in all U.S. wars, and the U.S. firearms death rate is ten times that of other high-income, developed countries, meaning that, among these countries, 82 percent of people killed by firearms were killed in the United States (Grinshteyn and Hemenway 2016). Not only does the United States have a disproportionate share of gun deaths but also within the United States gun violence is concentrated. Boys and men of color in urban areas are disproportionately the victims of homicides; according to 2008 U.S. Department of Justice figures, a black male teen was seven times more likely to die from homicide than a white male teen (Cooper and Smith 2011, 14). Meanwhile, middle-aged white rural men are disproportionately the victims of suicide; white people commit gun suicide in a ratio of 3:1 compared to African Americans, according to CDC data analyzed by the *Washington Post* (Keating 2013).

As stunning as this death toll is, measuring gun violence in deaths alone underestimates the breadth of the impact of gun violence. For example, scholars estimate that there are roughly one hundred shootings for every homicide. Individuals who survive gun violence often experience significant stigma, shame, and hardship related to ongoing social and medical complications resulting from gunshot wounds (Lee 2012). In economic terms, wounded individuals also suffer from lost wages and reduced quality of life. A 2015 report led by Ted Miller of the Pacific Institute for Research and Evaluation and profiled in *Mother Jones* attempted to quantify these costs, estimating that the price of gun violence roughly equates to $700 per American, or $229 billion, per year, once direct costs (emergency response, healthcare, court fees, family mental healthcare, prison) and indirect costs (lost wages, reduced quality of life) are calculated (Follman et al. 2016). However, this cost is not shared equally: given the concentration of gun homicides and assaults in impoverished communities of color, communities least resourced to cope with the long-term costs of nonlethal gun violence disproportionately bear its burden.

Finally, individuals who are indirectly touched by gun violence are also harmed. Children who grow up in areas of concentrated gun violence—even if they do not directly experience gun violence—suffer diminished reading ability, cognitive function, and long-term health outcomes, as well as increased risks of anxiety, depression, tremors, nightmares, and other symptoms associated with post-traumatic stress disorder (Boynton-Jarrett et al. 2008; Duncan 1996; Sharkey 2010; Sharkey et al. 2012). As children and young teens live with ongoing violence, they cope in a variety of ways—from turning gun violence into a childhood game (e.g., playing "funeral") to adopting a so-called war-zone mentality that normalizes a kill-or-be-killed attitude as a means of survival (Garbarino 2015; see also Anderson 2000; Collins 2009; Contreras 2012). Thus, the cost of violence is not just lives lost and injuries sustained disproportionately among poor racial minorities but also *more* trauma and violence.

Gun Stock

While there is no national registration or log of all guns[2]—legal or illegal—in circulation in the United States, recent estimates suggest that there are "more guns than people" (Ingraham 2015) in the United States (Krause 2012). Roughly two-thirds of these firearms are long guns (rifles and shotguns);

about one-third are handguns (Krause 2012). Going by background checks conducted via the FBI NICS, gun sales have spiked dramatically since 2008 and tend to be particularly high during holiday shopping periods (especially Black Friday) and in the days following a highly publicized mass shooting. As of this writing, the all-time high for NICS checks was on November 24, 2017, with 203,086 requests (Johnson 2017). Note that this figure does not reflect multiple firearms bought in a single purchase; nor does it reflect purchases that require no background check, which in some states may include private sales and sales to concealed-pistol license holders.

Just as we do not know exactly how many guns are in circulation in the United States, we also do not know with precision the social profile—or even the raw numbers—of Americans who legally own guns. Gallup and General Social Survey (GSS) data, both of which cover personal and household gun ownership, conflict as to whether household gun ownership and personal gun ownership are down (GSS) or erratic (Gallup; Pew Research Center 2013). (Some scholars suggest that measured declines may be attributed, at least in part, to gendered reporting disparities rather than changes in ownership [Legault 2013; Ludwig, Cook, and Smith 1998].) Regardless, the discrepancy between the surveys highlights a surprising lack of consensus surrounding such basic metrics as gun ownership. Nevertheless, when paired with NICS data indicating an increased gun stock, these self-reported gun-ownership measures suggest that Americans own more guns—even if the number of Americans who own them has not increased.

What do we know about these gun-owning Americans other than that they own guns? We know that motivation for gun ownership has swung toward personal protection and away from hunting: in 2013, 48 percent of gun owners surveyed by the Pew Research Center said they own firearms for personal safety or protection, while 32 percent said they own them for hunting. This contrasts with data collected in 1999, which showed only a quarter of gun owners motivated by personal protection and half motivated by hunting (Pew Research Center 2013). According to 2014 Pew data, gun-owning households are disproportionately white as compared to black or Hispanic (41 percent versus 19 percent versus 20 percent); rural versus suburban or urban (51 percent versus 36 percent versus 25 percent) and conservative as compared to moderate or liberal (41 percent versus 36 percent versus 23 percent) (Morin 2014). Surveys on individual gun ownership, such as those conducted annually by Gallup, have found that southern married men and southern white men have particularly high rates of gun ownership (64 percent and 61 percent), while nonsouthern white women; nonwhite women; and nonsouthern unmarried women have particularly low rates of individual gun ownership (13 percent, 12 percent, and 10 percent) (Jones 2013). Overwhelmingly, Gallup found that the single most powerful factor in determining individual gun ownership was gender: men are five times more likely than women to own guns; region, marital status, race, ethnicity, age, and even political ideology were also significant but paled in comparison to the power of gender, impacting the odds of gun ownership by factors of roughly 1.5 to 1.7 (Jones 2013). Pew Research Center (2013) data also suggest that white married southern and midwestern men are particularly likely to own guns: three times as many men as women own guns; twice as many white people as African Americans own guns;[3] and southerners (29 percent) together with midwesterners (27 percent) account for more than half of gun owners.

Gun Attitudes

Who owns guns, and whether fewer Americans own more guns, must also be contextualized within broader public opinion on guns. According to the Pew Research Center (2016), the balance between Americans who favor controlling gun ownership and those who favor protecting individual rights has hovered around 50/50 since 2010. Gun owners, men, conservatives and moderates, and white people are much more likely to support gun rights over gun control (Pew Research Center 2016). However, the picture of public opinion changes once the topic narrows from abstract ideological commitments to specific policies. Nearly three-quarters of Americans oppose a ban on handguns (Swift 2015). In 2015, 56 percent of respondents told Gallup they agree that "if more Americans carried concealed weapons," the United States would be safer, which reflects majorities or near-majorities (within the margin of error) among gun owners and non–gun owners, among men and women, across all age groups, and across rural, suburban, and urban areas (Newport 2015).[4] Another poll querying Americans' views on guns in the home reveals a similar sentiment: men and women; whites and nonwhites; easterners, midwesterners, southerners, and westerners; and Republicans and Independents all agreed in the majority that a gun makes a home a safer place (only 41 percent of Democrats, however, agreed with this statement) (McCarthy 2014). Meanwhile, Americans—57 percent of all adults, 68 percent of gun owners, and 49 percent of non–gun owners—agree that stricter gun laws "give too much power to government over average citizens" (Pew Research Center 2013). In some cases, Americans—gun owners and non–gun owners alike—are united in supporting certain gun-control mechanisms, such as background checks for private gun sales and laws preventing people with mental illness from buying firearms (Pew Research Center 2013, 2015). Finally, policy proposals such as assault-style weapons bans and federal databases to track gun sales are more contentious, especially along the divide between gun owners and non–gun owners and between Republicans and Democrats (Pew Research Center 2015).

GUN-POLICY PARADIGMS

Contemporary gun policy reflects and reinforces the complex U.S. gun context in terms of gun violence, gun stock, and gun attitudes. Before heading into the complex maze of gun policy at the federal, state, and local levels, some orientation toward different gun-policy paradigms is helpful. While gun policy is often presented as a binary opposition between gun rights (meaning less regulation) and gun control (meaning more regulation), this presentation can obscure more than it reveals with regard to gun policy. On the one hand, some gun-policy approaches—such as banning gun ownership by convicted violent felons—enjoy support across both sides of the gun debate. On the other hand, de jure gun regulations may in fact *expand* de facto gun rights. Consider concealed-carry laws: so-called "shall-issue" concealed-carry legislation creates a regulatory system (a licensing system for would-be gun carriers) that facilitates more guns in public. While this vastly expands what licensees can do with the guns they own (and thus is largely viewed as in line with a gun-rights perspective), at the state level these National Rifle Association (NRA)-backed laws create with regard to gun carriers what at the federal level the gun lobby has vigorously opposed with regard to gun owners: a registration system.

To move beyond the gun rights/gun control dichotomy, it is helpful to think of three different paradigms that have driven gun policy: a targeted-enforcement approach, a preventive approach, and a self-defense approach. The targeted-enforcement approach, rooted in a criminological perspective, refers to the development and use of strategic, problem-oriented policing tools and tactics aimed at identifying and disarming individuals who commit—or are likely to commit—criminal gun offenses. These policies often overlap with policies aimed at gang-related and drug-related offenses. The preventive approach, rooted in a public health perspective, refers to policies aimed at reducing primary, secondary, and tertiary risk related to firearms. Instead of disarming *people* (as in the case of targeted enforcement), these policies are more focused on removing guns from *situations* that have a high potential for injury or death. Finally, the self-defense approach aims at expanding access to firearms for the purpose of self-defense. This approach involves not only expanding where individuals may carry guns and the parameters under which individuals may lawfully engage in self-defense but also—at least in states that license gun carriers—vetting individuals interested in carrying guns. In this regard, the self-defense approach flips both the preventive approach and the targeted-enforcement approach on their heads, focusing instead on *arming* vetted individuals and *increasing* the proliferation of guns into settings from which they were formerly prohibited.

Contemporary gun policy at the federal, state, and local levels is a messy, uneven, and at times contradictory amalgam of these three approaches. Nevertheless, public policy, albeit with notable exceptions, trends toward facilitating gun access and gun use.

Federal Policies

The most well-known and widely cited federal dictum on American gun policy is the Second Amendment:

> A well-regulated militia being necessary to the security of a free State, the right of the People to keep and bear arms shall not be infringed.

Legal scholars and historians alike have debated at length whether the Second Amendment is individualist (applying to individual gun owners) or collectivist (applying only to organized militias), culminating in the 2008 Supreme Court case *Heller v. District of Columbia*, which interpreted the Second Amendment as providing an individual the right to own handguns (Winkler 2011). This decision was subsequently incorporated to the states in 2010 in *McDonald v. Chicago*. Justice Antonin Scalia, who wrote the majority opinion in *Heller*, clarified that the affirmation established neither a constitutional right to carry nor a constitutional bar to gun regulations: "nothing in our opinion should be taken to cast doubt on longstanding prohibitions on the possession of firearms by felons and the mentally ill, or laws forbidding the carrying of firearms in sensitive places such as schools and government buildings, or laws imposing conditions and qualifications on the commercial sale of arms."

Other than overturning the District of Columbia's effective ban on handgun ownership, *Heller* did little to change gun policy at the federal level. National gun policies largely revolved around (1) restricting (and, at times, banning) certain kinds of guns and gun accessories,[5] (2) restricting gun possession in certain public areas, (3) banning certain people from firearms possession, (4) imposing additional penalties on individuals who commit crime with guns, and (5) regulating the records-keeping capacity of federal agents to vet and track gun purchasers.

The first landmark federal legislation, the National Firearms Acts of 1934 and 1938, regulated and taxed fully automatic firearms, silencers, and short-barrel rifles and shotguns; regulated gun businesses by requiring firearms sellers and manufacturers to hold a federal firearms license and maintain other records-keeping standards; and forbid the sale of firearms to felons (Cook and Goss 2014). The 1968 Gun Control Act reintroduced and expanded many of these regulations by, for example, extending the prohibition on firearms ownership from felons to persons with mental illnesses (Goss 2015; Zimring 1975). It also outlawed interstate commerce of firearms except between licensed dealers and prohibited the importation of military surplus fully automatic guns. Subsequent laws have further tightened restrictions on certain kinds of firearms. The 1986 Firearms Owner Protection Act prohibits the manufacturing of fully automatic guns for the civilian market (Hardy 1986), while the 1994 Federal Assault Weapons Ban, which expired in 2004, prohibited the manufacturing of firearms defined as "assault weapons" and "high-capacity" magazines (Cook and Goss 2014). Finally, the 1990 Gun-Free School Zones Act, which was overturned by the U.S. Supreme Court in 1995 and amended in 1996, forbids any "unauthorized" person from possessing a firearm in a school zone (Kopel 2009).

Also passed in the early 1990s, the 1993 Brady Handgun Violence Prevention Act requires a federal background check on individuals purchasing guns from a licensed firearms dealer and establishes a mechanism for conducting these checks through the National Instant Criminal Background Check System (Cook and Goss 2014; Jacobs and Potter 1995). Unfortunately, these checks often rely on incomplete databases. For example, the Virginia Tech shooting revealed a critical failure of the NICS system: many states were not populating their mental health records into the national system (Goss 2015, 205). In response, Congress passed the 2007 NICS Improvement Amendments Act to incentivize states to add mental health records to the national background check database.

Background checks for firearms purchases are not universal, as private sales are not included under the act's mandate. Furthermore, the establishment of a searchable registry of gun owners or gun sales is prohibited by the 1986 Firearms Owner Protection Act and subsequent amendments, which restrict the regulatory capacity of the Bureau of Alcohol, Tobacco, and Firearms (BATF) by limiting BATF site visits to licensed firearms dealers, reducing criminal penalties for noncompliant dealers, and placing restrictions on the kinds of information that can be released to the public. This has created a bureaucratic impasse, as the BATF is also charged with tracing crime guns (as per the 1968 Gun Control Act) with the sales paperwork it collects from gun dealers. But in order to be legally compliant, the bureau cannot computerize this paperwork in a systematic, searchable manner (Goode and Stolberg 2012).

The federal imposition of gun bans and gun background checks tends to dominate debate about gun policy. But another area of active gun policy that has generally enjoyed public approval involves policies targeted at criminal offenders, especially gun offenders. The Gun Control Act of 1968 established a mandatory minimum sentence for gun offenders as well as offenders who unlawfully carry a firearm in the commission of a felony; the Armed Career Criminal Act of 1984 established further sentencing enhancements for gun offenders with prior violent or serious drug convictions. During the 1980s, 1990s, and into the 2000s, sentencing enhancements were strengthened to target the use of certain firearms, firearms devices, and ammunition, such as sawed-off shotguns, fully automatic firearms, silencers, and armor-piercing ammunition (Hofer et al. 2000). Rather than gun-control restrictions, these mandatory minimums and sentencing enhancements have been passed as sensible "tough on crime" policies. Another policy that has enjoyed widespread public consensus, the ban on possession of firearms by convicted felons, has been in place since 1968. The only exception to this general public approval involves the prohibition of gun possession by domestic violence misdemeanants, passed as part of the 1994 Violence Against Women Act. Instead of treating this as another "tough on crime" proposal, gun-rights advocates aggressively opposed the measure. In his dissenting opinion in the 2016 Supreme Court case *Voisine v. United States*, conservative Justice Clarence Thomas wrote that this prohibition "is already very broad. It imposes a lifetime ban on gun ownership for a single intentional nonconsensual touching of a family member. A mother who slaps her 18-year-old son for talking back to her—an intentional use of force—could lose her right to bear arms forever if she is cited by the police under a local ordinance." Nevertheless, the prohibition remains over twenty years since the passage of the 1994 Violence Against Women Act.

State Policies

The labyrinth of state-level policies on guns makes the complex federal picture seem almost straightforward. The vast majority of gun regulation happens at the state level. In fact, the majority of states have Second Amendment equivalents within their state constitutions, many of which explicitly recognize a right to self-defense (Kopel 1998). For example, Article 6 of Michigan's state constitution reads, "Every person has a right to keep and bear arms for the defense of himself and the state." Just a handful of states, including California, New Jersey, and New York, have no such provision within their state constitutions.

Beyond these articles within state constitutions, gun policy covers areas as diverse as gun bans, gun-carry laws, self-defense use, mental health precautions, domestic violence precautions, and mandatory minimum sentencing laws. Somewhat simplifying this complicated terrain, many states have so-called firearms preemption, which means that local municipalities cannot pass regulations that are stricter than those mandated by state law.

Assault Weapons

After the Assault Weapons Ban expired in 2004, a variety of firearms and firearms accessories became deregulated in most states. However, in states that already had passed a state-level ban or would subsequently pass such a ban, many of these weapons remained illegal. California, Connecticut, Hawaii, Maryland, Massachusetts, New Jersey, and New York have banned weapons by either name or according to the presence of generic features, such as folding stocks or pistol grips. Minnesota and Virginia more heavily regulate these guns but do not ban them. The other forty-one states do not impose particular regulations on this class of firearms (Law Center to Prevent Gun Violence 2016a).

Gun Carry

Most states issue licenses to residents to carry a firearm concealed on a so-called "shall-issue" basis (National Rifle Association 2016). Prior to the 1970s, states generally issued gun-carry licenses on a "may-issue" basis, which meant that gun licenses were granted at the discretion of licensing officials. At the time of this writing, shall-issue laws in effect in forty states remove that discretion and instead require states to grant licenses if statutory requirements regarding age, residency, criminal history, and mental health are satisfied. Relatively few states, including California, Delaware, Hawaii, Maryland, Massachusetts, New Jersey, New York, and Rhode Island, issue licenses on a limited, discretionary basis (although some of these states have significant within-state variation). Connecticut is an exception: although it is legally a may-issue state, in practice it tends to issue licenses on a shall-issue basis. Vermont's system is also noteworthy: it has no system for issuing licenses and allows anyone who can legally possess a firearm to carry it; however, residents under the age of sixteen require the permission of a parent or guardian (Law Center to Prevent Gun Violence 2016b). Eleven additional states—Alaska, Arizona, Idaho, Kansas, Maine, Missouri, Mississippi, New Hampshire, North Dakota, West Virginia, and Wyoming—have further deregulated their permitting systems, allowing lawful gun owners to carry a firearm without a permit; unlike Vermont, however, these so-called permit-less or constitutional carry states retain the permitting system for residents wishing to obtain a license for out-of-state carry or other purposes. Finally, thirty states allow residents to openly carry a handgun without a permit. While no one knows how many people legally carry without a license, the latest estimates from the Crime Prevention Research Center estimate over 16.3 million licensed gun carriers in the United States (Lott 2017).

Justifiable Gun Use

Most justifiable homicides are committed using firearms; from 2010 to 2014, firearms were involved in 81 percent of the 1,433 justifiable homicides reported to the FBI (Uniform Crime Report 2014). In parallel with the expansion of gun carry, the use of guns in self-defense has also undergone significant legal changes. The United States inherited the "duty to retreat" and "castle" doctrines from England; while the duty to retreat doctrine required that a person—usually, a man—attempt to retreat before resorting to the use of lethal force, the castle doctrine recognized that insofar as "a man's house is his castle," a person cannot retreat within his or her own home. Therefore, the duty to retreat was suspended in the domicile. By late nineteenth-century and early twentieth-century America, the castle doctrine was extended in several states to apply to public areas, which marked the emergence of the "no duty to retreat" doctrine in the United States (Brown 1991). According to the American Bar Foundation, by 2015 there were seventeen states that place a duty to retreat on would-be victims; thirty-three states require no such duty (National Task Force on Stand Your Ground Laws 2015). Twenty-four of these states have enacted so-called "stand your ground" laws. According to Florida's statute, which passed in 2005 and prompted a wave of copycat laws in other states, "a person is justified in the use of deadly force and does not have a duty to retreat if...He or she reasonably believes that such force is necessary to prevent imminent death or great bodily harm to himself or herself or another or to prevent the imminent commission of a forcible felony."[6] In addition to removing the duty to retreat and sanctioning individuals to intervene in certain felonies, the statute grants immunity from criminal prosecution and civil action if force is deemed justifiable. John Roman (2013) of the Urban Institute found that white-on-black homicides were more likely to be deemed "justifiable" in states with Stand Your Ground laws.

Mental Health

Although gun policy tends to ignite partisan divides, regulations on firearms and mental health have enjoyed bipartisan support at the state level (Goss 2015). During the ten-year period from 2004 to 2014, new laws in thirty-six states required the reporting of relevant mental health records, clarified prohibition criteria relating to mental illness in nine states, and stipulated the protocol for the seizure or surrender of firearms (or revocation of firearms license) due to mental health issues in eight states (See Table 2 in Goss 2015). In addition, twenty-seven states enacted laws that included a rights restoration protocol for people who at some point had been disqualified because of mental health reasons (See Table 2 in Goss). As of 2016, forty-seven states authorize or require mental health records to be reported either to NICS (in forty-two states) or an in-state database (Arkansas, California, Michigan, Ohio, and Utah). Colorado, Florida, Nebraska, Missouri, Pennsylvania, and West Virginia authorize but do not require reporting; Montana, New Hampshire, and Wyoming have not authorized or required reporting (Law Center to Prevent Gun Violence 2016c). In line with Goss's (2015) analysis, there is relatively broad consensus regarding mental health reporting, and in contrast to the policy picture for most other state-level gun laws, the outliers are states favoring loosened gun restrictions rather than tightened gun restrictions.

Safe Storage and Child Access Prevention (CAP)

Unintentional shooting deaths appear to have undergone a dramatic decline over the past hundred years (note that changing data collection techniques make direct comparisons unfeasible). According to CDC figures, around 16,000 injuries and 600 deaths result each year from unintentional, accidental, or negligent firearms discharge (see Carlson and Cobb 2017 for details on these firearms injuries and deaths). In order to prevent injuries and deaths resulting from gun accidents involving children, individual states have mandated child access prevention laws, which assign criminal liability to adults in certain cases of gun misuse involving children. Though twenty-seven states and the District of Columbia have these laws, however, they vary significantly in terms of whether they emphasize safe storage versus access and misuse. At the strictest end, gun owners in Massachusetts who do not store their guns with a lock or safe may face up to eighteen months of prison and up to $7,500 in fines, with additional fines and prison time for "large capacity weapon[s] or machine gun[s]" and for guns stored in areas accessible to children.[7] No other state requires all guns to be locked at all times. Seven states, including California, Minnesota, and Texas, and the District of Columbia hold adults criminally liable if a child gains access to a firearm, regardless of the consequences, while seven other states impose criminal liability only if the child uses or carries the firearm. An additional thirteen states prohibit the intentional, knowing, or reckless provision of firearms to children, although this law only applies to handguns in Colorado, Georgia, Kentucky, Mississippi, and Tennessee. The other twenty-three states, including Arizona, Michigan, and others, have no laws in effect.

Domestic Violence

While federal law prohibits people with domestic violence convictions from purchasing or possessing a firearm, several states have expanded the federal mandate to broaden the definition of domestic violence to include violence against any family member, regardless of cohabitation; to include victims beyond the immediate family, including current and former dating partners and household members; and to include prohibitions not just on firearms but also on ammunition (Law Center to Prevent Gun Violence 2016d). Fourteen states authorize or require that individuals surrender firearms and/or ammunition if they are prohibited from possessing them due to domestic violence misdemeanors. In addition, thirty-five states authorize or require courts to prohibit individuals under domestic violence protective orders from possessing or purchasing firearms. These laws vary significantly, from authorizing or requiring police to remove firearms from persons under protective orders to authorizing (but not requiring) judges to inform abusers of the requirement to surrender firearms. Meanwhile, some states, such as Kentucky, Michigan, Ohio, and Washington, have procedures in place to issue temporary emergency concealed-pistol licenses to domestic violence victims who have taken out protective orders against their abusers.

Mandatory Minimums for Gun Crimes

Finally, states also vary in the extent to which they apply criminal penalties for possession of a firearm in the commission of a crime (even if that firearm is not used) and for possession of a firearm by convicted felons. California's colloquially named "use a gun and you're done" law increases sentences by ten years if the offender is in possession of a firearm in the commission of a crime, by twenty years if the offender discharges the firearm, and twenty-five years to life if the firearm is discharged and causes great bodily injury or death.[8] When it was implemented in 1998, this "10-20-life" enhancement scheme was the toughest state-level law targeting gun offenders (Clairborne 1998). Mandatory minimums and sentencing enhancements once enjoyed widespread popularity as part of "tough on crime" policies in the 1970s, 1980s, and 1990s, although pressure to reduce prison populations, combined with sparse evidence that sentencing guidelines impact crime, has led to rollbacks on mandatory minimums. Remarkably, California Governor Jerry Brown, who signed into law determinate sentencing in the 1970s, has recommended that parole boards no longer consider enhancements in their decisions, even for offenses involving firearms (Walters 2016). Seemingly bucking this trend toward decarceration, support remains for "tough on crime" initiatives for gun-involved crimes from both gun-control and gun-rights interests (Borden 2015; *NRA News* 2016).

Local Regulations

Most states have so-called "preemption" laws related to gun regulation, meaning that local jurisdictions cannot pass laws that are more restrictive than state laws. While this standardizes regulations and simplifies enforcement, it also means that cities may be unable to create policies specific to the issues of violence that they face. Nevertheless, local jurisdictions have attempted to forge gun policy, even in states with preemption. For example, because preemption in California forbids localities from regulating firearms, Los Angeles County instead passed its own ban on magazines holding more than ten rounds (Reyes 2016).[9] Relatedly, local jurisdictions may initiate efforts through public law enforcement; gun buybacks and hot spots policing, along with more general initiatives aimed at stemming gun violence, are orchestrated at the local level and thus largely depend on the enforcement capacities and resources of these jurisdictions. As particularly notable examples, the Kansas City Gun Experiment and Boston's Project Ceasefire marshal problem-oriented policing to proactively identify and reach out to networks of high-incident gun offenders with a zero-tolerance approach.

LAWS ON THE BOOKS, POLICIES IN PRACTICE

The complexity of American gun policy at local, state, and federal levels adds difficulty to the already intractable question of what impacts crime, particularly gun crime. Gun laws are often as much about political objectives as they are about policy impact. What is the impact of these laws?

Gun Violence

Let's start by considering the impact of these laws on gun violence. Can public policy lessen the costs of gun violence, whether measured in lives lost or dollars spent? One starting point is whether the presence of firearms changes the contours of crime, both at individual and aggregate levels. Scholars have found evidence that gun ownership rates correlate with higher gun-involved crime rates, especially homicides against women (Hepburn and Hemenway 2004; Killias, van Kesteren, and Rindlisbacher 2001; Miller, Azrael, and Hemenway 2002), assault rates (Killias, van Kesteren, and Rindlisbacher 2001), and robbery rates (Cook 1987) but not necessarily other kinds of violence (i.e., non-gun-related assaults; Killias, van Kesteren, and Rindlisbacher 2001; see also Cook and Goss 2014). This finding is in line with what Frank Zimring (1972; see also Cook 1991) calls instrumentality effect: the weapon *matters*, independently of the intentions of the person wielding it. Assaults are more likely to become homicides, and suicide attempts are more likely to be completed when a gun, as opposed to another weapon, is chosen. Scholars find that rates of violent crime and suicides with a firearm track weapon stock, but non-firearm-involved crime and suicides do not. Meanwhile, scholars evaluating the self-defense approach and examining *individual,* rather than *aggregate,* access to guns suggest there are positive outcomes associated with firearms presence, such as lower exposure to victimization (Kleck 1997; Kleck and Gertz 1995) and lower rates of completion of rape (Kleck and Sayles 1990; see also McCaughey 1998). Meanwhile, the hotly debated impact of gun carry on crime rates has resulted in "evidence [that is] far from definitive" (Ludwig 2000, 410), but it has generated many pithy slogans, including "more guns, less crime" (the title of Lott's [1998 (2013)] book); "more guns, more crime" (Duggan 2001: 1086); and even "more statistics, less persuasion" (Kahan and Braman 2003: 1291). A 2016 study captures the mismatch between the public frenzy over concealed carry's impact and the size of its effects with this summary: "large debate and small effects" (Carter and Binder 2016: 1).

Jettisoning the political hot-button issue of general gun bans and broad gun restrictions while also recognizing that violent crime would decline if fewer criminals committed crimes using guns (Cook 1991; Zimring 1972), criminologists have turned to a targeted enforcement approach by examining law enforcement efforts to target individuals engaged in gun crime, especially gang-related and drug-related gun crime (Braga et al. 2008; Weisburd and Green 1995). In 1992 and 1993, the Kansas City Gun Experiment tested whether the targeted policing of illegally carried guns impacted gun crimes. The study found that after dramatically increasing the number of guns seized, primarily through more proactive traffic stops, gun crimes dropped significantly in the targeted area as compared to the control beats (Sherman, Shaw, and Rogan 1995). Perhaps the most well-known example, Project Ceasefire, is credited with dramatic drops in youth gun violence in Boston and elsewhere (Kennedy et al. 2001; Rosenfeld, Fornango, and Baumer 2005); Zimring (2011) likewise credits hot spots policing that targeted gun offenders with New York City's striking drop in crime—the "New York Difference"—by which the city beat national averages in terms of crime decline. However, while these strategic policing initiative programs appear to have meaningful impacts on gun violence, other scholars have raised concerns that such programs increase fear, reduce community efficacy, and undermine police legitimacy. For example, one 1994 study focused on the Consent-to-Search program in St. Louis, which involved police going door-to-door to parents of high-risk youth to ask for consent to search for guns; despite initially promising results, the study could not be completed partly because of eroding community support and increasing officer resistance (Decker and Rosenfeld 2004; see also Hinkle and Weisburd 2008; note that Weisburd et al.[2011], however, find these concerns to be overblown, with no meaningful impact of hot spots policing on fear, community efficacy, or police legitimacy). Finally, interventions such as stop and frisk policing, allegedly intended to find contraband such as drugs or guns, have become vehicles for racial profiling (Butler 2017), with some commentators pointing to dramatic racial disparities in gun law enforcement (Balko 2014; Schenwar 2014). Indeed, as Leonardatos (1999) shows, laws such as California's Mulford Act of 1967, which outlawed loaded open carry, were directly targeted at armed black groups such as the Black Panthers. However, as compared to research documenting racial disparities in drug law enforcement, there is less scholarly interest in racial disparities in gun law enforcement.

Another body of scholarship has looked at the impact of background checks and waiting periods (Cook and Ludwig 1996; McDowall, Loftin, and Wiersem 1995; Tita et al. 2006; Wright et al. 1999). Examining handgun purchasers with prior felonies and prior felony arrests in California, Wright et al. (1999, 89) estimated that "that denial of handgun purchase is associated with a reduction in risk for later criminal activity of approximately 20 percent to 30 percent." These results also extend to ammunition regulations. One study exploiting Los Angeles's unique ammunition background check provision found that both criminal access to ammunition and injuries from felonious gun assaults declined as a result (Tita et al. 2006).

A third body of research examines gun buyback programs. While some criminologists see their effectiveness as still an open question (e.g., Zimring 2011), several studies suggest these programs have minimal impact; one reason is that unlike hot spots policing or background check measures, gun buybacks are not targeted toward gun offenders (see Sherman 2001).

Alongside criminological studies that evaluate different kinds of enforcement efforts, public health scholars have developed and examined targeted preventive measures aimed at reducing gun violence, measured not just in terms of gun street crime. Public health scholars imagine risk more broadly and seek to minimize gun death and injury in contexts of suicide, domestic violence, unintentional shootings, and so forth. Consider suicide: because most suicides are impulsive and most suicide attempts with firearms are completed, public health scholars have investigated whether risk-based warrants, which allow for the seizure of firearms in the event of a mental health crisis, reduce suicide. Swanson et al. (2017, 203) examined Connecticut's protocol for seizing firearms and calculated that roughly for every ten to eleven gun seizure cases, one suicide is averted. As Swanson notes, this balance between rights and risk may be too high or too low, depending on the value one places on rights versus risk, but Swanson's approach reveals that, despite the often abstract nature of the gun debate, this balance can be precisely measured and quantified. Likewise, the ban on gun purchase and possession by people under a domestic violence restraining order is grounded in research showing that increased risk of intimate partner femicide is associated with the perpetrator's gun access; child access prevention laws are based on research showing that unintentional shootings are reduced when access by unauthorized users, such as children, is prevented. Across these examples, the logic is the same: remove a gun from a dangerous situation and/or dangerous person, and the risk of violence is reduced. That said, assessments of risk-based measures have been mixed, at times because enforcement "bite" is lacking and at other times because of uneven enforcement protocols. For example, even though public health scholars show that child access prevention *mechanisms* can reduce unintentional shootings, child access prevention *laws* do not necessarily reduce these shootings, except in cases with severe penalties such as Florida's felonization of child access (Webster and Starnes 2000). As a second example, consider domestic violence gun prohibitions: Vigdor and Mercy (2006) found that because of poor database interoperability and inadequate enforcement protocols, the effect of these laws was difficult to assess. Meanwhile, May (2005) suggests that in some cases, judges became more reluctant to issue domestic violence restraining orders after gun prohibitions were implemented.

Gun Publics

While much of gun-policy evaluation focuses on the impact of gun policy on gun violence, this is not the only impact of gun laws. According to the public policy feedback perspective, public policies (Mettler and Soss 2004) create constituencies, shape political beliefs, galvanize voters, and cultivate new civic capacities. In many ways, gun policy provides a stunning example of how policy politicizes publics. Gun-control laws, or fears of their passage, have the unintended effect of galvanizing pro-gun politics and even increasing the number of guns in public, as indicated by the surges in gun sales directly as well as increases in gun carry license applications following high-profile mass shootings (Steidley and Kosla 2018; Turchan et al. 2017). Indeed, the gun-control laws passed by the Clinton administration with the help of the National Rifle Association (NRA) in the early 1990s are often credited with galvanizing the pro-gun American public, which has rallied behind the logic of the "slippery slope" argument to oppose incremental restrictions (a piecemeal policy strategy favored by gun-control advocates that, Goss [2004] shows, results from the institutional barriers to comprehensive gun control).

Policy that has expanded the place of guns in everyday life has also contributed to shifting the public mood on guns. By pressing for concealed carry laws at the state level, the NRA and other pro-gun organizations have changed not just gun policy but also gun practice (Carlson 2015). As hunting has declined in the United States both as a pastime and as a reason for owning guns, the shift toward concealed carry—alongside the broader "tough on crime" politics that unfolded in the United States from the 1970s onward—has oriented gun culture toward personal protection and situated guns as everyday objects of self-defense (Simon 2003). The NRA has promoted gun rights as a key battleground in the culture wars (Sugarman 1992) using "frontier masculinity" (Melzer 2012; see also O'Neill 2007) to frame defensive gun use as the mark of a good and responsible citizen, especially for men. These cultural messages circulate in the pages of NRA magazines, in shooting ranges, through gun online forums, and in gun training. Given that loosened concealed carry laws sustain the spaces and practices (Carlson 2015) that encourage pro-gun sensibilities that, in turn, engender further support for gun rights, the transformation of U.S. gun policy can be understood as not just expanding gun rights but also as expanding the pro-gun public.

This observation is born out in shifts in public opinion data on American attitudes on guns, which show a general swing toward pro-gun sentiment among Americans. The proportion of Americans opposing a handgun ban has grown steadily since the 1960s, the last time a majority of Americans supported such a ban. Available polling data suggest that this drop has occurred, albeit somewhat unevenly, across gender, age, educational, regional, political, and gun-owning/non-gun-owning demographic divides. By 2011, the number of women who supported a handgun ban was fewer than the number of men who had supported one in 1991 (Jones 2011). A similar shift has occurred with regard to how Americans imagine guns as objects of safety versus danger. Although two-thirds of Americans said guns make homes safer in 2014, only a third agreed in 2000. These historical shifts reflect an increase among demographics already disproportionately supportive of gun-rights measures (e.g., the percentage of Republicans saying that a gun in the home makes that home safer almost doubled from 2000 to 2014). But these shifts also reflect erosion among demographics that have historically supported gun control (McCarthy 2014). As crime rates have dropped and the American gun supply has surged, Americans on the whole appear to have grown more in favor of loosened gun laws and more comfortable with guns in their homes and in their streets. A key part of this comfort is the increased presence and thus normalization of guns that loosened gun laws, especially gun carry laws, have helped to facilitate.

CONCLUSION

On June 12, 2016, a gunman opened fire at a gay night club in Orlando, FL, killing forty-nine people. Aware that the heinous shooting was unlikely to move the policy needle at the federal level, a group of Democrats held a sit-in in the U.S. Congress. They chanted "Shame! Shame!" at Speaker of the House Paul Ryan for refusing to schedule votes on gun regulation, and after he shut off congressional cameras on the politicians-turned-protestors, they broadcasted the event using smartphones. Despite the public spectacle the event created and the public attention it garnered, the policy needle stayed stubbornly put: there would be no vote and no major changes to federal gun policy. Meanwhile, states have undertaken strikingly different gun policy approaches. In the year after the Sandy Hook mass shooting, which left twenty-six elementary school teachers and students dead (in addition to the deaths of shooter Adam Lanza and his mother, Nancy Lanza), lawmakers passed laws that loosened, rather than tightened, gun regulations in a roughly 2:1 ratio (Yourish et al. 2013). Coastal states—New York, California, and others—tended to tighten regulations; other states in the South, the Midwest, and Rocky Mountain regions tended to loosen them.

At the federal, state, and local levels, then, the policy world of guns ranges from deadlocked to highly uneven. While policy makers may look to evaluations of policy impacts and implications to adjudicate between different initiatives, gun policy brings into stark relief the role of culture in shaping which policies are appealing and thus politically feasible. Kahan and Braman (2003) apply the cultural theory of risk to gun policy to argue that people do not support gun policies out of cold, rational evaluation of the evidence regarding policy consequences. Instead, people evaluate gun policy on the basis of *what kinds of risks they are willing to tolerate* and *what it says about them to tolerate those risks.* They hypothesize that gun-control advocates weigh the collective risks of gun availability more heavily than concerns regarding individual victimization, while they wager that for gun-rights proponents, the opposite risk calculation is made. To test the theory, Kahan and Braman (2003) use GSS data to show that people valuing individual responsibility (rather than collective decision making) and hierarchical authority structures (rather than egalitarianism) are more likely to support gun rights (rather than gun control). Their analysis reveals that cultural perceptions of risk are at least as important as evidence—one way or another—regarding gun policy.

This theory helps explain why public discourse over guns so often feels intractable. The gun debate is uniquely marked by a great deal of vehement disagreement among Americans; the politics of abortion represents the other policy debate that perhaps resembles the acrimony of the gun debate (for more on the intersection between these two debates, see Johnson [1997]). Yet Kahan and Braman (2003, 30) also suggest a way out of this deadlocked disagreement, what they call a "pluralistic expressive idiom." They ask readers to imagine a different gun discourse, one that accommodates and acknowledges the plurality of risks that gun policy across the spectrum can pose, whether it loosens or strengthens gun restrictions. Though they are vague on what this may look like in practice, the recent surge in public discourse surrounding guns has galvanized Americans interested in this debate to be more creative about bridging divides. The Center for Peace Studies and Violence Prevention at Virginia Tech, founded in the aftermath of the 2007 shootings on that campus, holds regular events aimed at bridging the gun divide, inviting Americans across the debate to sit down for dinner and conversation. As another example, the Gun Shop Project, spearheaded by the New Hampshire Firearms Safety Coalition, brings together public health practitioners and firearm retailers to promote suicide awareness and prevent gun suicide. Pro-gun National African American Gun Association makes it a point to open its doors to people on all sides of the issue and links guns to other social justice issues. To the extent that public policy is judged both by its practical impact and political feasibility, the best policy on guns will likely result not from deepening the gun debate but from creatively and conscientiously bridging the divides.

NOTES

1. Mass Shootings is a website that tabulates annual mass shootings from media reports. Available at http://www.shootingtracker.com/Main_Page.
2. Note, however, that the Bureau of Alcohol, Tobacco, and Firearms does require the registration of certain firearms, including fully automatic firearms and short-barreled shotguns and rifles.
3. Note that this varies by firearm type. The racial disparity is greatest for long guns, while this difference narrows for handguns.
4. The outliers were respondents who identified as Democrats and who had a postgraduate degree. Only about a third agreed that concealed gun carry makes Americans safer.
5. Note that trade treaties may also have the effect of banning or restricting certain kinds of firearms; this quietly occurred, for example, when the Bush administration banned imports in 2003 from Norinco, a Chinese conglomerate that manufactured a replica SKS rifle that sold for less than the Russian original. See Barbara Slavin, "US Bans Imports from Huge Chinese Conglomerate," *USA Today*, May 22, 2003, available at http://usatoday30.usatoday.com/news/washington/2003-05-22-norinco-usat_x.htm.
6. See Florida State Statute 776.031, available at https://www.flsenate.gov/Laws/Statutes/2011/Chapter776.
7. See Massachusetts State Statute 140.131L, available at https://malegislature.gov/Laws/GeneralLaws/PartI/TitleXX/Chapter140/Section131L.
8. See California State Penal Code 12022.53, available at http://leginfo.legislature.ca.gov/faces/codes_displaySection.xhtml?sectionNum=12022.53.&lawCode=PEN.
9. This regulation in turn inspired state lawmakers to enact a similar law statewide in 2016.

REFERENCES

Anderson, E. 2000. *Code of the Street: Decency, Violence, and the Moral Life of the Inner City.* New York: W. W. Norton.

Balko, R. 2014. Shaneen Allen, race and gun control. *The Washington Post,* July 22. Available at https://www.washingtonpost.com/news/the-watch/wp/2014/07/22/shaneen-allen-race-and-gun-control/?utm_term=.13855f6508b5.

Borden, J. 2015. Mandatory minimums are unpopular with everyone—except mayors of gun-ravaged cities. *Trace,* October 26. Available at https://www.thetrace.org/2015/10/mandatory-minimum-sentences-for-gun-crimes-mayors-support/.

Boynton-Jarrett, R., L. M. Ryan, L. F. Berkman, and R. J. Wright. 2008. Cumulative violence exposure and self-rated health. *Pediatrics* 122 (5): 961–970.

Braga, A. A., G. L. Pierce, J. McDevitt, B. J. Bond, and S. Cronin. 2008. The strategic prevention of gun violence among gang-involved offenders. *Justice Quarterly* 25 (1): 132–162.

Brown, R. M. 1991. *No Duty to Retreat: Violence and Values in American History and Society.* New York: Oxford University Press.

Butler, P. 2017. *Chokehold: Policing Black Men.* New York: The New Press.

Carlson, J. 2015. *Citizen-Protectors: The Everyday Politics of Guns in an Age of Decline.* New York: Oxford University Press.

Carlson, J., and Cobb, J. 2017. From play to peril: A historical examination of media coverage of accidental shootings involving children. *Social Science Quarterly* 98 (2): 397–412.

Carter, J. G., and M. Binder. 2016. Firearm violence and effects on concealed gun carrying: Large debate and small effects. *Journal of Interpersonal Violence,* February 24. https://doi.org/10.1177/0886260516633608.

Clairborne, W. 1998. Starting today, California packs toughest gun-sentencing law. *Washington Post,* January 1. Available at https://www.washingtonpost.com/archive/politics/1998/01/01/starting-today-california-packs-toughest-gun-sentencing-law/cef57ead-f714-4546-b938-89c86aea26ac/.

Collins, R. 2009. *Violence: A Micro-Sociological Theory.* Westport, CT: Greenwood Publishing Group.

Contreras, R. 2012. *The Stickup Kids: Race, Drugs, Violence, and the American Dream.* Oakland, CA: University of California Press.

Cook, P. J. 1987. Robbery violence. *Journal of Criminal Law and Criminology* 78 (2): 357–376.

———. 1991. The technology of personal violence. *Crime and Justice* 1–71.

Cook, P. J., and K. A. Goss. 2014. *The Gun Debate: What Everyone Needs to Know.* New York: Oxford University Press.

Cook, P. J., and J. Ludwig. 1996. *Guns in America: Results of a Comprehensive National Survey on Firearms Ownership and Use.* Washington, DC: Police Foundation.

Cooper, A., and E. L. Smith. 2011. *Homicide Trends in the United States, 1980–2008.* Washington, DC: Bureau of Justice Statistics.

Decker, S. H., and R. Rosenfeld. 2004. *Reducing Gun Violence: The St. Louis Consent-to-Search Program.* Washington, DC: U.S. Department of Justice, Office of Justice Programs, National Institute of Justice.

Duggan, M. 2001. More guns, more crime. *Journal of Political Economy* 109 (5): 1086–1114.

Duncan, D. F. 1996. Growing up under the gun. *Journal of Primary Prevention* 16 (4): 343–356.

Follman, M., J. Lurie, J. Lee, and J. West. 2016. What does gun violence really cost? *Mother Jones,* April. Available at http://www.motherjones.com/politics/2015/04/true-cost-of-gun-violence-in-america.

Garbarino, J. 2015. *Listening to Killers.* Oakland, CA: University of California Press.

Goode, E., and S. G. Stolberg. 2012. Legal curbs said to hamper ATF in gun inquiries. *New York Times,* December 12. Available at http://www.nytimes.com/2012/12/26/us/legislative-handcuffs-limit-atfs-ability-to-fight-gun-crime.html.

Goss, K. A. 2004. Policy, politics and paradox: The institutional origins of the great American gun war. *Fordham Law Review* 73: 681.

———. 2015. Defying the odds on gun regulation: The passage of bipartisan mental health laws across the states. *American Journal of Orthopsychiatry* 85 (3): 203–210.

Grinshteyn, E., and D. Hemenway. 2016. Violent death rates: the US compared with other high-income OECD countries, 2010. *American Journal of Medicine* 129 (3): 266–273.

Hardy, D. T. 1986. The Firearms Owners' Protection Act. *Cumberland Law Review* 17: 585–682.

Hepburn, L. M., and D. Hemenway. 2004. Firearm availability and homicide. *Aggression and Violent Behavior* 9 (4): 417–440.

Hinkle, J. C., and D. Weisburd. 2008. The irony of broken windows policing. *Journal of Criminal Justice* 36 (6): 503–512.

Hofer, P. J., K. Blackwell, K. Burchfield, J. Gabriel, and D. Stevens-Panzer. 2000. Sentencing for the possession or use of firearms during a crime. Washington, DC: United States Sentencing Commission, January 6. Available at http://www.ussc.gov/sites/default/files/pdf/research/working-group-reports/firearms/20000106-use-firearms-during-crime/firearms.pdf.

Ingraham, C. 2015. There are now more guns than people in the United States. *Washington Post,* October 5. Available at https://www.washingtonpost.com/news/wonk/wp/2015/10/05/guns-in-the-united-states-one-for-every-man-woman-and-child-and-then-some/.

Jacobs, J. B., and K. A. Potter. 1995. Keeping guns out of the "wrong" hands. *Journal of Criminal Law and Criminology* 86 (1): 93–120.

Jacobson, L. 2013. PBS commentator Mark Shields says more killed by guns since '68 than in all U.S. wars. *Politifact,* January 18. Available at http://www.politifact.com/truth-o-meter/statements/2013/jan/18/mark-shields/pbs-commentator-mark-shields-says-more-killed-guns/.

Johnson, K. 2017. Black Friday posts new single day record for gun checks at more than 200,000. *USA Today.* November 25. Available at: https://www.usatoday.com/story/news/politics/2017/11/25/black-friday-posts-new-single-day-record-gun-checks-more-than-200-000/894706001/

Johnson, N. J. 1997. Principles and passions: The intersection of abortion and gun rights. *Rutgers University Law Review* 50: 97–197.

Jones, J. 2011. Record-low 26% in US favor handgun ban. Gallup, October 26. Available at http://www.gallup.com/poll/150341/record-low-favor-handgun-ban.aspx.

———. 2013. Men, married, southerners most likely to be gun owners. Gallup, February 1. Available at http://www.gallup.com/poll/160223/men-married-southerners-likely-gun-owners.aspx.

Kahan, D. M., and D. Braman. 2003. More statistics, less persuasion. *University of Pennsylvania Law Review* 151 (4): 1291–1327.

Keating, D. 2013. Gun deaths shaped by race in America. *Washington Post,* March 22. Available at http://www.washingtonpost.com/sf/feature/wp/2013/03/22/gun-deaths-shaped-by-race-in-america/.

Kelly, G. 2015. Here's why no one can agree on the number of mass shootings. *New Republic,* October 3. Available at https://newrepublic.com/article/123027/heres-why-no-one-can-agree-number-mass-shootings.

Kennedy, D. M., A. A. Braga, A. M. Piehl, and E. J. Waring. 2001. *Reducing Gun Violence: The Boston Gun Project's Operation Ceasefire,* 20–23. Washington, DC: U.S. Department of Justice, Office of Justice Programs.

Killias, M., J. van Kesteren, and M. Rindlisbacher. 2001. Guns, violent crime, and suicide in 21 countries. *Canadian Journal of Criminology* 43 (4): 429–429.

Kleck, G. 1997. *Targeting Guns: Firearms and Their Control.* Piscataway, NJ: Transaction Publishers.

Kleck, G., and M. Gertz. 1995. Armed resistance to crime. *Journal of Criminal Law and Criminology* 86 (1): 150–187.

Kleck, G., and S. Sayles. 1990. Rape and resistance. *Social Problems* 37 (2): 149–162.

Kopel, D. B. 1998. Second Amendment in the Nineteenth Century. *Brigham Young University Law Review* 1359.

———. 2009. Pretend "gun-free" school zones. *Connecticut Law Review* 42 (2): 515–584.

Krause, W. 2012. *Gun Control Legislation: Congressional Research Service Report.* Washington, DC: Congressional Research Service.

Law Center to Prevent Gun Violence. 2016a. Assault weapons. Available at http://smartgunlaws.org/gun-laws/policy-areas/classes-of-weapons/assault-weapons/.

———. 2016b. Minimum age to purchase and possess in Vermont. Available at http://smartgunlaws.org/minimum-age-to-purchase-or-possess-firearms-in-vermont/.

———. 2016c. Mental health reporting. Available at http://smartgunlaws.org/gun-laws/policy-areas/background-checks/mental-health-reporting/.

———. 2016d. Domestic violence and firearms. Available at http://smartgunlaws.org/gun-laws/policy-areas/background-checks/domestic-violence-firearms/.

Lee, J. 2012. Wounded life after the shooting. *Annals of the American Academy of Political and Social Science* 642 (1): 244–257.

Legault, R. L. 2013. Reporting error in household gun ownership in the 2000 General Social Survey. *Crime and Delinquency* 59 (6): 811–836.

Leonardatos, C. D. 1999. California's attempts to disarm the Black Panthers *San Diego Law Review* 36: 947–1109.

Lott, J. R. 1998 [2013]. *More Guns, Less Crime.* Chicago: University of Chicago Press.

———. 2017. Concealed carry permit holders across the United States: 2017. Crime Prevention Research Center. Available at https://ssrn.com/abstract=3004915.

Ludwig, J. 2000. Gun self-defense and deterrence. *Crime and Justice* 27: 363–417.

Ludwig, J., P. J. Cook, and T. W. Smith. 1998. The gender gap in reporting household gun ownership. *American Journal of Public Health* 88 (11): 1715–1718.

McCarthy, J. 2014. More than six in 10 Americans say guns make homes safer. Gallup, November 7. Available at http://www.gallup.com/poll/179213/six-americans-say-guns-homes-safer.aspx.

McCaughey, M. 1998. The fighting spirit women's self-defense training and the discourse of sexed embodiment. *Gender and Society* 12 (3): 277–300.

McDowall, D., C. Loftin, and B. Wiersem. 1995. Easing concealed firearms laws. *Journal of Criminal Law and Criminology* 86 (1): 193–206.

Melzer, S. 2012. *Gun Crusaders: The NRA's Culture War*. New York: New York University Press.

Mettler, S., and J. Soss. 2004. The consequences of public policy for democratic citizenship. *Perspectives on Politics* 2 (1): 5–73.

Miller, M., D. Azrael, and D. Hemenway. 2002. Firearm availability and suicide, homicide, and unintentional firearm deaths among women. *Journal of Urban Health* 79 (1): 26–38.

Morin, R. 2014. The demographics and politics of gun-owning households. Pew Research Center for the People and the Press, July 15. Available at http://www.pewresearch.org/fact-tank/2014/07/15/the-demographics-and-politics-of-gun-owning-households/.

National Rifle Association. 2016. Right to carry laws. National Rifle Association Institute for Legislative Action. Available at https://www.nraila.org/gun-laws/.

National Task Force on Stand Your Ground Laws. 2015. Final report and recommendations. American Bar Foundation. Available at http://www.americanbar.org/content/dam/aba/images/diversity/SYG_Report_Book.pdf.

Newport, F. 2015. Majority say more concealed weapons would make US safer. Gallup, October 20. Available at http://www.gallup.com/poll/186263/majority-say-concealed-weapons-safer.aspx.

O'Neill, K. L. 2007. Armed citizens and the stories they tell. *Men and Masculinities* 9 (4): 457–475.

Pew Research Center. 2013. Why own a gun? Protection is now top reason: Perspectives of gun owners, non-owners. Pew Research Center for the People and the Press, March 12. Available at http://www.people-press.org/files/legacy-pdf/03-12-13%20Gun%20Ownership%20Release.pdf.

———. 2015. Continued bipartisan support for expanded background checks on gun sales. Pew Research Center for the People and the Press, August 13. Available at http://www.people-press.org/2015/08/13/continued-bipartisan-support-for-expanded-background-checks-on-gun-sales/.

———. 2016. Gun rights vs. gun control. Pew Research Center for the People and the Press, August 26. Available at http://www.people-press.org/2016/08/26/gun-rights-vs-gun-control/#total.

Reyes, E. A. 2016. LA City Council bans large-capacity ammunition magazines. *Los Angeles Times,* September 24. Available at http://www.latimes.com/local/lanow/la-me-ln-ammunition-magazines-20150728-story.html.

Roman, J. 2013. Race, justifiable homicide, and stand your ground laws: Analysis of FBI supplementary homicide report data. *Urban Institute*. Available at https://www.urban.org/research/publication/race-justifiable-homicide-and-stand-your-ground-laws/view/full_report.

Rosenfeld, R., R. Fornango, and E. Baumer. 2005. Did Ceasefire, Compstat, and Exile reduce homicide? *Criminology and Public Policy* 4 (3): 419–449.

Schenwar, M. 2014. Reduce Gun Penalties. *The New York Times,* March 14. Available at https://www.nytimes.com/2014/03/15/opinion/reduce-gun-penalties.html?_r=0.

Sharkey, P. 2010. The acute effect of local homicides on children's cognitive performance. *Proceedings of the National Academy of Sciences* 107 (26): 11733–11738.

Sharkey, P. T., N. Tirado-Strayer, A. V. Papachristos, and C. C. Raver. 2012. The effect of local violence on children's attention and impulse control. *American Journal of Public Health* 102 (12): 2287–2293.

Sherman, L. W. 2001. Reducing gun violence. *Criminology and Criminal Justice* 1 (1): 11–25.

Sherman, L. W., J. W. Shaw, and D. P. Rogan. 1995. The Kansas City Gun Experiment. *Population* 4: 8–142.

Simon, J. 2003. Gun rights and the constitutional significance of violent crime. *William and Mary Bill of Rights Journal* 12: 335–356.

Spitzer, R. 2015a. *Guns Across America: Reconciling Gun Rules and Rights*. New York: Oxford University Press.

———. 2015b. *Politics of Gun Control*. New York: Routledge.

Steidley, T., and M. T. Kosla. 2018. Toward a status anxiety theory of macro-level firearm demand. *Social Currents* 5 (1): 86–103.

Sugarman, J. 1992. *National Rifle Association: Money, Firepower, Fear*. Washington, DC: National Press Books.

Swanson, J. W., M. A. Norko, H. J. Lin, K. Alanis-Hirsch, L. K. Frisman, M. V. Baranoski, and R. J. Bonnie. 2017. Implementation and effectiveness of Connecticut's risk-based gun removal law: Does it prevent suicides? *Law and Contemporary Problems*. 80 (2): 179–208.

Swift, A. 2015. Americans' desire for stricter gun laws up sharply. Gallup, October 19. Available at http://www.gallup.com/poll/186236/americans-desire-stricter-gun-laws-sharply.aspx?utm_source=genericbutton&utm_medium=organic&utm_campaign=sharing.

Tita, G. E., A. A. Braga, G. Ridgeway, and G. L. Pierce. 2006. The criminal purchase of firearm ammunition. *Injury Prevention* 12 (5): 308–311.

Turchan, B., A. M. Zeoli, and C. Kwiatkowski. 2017. Reacting to the improbable: Handgun carrying permit application rates in the wake of high-profile mass shootings. *Homicide Studies* 21 (4): 267–286.

Uniform Crime Report. 2014. Justifiable homicide by weapon, private citizen, 2010–2014. Federal Bureau of Investigation. Available at https://ucr.fbi.gov/crime-in-the-u.s/2014/crime-in-the-u.s.-2014/tables/expanded-homicide-data/expanded_homicide_data_table_15_justifiable_homicide_by_weapon_private_citizen_2010-2014.xls.

Vigdor, E. R., and J. A. Mercy. 2006. Do laws restricting access to firearms by domestic violence offenders prevent intimate partner homicide? *Evaluation Review* 30 (3): 313–346.

Walters, D. 2016. Jerry Brown's "nonviolent" parole measure would apply to violent crimes. *Sacramento Bee*, May 23. Available at http://www.sacbee.com/news/politics-government/politics-columns-blogs/dan-walters/article79420247.html.

Webster, D. W., and M. Starnes. 2000. Reexamining the association between child access prevention gun laws and unintentional shooting deaths of children. *Pediatrics* 106 (6): 1466–1469.

Weisburd, D., and L. Green. 1995. Policing drug hot spots. *Justice Quarterly* 12 (4): 711–735.

Weisburd, D., J. C. Hinkle, C. Famega, and J. Ready. 2011. The possible "backfire" effects of hot spots policing. *Journal of Experimental Criminology* 7 (4): 297–320.

Winkler, A. 2011. *Gunfight: The Battle over the Right to Bear Arms in America*. New York: W. W. Norton.

Wright, M. A., G. J. Wintemute, and F. P. Rivara,. 1999. Effectiveness of denial of handgun purchase to persons believed to be at high risk for firearm violence. *American Journal of Public Health* 89 (1): 88–90.

Yourish, K., W. Andrews, L. Buchanan, and A. McLean. 2013. State laws enacted in the year after Newtown. *New York Times,* December 10. Available at http://www.nytimes.com/interactive/2013/12/10/us/state-gun-laws-enacted-in-the-year-since-newtown.html.

Zimring, F. E. 1972. The medium is the message. *Journal of Legal Studies* 1 (1): 97–123.

———. 1975. Firearms and federal law. *Journal of Legal Studies* 4 (1): 133–198.

———. 2011. *The City That Became safe: New York's Lessons for Urban Crime and Its Control.* New York: Oxford University Press.

17

Thinking Outside the Prison Walls

The Value of the Inside-Out Prison Exchange Program to Solve Old Problems

Kevin A. Wright and
Cheryl Lero Jonson

WHAT'S THE PROBLEM?

Time does not actually stop in prison—it dictates prison and prison life. Time spent in prison is one of two components that meaningfully impact the size of prison populations (the other being how many are sent to prison) (Clear and Austin 2009). Time served. Time to be served. Time to count. Time to be idle. Hurry up and wait. The phrase "doing time" is familiar to both the incarcerated and nonincarcerated. It is an odd phrase if you actually think about it: what is being done to time? More time served in prison means more time away from society. And as Red from *The Shawshank Redemption* warns us, if enough of it passes while you are in prison, then you begin to depend on that prison for survival. "That's institutionalized."

Consider alone what is now being accomplished through technology that in the past required human interaction: shopping, dating, applying for jobs, paying bills, managing a bank account, holding a real-time conversation, and the list goes on. When human interaction *is* required, the simplest exchanges can become complicated (yes, even violent) when you have spent years talking to only officers and other people who are incarcerated. Antisocial tendencies held prior to prison can become hardened in the prison environment, and prosocial tendencies—those that are required to live lawfully in the community to which nearly all incarcerated will one day return—can become weakened and even extinguished. Any quality prison program would broadly address the risks and needs of incarcerated persons, and it would also address the time spent away from an ever evolving society that is not arrested by prison walls.

Risk, Need, Responsivity for Individuals

The current cohort of prisoners returning to society has more risks and needs than any prior release group (Petersilia 2003). Physical health concerns, mental health concerns, lack of education, lack of employable job skills, and drug and alcohol addictions are some of the critical baggage carried by returning men and women. Longer sentences can create and exacerbate each of these concerns and potentially contribute to higher rates of recidivism (c.f. Nagin, Cullen, and Jonson 2009). It is likely more difficult to secure affordable and stable housing, to obtain gainful employment, and to establish loving relationships the longer an individual has been removed from society. These critical issues notwithstanding, prison programming is typically geared toward modifying the thought processes and behaviors that led to imprisonment in the first place.

By now, most criminologists and many practitioners are at least broadly familiar with Risks-Need-Responsivity (RNR) models of offender classification, management, and treatment (e.g., Andrews, Bonta, and Hoge 1990). Appropriate treatment, as identified by these models, involves matching treatment intensity to risk level (with higher-intensity treatments reserved for higher-risk offenders), targeting malleable criminogenic needs (such as the modification of antisocial attitudes), and matching style and mode of treatment to the offender's learning style and abilities (with cognitive behavioral therapy generally regarded as the gold standard approach and consideration given for individual differences such as mental illness). These models have contributed to a theory of effective correctional intervention (Gendreau, Smith, and French 2011), which is firmly rooted in a strong tradition of correctional psychology and applied cognitive-social learning theory (Cullen et al. 2003).

Programming based on "what works" has been shown to produce sizeable reductions in recidivism (Lipsey and Cullen 2007). A number of inventories and assessment tools are now available to determine whether programming meets the standards of principles of effective intervention in both prison and community settings (e.g., Gendreau, Andrews, and Theriault 2010). These, too, have shown that programs high in treatment integrity are associated with reductions in recidivism (Lowenkamp, Latessa, and Smith 2006). Equally important, programming based on neither the causes of crime (i.e., criminogenic needs) nor modes of effective behavior change (i.e., general responsivity) is said to be "correctional quackery" (Latessa, Cullen, and Gendreau 2002) and is unlikely to impact recidivism in a meaningful way (see also "inappropriate correctional service" of Andrews, Zinger et al. 1990). Further, some evidence exists that ignoring the risk principle by focusing on low-risk offenders may potentially make matters worse for them (Cullen and Jonson 2014).

The RNR model and its offshoots will likely guide prison programming for the foreseeable future; however, even the very best in-prison programming cannot approximate life in free society—perhaps one reason that treatment is often said to be more effective in community settings than in prison. At a minimum, the rehabilitated prisoner may be returning to a community or peer or family environment that has not been rehabilitated (Wright et al. 2012). Human interaction does not occur in a vacuum, and it is difficult to replicate all of the unpredictable factors that contextualize life on the outside while at the same time eliminating the drab and hostile environment that contextualizes life on the inside. Role-playing and "what would you do?" scenarios may be facilitated by a trained therapist, but due to resource constraints are more likely to be taught by officers who balance their work with security concerns or by other incarcerated individuals in a peer-programming setting. Truth be told: most programs have pretty lousy scores on integrity inventories (Smith and Schweitzer 2012). Finally, and perhaps most importantly, prison programming is unlikely to involve any significant actors who will play a role in the post-prison life of the incarcerated individual. Doing so would require bringing the outside into prison, which is currently best accomplished through visitation.

Maintaining Contact with Communities

When an individual is incarcerated, he or she is typically viewed as that: an individual. It is often forgotten that people who are incarcerated are parents and children, employers and employees, friends, neighbors, and citizens. It is easier instead to think of them as simply a convicted criminal and to desire the worst for them, which allows for the necessary retribution and incapacitation that follow crime, especially violent crime. In this regard, the American approach to corrections is very much in line with what Braithwaite (1989) identified as disintegrative shaming. Prisoners become outcasts, they identify with their criminality as their primary status, and there are few efforts to downplay this criminality or welcome prisoners back into the community. But again, "they all come back" (Travis 2005). Disintegrative shaming, coupled with felony restrictions, is likely to result in blocked prosocial opportunities for the returning prisoner and an increased likelihood that criminal behavior will continue (Wakefield and Uggen 2010).

One option to avoid severing ties with the community is to allow the community to continue contact with the prisoner during incarceration. Visits from family and friends can directly maintain ties between prisoners and their critical social supports in society and indirectly keep prisoners connected to the advancements and changes of that society (Arditti 2012). And unlike temporary community programs such as work furlough that are typically unavailable to those deemed high risk, prison visitation can occur at all security levels and reach those who stand to benefit most from maintained contact with the community. Indeed, visitation has been shown to be associated with improved prisoner mental and physical health (Poehlmann 2005), reduced institutional misconduct (Cochran 2012), and reduced recidivism (Mitchell et al. 2016). Prison visitation may help to ensure that time passed in prison does not lead to a dependence on that prison for survival; prison visitation may help to prolong or prevent institutionalization.

Currently, visitation is usually not viewed as a form of programming. There is no assessment tool available to guide the integrity of prison visitation and there is no guarantee that it will lead to positive behavioral outcomes for prisoners. In fact, the literature on prison visitation includes a number of perplexing findings—such as an association between visits from children and increased recidivism (Bales and Mears 2008). Visits can be stressful and can be characterized by disagreements and fights; they can also be mundane and relatively unproductive when it comes to changing antisocial attitudes and behaviors (Tasca et al. 2016). To that end, visitation may be accomplishing little more than maintaining the status quo among nonrehabilitated prisoners, their families, and their communities. No shaming has occurred—of either the disintegrative or reintegrative variety (for a similar discussion, see Cullen and Jonson 2017, chapter 6). Visitation as evidence-based programming would require structured interaction between prisoners and visitors that addresses criminogenic needs.

The problem, then, is one that dates back to the inception of corrections in America. How can the often competing goals of deterrence, incapacitation, retribution, and rehabilitation be accomplished? Incapacitation and rehabilitation in particular are difficult to achieve simultaneously. The solution offered by early U.S. penitentiaries was to remove the offenders from society (incapacitate) and provide them with a steady dose of work and religion (rehabilitate). Today, the science is better, but the limits of RNR programming discussed above identify the challenges of rehabilitating prisoners after they have been removed from society. The stigmatization and institutionalization that can be brought on by removal and incapacitation can be lessened through opportunities like prison visitation that serve to break down the walls. Here again, the approach is incomplete: without some form of structured programming, it is unlikely that rehabilitation would be achieved through sustained community contact alone. With over 1.6 million people incarcerated in prisons, over 600,000 released each year, and return-to-prison rates that exceed 50 percent within five years, it is necessary to identify prison programming that can address the risks and needs of individuals while keeping them connected to the communities to which they will one day return.

WHAT'S THE THEORY?

So what theory would guide programming that accounts for the above problem? Part of the difficulty in identifying this theory begins with the challenge of knowing what type of theory is needed. Is it a theory of criminal behavior or a theory of behavioral change? Similar to those who caution against correctional quackery, we contend that it requires both. Borrowing from the theories surrounding place-based pedagogic techniques (Knapp 2005; Sobel 2005; Wurdinger and Carlson 2010), social support (Cullen 1994), and desistance (Giordano, Cerknovich, and Rudolph 2002; Maruna 2001; Sampson and Laub 1993), we demonstrate the potential that correctional education has to transform law-violating into law-abiding individuals, while increasing their connectedness to the outside world to which they will eventually return.

Place-Based Learning

Walking into a prison education wing, outsiders are often taken aback by the normalcy they witness. Although the walls are still made of concrete and often painted institutional white or grey, motivational posters, colorful artwork, and inspirational quotes are sprinkled around the room. Tables with chairs are positioned throughout, with a teacher's desk prominently assuming the helm of the classroom. Mathematical equations, conjugation of verbs, and outlines of the day's goals are commonplace on the chalkboard or whiteboard. The commonalities between these rooms and classrooms found in K–12 schools are striking, almost allowing individuals who enter these rooms to forget for a brief moment that they are surrounded by walls and razor-wire fences outside. For a few hours, the role of prisoner is replaced with that of student, and prisoners are fully immersed in an environment that is foreign to the daily grind of the larger institution.

Why is it that prison education providers go to such great lengths to transform their classrooms into warm and inviting environments? Realistically, the sights, sounds, and smells of the prison permeate every nook and cranny of the institution. Prisoners are served questionable food and wear faded and ill-fitting state uniforms, every single day. So, what good are a few posters, some motivational quotes, and a teacher from the outside really going to achieve? One answer can come from the theory surrounding place-based education (Wurdinger and Carlson 2010). "Characterized as the pedagogy of community, the reintegration of the individual into her homeground and the restoration of the essential links between a person and her places," place-based educational approaches emphasize the importance of the environment itself as a resource to learning (Podder 2016, 1). By immersing and educating students in natural as opposed to artificial settings, a deeper understanding, appreciation for, and commitment to the topics being taught as well as a greater connection to the community can be achieved (Sobel 2005).

Originating in the 1960s and 1970s as an offshoot of environmental education, this pedagogical approach contends that traditional school settings tend to isolate individuals and stunt learning as classrooms do not provide an opportunity for students to intimately experience the outside natural environment (Gruenewald 2003; Kemp 2006). By breaking out of traditional classroom settings and engaging with places and, at times, people, in their natural state, place-based educators hope to increase their students' motivation for learning and pique their interest, curiosity, and knowledge about a topic (Sarkar and Fraizer 2008). Taking an ecological course as an example, place-based approaches argue that having students sit in a classroom with their notebooks open, frantically jotting down every word the teacher orates, is ineffective and will not result in a deeper understanding of the topic. If educators want to facilitate that higher-level learning, they must force their students to leave the confines of the school and become immersed in the environment being studied. By thrusting students into a forest or wooded area to see and experience firsthand the concepts and topics being taught in the course, students will become more engaged, more motivated, and form a greater connection between the learning outcomes of the course and their connection or applicability to the larger world (Griset 2007).

So, what does this have to do with correctional populations? Without a doubt, correctional education programs are a unique form of place-based learning. After all, it is not as if we can load up all the people in prison on a bus and take them beyond the prison gates in order to immerse them in a different environment to facilitate their learning. But the prison environment is a unique place, and one that is not the most conducive to prosocial knowledge construction. While traditional place-based learning experiences involve replacing conventional academic settings with those located within the community, correctional education programs seek to provide environments that tend to mirror the traditional classroom settings found on the outside (Place-Based Educational Evaluation Collaborative 2010).

The daily environment of the prison is often marked by violence, oppression, and control, which may result in the hardening of antisocial tendencies and the view that the outside world is cruel and unforgiving. Thus, place-based pedagogical approaches to learning in prison involve the removal of individuals from the punitive environment they endure each day, even if for a few short hours. The classroom setting, with its warm, inviting atmosphere, is similar to leaving the prison and experiencing something outside the norm for offenders. In this environment, educators seek to teach not only basic academic skills but also to foster an attachment to this setting that may translate to positive associations with the outside world.

The people who are interacting with the students in these place-based approaches also take on an important role (Place-Based Educational Evaluation Collaborative 2010; Wurdinger and Carlson 2010). Correctional education programs are marked with the presence of educators who are human service oriented from the outside community rather than the agents of control that characterize the prison (Zoukis 2014). And, in the rare cases where outside students learn alongside incarcerated men and women, offenders are immersed in an environment where opportunities to engage in authentic and genuine interactions with members of the community are made possible (Zoukis 2014). The classroom then provides a dual purpose: it is a place where the knowledge and skills needed to alter criminal trajectories can be obtained, while simultaneously establishing connections to the community beyond the prison walls.

Social Support Theory

While place-based pedagogical approaches emphasize the importance of learning and interacting with others in authentic environments, they often do not acknowledge the direct impact that relationships among people, particularly prosocial relationships, can have on behavioral change. This omission is surprising as the importance of appropriate relationships is highlighted not only in the wider pedagogical research but also in the correctional literature (Bain 2004; Skeem et al. 2007; Smith and Schweitzer 2012). Looking back over our own life course, we can all identify how a relationship, and the support associated with it, changed the pathway our life was following. Many of us are reminded instantly of that one teacher who challenged us to be better versions of ourselves; who saw the potential within us that we had not yet discovered; who guided us and nudged us to experience something out of our comfort zone that broadened our horizons more than we ever thought possible.

Consequently, social support mattered, even for those of us walking the line. But are social supports just as influential for those who are already leading a life of crime? Can supportive, prosocial relationships trigger a departure from a criminal pathway? According to Cullen's 1994 theory of social support, the answer to both of these questions is "yes." Cullen argues that "whether social support is delivered through governmental social programs, communities, social networks, families, interpersonal relations, or agents of the criminal justice system, it reduces criminal involvement" (1994, 527). Social supports act as a protective factor, insulating people from crime by reducing the impact of criminogenic strains and increasing the effectiveness of informal social controls generated by families, communities, and schools (Makarios and Livelsberger 2012).

When taking a look inside the prison walls, it is clear that correctional education programs embody many of the propositions put forth by social support theory. Instrumental social support is provided through the ability to obtain GED and collegiate degrees, while expressive support occurs through the interactions between teachers and their pupils (Cullen 1994; Lin 1986). The words of encouragement, notes providing constructive criticism at the end of an assignment, and confirmatory nods of the head reinforce offenders' self-worth and sense of belonging in the classroom.

The fact that correctional educational programs serve as a major source of social support in the prison should come as no surprise. Educators often are not assigned or obligated to teach in a prison; rather, they volunteer and seek out this type of work. A sense of caring and compassion toward this traditionally neglected population are often at the "heart" of prison education programs (Wright 2004). Furthermore, many prison educators perceive themselves as agents of change with their work standing in direct opposition to the prevailing antisocial prison norms. Rather than contributing to the punitive nature of the prison, prison educators contend that their teaching, marked by a sense of caring and support, "highlights the importance of connection and community-inclusiveness" (Wright 2004, 202).

Social support, thus, is an important underlying theme in how teachers approach their students. And, for a population that often interacts with antagonistic and hostile individuals on a regular basis, the social support they experience in the classroom may be life altering. As argued by Cullen (1994), the social supports received in the classroom may shield offenders from the criminogenic strains that surround them, as well as increasing their informal social controls through teachers holding their pupils accountable and expecting them to continue their prosocial behaviors once they return to their cell blocks. The social supports present in the classroom thus create an environment where students become invested in their education (targeting their criminogenic needs) and value the contact with the outside world (addressing the isolation many offenders often endure) (Zoukis 2014).

Desistance from Crime

Most offenders will eventually retire from their life of crime (Laub and Sampson 2003). However, just like athletes, the reasons vary by the individual, and what makes one offender desist may be different from what makes others leave their criminal behavior in the rearview mirror (Cullen, Agnew, and Wilcox 2014). As a result, various theories have been developed to explain the desistance process (Giordano, Cernkovich, and Rudolph 2002; Maruna 2001; Sampson and Laub 1993).

In 1993 and, again, in 2003, Sampson and Laub changed the criminological landscape with the introduction of their age-graded social bond theory. Unlike Gottfredson and Hirschi's (1990) theory that contends there is continuity in criminal behavior, and Moffitt's (1993) theory that splits offenders into two groups, one defined by their change in offending (adolescence-limited offenders) and one defined by their continuity of offending (life-course-persistent offenders), Sampson and Laub argue that all individuals can desist from or alter their criminal pathway if they form meaningful social bonds (e.g., marriage, employment). These "turning points" can set the stage for a change in behavior, as they can create informal social controls and provide social support.

For example, saying "I do" changes many aspects of a person's life. The married man's structural routines often change; no more staying out all night! No longer can the man think only of himself; he now must consider how his actions and decisions will impact his spouse and children. The marriage provides both tangible and intangible resources, as well as a constant source of social support. The coalescing of all these factors often results in "desistance by default," where the criminal lifestyle of offenders becomes a distant memory without the offender even realizing it.

However, simply getting married or finding employment (along with their associated informal social controls) does not always result in the desistance of criminal offending. After all, there are still married, employed men engaging in criminal behavior. Therefore, something else must occur for individuals to leave their life of crime behind. Giordano and colleagues (2002) argue that the missing factor in Sampson and Laub's (1993) theory is the corresponding "cognitive transformation" that accompanies exposure to prosocial opportunities, or what Giordano and colleagues refer to as "hooks for change." Offenders must be receptive and willing to both seek out and utilize these hooks as a catalyst to change their behavior. Once they have been hooked, offenders then must be able to create a "replacement self" where they develop a new prosocial identity and view their past lifestyle as undesirable and unappealing (Giordano, Cernkovich, and Rudolph 2002; c.f. Maruna 2001). When that replacement self is embraced and internalized, the desistance process is complete, with the criminal transformed, both in thought and in behavior, to a prosocial, law-abiding individual.

At first glance, it appears that this theoretical foundation is largely ignored by the prison system. Prosocial opportunities are scarce: jobs in prison are often unfulfilling and do not involve meaningful work, a lack of intimate relationships is one of the pains of imprisonment (Sykes 1958), interactions between offenders and staff are often hostile, and the friendships that do emerge are frequently with other antisocial individuals. However, there are treatment, religious, and educational programs that could potentially be turning points or hooks for change. These prosocial outlets allow offenders to engage with therapists, religious leaders, and educators who focus on the growth that offenders are capable of making (Smith and Schweitzer 2012; Wright 2004). Rather than continually punishing individuals for their wrongdoing, these agents of change hold offenders accountable, while exposing them to a different, noncriminal pathway. They provide informal social controls and social support, while trying to inspire individuals to take advantage of opportunities to alter their criminal lifestyle. Thus, in accordance with desistance theories, meaningful social bonds, along with encouragement that can facilitate cognitive transformations, are pillars of these types of programs.

Looking across the theoretical foundations presented above, there appear to be some common threads that weave each one of them together. Insulating individuals from the damaging prison environment, offering social support, and providing prosocial opportunities that individuals can connect with are consistently recognized as important factors in accomplishing cognitive and behavioral change. When offenders are immersed in warm, caring environments, engaged with members from the outside community who treat them with respect and kindness, and are provided with the skills that can help them navigate life outside the prison walls in a prosocial manner, two major goals are accomplished: the various needs and deficits possessed by incarcerated offenders are addressed, while simultaneously reducing the isolation many offenders feel from the outside community. With this as a theoretical foundation, attention must be turned to how this translates into practice. In other words, what specific programs can be implemented to target the needs of offenders as well as the alienation of incarcerated individuals from the community produced by long prison sentences?

WHAT'S THE ANSWER?

We contend that one answer to the above problem may be found in correctional education programs for two compelling reasons. First, these programs have the ability to equip individuals with the knowledge and skills needed to alter their criminal trajectories, resulting in decreased post-release criminal behavior (Chappell 2004; Davis et al. 2013; MacKenzie 2006; Wilson, Gallagher, and MacKenzie 2000). While a lack of education is considered to be one of Andrews and Bonta's (2010, 58–60) "Central Eight" criminogenic risk factors, viewing educational programs as simply learning the basics of reading, writing, and arithmetic is narrow-minded. Both inside and outside the prison walls, educators have been assigned with the additional task of creating environments that cultivate the development of "soft skills," or "the diverse habits, mindset, and nontechnical skills that can help individuals be more successful in all aspects and stages of life" (Tooley and Bornfreund 2014, 7; see also Crawford and Dalton 2016; Evenson 1999; Heckman and Kautz 2012; Lopez and Calderon 2013). These soft skills can be characterized as *internal*, such as critical thinking and problem-solving skills, emotion management, the ability to accept criticism, and resilience, or *external*, which involve the ability to work collaboratively, communicate effectively, negotiate, and manage conflict (Tooley and Bornfreund 2014). As a result, correctional education programs possess the unique ability for offenders to obtain high school or, in some cases, collegiate degrees, which is crucial for securing living wage employment, while equipping them with the skills needed to foster successful personal and professional relationships (Heckman and Kautz 2012).

Second, correctional education programs can address the feelings of isolation from the outside world by providing a conduit for which offenders and members from the community can come into contact with one another. Teachers and college professors often are tapped to enter the prison walls and teach courses, and the interactions with these non-prison-affiliated individuals stand in stark contrast to those that the incarcerated have grown accustomed to (Wright 2004; Zoukis 2014). Expressions of control, dominance, and oppression are replaced with words of support, encouragement, and inspiration. Critical thinking and challenging the status quo are rewarded rather than punished. Harsh disciplinary reprimands are exchanged for reinforcements and letter grades on assignments. Once a person enters the classrooms, the label of "prisoner" is often substituted with that of "student," and some semblance to the outside world is experienced (Fraley 1991). Prisoner-students, who in their youth may have not been the most stellar of pupils, gain confidence in their ability to succeed and become invested in their education. Attachments often form with the teachers, providing a prosocial role model in the community who also can hold them accountable in a firm but fair manner (Jonson and Moon 2014; Zoukis 2014).

Inside-Out Prison Exchange Program

There is a particular type of correctional education program, however, that best exemplifies the above theories in addressing the problem of how to rehabilitate offenders without further alienating them from the communities to which they will return. In the Inside-Out Prison Exchange Program, college students ("outside students") enter the prison gates and learn alongside the incarcerated ("inside students"). These classes connect prisoners to the outside world through dialogue, collaboration, and informed action, while simultaneously and implicitly addressing various criminogenic needs that they may hold. Inside-Out was developed by Lori Pompa at Temple University and first taught in the Philadelphia jail system in 1997 (for a more complete description of Inside-Out see Pompa 2013; http://www.insideout-center.org). At the time of writing, the program has since grown to reach more than thirty thousand students across more than forty states and six other countries. Courses using the Inside-Out method have been offered in everything from criminology to nursing, and the courses typically lead to a class project that is collaboratively designed by outside and inside students—often with a focus toward improving correctional environments and the communities to which incarcerated men and women will return.

The culmination of the course is a celebration, often marked by a graduation ceremony in which certificates are awarded to program graduates. Inside-Out courses are so meaningful and so impactful that they often do not end when the semester is over. A number of think tanks have been developed across the nation to bring together interested outside and inside individuals to continue the ideals of Inside-Out. The first of these—the Graterford Think Tank—was created after a summer 2002 Inside-Out course and has met weekly ever since. The group acts as an advisory committee for the national organization and is a critical component to the Inside-Out Training Institute that takes place in Philadelphia. At the time of writing, other think tanks across the nation include the Michigan Theory Group, Another Chance at Education (ACE) in Oregon, and the Arizona Transformation Project. These groups perform a variety of functions, from improving Inside-Out curriculum to engaging in original research and writings on criminal justice topics.

Taken altogether, the Inside-Out Prison Exchange Program provides a place-based educational setting in which cognitive transformation may take place through the social support and collective efficacy provided by learning alongside members of the community. This can be seen through the words of incarcerated men who have graduated from the program.

Inside-Out can help foster a correctional environment that is more conducive to behavioral change:

> *It is so meaningful; we are going to change so many peoples' perspectives and lives. It has already begun. This is being talked about on the yard, with our families and friends* (Inside Student). *I love the excitement I see in my*

> *inside brothers, most of whom I've known for years in here. To see them just as excited as I am and the way I get to see them truly express themselves in class is very nice to watch, along with the conversations we have amongst ourselves after class* (Inside Student).

Inside-Out allows inside students to envision themselves as members of a community:

> *One class at a time, we are able to apply our experiences to help restore, enrich, and rebuild our society together* (Inside Student). *Learning from friendly, non-judgmental, non-condescending outside students that I can fit in and be accepted in society again, that I don't have to be afraid...I can do anything I put my mind to. I can get an A. I don't have to fail in school just because I did as a youth* (Inside Student).

Inside-Out allows graduates to see a future self that is different from the one who ended up incarcerated:

> *The insights I have gained from this course have changed my life. My new understanding of criminal justice and crime is paving a new outlook on life and society that is hopeful. This class is making a real difference and touching students' lives as well as others* (Inside Student).

To be more direct, Inside-Out is implicitly a form of correctional programming:

> *This class is not just about academia. Intended or not, this class has a therapeutic aspect embedded in it that teaches us to reconcile the past, learn about the present, and grow for the future. This therapeutic aspect turned out to be the ingredients for HOPE. Hope in humanity; hope in self; and hope in the future; exactly that which is needed in prison* (Inside Student). *I've found through the questions and answers this class offers some genuine healing for the soul* (Inside Student).

We would be remiss if we did not point out that Inside-Out is transformative for traditional college students as well. It is common to hear themes similar to that expressed by this outside student:

> *It has been amazing to work with and get to know the inside students and learn not only how similar we are as people but also how similar our views can be on crime, its causes, and punishment. Their input and life experi-*

ences they have shared have been invaluable, speaking with great insight of many social programs and aspects of the criminal justice system which I would have never even given a second thought.

This is consistent with recent calls for correctional interventions that incorporate interpersonal contact from the community to reduce criminal stigma (Rade, Desmarais, and Mitchell 2016). Indeed, outside students often leave the class with a new appreciation for the prisoners who will return to their community—and so do those students' friends, neighbors, and family members.

One of the criticisms of correctional educational programming is that those who succeed in learning behind bars (especially at the collegiate level) are also those who were unlikely to recidivate in the first place. It is fair to be cynical when a particular program touts its graduates as having a recidivism rate of less than 10 percent, for example (Wright and Khade 2018). Inside-Out, however, does not necessarily need to be reserved for those who were already well on the path to returning to society as a law-abiding citizen. Welcomed into Inside-Out are individuals whom Werts (2013, 137), a former inside student, termed as "throw-away people"—those men and women who recidivate because "no one showed them any kindness or compassion or demonstrated a belief that they could survive the rigors of a higher education." Inside-Out programs have occurred in all levels of security—from work release programs to maximum security prisons—and often the minimum requirement for course admittance is the willingness to work and participate in class discussions. To that end, men and women who would otherwise be considered "high risk" are eligible to participate in Inside-Out—exactly the individuals that RNR programming would suggest might benefit most from this type of program. This includes men and women whose crime or the amount of time they have left to serve might ordinarily prohibit them from programming based on priority-ranking systems.

If Inside-Out is to be conceived of as correctional programming, then the challenge for its proponents is to more explicitly document its program integrity as well as its impact on the attitudes and behaviors of program graduates. To date, the bulk of scholarly works that has been published on Inside-Out has focused on describing the program or presenting anecdotal evidence of its effectiveness (e.g., Davis and Roswell 2013; Hilinski-Rosick and Blackmer 2014; Van Gundy, Bryant, and Starks 2013). An exception to this is Allred, Harrison, and O'Connell's (2013) study on changes in levels of self-efficacy among forty-eight eligible inside and forty-seven outside students across three separate courses based on the Inside-Out model.

Assessing self-efficacy with ten items such as "I can solve most problems if I invest the necessary effort," the authors documented a significant difference at the start of the classes where inside students scored lower on aggregate mean levels of self-efficacy than outside students. By the end of the classes, however, the aggregate mean level of self-efficacy for inside students was a statistically significant increase from their mean level of self-efficacy at the start of classes. There was no parallel change in self-efficacy among outside students. Indeed, by the end of the classes, inside students scored higher on self-efficacy than outside students.

This research is an important foundational start, but more needs to be done using more rigorous methods to establish the processes and outcomes of Inside-Out. Program integrity assessment tools could be used to identify how well Inside-Out stacks up against current effective interventions. Program evaluations could work to document attitudinal changes on items and scales known to be correlated with antisocial behavior, such as self-control indices (e.g., MacKenzie, Bierie, and Mitchell 2007). Program evaluations could determine whether program completion affects behavior in the short term in the form of prison misconduct. Most importantly, research is needed to document the long-term impact of Inside-Out—especially whether it reduces recidivism of program participants as compared to similarly situated nonparticipants. We are unaware of any study or report at the time of writing that examines the impact of Inside-Out on in-prison or post-prison behavior.

Perhaps those who are trained in the Inside-Out method prefer to keep the research out of it and maintain it as simply a college-level class that educates outside and inside students on a wide variety of topics. If so, we believe that this line of thinking presents a missed opportunity to document the transformative nature of a program that to so many students has been more than just a class. In a resource-tight, results-driven correctional environment, adding Inside-Out to the "what works" roster would go a long way toward elevating its status to rehabilitative programming. In the process, many of the barriers and challenges to developing and implementing the program could be removed should it be known that it improves both in-prison and post-prison behavior. We also note that the national Inside-Out website acknowledges the need to document the impact of the program from a research standpoint. At a time when prominent criminologists are suggesting that activism be a part of teaching, research, and service (Belknap 2015), and Lori Pompa is awarded the 2016 Lifetime Achievement in Teaching Award from the American Society of Criminology, programs like the Inside-Out Prison Exchange may be the answer to the problem of how we best rehabilitate prisoners without allowing them to become institutionalized.

CONCLUSION

Programs like Inside-Out are not the only answer. They should not replace existing effective interventions, nor should they be implemented to such a large scale in any one system that program fidelity is lost. But they can tell us something important about how to improve existing programming. Nearly every prisoner returns to the community, so it is important that offenders are not ostracized from that community through the process of incarceration. Programs like Inside-Out have the teeth of retribution, deterrence, and incapacitation through incarceration and the heart of rehabilitation through effective programming. These programs represent reintegrative shaming, and they do so by reminding community members of the importance and place of removed citizens. It is an approach that recognizes that removal from the community is the punishment and that further punishment during incarceration will eventually do more harm to the community than good. The programmatic elements that make Inside-Out unique could be borrowed and implemented into structured prison visitation programs that address criminogenic needs, parenting programs that allow family members into the institution so that skills can be practiced, or work release programs that integrate prisoner employees with employees of the free world.

We both teach classes modeled on the Inside-Out Prison Exchange Program and have seen firsthand the effect that it can have on inside and outside students. So yes, we are biased in suggesting that Inside-Out be thought of as an effective correctional intervention. But we also both have researched and written about correctional programming, rehabilitation, and recidivism, and our work has taken us out of our offices and into the correctional facilities where men and women live and work. The evidence-based movement in corrections can be traced back to individuals who interacted with prisoners and knew that behavior change was possible (see Cullen 2005). The objective evidence that was then marshalled in support of this insider knowledge contributed to the characteristics of appropriate treatment and eventually a theory of effective intervention. In this regard, it is necessary for those who teach and do research as part of Inside-Out—both of us included—to work to examine the true effectiveness of the program so that we may complete the feedback loop from theory to policy and back again.

REFERENCES

Allred, S., L. Harrison, and D. O'Connell. 2013. Self-efficacy: An important aspect of prison-based learning. *Prison Journal* 93: 211–233.

Andrews, D., and J. Bonta. 2010. *The Psychology of Criminal Conduct.* 5th ed. New Providence, NJ: Anderson.

Andrews, D., J. Bonta, and R. Hoge. 1990. Classification for effective rehabilitation: Rediscovering psychology. *Criminal Justice and Behavior* 17: 19–52.

Andrews, D., I. Zinger, R. Hoge, J. Bonta, P. Gendreau, and F. Cullen. 1990. Does correctional treatment work? A clinically relevant and psychologically informed meta-analysis. *Criminology* 28: 369–404.

Arditti, J. 2012. *Parental Incarceration and the Family: Psychological and Social Effects of Imprisonment on Children, Parents, and Caregivers.* New York: New York University Press.

Bain, K. 2004. *What the Best College Teachers Do.* Cambridge, MA: Harvard University Press.

Bales, W., and D. Mears. 2008. Inmate social ties and the transition to society: Does visitation reduce recidivism? *Journal of Research in Crime and Delinquency* 45: 287–321.

Belknap, J. 2015. Activist criminology: Criminologists' responsibility to advocate for social and legal justice. *Criminology* 53: 1–22.

Braithwaite, J. 1989. *Crime, Shame, and Reintegration.* New York: Cambridge University Press.

Chappell, C. A. 2004. Post-secondary correctional education and recidivism: A meta-analysis of researched conducted 1990–1999. *Journal of Correctional Education* 55: 148–169.

Clear T., and J. Austin. 2009. Reducing mass incarceration: Implications of the iron law of prison populations. *Harvard Review of Law and Policy* 3: 307–324.

Cochran, J. 2012. The ties that bind or the ties that break: Examining the relationship between visitation and prisoner misconduct. *Journal of Criminal Justice* 40: 433–440.

Crawford, P., and R. Dalton. 2016. Providing built environment students with the necessary skills for employment: Finding the required soft skills. *Current Urban Studies* 4: 97–123.

Cullen, F. T. 1994. Social support as an organizing concept for criminology: Presidential address to the Academy of Criminal Justice Sciences. *Justice Quarterly* 11: 527–560.

———. 2005. The twelve people who saved rehabilitation: How the science of criminology made a difference. *Criminology* 43: 1–42.

Cullen, F. T., R. Agnew, and P. Wilcox. 2014. *Criminological Theory: Past to Present.* 5th ed. New York: Oxford University Press.

Cullen, F. T., and C. L. Jonson. 2014. Labeling theory and correctional rehabilitation: Beyond unanticipated consequences. In *Empirical Tests of Labeling Theory: Advances in Criminological Theory,* vol. 18, edited by D. Farrington and J. Murray, 63–85. New Brunswick, NJ: Transaction.

———. 2017. *Correctional Theory: Contexts and Consequences.* 2nd ed. Thousand Oaks, CA: Sage.

Cullen, F. T., J. Wright, P. Gendreau, and D. Andrews. 2003. What correctional treatment can tell us about criminological theory: Implications for social learning theory. In *Social Learning Theory and the Explanation of Crime: Advances in Criminological Theory,* vol. 11, edited by R. Akers and G. Jensen, 339–362. New Brunswick, NJ: Transaction.

Davis, L. M., R. Bozick, J. L. Steele, J. Saunders, and J.N.V. Miles. 2013. *Evaluating the Effectiveness of Correctional Education: A Meta-Analysis of Programs That Provide Education to Incarcerated Adults.* Santa Monica, CA: RAND Corporation.

Davis, S., and B. Roswell, eds. 2013. *Turning Teaching Inside Out: A Pedagogy of Transformation for Community-Based Education.* New York: Palgrave Macmillan.

Evenson, R. 1999. Soft skills, hard sell. *Making Education & Career Connections* 74 (3): 29–31.

Fraley, S. E. 1991. From self-blame to self-acceptance: Benefits of learning psychology in a prison undergraduate program. *Teaching of Psychology* 18: 234–235.

Gendreau, P., D. Andrews, and Y. Theriault. 2010. *Correctional Program Assessment Inventory—2010* (CPAI-2100). Saint John, Canada: University of New Brunswick.

Gendreau, P., P. Smith, and S. French. 2006. The theory of effective correctional intervention: Empirical status and future directions. In *Taking Stock: The Status of Criminological Theory—Advances in Criminological Theory,* vol. 15, edited by F. T. Cullen, J. P. Wright, and K. Blevins, 419–446. New Brunswick, NJ: Transaction.

Giordano, P. C., S. A. Cernkovich, and J. L. Rudolph. 2002. Gender, crime, and desistance: Toward a theory of cognitive transformation. *American Journal of Sociology* 107: 990–1064.

Gottfredson, M. R., and T. Hirschi. 1990. *A General Theory of Crime.* Stanford, CA: Stanford University Press.

Griset, O. 2007. Meet us outside! *The Science Teacher* 77 (2): 40–46.

Gruenewald, D. A. 2003. Foundations of place: A multidisciplinary framework for place-conscious education. *American Educational Research Journal* 40: 619–654.

Heckman, J. J., and T. Kautz. 2012. Hard evidence on soft skills. *Labour Economics* 19: 451–464.

Hilinski-Rosick, C., and A. Blackmer. 2014. An exploratory examination of the impact of the Inside-Out Prison Exchange Program. *Journal of Criminal Justice Education* 25: 386–397.

Jonson, C. L., and M. M. Moon. 2014. How to be a successful classroom teacher. *Journal of Contemporary Criminal Justice* 30: 392–408.

Kemp, A. T. 2006. Engaging the environment: A case for a place-based curriculum. *Curriculum and Teaching Dialogue* 8: 125–142.

Knapp, C. E. 2005. The "I-thou" relationship, place-based education, and Aldo Leopold. *Journal of Experimental Education* 27: 277–285.

Latessa, E. J., F. T. Cullen, and P. Gendreau. 2002. Beyond correctional quackery. *Federal Probation* 66: 43–49.

Laub, J. H., and R. J. Sampson. 2003. *Shared Beginnings, Divergent Lives: Delinquent Boys to Age 70.* Cambridge, MA: Harvard University Press.

Lin, N. 1986. Conceptualizing social support. In *Social Support, Life Events, and Depression,* edited by N. Lin, A. Dean, and W. Edsel, 17–30. Orlando, FL: Academic Press.

Lipsey, M., and F. T. Cullen. 2007. The effectiveness of correctional rehabilitation: A review of systematic reviews. *Annual Review of Law and Social Science* 3: 297–320.

Lopez, S. J., and V. J. Calderon. 2013. *Americans Say U.S. Schools Should Teach "Soft" Skills.* Washington, DC: Gallup World Headquarters.

Lowenkamp, C., E. J. Latessa, and P. Smith. 2006. Does correctional program quality really matter? The impact of adhering to the principles of effective intervention. *Criminology & Public Policy* 5: 201–220.

MacKenzie, D. L. 2006. *What Works in Corrections: Reducing the Criminal Activities of Offenders and Delinquents.* New York: Cambridge University Press.

MacKenzie D. L., D. Bierie, and O. Mitchell. 2007. An experimental study of a therapeutic boot camp: Impact on impulses, attitudes and recidivism. *Journal of Experimental Criminology* 3: 221–246.

Makarios, M. D., and T. Livelsberger. 2012. Social support and crime. In *Oxford Handbook of Criminological Theory,* edited by F. T. Cullen and P. Wilcox, 160–188. New York: Oxford University Press.

Maruna, S. 2001. *Making Good: How Ex-Convicts Reform and Rebuild Their Lives.* Washington, DC: American Psychological Association.

Mitchell, M., K. Spooner, D. Jia, and Y. Zhang. 2016. The effect of prison visitation on reentry success: A meta-analysis. *Journal of Criminal Justice* 47: 74–83.

Moffitt, T. E. 1993. Adolescence-limited and life-course-persistent antisocial behavior: A developmental taxonomy. *Psychological Review* 100: 674–701.

Nagin, D., Cullen, F. T., and C. L. Jonson. 2009. Imprisonment and reoffending. In *Crime and Justice: An Annual Review of Research,* vol. 38, edited by M. Tonry, 115–200. Chicago: University of Chicago Press.

Petersilia, J. 2003. *When Prisoners Come Home: Parole and Prisoner Reentry.* New York: Oxford University Press.

Place-Based Educational Evaluation Collaborative. 2010. *The Benefits of Place-Based Education: A Report from the Place-Based Education Evaluation Collaborative.* 2nd ed. Available at http://www.litzsinger.org/PEEC2010_web.pdf.

Podder, A. 2006. *Place-Based Education, Entrepreneurship and Investing for an "Impact Economy."* Salt Lake City, UT: Your Mark on the World.

Poehlmann, J. 2005. Incarcerated mothers' contact with children, perceived family relationships, and depressive symptoms. *Journal of Family Psychology* 19: 350–357.

Pompa, L. 2013. One brick at a time: The power and possibility of dialogue across the prison wall. *Prison Journal* 93: 127–134.

Rade, C., S. Desmarais, and R. Mitchell. 2016. A meta-analysis of public attitudes toward ex-offenders. *Criminal Justice and Behavior* 43: 1260–1280.

Sampson, R. J., and J. H. Laub. 1993. *Crime in the Making: Pathways and Turning Points through Life.* Cambridge, MA: Harvard University Press.

Sarkar, S., and R. Fraizer. 2008. Place-based investigations and authentic inquiry. *Science Teacher* 75 (2): 29–33.

Skeem, J. L., J. E. Louden, D. Polaschek, and J. Camp. 2007. Assessing relationship quality in mandated community treatment: Blending care with control. *Psychological Assessment* 19: 397–410.

Smith, P., and M. Schweitzer. 2012. The therapeutic prison. *Journal of Contemporary Criminal Justice* 28: 7–22.

Sobel, D. 2005. *Place-Based Education: Connecting Classrooms and Communities.* Great Barrington, MA: The Orion Society.

Sykes, G. M. 1958. *The Society of Captives: A Study of Maximum Security Prison.* Princeton, NJ: Princeton University Press.

Tasca, M., K. Wright, J. Turanovic, C. White, and N. Rodriguez. 2016. Moving prison visitation research forward: The Arizona Prison Visitation Project. *Criminology, Criminal Justice, Law & Society* 17: 55–67.

Tooley, M., and L. Bornfreund. 2014. *Skills for Success: Supporting and Assessing Key Habits, Mindsets, and Skills in PreK-12.* Washington, DC: New America.

Travis, J. 2005. *But They All Come Back: Facing the Challenges of Prisoner Reentry.* Washington, DC: The Urban Institute Press.

Van Gundy, A., A. Bryant, and B. Starks. 2013. Pushing the envelope for evolution and social change: Critical challenges for teaching Inside-Out. *Prison Journal* 93: 189–210.

Wakefield, S., and C. Uggen. 2010. Incarceration and stratification. *Annual Review of Sociology* 36: 387–406.

Werts, T. 2013. Tyrone Werts: Reflections on the Inside-Out Prison Exchange Program. *Prison Journal* 93: 135–138.

Wilson, D. B., C. A., Gallagher, and D. L. MacKenzie. 2000. A meta-analysis of corrections-based education, vocation, and work programs for adult offenders. *Journal of Research in Crime and Delinquency* 37: 347–368.

Wright, K., and N. Khade. 2018. Offender recidivism. In *Handbook of Corrections in the United States*, edited by H. Griffin and V. Woodward, 494–502. New York: Routledge.

Wright, K., T. Pratt, C. Lowenkamp, and E. Latessa. 2012. The importance of ecological context for correctional treatment programs: Understanding the micro- and macro-level dimensions of successful offender treatment. *Justice Quarterly* 29: 775–798.

Wright, R. 2004. Care as the "heart" of prison teaching. *Journal of Correctional Education* 55: 191–209.

Wurdinger, S. D., and J. A. Carlson. 2010. *Teaching for Experiential Learning.* Lanham, MD: Rowman & Littlefield Education.

Zoukis, C. 2014. *College for Convicts: The Case for Higher Education in American Prisons.* Jefferson, NC: McFarland & Company.

18

Toward a Theory of Mental Illness and Crime

Robert D. Morgan
and Robert K. Ax

It is well established in the U.S. corrections and criminology literature, as well as the popular media, that persons with severe and persistent mental illness are disproportionately represented in the criminal justice system. With nearly 7 million adult offenders in the U.S. criminal justice system, including approximately 2.1 million incarcerated adults (Kaeble and Glaze 2015), and prevalence estimates of mental health concerns in jails and prisons ranging broadly from 10–60 percent (James and Glaze 2006; Prins 2014), criminal justice involved persons with mental illness (CJ-PMI) is a clinical population warranting special consideration.

With regard to prevalence of mental health concerns in corrections, it is relevant to note that rates will differ based on how one defines mental health concern. For example, if mental health concern is restricted to serious mental illness (i.e., serious mood disorders such as major depressive disorder and bipolar disorder, as well as psychotic disorders such as schizophrenia, schizoaffective disorder, and other psychotic disorders), the prevalence rate is approximately 10 percent in prisons. Notably, this is consistent with prior findings regarding the number of inmates receiving psychotropic medications (Beck and Maruschak 2001). A significantly higher proportion of jail inmates (i.e., 31 percent), a population considered to be significantly more volatile, met *DSM-IV-TR* diagnostic criteria for a serious mental illness (Steadman et al. 2009). Further, approximately 15–25 percent of federal and state prison inmates reported previous diagnosis of at least one mental disorder (Wilper et al. 2009). On the other end of the spectrum, when not limiting estimates to severe mental illness, it has been reported that as many as 60 percent of prison inmates have a "mental health problem" broadly defined (James and Glaze 2006). Given that 4 percent of the general U.S. population (i.e., non-CJ involved) reported a diagnosis (current or recent) of a serious mental illness, and 18.5 percent reported a current or recent diagnosis of any psychiatric disorder (Substance Abuse and Mental Health Services Administration 2014), the overrepresentation of persons with mental illness in corrections specifically and in the criminal justice system broadly is clear.

TOWARD A THEORY OF MENTAL ILLNESS AND CRIME

Limited community mental health resources and deinstitutionalization are frequently cited as the reasons for the increased numbers of persons with mental illness (PMI) in the criminal justice system (Abramson 1972; Bloom 2010; Lamb and Bachrach 2001; Lamb and Weinberger 1998; Munetz, Grande, and Chambers 2001; Teplin 1984, 1990; Torrey 1995); however, others have contended that other factors may contribute to involvement of persons with mental illness in the criminal justice system and that these criminogenic needs, neglected in prior treatment efforts with CJ-PMI, warrant clinical consideration (e.g., Draine et al. 2002; Hodgins et al. 2007). Morgan and colleagues established a program of research to examine the prevalence of criminal risk factors in criminal justice and non–criminal justice populations of persons with mental illness as an alternative perspective for why these individuals are involved in the criminal justice system at disproportionate rates.

When examining the psychiatric presentation of adult inmates in state prison compared to persons with mental illness in psychiatric hospitals, not surprisingly, CJ-PMI demonstrate a similar clinical profile as persons with mental illness who are not justice involved (Morgan et al. 2010; see also Wolff et al. 2011). More significantly and surprisingly, given previous assumptions that persons with mental illness were justice involved as a result of their mental illness or due to a lack of adequate mental health resources, CJ-PMI in state prisons exhibited criminal thinking and antisocial attitudes comparable to inmates without mental illness (Morgan et al. 2010; Wolff et al. 2011). These findings, consistent across two populations of state prison inmates, suggested that criminogenic risk and not mental illness may be a more significant contributor to justice involvement for this population of offenders. Notably, these findings were from adult prison inmates, a population that would be expected to present more criminogenic risk, but what about youthful inmates in a county jail setting (i.e., would this finding hold for a volatile population in a volatile setting)? Results from a measure of criminal thinking from 122 low-level offenders with co-occurring serious mental illness and substance abuse in a county jail were compared to inmates in Morgan et al. (2010). Results indicated that young persons with mental illness in a large county jail presented with thinking styles that support a criminal lifestyle and that these criminal thinking styles follow a pattern that is very similar to adult persons with mental illness in state prison.

These studies focused on criminal thinking among incarcerated persons with mental illness, but what about CJ-PMI in community placements (e.g., psychiatric hospitals)? Gross and Morgan examined this issue in two separate studies. The first study (Gross and Morgan 2013) examined criminal thinking in a short-term, inpatient psychiatric sample with and without criminal justice involvement. In this study psychiatric patients were matched with participants from the Morgan et al. (2010) sample on a number of sociodemographic variables (e.g., gender, diagnosis, ethnicity, and years of formal education). Comparisons between the two groups (i.e., incarcerated persons with mental illness and short-term psychiatric inpatients) indicated that CJ-PMI in an acute psychiatric facility present similarly to incarcerated persons with mental illness with regard to both psychiatric symptomatology and criminal thinking. Furthermore, persons with mental illness without criminal justice involvement were distinguished from the incarcerated persons with mental illness in the Morgan et al. study (2010) by lower levels of criminal thinking and lower levels of antisocial personality disorder but presented similarly with regard to other psychiatric symptoms. In a follow-up study (Bartholomew, Morgan, and Mitchell 2017), participants consisted of male and female consumers enrolled in Assertive Community Treatment (ACT) and Forensic Assertive Community Treatment (FACT; or programs with a like model of service delivery) programs in four separate states. Although results of this study revealed no differences in criminal thinking when comparing participants with and without a history of criminal justice involvement, there was a significant relationship between general criminal thinking and mental health symptomatology. Specifically, both the overall level of symptom distress and the number of mental health symptoms experienced were positively associated with general criminal thinking. This latter finding supports the contention made by several that criminal thinking and mental health symptomatology should be conceptualized as comorbid disorders (Draine et al. 2002; Epperson et al. 2011; Hodgins et al. 2007; Morgan et al. 2010; Morgan et al. 2012; Wilson et al. 2014) and treated concurrently.

A primary limitation with the above studies was an overreliance on one aspect of criminogenic risk—antisocial attitudes/criminal thinking. It is relevant to examine other criminal risk factors (e.g., history of criminal justice involvment, antisocial associates, and substance abuse) to further elucidate the presence of criminogenic needs as it pertains to the criminal justice involvement of persons with mental illness. Thus, Bolanos, Morgan, and Mitchell (2017) examined a number of criminogenic risk factors in persons with mental illness in an acute inpatient psychiatric unit who were and were not involved with the criminal justice system and found that, although there were no statistically significant differences on psychiatric symptomatology, CJ-PMI endorsed significantly more criminogenic risk than their counterparts who were not involved with the criminal justice system. Specifically, CJ-PMI reported significantly more antisocial associates and they spent more time with these associates. They also produced significantly higher scores on a measure of criminal risk (Self-Appraisal Questionnaire) and, consistent with the previously summarized findings, CJ-PMI produced significantly higher scores on measures of criminal risk.

Collectively, results of this series of studies provide clear evidence that CJ-PMI differ from their peers with mental illness who are not involved with the criminal justice system on variables associated with criminal risk despite no significant differences in their psychiatric functioning. Furthermore, these antisocial tendencies are linked to recidivism regardless of mental health status (Skeem et al. 2013). In fact, the evidence is so compelling that it is now recognized that cases in which persons with mental illness are incarcerated due to complications with mental illness is the exception rather than the rule (Skeem, Manchak, and Peterson 2011); thus, when working with offenders with mental illness, service providers must target dual issues of mental illness and criminal propensity. In other words, the preponderance of the data seems to support the contention that CJ-PMI have both psychiatric and criminal risk concerns, such that they have different treatment needs than either non–justice involved persons with mental illness or justice-involved individuals without mental illness.

TREATMENT IMPLICATIONS

When treating CJ-PMI, service providers have historically placed greater emphasis on symptom management and mental health stabilization than on criminogenic needs (see Bewley and Morgan 2011). Although it may be that service providers opt for providing mental health services aimed at psychiatric stability and the immediate clinical presentation (e.g., active psychosis, mania, depressed mood), it may also be the case that service providers are providing mental health services at the exclusion of criminogenic needs based on previously noted assumptions common in the mental health and criminal justice fields that the criminal behavior of persons with mental illness is driven by an absence of adequate mental health services and destabilization (Lamb and

Bachrach 2001; Lamb and Weinberger 1998; Teplin 1984). Regardless of the rationale for focusing services on issues related to mental health functioning, as discussed above, the totality of the clinical presentation should be considered in treatment planning. That is, issues of mental illness and criminogenic need are co-occurring and should be dually targeted.

With regard to providing services aimed at co-occurring issues of mental illness and criminogenic need, a comprehensive meta-analytic review of interventions for incarcerated persons with mental illness found significant improvements for general mental health outcomes, improved coping skills, improved institutional adjustment with fewer behavioral problems, as well as an appreciable effect on criminal and psychiatric recidivism (Morgan et al. 2012). Similar mental health outcomes were obtained in a separate meta-analysis with noted reductions in symptom distress and improved functioning (Martin et al. 2012). Although tentative and inconclusive, the most significant treatment gains with respect to effect size in Morgan et al. (2012) were produced in the one and only study that targeted both mental health needs and criminal behavior. The meta-analyses by Morgan et al. (2012) and Martin et al. (2012) also provided important insights into effective therapeutic strategies. Morgan et al. (2012) found that having CJ-PMI practice new behaviors, including practicing learned behaviors in their real-world environment (e.g., via homework), contributed to more favorable outcomes. Martin et al. (2012) found that continuity of services between institutions and community, when feasible, led to more favorable outcomes.

Mental health professionals attempting to provide integrated services (i.e., services targeting the co-occurring issues of mental illness and criminal risk) have few options available in the treatment literature. Notably, some professionals have attempted to modify correctional rehabilitation programs known to effectively reduce criminal recidivism (e.g., Thinking for a Change; Bush, Glick, and Taymans 1997) by including information relevant to offenders with mental illness (i.e., supplementing the treatment program with information regarding mental illness and psychiatric stability). Although commendable in effort, such approaches fail to recognize the reciprocal relationship between criminal behavior and mental illness and that these issues co-occur in an individual (see Morgan et al. 2013). Thus, these co-occurring issues cannot be treated in isolation. This was the intent of Changing Lives and Changing Outcomes (CLCO): A Therapeutic Program for Justice Involved Persons with Mental Illness (Morgan, Kroner, and Mills 2017)[1]—the first intervention developed to treat problems of mental illness and criminal risk as co-occurring treatment targets in CJ-PMI.

CLCO utilizes a bi-adaptive model of intervention by targeting dual (bi) issues of mental illness and criminal propensity to improve functional (adaptive) outcomes for offenders with mental illness. Psychosocial and cognitive-behavioral theoretical orientations are used to increase these offenders' understanding of their mental illness and criminal risk and to provide the knowledge and skills necessary to cope with their illness and "criminalness." The aim of this treatment model is to maximize adaptive behaviors to optimize functioning while reducing both criminal and psychiatric recidivism. CLCO has a structured treatment manual and client workbook and consists of seventy-seven sessions with the target length of each session lasting between 1.5 and 2 hours. The authors recommend two to three sessions per week for an approximate treatment delivery time of four to six months. Changing Lives and Changing Outcomes (CLCO; Morgan, Kroner, and Mills 2017) is a comprehensive, manualized treatment program designed to help CJ-PMI address issues related to both their mental illness and their "criminalness" (i.e., behaviors that violate the rights of others, laws, and/or social norms, regardless if the behavior results in arrest; Morgan et al. 2010). CLCO incorporates elements of best practices for both correctional and clinical populations to help CJ-PMI understand and cope with their mental illness, identify and challenge antisocial thought patterns, learn basic social skills (e.g., how to interview for a job, how to initiate and maintain prosocial friendships), abstain from substance use, and proactively manage signs of their own psychiatric and criminal relapse.

Preliminary examinations of CLCO are promising. CJ-PMI who participated in CLCO were satisfied that the intervention helped them meet their treatment goals, and they endorsed positive therapeutic bonds with treatment providers as assessed on standardized measures (Morgan et al. 2014). From a therapeutic process perspective, CJ-PMI in CLCO were, on average, engaged and active in the treatment process (e.g., $M = 8.07$, $SD = 2.52$ on a ten-point Likert-type scale rating session participation). Even more significantly, initial evaluation found that CJ-PMI experienced significant improvements over time with small to moderate effect sizes noted on measures of symptom distress, psychopathology, and some aspects of criminal thinking (Morgan et al. 2014). Notably, not only does CLCO facilitate change (reduced symptoms and criminal thinking as endorsed on self-report measures), but CJ-PMI also learned the content and principles taught to them during the various therapeutic modules. That is, participants in CLCO demonstrated increased knowledge acquisition as assessed from pre-module to post-module content tests (Van Horn et al. 2017). Finally, and most significantly, CJ-PMI who successfully completed CLCO were over two times as likely to successfully meet the terms of their probation compared to CJ-PMI who were unsuccessfully discharged from the CLCO program (Morgan and Van Horn 2017). CJ-PMI who successfully completed CLCO also had significantly fewer positive drug screenings (M = 0.66, SD = 1.26) than did those who did not complete the program (M = 1.36, SD = 2.10), $t(110.39) = -2.30$, p = .02, d = 0.40). Furthermore, CJ-PMI who completed the treatment program evidenced a 71 percent decrease in the rate of positive drug screenings before and after treatment. No significant decrease was noted among CJ-PMI discharged from the program. It is important to note that individuals who completed the program had significantly more pretreatment positive drug screenings than those who did not complete the program. Thus, the intensive nature of CLCO may be most helpful for individuals who are at increased risk for probation failure.

Thus, CLCO and other interventions specifically developed to target the co-occurring issues of mental illness and criminal risk offer promising approaches for reducing psychiatric symptomatology, improving psychiatric and criminal justice outcomes, and most significantly, potentially improving quality of life for persons with mental illness who are involved with the criminal justice system.

POLICY IMPLICATIONS

Persons with mental illness present significant concerns both during incarceration and after release from prison. While incarcerated, individuals with mental illness experience poorer institutional adjustment, as they receive more disciplinary infractions (Matejkowski, Caplan, and Wiesel-Cullen 2010), spend more time in segregation (Stone 2003), and are prone to physical and sexual victimization (Wolff et al. 2007). As a result, these inmates are less likely to receive early release and, on average, serve longer sentences in prison than their peers without mental illness (Matejkowski, Caplan, and Wiesel-Cullen 2010). Compounding the problem is that increased time in prison is associated with increased psychiatric symptomatology and aggressive and antisocial personality traits for inmates suffering from mental illness (Bauer, Morgan, and Bolanos 2016). Furthermore, individuals with mental illness who are released from prison encounter numerous transitional difficulties such as housing concerns, financial stress, and social disruption (Draine et al. 2005; Haimowitz 2004) and are at increased risk for reincarceration (Skeem and Louden 2006). Thus, public policy aimed at targeting this unique population must account for the co-occurring needs of individuals presenting with issues of mental illness *and* criminal proclivity.

With regard to criminal justice policy, a caveat is warranted. Get tough on crime policies of the 1980s and 1990s have contributed to an incarceration epidemic in the United States. It is not by accident that the United States leads the world in incarceration rates (see Walmsley, 2013). Furthermore, significant iatrogenic effects result from such policies (e.g., one in six black males had been incarcerated by 2001 with current projections of one in three black males being involved with the criminal justice system; National Association for the Advancement of Colored People 2017). As policy approaches throughout the beginning of the twenty-first century sought to reduce the national incarceration rate (see, e.g., Eaglin 2016; Eisen and Cullen 2016), the Trump administration favors reverting to a tough-mindedness approach to crime.

Although get tough on crime approaches work if the goal is to keep persons who break the law in prison for as long as possible, such policies neither reduce crime nor provide optimal opportunities for rehabilitation (i.e., to help offenders to become contributing members of society), and it is very expensive to maintain policies that result in overcrowding prisons and jails. We submit that, contrary to U.S. Senator Tom Cotton, the United States does not have an "under-incarceration" problem (Manchester 2016). Recent attempts to reduce the national incarceration rate are not only fiscally responsible but smart policy as well. Interventions reduce criminal offending (see, e.g., McGuire 2003), which in turn will save taxpayer dollars. Incarcerating one individual for one year costs American taxpayers approximately $31,286 (Henrichson and Delaney 2012). The more we can keep offenders out of prison and in the workforce, the more we gain as a society.

It is important to note that get-tough legislation (e.g., "three-strikes" laws, federal guidelines for mandatory minimum sentencing) has been well received, or at least tolerated, by taxpaying citizens over the past four decades. This suggests that many Americans believe they receive acceptable returns on their investment in prisons and jails. These might include an increased sense of safety or one of satisfaction in the protracted punishment of offenders. In some economically depressed localities, prisons provide job opportunities. Researchers and clinicians in the criminal justice field must recognize and respond to the public's "willingness to pay" for retribution and a sense of safety.

Prevention and Collaboration

To counter get-tough policies and legislation it is part of our professional community's responsibility to communicate the data documenting that it is both fiscally beneficial and broadly effective from *a public safety perspective* to divert nonviolent offenders from prison. Diversion courts (e.g., drug courts, mental health courts, and veterans' courts) have proven effective for reducing substance use (Rossman et al. 2011) and criminal behavior (see Gottfredson, Najaka, and Kearly 2003; Hiller et al. 2009; Latessa et al. 2001; Rossman et al. 2011). Just as desirable are primary prevention strategies (i.e., preventing the onset of psychopathology; Ax 2011) targeting at-risk individuals and families *before* the point of arrest, interventions that could be undertaken in collaboration with community providers (Washington State Institute for Public Policy Research 2016). Ultimately, our value as correctional healthcare professionals lies in our ability to formulate, implement, and document effective, portable treatments. To do so, we believe that the future of criminal justice mental health involves increased collaboration within and across disciplines, and in particular partnering with professionals working in the communities where preventive strategies are implemented.

Advocacy: An Evolving Role for Criminal Justice Professionals

The authors maintain that the community of criminal justice healthcare professionals must advocate on behalf of enlightened criminal justice policies and perspectives, based as much as possible on robust outcome data, taking into account the range of rewards a skeptical public may feel it receives for its investment in prisons and jails and dealing honestly with their concerns.

A common question with regard to policy, however, is how to best disseminate the information that we as criminologists and criminal justice professionals know will improve the lives of those involved in the justice system. Advocacy can take many forms. In addition to writing or visiting individual legislatures (see, e.g., state psychological associations legislative days), criminal justice advocates may write for popular consumption (see, e.g., Dr. Carl Hart's op-eds in the *New York Times* and his consumer-driven website http://drcarlhart.com/), volunteer and accept invitations to testify before legislators, and consult or collaborate with nongovernmental organizations, such as the National Alliance on Mental Illness (NAMI), to contribute to criminal justice policy initiatives. We can use innovative platforms (e.g., social media, podcasts) and interdisciplinary collaboration to move beyond our silos to share our knowledge, expertise, and data with partner-professionals in advocacy.

Ultimately, to be successful, we must be *active*, and we should start with our own institutions. We do not teach about these opportunities or the requisite skills in graduate school, nor are they session topics at our national/international criminology, criminal justice, or corrections conferences. To create a professional culture whereby advocating for smarter criminal justice policies is the rule rather than the exception, we need to begin educating one another about how to formulate and promote effective, beneficial, and empirically sound policy.

CONCLUSIONS

Implicit in any approach to reducing mass incarceration is the perspective that all lives have value and that removing individuals who violate our laws and social mores from society for extended periods of time (especially in cases that involve no violence) is not the most effective or humane approach to dealing with problem people, many of whom are already marginalized.

Extended periods of incarceration, while consistent with the criminal justice missions of punishment, incapacitation, and deterrence, do not teach alternative, prosocial behaviors. Incarceration has predictably adverse consequences for CJ-PMI resulting in increased psychiatric symptomatology and aggressive, antisocial, and negativistic personality traits (Bauer, Morgan, and Bolanos 2017). Rehabilitation, the province of correctional and criminal justice researchers and practitioners, emphasizes change through positive reinforcement (among other clinical strategies), and in that respect is at variance with the other correctional missions.

Accordingly, it is not merely abolishing "get tough on crime" policies that must happen. We also need to expend resources on preventing involvement with the criminal justice system, diverting those individuals from incarceration to alternate programs where appropriate, and reprioritizing correctional resources to focus on transitional programming that assists incarcerated persons to return to society. Good research should find its way into practice. To make this happen we must become effective advocates, engaging in honest dialogues with stakeholders justifiably concerned about public safety, and make our case for empirically based and, broadly speaking, cost-effective criminal justice policies.

NOTE

1. Disclaimer: CLCO was developed by the lead author of this chapter with support from Texas Tech University (TTU) and the National Institute of Mental Health. CLCO will be commercially available in 2017 and all revenue from sales (royalties) will be placed in a research account at TTU to support graduate students CJ-PMI research efforts.

REFERENCES

Abramson, M. F. 1972. The criminalization of mentally disordered behavior. *Psychiatric Services* 23 (4): 101–105.

Ax, R. K. 2011. Correctional mental health: A best practices future. In *Correctional Mental Health: From Theory to Best Practice*, edited by T. J. Fagan and R. K. Ax, 353–378. Thousand Oaks, CA: Sage.

Bartholomew, N. G., R. D. Morgan, and S. Mitchell. 2017. Criminal thinking in a community mental health sample: Effects on treatment engagement, psychiatric recovery, and criminality. Manuscript under review for publication.

Bauer, R. L., R. D. Morgan, and A. B. Bolanos. 2016. Implications of long-term incarceration for persons with mental illness. Manuscript in preparation for publication.

Beck, A. J., and L. M. Maruschak. 2001. *Mental Health Treatment in State Prisons, 2000.* Washington, DC: U.S. Department of Justice, Office of Justice Programs, Bureau of Justice Statistics.

Bewley, M. T., and R. D. Morgan. 2011. A national survey of mental health services available to offenders with mental illness: Who is doing what? *Law and Human Behavior* 35 (5): 351–363.

Bloom, J. D. 2010. "The incarceration revolution": The abandonment of the seriously mentally ill to our jails and prisons. *Journal of Law, Medicine & Ethics* 38 (4): 727–734.

Bolanos, A., R. D. Morgan, and S. Mitchell. 2017. Shared risk factors among persons with mental illness who are and are not criminal justice involved. Manuscript in preparation for publication.

Bush, J., B. Glick, and J. Taymans. 1997. *Thinking for a Change.* Longmont, CO: National Institute of Corrections, U.S. Department of Justice.

Draine, J., M. S. Salzer, D. P. Culhane, and T. R. Hadley. 2002. Role of social disadvantage in crime, joblessness, and homelessness among persons with serious mental illness. *Psychiatric Services* 53 (5): 565–573.

Draine, J., N. Wolff, J. E. Jacoby, S. Hartwell, and C. Duclos. 2005. Understanding community re-entry of former prisoners with mental illness: A conceptual model to guide new research. *Behavioral Sciences & the Law* 23: 689–707.

Eaglin, J. 2016. California quietly continues to reduce mass incarceration. Brennan Center for Justice, February 15. Available at https://www.brennancenter.org/blog/california-quietly-continues-reduce-mass-incarceration.

Eisen, L. B., and J. Cullen. 2016. Update: Changes in state imprisonment rates. Brennan Center for Justice, June 7. Available at https://www.brennancenter.org/analysis/update-changes-state-imprisonment-rates.

Epperson, M., N. Wolff, R. Morgan, W. Fisher, B. C. Frueh, and J. Huening. 2011. The next generation of behavioral health and criminal justice interventions: Improving outcomes by improving interventions. Center for Behavioral Health Services & Criminal Justice Research. New Brunswick, NJ: Rutgers University.

Gottfredson, D. G., S. S. Najaka, and B. Kearley. 2003. Effectiveness of drug treatment courts: Evidence from a randomized trial. *Criminology and Public Policy* 2 (2): 171.

Gross, N. G., and R. D. Morgan. 2013. Understanding persons with mental illness who are and are not criminal justice involved: A comparison of criminal thinking and psychiatric symptoms. *Law and Human Behavior* 37: 175–186.

Haimowitz, S. 2004. Slowing the revolving door: Community reentry of offenders with mental illness. *Psychiatric Services* 55: 373–375.

Henrichson, C., and R. Delaney. 2012. The price of prisons: What incarceration costs taxpayers. *Federal Sentencing Reporter* 25: 68.

Hiller, M. L., E. Narevic, J. M. Webster, P. Rosen, M. Staton, C. Leukefeld, T. F. Garrity, and R. Kayo. 2009. Problem severity and motivation for treatment in incarcerated substance abusers. *Substance Use & Misuse* 44 (1): 28–41.

Hodgins, S., R. Müller-Isberner, R. Freese, J. Tiihonen, E. Repo-Tiihonen, M. Eronen, M. D. Eaves, S. Hart, C. Webster, S. Levander, E. Tuninger, D. Ross, H. Vartiainen, and R. Kronstrand. 2007. A comparison of general adult and forensic patients with schizophrenia living in the community. *International Journal of Forensic Mental Health* 6 (1): 63–75.

James, D. J., and L. E. Glaze. 2006. Mental health problems of prison and jail inmates. Washington, DC: U.S. Department of Justice, Office of Justice Programs, Bureau of Justice Statistics.

Kaeble, D., and L. Glaze. 2016. *Correctional Populations in the United States, 2015*. Washington, DC: U.S. Department of Justice, Office of Justice Programs, Bureau of Justice Statistics.

Lamb, H. R., and L. L. Bachrach. 2001. Some perspectives on deinstitutionalization. *Psychiatric Services* 52:1039–1045.

Lamb, H. R., and L. E. Weinberger. 1998. Persons with severe mental illness in jails and prisons: A review. *Psychiatric Services* 49: 483–492.

Latessa, E. J., S. J. Listwan, D. K. Shaffer, C. Lowenkamp, and S. Ratansi, S. 2001. Preliminary evaluation of Ohio's drug court efforts. Center for Criminal Justice Research, Division of Criminal Justice, University of Cincinnati.

Manchester, J. 2016. Senator: We have an under-incarceration problem. May 20, CNN. Available at http://www.cnn.com/2016/05/20/politics/tom-cotton-under-incarceration-problem-prison-reform/.

Martin, M., S. Dorken, A. Wamboldt, and S. Wootten. 2012. Stopping the revolving door: A meta-analysis on the effectiveness of interventions for criminally involved individuals with major mental disorders. *Law and Human Behavior* 36 (1): 1–12.

Matejkowski, J., J. M. Caplan, and S. Wiesel-Cullen. 2010. The impact of severe mental illness on parole decisions: Social integration within a prison setting. *Criminal Justice and Behavior* 37: 1005–1029.

McGuire, J., ed. 2003. *Offender Rehabilitation and Treatment: Effective Programmes and Policies to Reduce Re-Offending*. Chichester, UK: Wiley.

Morgan, R. D., W. H. Fisher, N. Duan, J. T. Mandracchia, and D. Murray. 2010. Prevalence of criminal thinking among state prison inmates with serious mental illness. *Law and Human Behavior* 34: 324–336.

Morgan, R. D., D. B. Flora, D. G. Kroner, J. F. Mills, F. Varghese, and J. S. Steffan. 2012. Treating offenders with mental illness: A research synthesis. *Law and Human Behavior* 36: 37–50.

Morgan, R. D., D. G. Kroner, and J. F. Mills. 2017. Changing Lives and Changing Outcomes: A Treatment Guide for Offenders with Mental Illness. Treatment manual submitted for publication.

Morgan, R. D., D. G. Kroner, J. F. Mills, and A. B. Batastini. 2013. Treating criminal offenders. *Handbook of Forensic Psychology*, 4th ed., edited by I. B. Weiner and R. K. Otto, 795–838. Hoboken, NJ: Wiley.

Morgan, R. D., D. G. Kroner, J. F. Mills, R. Bauer, and C. Serna. 2014. Treating justice involved persons with mental illness: Preliminary evaluation of a comprehensive treatment program. *Criminal Justice and Behavior* 41: 902–916.

Morgan, R. D., and S. A. Van Horn. 2017. Changing lives and changing outcomes: Community outcomes from an intervention for justice involved persons with mental illness. Manuscript in preparation for publication.

Munetz, M. R., T. P. Grande, and M. R. Chambers. 2001. The incarceration of individuals with severe mental disorders. *Community Mental Health Journal* 37: 361–372.

National Organization for the Advancement of Colored People. 2017. Criminal justice fact sheet. Baltimore: NAACP.

Prins, S. J. 2014. Prevalence of mental illnesses in U.S. state prisons: A systematic review. *Psychiatric Services* 65 (7): 862–872.

Rossman, S. B., J. K. Roman, J. M. Zweig, M. Rempel, and C. H Lindquist. 2011. *The Multi-Site Adult Drug Court Evaluation: Executive Summary*. Washington, DC: Urban Institute.

Skeem, J. L., and J. E. Louden. 2006. Toward evidence-based practice for probationers and parolees mandated to mental health treatment. *Psychiatric Services* 57: 333–342.

Skeem, J. L., S. M. Manchak, C. W. Lidz, and E. P. Mulvey. 2013. The utility of patients' self-perceptions of violence risk: Consider asking the person who may know best. *Psychiatric Services* 64 (5): 410–415.

Skeem, J. L., S. M. Manchak, and J. K. Peterson. 2011. Correctional policy for offenders with mental illness: Creating a new paradigm for recidivism reduction. *Law and Human Behavior* 35: 110–126.

Steadman, H., F. Osher, P. C. Robbins, B. Case, and S. Samuels. 2009. Prevalence of serious mental illness among jail inmates. *Psychiatric Services* 60 (6): 761–765.

Stone, N. 2003. *A Companion Guide to Mentally Disordered Offenders*. Shaw and Sons.

Substance Abuse and Mental Health Services Administration. 2014. National Survey on Drug Use and Health: Comparison of 2011–2012 and 2012–2013 Model Based Prevalence Estimates (50 States and the District of Columbia). Washington, DC.

Teplin, L. A. 1984. Criminalizing mental disorder: The comparative arrest rate of the mentally ill. *American Psychologist* 39: 794–803.

———. 1990. Detecting disorder: The treatment of mentally ill among jail detainees. *Journal of Consulting and Clinical Psychology* 58: 233–236.

Torrey, E. F. 1995. Editorial: Jails and prisons—America's new mental hospitals. *American Journal of Public Health* 85: 1611–1613.

Van Horn, S. A., R. D. Morgan, L. Brusman-Lovins, A. Littlefield, J. Hunter, G. Gigax, and K. Ridley. 2017. Changing Lives and Changing Outcomes: "What Works" in an Intervention for Justice Involved Persons with Mental Illness. Manuscript submitted for publication.

Walmsley, R. 2013. *World Prison Population List*. 10th ed. London: International Centre for Prison Studies.

Washington State Institute for Public Policy. 2016. Updated inventory of evidence-based, research-based, and promising practices: For prevention and intervention services for children and juveniles in the child welfare, juvenile justice, and mental health systems, June. Olympia, WA: University of Washington. Available at http://www.wsipp.wa.gov/ReportFile/1639/Wsipp_Updated-Inventory-of-Evidence-Based-Researched-Based-and-Promising-Practices-For-Prevention-and-Intervention-Services-for-Children-and-Juveniles-in-the-Child-Welfare-Juvenile-Justice-and-Mental-Health-Systems_Report.pdf.

Wilper, A. P., S. Woolhandler, J. W. Boyd, K. E. Lasser, D. McCormick, D. H. Bor, and D. U. Himmelstein. 2009. The health and health care of U.S. prisoners: Results of a nationwide survey. *American Journal of Public Health* 99 (4): 666–672.

Wilson, K., M. Freestone, C. Taylor, F. Blazey, and F. Hardman. 2014. Effectiveness of modified therapeutic community treatment within a medium-secure service for personality-disordered offenders. *Journal of Forensic Psychiatry and Psychology* 25 (3): 243–261.

Wolff, N., R. D. Morgan, J. Shi, W. Fisher, and J. Huening, J. 2011. Comparative analysis of thinking styles and emotional states of male and female inmates with and without mental disorders. *Psychiatric Services* 62: 1485–1493.

Wolff, N., J. Shi, C. L. Blitz, and J. Siegel, J. 2007. Understanding sexual victimization inside prisons: Factors that predict risk. *Criminology and Public Policy* 6: 535–564.

Conclusion

When Theory Fails

Scott H. Decker

The first college course I taught had thirty-five students. All of them were police officers, and all of them came to class in uniform, with their sidearm. I started the course with some arcane lecture about the importance of theory. About halfway through my lecture, a student raised his hand and offered his views about theory. They were, needless to say, quite different than my own. "Theories don't get things done." "Theories waste time when real efforts are called for." "Theories are abstract." When the student finished, I told him that it seemed to me that he had a theory about theory. His theory about theory had several variables that taken together formed propositions that were testable. He acknowledged that he had some ideas about theory but that those ideas did not form a theory. As twenty-four-year-olds often do, I pressed on. "What is your assignment in the police department?" He told me that he was a detective who was assigned to the burglary division. I asked him what burglars were like. "Opportunistic." "Not big risk takers; they look for easy scores that are quick. They seldom plan extensively and find a routine and stick with it." This being 1974, it was well before the theory known today as routine activity theory. When I asked how he learned these things about burglars, he told me that by talking to other detectives and burglars he had put these things together. Of course, he had a theory about burglars. He said that when he began to work a new burglary, he gathered as many facts as he could from the crime to develop a description of the offense, so he could match it against known burglars whose methods of operation would fit the pattern of the burglary. Of course, this is the inductive method of reasoning that we describe throughout the book: move from the specific to the general and back again. As I came to study burglars some twenty years later, I wish I had paid more attention to what this burglary detective knew as he described an early version of how routine activity theory applied to burglars. Despite his continued reluctance to accept that he had a theory of theories or a theory of burglars, his method of thinking about these issues fits such a pattern.

We believe that this book illustrates a number of important ways of thinking about offenders and the way the criminal justice system responds to offenders. In its classic formulation, theory is created *a priori* and before a project begins. That theory is tested with data that are collected to measure the tenets of the theory. It is hardly so clean and clear. We believe that just as often, theory is derived from a set of facts as it is laid out in advance of a research project. In addition, we believe that theory is as important, perhaps more important, in dealing with aspects of the criminal justice system as it is in describing offenders. Most programs need a blueprint to be successful. Such a blueprint lays out the key elements of a program, policy, or intervention, as well as the interrelationship between those elements. In many cases, a well-developed description is a "logic model," something that identifies the sequences, dosages, and targets of an intervention. Unless it is by chance, no intervention can be successful without a blueprint or logic model. A logic model is essentially an operational theory of the program, policy, or intervention. Many programs fail for lack of such a plan; what we argue for is a theory of how change would operate. In order for such a theory to be useful, it would have to specify the concepts as well as their timing and relationships to other concepts. Similarly, many theories fail for lack of realization in practice. In our minds, the two are inimitably linked.

An example may make this process more clear. Race has been a central concept in criminology since its inception. At least five of the chapters in this book deal explicitly with race (Brunson and Block; Trager and Kubrin; Braga and Drakulich; Farrel, Warren, and Cronin; and Spohn). These chapters provide a treatment of race as both an independent and dependent variable. But more importantly, the chapters provide a theory of race and how it is theoretically correlated with a program or policy. The Braga and Drakulich chapter is a good example of how treating race on both sides of the equation can enhance our understanding of the concept. There are actual characteristics of race, perceptions of race, and treatment of race in the reaction of a criminal justice system, process, or program. The best way to sort the differences is to have a theory of how race affects and is affected by external measures. Such an approach effectively addresses concerns about reductionism, a key issue in theory construction and testing.

One of the notable features of the book is its broad applicability of the approach to integrating theory with practice. While descriptions of sentencing, policing hot spots, firearms and police misconduct are staples in criminological analysis, we include several nontraditional topics. These include global warming, wildlife crime, critical race theory, mass shootings, and mental illness. These important topics have not made it into the mainstream on a consistent basis.

It is easier to identify major areas of criminal justice policy that have not been successful than those that have succeeded. Three areas come to mind: mass incarceration, boot camps, and gang programming. In each of these areas there has been substantial investment in criminal justice policy and practice. In each of these areas there is consensus that the policy/practice does not work and in, many cases, it makes things worse. While political considerations had a role in promulgating these policies, each lacked a sound theory of individual adaptation and change. In the case of mass incarceration, we lacked theories of institutional and individual change to guide the American experiment with expanding imprisonment so rapidly and into so many new areas. The creation of the "school to prison" and "family to prison" pipelines was unanticipated, largely as a consequence of the lack of good theory. Theories of adolescent development, family dysfunction, and institutional failure should have led us to at least doubt the wisdom of embarking on the mass incarceration binge. Similarly, boot camps have been a dismal failure, arguably making youth who participate in them worse than before they entered the camps. Despite this, criminologists were silent early in the boot camp movement. There was no attempt to develop a program theory that articulated theories of adolescent development. Gang programming followed a similar path. Largely isolated from theories of group process (save for Jim Short's work) and adolescent development, gang programming was an admixture of suppression and support. There was little coordination between the two approaches and minimal effort at assessment of assets and deficits. The risk assessment that has made probation and parole more successful was not integrated into such approaches. Now, the integration of theory with these three approaches would not magically have altered the course of mass incarceration, boot camps, and gang programming. But doing so would have made room for and provided support for alternatives.

Of course, in retrospect, theory seems like a useful addition to each of these approaches. But why was theory not integrated? There are several reasons. First, "theorists" and "practitioners" remain isolated. But it is also the case that theorists and researchers in general fail to do an adequate job making theory accessible, testable, and useful. This isolation can be laid at the feet of researchers who fail to integrate theories outside their own discipline into their work. Recent criminological work on life-course theory is a good case in point. Little criminological work in this area integrates psychological theories and research on the life course. Similarly, a doctoral course on life-course theories in a top-ranked psychology program included not a single mention of crime, delinquency, or deviance. If researchers don't reach out across disciplines or departments, it hardly seems realistic to expect practitioners to do so. A second reason for the failure of theory to inform program and policy development is the lack of interest in the development of policies and programs. Such development is "where the sausage is made," a messy process that involves politics, funding priorities, past practice, and some attention to best practices. The "public criminology" and "translational criminology" efforts in some settings are recent; generally they enjoy low levels of support and do not articulate clearly with university reward structures. Tenure and promotion, raises and recognition in the research community go to the highest citation count, the most prestigious publications, and the largest grant portfolio—not to the individual who spends the most hours slogging through agency protocol to develop and fine-tune interventions. It is also the case that program failure is the modal outcome in any criminal justice intervention. As such, development and evaluation of programs and policies do not attract a large following among researchers.

There is hope on the horizon. Translational criminology has a toehold in the discipline, largely on Twitter through George Mason University (@cebcp) and the Center for Public Criminology (@PublicCrim) and others. We hope when the next edition of the book comes out, it will reflect considerable development in this area.

Contributors

Robert K. Ax received his Ph.D. in clinical psychology at Virginia Tech. He is retired from the Federal Bureau of Prisons and is the coeditor, with Thomas J. Fagan, Ph.D., of *Correctional Mental Health: From Theory to Best Practice* (Sage, 2011).

Michelle N. Block is a doctoral candidate in the Criminal Justice and Criminology Department at Georgia State University. Her research interests focus on neighborhood crime, community perceptions of criminal justice, and law enforcement strategies. She studies the effects of neighborhood context and police legitimacy on a variety of outcomes, such as informal social control, neighborhood culture, and crime.

Anthony A. Braga is a Distinguished Professor and Director of the School of Criminology and Criminal Justice at Northeastern University. He is a fellow of the American Society of Criminology. Professor Braga is also a past president and fellow of the Academy of Experimental Criminology and the 2104 recipient of its Joan McCord Award. He received his M.P.A. from Harvard University and Ph.D. in criminal justice from Rutgers University.

Rod K. Brunson is Dean of the School of Criminal Justice at Rutgers, the State University of New Jersey. His research examines youths' experiences in neighborhood contexts, with a specific focus on the interactions of race, class, and gender and their relationship to criminal justice practices.

Jennifer Carlson is an Assistant Professor in Sociology and Government and Public Policy at the University of Arizona. She received a Ph.D. in sociology from the University of California, Berkeley, in 2013. Her work examines American gun culture, policing and public law enforcement, and conservative politics. She is the author of *Citizen-Protectors: The Everyday Politics of Guns in an Age of Decline.* In addition to writing for popular audiences in venues such as the *Los Angeles Times* and the *Washington Post*, her work appears in *Law & Society Review, Social Problems, Theoretical Criminology,* and other scholarly outlets.

Ronald V. Clarke was employed for fifteen years in the British government's criminological research department, the Home Office Research and Planning Unit, before moving to the United States in 1984. While there, he led the team that originated situational crime prevention and is now considered to be the world's leading authority on that approach. In 2012, his colleagues and former students published a festschrift in his honor (*The Reasoning Criminologist*, Routledge) and in 2015 he was awarded the Stockholm Prize in Criminology. His current research focuses on prevention of wildlife crimes.

Shea Cronin is an Assistant Professor of Criminal Justice and a Program Coordinator at Boston University's Metropolitan College. He received his Ph.D. in justice, law, and society from American University, School of Public Affairs. His research interests include the administration of criminal justice, communities and crime, policing, and issues of democratic accountability. His research has been published in *Crime and Delinquency, Justice Quarterly*, and other academic journals.

Scott H. Decker is Foundation Professor of Criminology and Criminal Justice at Arizona State University. His main research interests are in gangs, violence, and criminal justice policy. He is a fellow in both the American Society of Criminology and the Academy of Criminal Justice Sciences. He is the author of seventeen books and over 120 scientific articles, including *Life in the Gang: Family, Friends and Violence* (Cambridge, 1996), *Confronting Gangs: Crime and Community* (Oxford, 2015), and *Policing Immigrants: Local Law Enforcement on the Front Lines* (University of Chicago, 2016). He served as a member of the Missouri Sentencing Commission for ten years and as a member of the Arizona POST Board for five years.

Megan Denver is an Assistant Professor in the College of Criminology and Criminal Justice at Florida State University. She received her Ph.D. from the School of Criminal Justice at the University at Albany. Her research interests include criminal record stigma, employment and recidivism, and theories of desistance and public policy.

Kevin M. Drakulich is an Associate Professor in the School of Criminology and Criminal Justice at Northeastern University. His work focuses on three interrelated lines of research on questions related to race, inequality, and justice: the social processes related to crime and its consequences across communities; perceptions of crime, disorder, and social control within communities; and perceptions of race, crime, control, and related policies more broadly. He is the 2014 recipient of the New Scholar Award from the American Society of Criminology's Division of People of Color and Crime, was awarded a W.E.B. Du Bois Fellowship by the National Institute of Justice, and is a member of the Racial Democracy, Crime, and Justice Network.

Grant Duwe is the Director of Research and Evaluation for the Minnesota Department of Corrections, where he evaluates correctional programs, develops risk assessment instruments, and forecasts the state's prison population. His recent work has been published in *Criminology & Public Policy, Criminal Justice Policy Review, Prison Journal, Journal of Offender Rehabilitation*, and *International Journal of Offender Therapy and Comparative Criminology.* He is a nonresident senior fellow with Baylor University's Institute for Studies of Religion and, along with Michael Hallett, Joshua Hays, Byron Johnson and Sung Joon Jang, a coauthor of the forthcoming book, *The Angola Prison Seminary: Effects of Faith-Based Ministry on Identity Transformation, Desistance, and Rehabilitation* (Routledge).

Amy Farrell, Ph.D., is an Associate Professor of Criminology and Criminal Justice at Northeastern University. Her scholarship seeks to understand arrest, adjudication, and criminal case disposition practices. Professor Farrell also conducts research on police legitimacy and law enforcement responses to new crimes, such as hate crime and human trafficking. She is the co-editor of *Deadly Injustice: Trayvon Martin, Race and the Criminal Justice System* and co-author of *Not Guilty: Are the Acquitted Innocent?* She was a corecipient of NIJ's W.E.B. DuBois Fellowship on crime justice and culture in 2006.

Cheryl Lero Jonson, Ph.D., is an Assistant Professor in the Department of Criminal Justice at Xavier University. Her current research interests focus on the impact of prison on recidivism, incentivizing justice, the use of meta-analysis to organize criminological knowledge, prison conditions, and active shooter responses. She has published over thirty-five articles as well as *Correctional Theory: Context and Consequences, The American Prison: Imagining a Different Future,* and *The Origins of American Criminology.* In addition, she has trained over three thousand people in active shooter responses in school and workplace settings.

Charis E. Kubrin is Professor of Criminology, Law and Society at the University of California, Irvine. In addition to her work in peer-reviewed journals, Professor Kubrin is coauthor of *Researching Theories of Crime and Deviance* (Oxford University Press, 2008) and *Privileged Places: Race, Residence, and the Structure of Opportunity* (Lynne Rienner, 2006) and coeditor of *Introduction to Criminal Justice: A Sociological Perspective* (Stanford University Press, 2013), *Punishing Immigrants: Policy, Politics, and Injustice* (New York University Press, 2012), and *Crime and Society: Crime,* 3rd ed. (Sage Publications, 2007).

Justin Kurland is currently a Senior Lecturer in Crime Science at the University of Waikato, New Zealand. He was previously a postdoctoral research associate at the School of Criminal Justice, Rutgers University, and before that conducted his doctoral training at University College London. Having worked within the field of criminology for several years now, he has particular interests in exploring how methods from other disciplines (e.g., complexity science) can inform understanding of crime and security issues and, in turn, how this knowledge can be harnessed for crime prevention.

Megan Kurlychek is an Associate Professor at the University at Albany's School of Criminal Justice where she also serves as Executive Director of the Hindelang Criminal Justice Research Center. Her research interests include juvenile justice and delinquency, courts and sentencing, quantitative research methods, and the collateral consequences of a criminal record. She is particularly focused on the ways in which criminal justice system involvement can impact criminal careers and in exploring the definitions and statistical modeling of a criminal career. Dr. Kurlychek also currently serves as the editor of *Justice Quarterly.*

Shannon Magnuson is a fourth-year doctoral student in the Department of Criminology, Law, and Society at George Mason University and currently works as a graduate research assistant at the National Institute of Justice. Her research interests include organizational change, implementation science, and translational criminology. While at George Mason, she worked for three years with Dr. Faye S. Taxman and Dr. Danielle Rudes at the Center for Advancing Correctional Excellence, working primarily to help state correctional agencies advance their use of evidence-based practices. Her dissertation will use mixed methods to understand the direct and indirect impacts of mandated prison reform on a subset of individual prisons specifically and the process of organizational change across the eastern states more broadly. Prior to coming to George Mason, Shannon received her master's degree in arts from John Jay College of Criminal Justice.

Daniel P. Mears, Ph.D., is the Mark C. Stafford Professor of Criminology at Florida State University's College of Criminology and Criminal Justice. He conducts research on crime and policy. His work has appeared in such journals as *Criminology* and *Journal of Research in Crime and Delinquency* and in *American Criminal Justice Policy* (Cambridge University Press, 2010) and *Prisoner Reentry in the Era of Mass Incarceration* (Sage, 2015).

Robert D. Morgan is the John G. Skelton Jr. regents endowed professor and Chair in the Department of Psychological Sciences at Texas Tech University. His research interests are in correctional mental health treatment, effects of incarceration, and forensic mental health assessment.

Kathleen Powell is a graduate student at Rutgers, Newark School of Criminal Justice. Her research focuses on punishment and inequality generated by the justice system, particularly for youth and adolescents.

Danielle Rudes, Ph.D., is an Associate Professor of Criminology, Law, and Society and the Deputy Director of the Center for Advancing Correctional Excellence (ACE!) at George Mason University. She received her Ph.D. from the University of California, Irvine, and is an expert qualitative researcher whose methods include ethnographic observation, interviews, and focus groups with nearly twenty years of experience working with adult and juvenile corrections agencies at the federal, state, and local county levels including prisons, jails, probation/parole agencies, and problem-solving courts. She is recognized for her work examining how social control organizations and their middle management and street-level workers understand, negotiate, and at times resist change. Her experience includes working with community corrections agencies during adoption, adaptation, and implementation of various workplace practices and reforms including contingency management (incentives/rewards/sanctions), risk needs assessment instruments, and motivational interviewing.

Cassia Spohn is a Foundation Professor and Director of the School of Criminology and Criminal Justice at Arizona State University. She is the author or coauthor of seven books, including *Policing and Prosecuting Sexual Assault: Inside the Criminal Justice System* and *How Do Judges Decide? The Search for Fairness and Equity in Sentencing.* Her research interests include prosecutorial and judicial decision making; the intersections of race, ethnicity, crime, and justice; and sexual assault case processing decisions. In 2013 she received ASU's Award for Leading Edge Research in the Social Sciences and was selected as a fellow of the American Society of Criminology.

Cody Telep is an Assistant Professor in the School of Criminology and Criminal Justice at Arizona State University. His research focuses on evaluating policing interventions, synthesizing evidence on what works in policing, and examining officer receptivity to research and evidence-based policing. His recent work has appeared in *Crime & Delinquency, Journal of Quantitative Criminology,* and *Journal of Experimental Criminology.*

Natalie Todak is an Assistant Professor of Criminal Justice at the University of Alabama at Birmingham. Her primary research area is policing with a focus on police-citizen interactions, de-escalation, and use of force. Her doctoral dissertation was a field study of de-escalation tactics in collaboration with the Spokane Police Department. She has also conducted research on police technologies including TASERs and body-worn cameras. Her recent work has been published in *Criminal Justice & Behavior, Women & Criminal Justice,* and *Police Quarterly.*

Glenn Trager is an Assistant Professor of Criminal Justice at the California State University East Bay. He is a former attorney with a background in East Asian studies who studies the role of law and legality in U.S. cities with immigrant communities.

Jillian J. Turanovic, Ph.D., is an Assistant Professor at Florida State University's College of Criminology and Criminal Justice. Her research examines victimization and offending over the life course and the collateral consequences of incarceration. Her recent publications have appeared in *Criminology, Journal of Quantitative Criminology, Justice Quarterly,* and *Journal of Pediatrics.*

Sara Wakefield is Associate Professor of Criminal Justice at Rutgers University, Newark. She received her Ph.D. from the Department of Sociology at the University of Minnesota in 2007. Her research interests focus on the consequences of mass imprisonment for the family with an emphasis on childhood well-being and racial inequality, culminating in a series of articles and book, *Children of the Prison Boom: Mass Incarceration and the Future of American Inequality* (Oxford University Press, with Christopher Wildeman). More recently, she is working on several original data collection projects. The Prison Inmate Networks Studies leverage a variety of methods and data sources to understand how social ties influence the conditions of confinement, community reintegration, and social inequality among former prisoners and their families.

Patricia Warren is an Associate Professor in the College of Criminology and Criminal Justice at Florida State University. Her research focuses on crime and social control with particular emphasis on the complex ways that race, ethnicity, and gender influence sentencing and policing outcomes. Her work has appeared in *Criminology, Journal of Research in Crime and Delinquency, Crime and Delinquency,* and other crime and policy journals.

David Weisburd is Distinguished Professor of Criminology, Law, and Society at George Mason University and Executive Director of its Center for Evidence-Based Crime Policy. He also serves as the Walter E. Meyer Professor of Law and Criminal Justice at the Hebrew University and Chief Science Advisor at the Police Foundation. Professor Weisburd is the recipient of the Stockholm Prize in Criminology (2010) and the Vollmer Award from the American Society of Criminology for his work on place-based crime prevention.

Michael D. White is a Professor in the School of Criminology and Criminal Justice at Arizona State University and is Associate Director of ASU's Center for Violence Prevention and Community Safety. He is also the codirector of Training and Technical Assistance for the U.S. Department of Justice Body-Worn Camera Policy and Implementation Program. He received his Ph.D. in criminal justice from Temple University in 1999. Prior to entering academia, Dr. White worked as a deputy sheriff in Pennsylvania. His primary research interests involve the police, including use of force, technology, and misconduct. His recent work has been published in *Justice Quarterly, Criminology and Public Policy, Criminal Justice and Behavior,* and *Applied Cognitive Psychology.*

Rob White is Professor of Criminology in the School of Social Sciences at the University of Tasmania, Australia. He has published extensively in criminology and youth studies. Among his recent books are *Environmental Harm: An Eco-justice Perspective* (2013); *Green Criminology* (with Diane Heckenberg, 2014); *Environmental Crime and Collaborative State Intervention* (with Grant Pink, eds., 2016); and *Media and Crime* (with Katrina Clifford, 2017).

Lauren Wilson is a doctoral student at Rutgers School of Criminal Justice, studying under Dr. Clarke. Lauren's background is in environmental science with a focus on population genetics and spatial ecology. She earned an M.S. in environmental science and policy from George Mason University and a B.S. in wildlife management from the University of Georgia.

Kevin A. Wright, Ph.D., is an Associate Professor in the School of Criminology and Criminal Justice at Arizona State University. His work focuses on improving the correctional environment for those working and living in prison and improving the opportunities for the formerly incarcerated. His published research on these topics has appeared in *Justice Quarterly, Criminology & Public Policy,* and *Journal of Offender Rehabilitation.* He developed and taught the first Inside-Out Prison Exchange Program class in the state of Arizona, is a cofounder of the Arizona Transformation Project, and is director of the Center for Correctional Solutions at ASU.

Index

Made in the USA
Middletown, DE
24 May 2022

66161522R00215